# How to Do Everything with

## Dreamweaver MX

# How to Do
## *Everything*
### with

# Dreamweaver®
# MX

## Michael Meadhra

**McGraw-Hill**/Osborne

New York  Chicago  San Francisco  Lisbon
London  Madrid  Mexico City  Milan  New Delhi
San Juan  Seoul  Singapore  Sydney  Toronto

**McGraw-Hill**/Osborne
2600 Tenth Street
Berkeley, California 94710
U.S.A.

To arrange bulk purchase discounts for sales promotions, premiums, or fund-raisers, please contact **McGraw-Hill**/Osborne at the above address. For information on translations or book distributors outside the U.S.A., please see the International Contact Information page immediately following the index of this book.

**How to Do Everything with Dreamweaver® MX**

34567890 FGR FGR 0198765432

ISBN 0-07-222470-3

| | |
|---|---|
| **Publisher** | Brandon A. Nordin |
| **Vice President** | |
| **& Associate Publisher** | Scott Rogers |
| **Acquisitions Editor** | Marjorie McAneny |
| **Project Editor** | Madhu Prasher |
| **Acquisitions Coordinator** | Tana Allen |
| **Technical Editor** | David Malmstrom |
| **Copy Editor** | Leslie Tilley |
| **Proofreader** | Pamela Vevea |
| **Indexer** | Valerie Robbins |
| **Computer Designers** | Tabitha M. Cagan, Melinda Moore Lytle, Kelly Stanton-Scott |
| **Illustrators** | Michael Mueller, Lyssa Wald |
| **Series Design** | Mickey Galicia |
| **Cover Series Design** | Dodie Shoemaker |
| **Cover Illustration** | Victor Stabin |

This book was composed with Corel VENTURA™ Publisher.

# About the Author

**Michael Meadhra** is an author, consultant, and web designer. After working as a photographer, graphic designer, media producer, and manager for a number of years, he discovered that his best efforts were directed toward writing and teaching others how to use the computer technology that figured so prominently in all those occupations. So he turned to writing as a full-time career, first as a writer/editor of technical journals and then as a freelance book author. To date, Michael has written or contributed to more than 35 computer books and countless articles on topics such as graphics, presentation, and publishing software.

Michael is also a consultant who provides advice, training, system administration, web design, and web-hosting services to small and midsize business clients. And, of course, he uses Dreamweaver in his web design work.

# Contents at a Glance

# Contents

# Acknowledgments

This book would not exist without the contributions of a lot of different people. I'm glad that tradition allows me this opportunity to acknowledge some of those people for their efforts.

Thanks to Roger Stewart for the vision that resulted in the original version of this book and to Margie McAneny for shepherding this update through the publishing process. Tana Allen, acquisitions coordinator, and Madhu Prasher, project editor, were my regular contacts and have been pleasant and professional to work with. David Malmstrom, technical editor, helped ensure the accuracy of the text. Leslie Tilley, the copy editor, saw to it that my prose was readable. I didn't have much direct contact with the rest of the Osborne staff working on this book, but their contributions are appreciated nonetheless. My thanks to all of you!

Fellow authors, Greg and Jennifer Kettell, helped ensure timely completion of this project by contributing their database and programming expertise and by revising and tech editing some chapters. I also want to thank my friends and colleagues, Michael Boatman and Michael Witt, for insights and suggestions that helped make this a better book. And finally, I wish to thank my agent, David Fugate, Waterside Productions, for getting me this gig and for his continued support and help to make it a reality.

# Introduction

This book is for anyone wanting to learn how to use Macromedia Dreamweaver MX, the leading web site development tool on the market today. It targets beginning-to-intermediate Dreamweaver users and assumes no previous experience with the software. It does presume, however, that the reader is an intelligent and interested person with basic computer skills and at least a beginner's understanding of the Web and web page design.

Dreamweaver is a versatile and powerful tool for developing web pages and web sites. But Dreamweaver is just a tool. It can't supply the vision of what your web site should be or what features will make your pages attractive and effective. Dreamweaver can, however, enable you to transform your vision for a web site into reality.

In some ways, Dreamweaver is like a car. A car gives you the means to make short trips quickly and easily and makes practical journeys too long to undertake on foot. Of course, you must learn to drive the car if you expect to use it as your primary means of transportation, but there wouldn't be much point in learning to drive if you didn't have somewhere to go. The destination is an essential element of the driving experience, yet selecting a destination and planning the trip have very little to do with the mechanics of steering, braking, and acceleration that are necessary to control the car.

This book is about learning to drive the car (using Dreamweaver); it's not about planning a road trip (designing a web site). Web site design is a huge topic, the exclusive subject of many books, and the art of design is beyond the scope of this book. Also, this book's focus is on using Dreamweaver MX to produce basic web sites, not on using the program's advanced features for producing web applications. However, it does include a brief overview of Dreamweaver MX's support for database-driven web pages and server-side programming technologies.

The book starts with an introduction to the Dreamweaver user interface: Part I, "Getting to Know Dreamweaver." This part covers how to work with the various windows and panels that make up the Dreamweaver working environment. You also learn how to define a site in Dreamweaver, which is the first step in developing a web site.

Part II, "Creating Basic Web Pages," covers the basics of how to create a web page, add and edit text, build hyperlinks, and add images. This is also where you discover how to access the HTML source code for your pages.

In Part III, "Going Beyond the Basics," you can learn how to work with tables in Dreamweaver, including Dreamweaver's Layout Table feature. You also discover how to use frames and framesets, how to build interactive forms, and how to use Dreamweaver templates to make creating and updating web pages fast and easy. You also learn how to use other external editors and how to add sounds, Flash animations, movies, and other media to your web pages.

In Part IV, "Expanding Your Horizons," you can learn how to use CSS style sheets and how to create layers and animate them with timelines. This part also covers Dreamweaver Behaviors, which enable you to create rollovers and other JavaScript effects without programming. Wrapping up this part is a chapter that introduces Dreamweaver's support for database connections and server-side programming technologies.

Part V, "Managing Your Site with Dreamweaver," covers how to publish your site using Dreamweaver's built-in file transfer features. You also learn how to use Dreamweaver's testing and reporting features to detect and correct problems on your web pages and how to use Design Notes and Check In/Out to work with files in a collaborative environment.

All the books in this series include special features that call out certain bits of information to make them easily accessible. Among them are the following:

- **How to...** A boxed section giving instructions on how to perform a specific task
- **Did you know...** A boxed section that provides background information or explores a topic related to the main text
- **Note** Supplemental information
- **Caution** Something to watch out for
- **Tip** A time-saving alternative
- **Shortcut** A keyboard shortcut for a command
- **New in MX** A new feature of Dreamweaver MX

Here are a few resources you might want to refer to as you read this book and go on to develop web pages and sites of your own. For web site design issues, check out *Web Design: The Complete Reference,* by Thomas A. Powell (McGraw-Hill/Osborne 2000; a new edition is due out in 2002.) You'll also need a good reference for HTML codes, such as the following books from McGraw-Hill/Osborne: *HTML: The Complete Reference*, by Thomas A. Powell (2001), or *HTML: A Beginner's Guide*, by Wendy Willard (2001). For information on the critical issue of browser compatibility, refer to www.webreview.com/browsers/browsers.shtml or hotwired.lycos.com/webmonkey/ reference/browser_chart/.

# Part I

# Getting to Know Dreamweaver

# Chapter 1

## Get Started with Dreamweaver

## How to...

- Get to know Dreamweaver
- Work with the Document window
- Work with the Site window
- Work with panels
- Set preferences

What is Dreamweaver anyway?

First and foremost, Dreamweaver is a graphical web page editing program that enables a web author to work with text, images, and other web page elements in a WYSIWYG (what you see is what you get) editing environment. Dreamweaver enables web authors to create and edit web pages in much the same way that desktop publishing programs enable layout artists to create page designs for print publication. Using Dreamweaver, you can design web pages without directly manipulating the HTML code that defines the web page. However, Dreamweaver also provides easy access to the HTML code, so you can work with it when you need to.

Dreamweaver MX is also a powerful development environment for building dynamic web sites that make full use of database-driven content, client-side scripts, and server technologies such as ASP (Active Server Pages), ColdFusion, and JSP (Java Server Pages). Dreamweaver MX incorporates all the features of the previous Dreamweaver and Dreamweaver UltraDev products, merged into a single program capable of handling the most sophisticated and demanding web design and development projects—from a simple home page to a large e-commerce site.

Dreamweaver is more than just a tool for web page layout and application development—it's also a complete solution for web site construction and maintenance. Besides making it easy to create and edit multiple web pages, Dreamweaver includes powerful features to help web developers manage all the related files for a site, post those files to a remote web server, and keep the local files and the files on the remote server synchronized. You don't need to use one program for creating web pages and then a host of separate utilities for diagramming the site, managing files, and transferring files to the web server—Dreamweaver does it all!

# The Three Faces of Dreamweaver

One of the most distinctive characteristics of most computer programs is its *user interface*—the collection of windows, menus, toolbars, dialog boxes, and other controls that the user sees onscreen and uses to access the program's features. The user interface may change from version to version as the program evolves, but the user interface is usually fixed in any one version of the product.

Dreamweaver MX is different. The Windows version of Dreamweaver MX offers its users a choice of three different user interfaces, called *workspaces*. (Dreamweaver MX for the Macintosh offers just one standard workspace.) Windows Dreamweaver MX users can elect to use the Floating Panel workspace, the Integrated workspace, or the Coder-Style workspace. The three workspaces don't change the capabilities or features of the Dreamweaver MX program, but

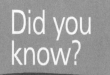

# Translating Windows Keys to the Macintosh

Dreamweaver MX is a cross-platform product that is available in both Windows and Macintosh versions (as are most of the other Macromedia products). The Windows version is Windows XP–compliant and the Mac version runs in OS X native mode.

All the figures, examples, and instructions in this book show the Windows version of the software. However, with few exceptions, the program looks and acts the same on both Windows and Macintosh computers. Sure, there are minor cosmetic differences imposed by the different operating systems and some differences in terminology, but other than that, the Windows and Macintosh versions are essentially the same. Here's a brief summary of the Macintosh counterparts for common Windows terms and keystrokes:

| Windows Key/Action | Macintosh Key/Action |
| --- | --- |
| CTRL key | COMMAND (⌘) key |
| ALT key | APPLE (⍟) key |
| SHIFT key | SHIFT key |
| DELETE key | BACKSPACE key |
| ENTER key | RETURN key |
| Click or left-click | Click |
| Right-click | Click and hold down the mouse button |

they do change the way the user controls are arranged on the computer screen. All three workspaces have their strengths, and each will undoubtedly appeal to some users.

## The Floating Panel Workspace

The Floating Panel workspace, or Floating workspace for short, (see Figure 1-1) continues the tradition of previous Dreamweaver versions by presenting a user interface composed of multiple, free-floating windows. There are separate windows for each document and for the various *panels*, which are smaller windows containing the objects and controls that you use to build web pages. You can open, close, resize, and move document windows and panels independently—and the panels can even overlap a document window.

Insert bar

Document toolbar

Menu

Panel group

HTML Styles panel

Document window

Panel dock

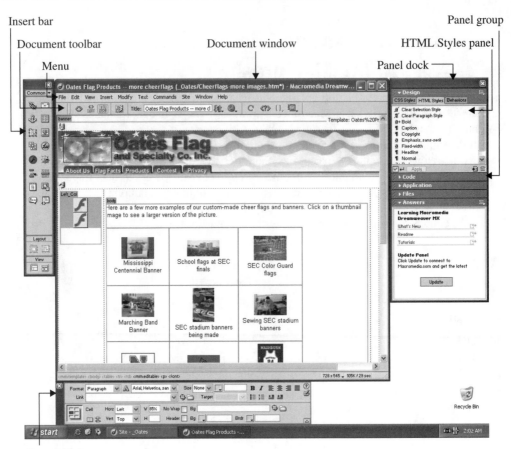

Properties Inspector panel

The Floating Panel workspace features multiple windows that you can move independently.

Despite the fact that the Floating Panel workspace is also referred to as the "Dreamweaver 4 workspace," it isn't an exact duplicate of the Dreamweaver 4 user interface. There are some significant changes, the largest of which is that most of the previously separate panels have been consolidated into a single window called the *panel dock*. The panel dock greatly simplifies panel management by allowing you to expand and collapse panel groups within the panel dock to access individual panels.

The Floating workspace is one of three workspace options on Windows. It is the sole workspace available on the Macintosh. The features of the Floating workspace will be explored in more detail in this chapter.

 NOTE    *Throughout this book, I use the Floating Panel workspace since it is the same on both Windows and Macintosh platforms. All illustrations and instructions in the book show the Floating Panel workspace.*

## The Integrated Workspace

 The Integrated workspace (see Figure 1-2) is the new user interface layout option introduced by Dreamweaver MX for Windows. It features a single large application window that uses a Multiple Document Interface (MDI) to present views of your document surrounded by the various Dreamweaver menus, toolbars, and panels. The result is similar to some of the Integrated Development Environment (IDE) user interface layouts that are popular among programmers, but with Dreamweaver's traditional emphasis on the graphical elements of a graphical user interface.

In the Integrated workspace, you can have multiple documents open in separate windows, just as you can in the Floating workspace, but they are confined to the large work area in the middle of the main Dreamweaver application window instead of floating free anywhere on the computer desktop. Similarly, you can have one or more panels open for easy access, but they are normally confined to specific locations in the Dreamweaver application window. The panel dock occupies a pane on the right side of the window, the Property Inspector panel is attached to the bottom of the application window, and the Insert bar is transformed from a floating panel to a toolbar above the open document.

In the Integrated workspace, there's a place for everything, and everything's in its place. Although Dreamweaver allows you to regroup panels, move them out of their normal positions, and "float" them over the workspace, the Integrated workspace is designed to work best with everything tucked into the Integrated workspace.

## The Coder-Style Workspace

 The Coder-Style workspace (see Figure 1-3) is a new option available in the Windows version of Dreamweaver MX. It bears a strong resemblance to the user interface found in HomeSite, the text-based code-editing environment originally developed by Allaire for its ColdFusion developers.

Like the Integrated workspace, the Coder-Style workspace features a single application window that integrates views of the current document and all the Dreamweaver panels in an MDI. In fact, the Coder-Style workspace is really just a variation on the Integrated workspace. The Coder-Style workspace shares all the features of the Integrated workspace, but the panel dock is positioned on the left instead of the right, and the Document window defaults to Code view.

Document window

Document toolbar          Menu     Dreamweaver application window

Insert bar

Panel group

HTML Styles panel

Panel dock

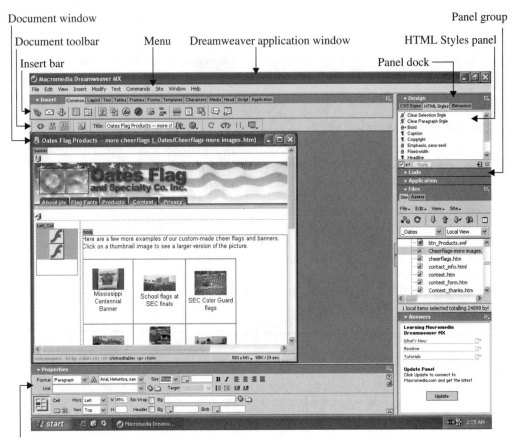

Properties Inspector panel

FIGURE 1-2    The Integrated workspace merges all the Dreamweaver Document windows and panels into one application window.

## Select Your Workspace

When you install Dreamweaver MX on a Windows system, the installer gives you the option to select your preferred workspace. The default is the Integrated (Dreamweaver MX) workspace, but you can select any one of the three workspaces you prefer.

Panel group

Panel dock    Menu    Dreamweaver application window

HTML Styles panel

Document window

Document toolbar

Insert bar

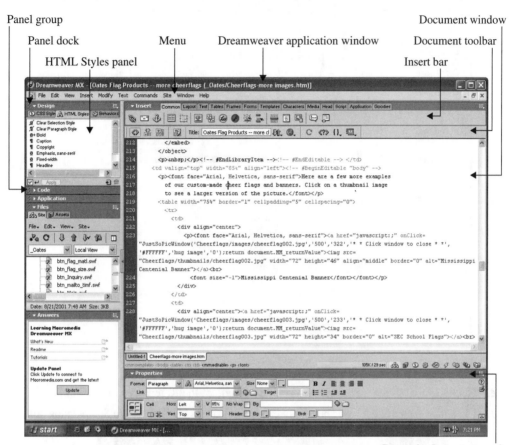

Properties Inspector panel

FIGURE 1-3    The Coder-Style workspace will look familiar to users migrating to Dreamweaver from HomeSite or ColdFusion Studio.

You can also change your workspace selection at any time. Here's how:

**1.** Choose Edit | Preferences from the Dreamweaver menu. (Obviously, Dreamweaver must be installed and running.) Dreamweaver opens the Preferences dialog box.

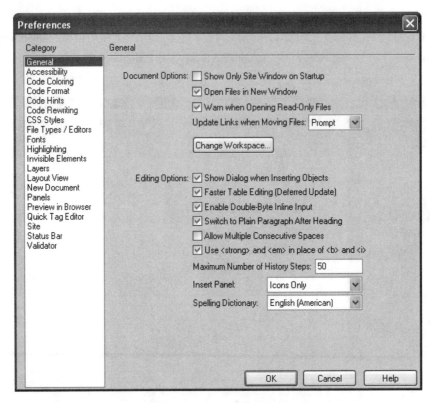

**2.** Click General in the Categories list on the left side of the References dialog box.

**3.** Click the Change Workspace button. Dreamweaver opens the Workspace Setup dialog box.

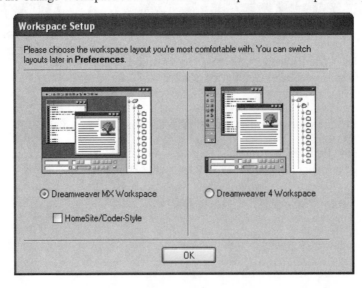

4. Click an option to select the workspace you prefer. To select the Floating workspace, click Dreamweaver 4 Workspace. To select the Integrated workspace, click Dreamweaver MX Workspace. To select the Coder-Style workspace, click Dreamweaver MX Workspace and then the check box labeled HomeSite/Coder-Style.

5. Click OK to close the Workspace Setup dialog box, and then click OK again to close the Preferences dialog box.

Dreamweaver doesn't change the workspace layout immediately, but you will see your new workspace selection the next time you launch the program.

# Get to Know Dreamweaver

Creating individual web pages, editing code, and managing all the files that make up an entire web site are obviously related activities, but they are very different tasks. Given the different natures of those tasks, it's not surprising that Dreamweaver presents you with different tools for handling them.

You can find a detailed exploration of how to perform all those tasks in other chapters of this book. This section gives you an introduction and overview of the various windows and menus that make up the Dreamweaver user interface, so you'll know where to find things. This section (and the rest of the book) assumes that you're working in the Floating (Dreamweaver 4) workspace. Actually, all the same major features exist in all three Dreamweaver workspaces, but they may be arranged differently.

## Get Acquainted with the Dreamweaver Floating Workspace

When you're working on an individual web page, you're in the Dreamweaver *Document window*. In the Floating workspace, the Document window is surrounded by an assortment of smaller windows, called *panels*, which contain the various tools and resources for creating and manipulating objects on the web page.

The combination of a document window and multiple panels, all open at once, is common to many graphics programs, but it's a stark contrast to the all-in-one-window approach of common word processing and spreadsheet software. The multiwindow nature of the Dreamweaver work area allows it to spread out across your entire screen, as shown in Figure 1-1, even though there is no application window enclosing all the component windows, and none of the individual windows are maximized to full-screen size. You can open, close, move, and even overlap the panels independent of the main document window.

When it comes time to deal with site-management chores, Dreamweaver presents a somewhat different face. Instead of an individual web page, the key feature of the Site window (see Figure 1-4) is a list of local files in the current web site, which is usually defined as a folder on your computer's hard drive.

Alongside the list of local files you can view either a site map diagram or a list of files on the remote web server that is linked to the local site. From the Site window, you can perform all sorts of site-management tasks, including posting newly created or edited files to the remote server. Chapter 2 covers defining a site in Dreamweaver, and Chapters 15 and 16 explore Dreamweaver's site-management capabilities in more detail.

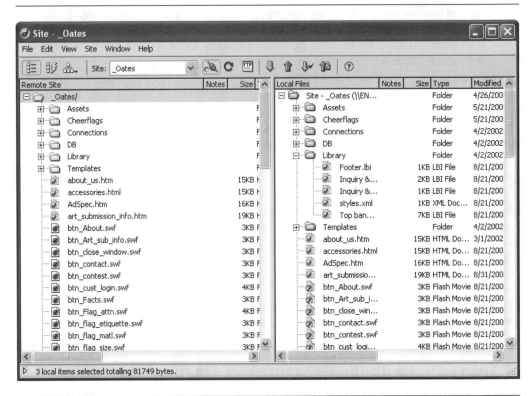

FIGURE 1-4    The Site window is where you tackle file management tasks for your web site.

As you might expect, the Dreamweaver Document window and Site window exhibit the common characteristics found in the windows of just about every program you've ever used. There's the usual title bar at the top, with its minimize, maximize, and close buttons; a menu bar below that; then a toolbar with buttons that give you quick access to commonly used commands; and a status bar at the bottom of the window. The interior of the Document window displays the web page you're editing, and the Site window displays the file list and site map. If necessary, scroll bars appear along the edge of the window to accommodate lists and pages that are too big to fit completely within the window. You can have multiple document windows open simultaneously, displaying different web pages. However, you can have only one Site window open at a time.

The panels and panel dock—the smaller windows surrounding the main Document window— are hybrids: half window, half dialog box. The panels display detailed information and options such as you might find in a dialog box in another programs, but, unlike dialog boxes, panels are designed to stay open on your computer desktop while you work on a web document in Dreamweaver. Some panels contain resources that you can use to develop your web page, while other panels display the properties of selected objects on the page. Panels enable you to do things like edit the properties of an object in a panel and see the changes reflected immediately in the Document window.

1

## Use Dreamweaver Menus and the Toolbar

Working with the menu bar in Dreamweaver is essentially the same as using the corresponding component of any other Windows (or Macintosh) program, so I won't rehash the general procedures here. In addition to the drop-down menus on the menu bar, Dreamweaver makes extensive use of context menus to present menu commands that are applicable to a selected object. To access a context menu, simply right-click (click and hold for Macintosh users) on an object in most any Dreamweaver window. A context menu will pop open showing a list of commands that are available for use with that object. Selecting a command from the context menu has exactly the same effect as selecting the same command from the menu bar—it's just faster and more convenient.

The Dreamweaver toolbar is relatively straightforward. The buttons on the toolbar provide shortcuts to several frequently used commands and options.

The standard Dreamweaver toolbar for the Document window, shown here, includes the following buttons:

- **Show Code View**   Switches the Document window into Code view so you can work with the raw text and HTML tags of the document file.
- **Show Code and Design View**   Switches the Document window into the split-screen Code and Design view.
- **Show Design View**   Switches the Document window into the WYSIWYG Design view, which approximates the way the page will appear in a browser.
- **Page Title**   A convenient editable display of the current document title.
- **File Management**   A drop-down list of file-management commands.
- **Preview/Debug in Browser**   A drop-down list of available browsers for previewing and debugging pages.
- **Refresh**   Refreshes the Design view display after you make changes to the HTML code in one of Dreamweaver's code windows.
- **Reference**   Displays context-sensitive reference information about the currently selected object in the Reference panel.
- **Code Navigation**   A drop-down list of code-navigation commands.
- **View Options**   A drop-down list of view options.

# Work with the Document Window

The Dreamweaver Document window is where you design and edit web page documents, so this is where you'll spend most of your time as you interact with the program to perform most web page development tasks. Normally, an empty document window appears when you launch Dreamweaver, but that's not always so. (Dreamweaver is highly adaptable to individual working styles, so you can configure the program to show the Site window first instead of the Document window.)

The Dreamweaver Document window can display a web page using one of three different views:

- **Design View**   Approximates the way a page will display in a browser
- **Code View**   Displays the HTML code for the page
- **Code and Design View**   Presents a split screen with the Design view in one portion and Code view in the other

Views are simply different ways of looking at the same document—the web page you're editing.

You can select which view Dreamweaver displays in the Document window by selecting the corresponding commands from the View menu of any Document window. (Choose View | Code, View | Design, or View | Code and Design.) You can also select a view by clicking one of the first three buttons on the Document Window toolbar. The button that looks recessed indicates the current view. You can change the view in one Dreamweaver document window without affecting other document windows.

## Understand Design View

Dreamweaver's Design view, shown in Figure 1-5, provides an intuitive graphical user interface for creating and editing web pages. Design view enables you to work with a graphical representation of your web page that approximates the way the page will look when viewed in a web browser.

In general, you interact with Dreamweaver in Design view in much the same way you use a modern word processor—with perhaps a little page layout program thrown in for good measure. For example, you can type text directly into the Document window, just as you would with a word processor. You can add graphics, tables, and other objects to the page with menu commands and with drag-and-drop techniques. You drag the mouse pointer across some text or an image to select it; then you can edit, move, delete, or reformat the selected object. In short, Dreamweaver Design view does just what you expect it to do under most circumstances.

However, the view of your web page that you see in Design view only approximates the page as it will appear in a web browser. Sometimes the Dreamweaver view and the browser view are a fairly close match, and other times the Dreamweaver view is significantly different.

Dreamweaver displays text and simple objects (such as images) in pretty much the same way as a web browser (aside from the subtle—and sometimes not so subtle—differences in the way different browsers render web pages). Consequently, if you're working on a very simple page, the Dreamweaver Design view might look similar to the same page viewed in a web browser.

But Dreamweaver is intended for creating and editing web pages, not just viewing them. So Dreamweaver includes an assortment of onscreen tools and visual aids to help you find, identify, and manipulate various objects on your web page. Dreamweaver Design view can include rulers and grids to aid in positioning objects on the page. Icons representing various hidden elements appear in Design view to give you easy access to otherwise invisible page elements. Table borders can be made visible in Design view, even when they are configured not to display in a browser.

**FIGURE 1-5**    A Dreamweaver document window in Design view

The same goes for the borders of frames, layers, and the hotspots in image maps. And Dreamweaver uses color coding and other visual clues to identify page elements and areas that are linked to templates and library objects.

The result is a Design view display, such as the one shown in Figure 1-5, that is rich in information about the page on which you're working. However, all this extra information makes the Design view representation of your web page look significantly different from what you expect to see in a browser (see Figure 1-6). Because of this difference between the appearance of your page in Design view and in a browser, you'll need to frequently check the page in a browser to see how the page will look to your viewers. Fortunately, Dreamweaver makes it very easy to preview your pages as you work.

**FIGURE 1-6**    The page shown in Figure 1-5 as it appears in a browser window

All the extra stuff that you see on your page in Design view can be a little distracting or disorienting at first. But there's no need to worry about it. As you work with Dreamweaver, you'll quickly become familiar with the onscreen markings and what they mean, and when you do, Design view ceases to be confusing at all.

## Use Rulers

As you might surmise from the name, *rulers* provide a convenient means of measuring things in the Design View window. When rulers are turned on, they appear as graduated scales on the top and left sides of the Design View window, as shown in Figure 1-7. As you move the pointer around on your page in Design view, a line moves on each ruler to indicate the precise position of the pointer.

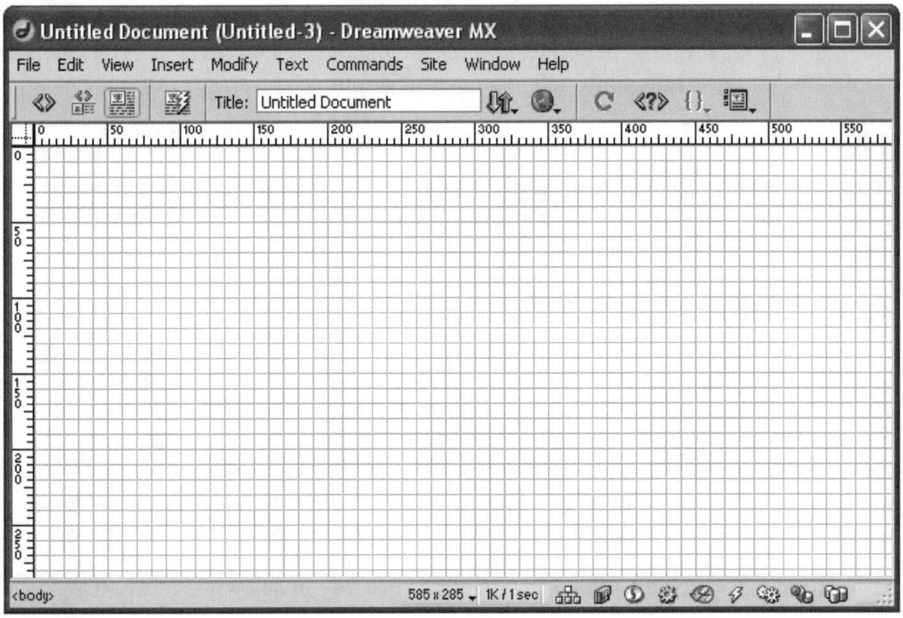

**FIGURE 1-7**    Rulers and grids aid in positioning objects in Design view.

You can reconfigure rulers to meet your individual needs and preferences. You can show or hide them, change the origin point (the zero mark), and display measurements in your choice of pixels, inches, or centimeters. Choose View | Rulers | *command*, and replace *command* with one of the following options:

- **Show**    Turns the ruler display on. (You can also press CTRL-ALT-R.) Repeating the same command hides the rulers.
- **Pixels**    Displays measurements in pixels.
- **Inches**    Displays measurements in inches.
- **Centimeters**    Displays measurements in centimeters.
- **Reset Origin**    Returns the rulers' origin (the zero marks) to the default position at the upper-left corner of the page.

TIP    *These same commands are available on the context menu that appears when you right-click the ruler.*

To move the rulers' origin, click and drag from the origin box (the place where the top and left rulers intersect in the upper-left corner of the Design View window) to the location on the page where you want the origin to be. When you release the mouse button, Dreamweaver adjusts the ruler scales so that the origin jumps to the pointer position.

## Use Grids

The *grid* is another handy tool that helps you position objects on your page in Design view. When you activate the grid, Dreamweaver displays a series of evenly spaced horizontal and vertical lines on your page (see Figure 1-7).

You can use these grid lines to help you align and position various elements on the page. The grid lines don't become a permanent part of the web page—they are simply a visual reference that helps you position objects in Design view.

If you need a little help aligning objects to the grid, you can activate the Snap to Grid feature. With Snap to Grid enabled, all you have to do is place or move an object close to a grid line— Dreamweaver automatically aligns the object precisely with the nearest grid line.

Dreamweaver gives you complete control over the grid. You can turn the grid display on and off and adjust the spacing and color of grid lines. You can also choose whether to enable Snap to Grid. Choose View | Grid | *command*, and replace *command* with one of the following options:

- **Show Grid** Toggles the grid display on or off. (You can also press CTRL-ALT-G.)
- **Snap to Grid** Toggles the Snap to Grid feature on and off. (You can also press CTRL-ALT-SHIFT-G.)
- **Edit Grid** Displays the Grid Settings dialog box.

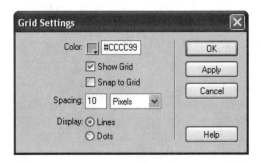

In this dialog box, you can adjust the color of the grid lines by selecting a color with the color picker or by entering the color value in the text box. The check boxes enable you to change the settings to show the grid and snap objects to the grid. To change the grid spacing, enter a number in the Spacing text box and select the appropriate measurement to go with it. The Display radio buttons enable you to choose between displaying the grid as lines or only as dots at each grid intersection. Adjust the settings and then click OK.

## Use Visual Aids

*Visual aids* is a catchall term for the various onscreen indicators that Dreamweaver uses to make otherwise invisible objects visible in Design view. Visual aids include outlines to mark the borders of tables, layers, and frames; indicators for the hotspots in image maps; and icons that show the location of invisible elements such as anchors, comments, embedded objects, and line breaks.

You have complete control over which visual aids are visible as you work with your page in Design view. You can activate some, or all, of the visual aids to make it easier to see and manipulate invisible page elements. Or you can hide the visual aids to reduce the clutter in the Design View window. Choose View | Visual Aids | *command*, and replace *command* with one of the following options to turn elements on and off:

- ■ **Table Borders**    Toggles the table border display on or off.
- ■ **Layer Borders**    Shows or hides the outlines showing the size and location of layers.
- ■ **Frame Borders**    Toggles the frame border display on or off.
- ■ **Image Maps**    Shows or hides the hotspots in image maps.
- ■ **Invisible Elements**    Toggles the invisible elements icon display on or off. Invisible elements include named anchors, scripts, comments, hidden form fields, and more. You can adjust settings in the Preferences dialog box to select which icons Dreamweaver displays when you enable viewing Invisible Elements.
- ■ **Hide All**    Suppresses the display of all the visual aids. (You can also press CTRL-SHIFT-I.) Repeat the command to restore the previously selected assortment of visual aids.

# Understand Code View

A web page may appear to be a graphically rich document when viewed in a web browser or in Dreamweaver's Design view, but that's only an illusion. When you peek behind the curtain, you find a file containing plain text and a bunch of embedded codes that tell the web browser how to format the text, where to find graphics files, and how to execute various special effects. Code view (shown in Figure 1-8) enables you to see your web document in its raw form so you can work directly with the HTML code.

Having access to the HTML code is essential for troubleshooting and highly desirable for routine page creation and editing. In Code view, you can edit the text and HTML code for your web page without the distraction or interference of a graphical user interface. Code view includes numerous features to facilitate working with the HTML code for your web page. Chapter 5 explores Dreamweaver's code-handling capabilities in more detail.

# Understand Code and Design View

Design view works well for many web page development tasks, and Code view is more appropriate for others. But sometimes it's nice to use a combination of the two views. Code and

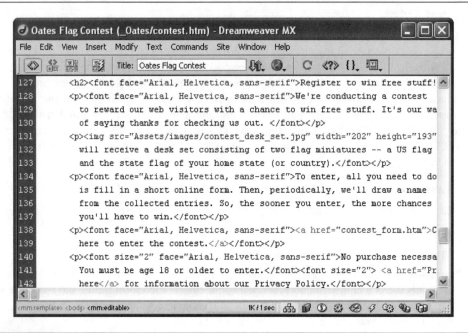

**FIGURE 1-8** The Document window in Code view

Design view (shown in Figure 1-9) divides the Document window into two panes and displays your web page in Design view in one pane and Code view in the other. The split-screen effect enables you to see simultaneously the page's HTML code and a graphic representation of the code instructions.

Splitting the Document window into two panes means you need to do more scrolling to access various portions of your web page. Each pane of the Code and Design view has separate scroll bars that act independently of the other pane's. However, selecting an object (or simply clicking) in either pane automatically scrolls the other pane so that it displays the corresponding portion of the page. You can select an object or text in either pane and let Dreamweaver move the other pane to highlight the corresponding object.

 *Pay attention to which pane of the Code and Design view has the focus before you start editing your page. Entering plain text is pretty much the same in both panes, but other editing actions can be quite different—especially within HTML codes. You can tell which pane is the active editing pane by the blinking insertion point cursor in that pane.*

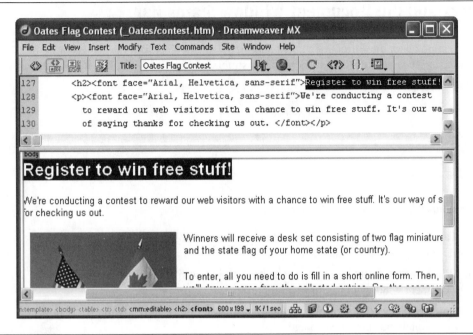

**FIGURE 1-9**    Code and Design view is the best of both worlds.

You can make changes in one pane—either the Design View pane or the Code View pane—and see those changes reflected in the other pane. This capability makes Code and Design view a great way to troubleshoot the HTML code, and it's also an invaluable tool for learning more about HTML. Here are a few tips for using Code and Design view:

- Choose View | Design View on Top to swap the locations of the Design View pane and the Code View pane. Choose the command again to return the Document window to its default configuration with the Code View pane on top.

- Drag the border between the two panes up or down to resize the panes.

- Edits that you make in the Design view pane are immediately and automatically reflected in the Code View pane, but you must manually refresh the Design View pane to reflect any changes that you make in Code view. To do so, click in the Design View pane, click the Refresh button in the Property Inspector panel, choose View | Refresh Design View, or press F5.

## Understand the Document Window Status Bar

You're probably accustomed to looking to the status bar at the bottom of a document window for information about the current document and the selected object. But the status bar in the Dreamweaver Document window is more than a simple informational display; it's an interactive toolbox packed with useful features.

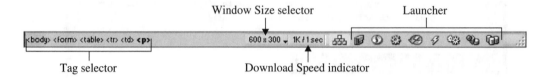

The status bar contains the following tools:

- **Tag selector**   Enables you to identify (and select) objects in Design view by the HTML tags enclosing them.

- **Window Size selector**   Shows the current window size and enables you to set the Document window to one of several preset sizes.

- **Download Speed indicator**   Shows an estimate of how long it will take to download and display the current web page.

- **Launcher**   Presents a row of icons representing Dreamweaver's various panels. Use the Launcher to open panels and keep track of which panels are active.

The Tag selector and Window Size selector are visible only when the Document window is displaying your page in Design view or Code and Design view. They're absent from the status bar when the Document window is in Code view. (You don't really need the Tag selector when the tags are directly available in Code view, and the window size is irrelevant in Code view.) The Download Speed indicator and Launcher are visible in all three views. You can customize the status bar tools with settings in the Preferences dialog box.

### Use the Tag Selector

The Tag selector occupies the left half of the Document window status bar. You may barely notice it at first, but once you become aware of its existence and how helpful it can be, you'll probably find yourself using it more and more. The Tag selector provides important information about the objects you work with in the Document window. But it's more than an informational display, it's an interactive tool that enables you to select page content for editing.

The structure of an HTML document relies on *tags*—embedded HTML codes—to define portions of the document and to convey instructions to the web browser on how to format and display the web page. The visible portion of the web page is enclosed between the <body> and </body> tags, which define the beginning and the end of the page body (visible page content) and separate it from the page header. Similarly, paragraphs, text formatting, graphics, hyperlinks, tables, table rows, table cells, and forms all have their own tags, which are often nested within other tags. For example, a paragraph might be nested within a table cell, which is within a table row, which is within a table, which is nested within the body tag.

The Tag selector shows all the HTML tags enclosing the object or text that is currently selected in the Document window when you're in Design view. Thus, the Tag selector supplies information that you might otherwise get only by carefully perusing the web document's HTML code in Code view.

```
<body> <form> <table> <tr> <td> <p>
```

While the Tag selector is certainly useful as a status display, it's even more useful as a tool for selecting things on your web page in Design view.

Selecting a few words of text in Design view is easy—you just drag the pointer across the text you want to select to highlight it. But selecting an object and its accompanying HTML tags can be tricky because the tags aren't visible in Design view. Another challenge is trying to select large objects, such as a table, that require scrolling the Design View window to view the entire thing.

The Tag selector gives you a quick and easy way to use the HTML tags to make your selections. Simply click on (or anywhere within) the object you want to select, then click a tag in the Tag selector. Dreamweaver highlights the contents of that tag in Design view.

> **TIP** *You can instantly select everything on a web page by clicking the <body> tag in the Tag selector.*

## Use the Window Size Selector

The Window Size selector is both a status display and a tool for adjusting the window size. Knowing the size of the Document window is handy when you're working in Design view because it helps you gauge the relative size of your web page and the objects on it. You can adjust the size of the Document window to approximate the size of a web browser window at different screen resolutions to get an idea of how much of your page will be visible at those resolutions.

The Window Size selector displays the current size of the Document window when you are using Design view. In Code and Design view, it displays the size of the Design View pane.

You can resize the Document window by dragging the window border. When you do, the Window Size selector displays the new window size in pixels. You can also use the Window Size selector to control the size of the Document window. When you click the Window Size selector, Dreamweaver displays a pop-up menu of preset window sizes. Just select a size from the list and Dreamweaver instantly resizes the Document window to match your selection.

Dreamweaver comes preprogrammed with an assortment of window sizes that correspond to typical browser window sizes at various standard screen resolutions. You can add to and edit the list of sizes in the Preferences dialog box.

### Use the Launcher

The Launcher consists of a row of icons at the right end of the status bar that represent the Site window and Dreamweaver's various floating panels. Basically, it provides an alternative to the Window menu for opening and keeping track of Dreamweaver's panels. At first, the icons may be cryptic, but you'll soon learn to recognize which icon corresponds to which panel.

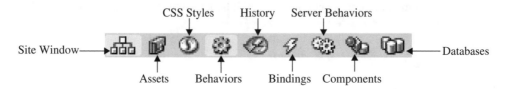

Using the Launcher is easy:

■ To open a panel or bring it to the foreground, click the corresponding Launcher icon.

■ A Launcher icon that looks like a recessed button indicates a panel that is currently open.

■ To close an open panel, click its Launcher icon.

By default, the Launcher is hidden. Most commonly used panels are available in the panel dock, and you can always open others using Dreamweaver's Window menu. You can enable the Launcher and configure it to show as many (or as few) of the available panels as you want by adjusting settings in the Preferences dialog box. (See "Set Preferences," at the end of the chapter.)

## View Pages with Browser Preview

Although Dreamweaver's Design view displays a graphical representation of your web page, it isn't an accurate rendering of the page as it will appear in a web browser. Even if Dreamweaver could match the output of one particular web browser, you'd still have to contend with significant differences in the way web pages are rendered by different browsers. As a result, it is *absolutely essential* to preview your web pages in a web browser as you work so you can see your pages as visitors to your site will see them.

Fortunately, Dreamweaver makes browser previews quick and easy to do. You don't need to manually save your page in a temporary file, open the browser, then locate and open the saved page so you can view it in the browser window. With a single key press or mouse click, you can instruct Dreamweaver to do all that for you automatically.

Dreamweaver gives you several ways to activate the browser preview feature:

■ Press F12 to preview the current page in your system's default browser.

■ Press CTRL-F12 to preview the current page in the secondary browser (if you have defined a secondary browser).

- Choose File | Preview in Browser | *browser name* to preview the page in the selected browser (if you have defined additional browsers).

- Click the Preview/Debug in Browser toolbar button and then choose the desired browser from the menu that appears.

The Dreamweaver installation routine normally detects your system's default browser and automatically configures Dreamweaver to use it as the primary browser for browser preview duties. However, most web authors use more than one web browser to preview pages under development. Dreamweaver can work with these other browsers, but first you must add them to Dreamweaver's browser list in the Preferences dialog box. See Chapter 15 for instructions.

# Work with the Site Window

While the Dreamweaver Document window is for creating and editing individual web pages, the Dreamweaver Site window is for creating and managing entire web sites. The Site window, shown earlier in Figure 1-4, is where you manage the collection of web documents and all the supporting files and folders that make up a web site.

*In the alternate Dreamweaver workspaces, the Site window appears as a panel in the panel dock instead of being a separate window—at least, that's its default location. It's easier to work with the Site panel if you click the Expand button to undock it and enlarge it to full window size.*

Chapter 2 explores the important concept of defining a site in Dreamweaver and the procedures for doing so. Chapters 15 and 16 cover publishing, testing, and maintaining your web site with Dreamweaver. Those chapters show the Dreamweaver Site window in action; this chapter gives you a brief get-acquainted tour of the user interface.

The Dreamweaver Site window is divided into two panes. One pane (usually the right) displays a list of files and folders in the local copy of your web site. The contents of the other Site window pane change depending on which of the two views you choose to display. The Site Files view (see Figure 1-4) shows a list of files and folders on the remote web server. The Site Map view, shown in Figure 1-10, shows a flowchart-style graphic representation of the links between pages in your web site.

## Understand the Menus and Toolbar

The menu bar near the top of the Dreamweaver Site window is an abbreviated version of the menu bar that appears in the Dreamweaver Document window. The Site window menu bar is missing a few menus (Insert, Modify, Text, and Commands) that apply only to the contents of individual web pages.

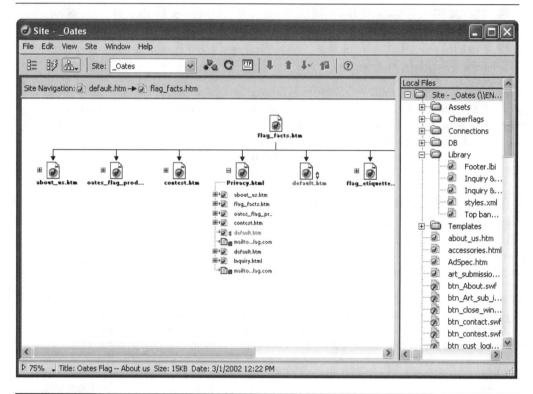

**FIGURE 1-10** The Dreamweaver Site window in Site Map view

The Site window also has a toolbar, like the one in the Dreamweaver Document window. But naturally, Dreamweaver populates the Site window toolbar with a different set of buttons.

Here's a list of the Dreamweaver Site window toolbar buttons (from left to right) and what they do:

- **Site Files** Selects Site Files view.
- **Testing Server** Shows the file list from the testing server (if you've defined one) in place of the Remote Site file list. (See Chapter 14 for information on configuring a testing server.)
- **Site Map** Selects Site Map view.

■ **Site Selector**   Drops down a list of sites that are defined in Dreamweaver. Select a site from the list to display it in the Site window.

■ **Connect to Remote**   Establishes a connection to the remote web server and updates the remote file list.

■ **Refresh**   Updates the Site window display after you make changes in the site.

■ **FTP Log**   Displays the FTP Log tab of the Results panel.

■ **Get Files**   Downloads selected files from the remote web server to the local site.

■ **Put Files**   Uploads selected files from the local site folder to the remote web server.

■ **Check Out**   Downloads selected files from the remote site and locks them to prevent editing by other team members.

■ **Check In**   Reverses the Check Out process by uploading selected files to the remote site.

■ **Help**   Opens a window displaying a Help file with information about the current window view.

## Understand Site Files View

Behind the scenes, a web site is really a collection of computer files and folders, so it makes sense that the key feature of the Dreamweaver Site window is a file list, or rather two lists. The Site Files view (Figure 1-4) shows a split screen view of your web site with a list of files on the remote web server in one half of the screen and a list of files in your local copy of the site shown in the other pane. This arrangement mirrors the way many web developers work: creating and editing web documents on their local hard drive and then publishing the site by copying documents to the main web server.

   To select Site Files view click Site | Site Files or press F8. (These techniques work even if the Site window isn't open.) You can also click the Site Files button in the toolbar if the Site window is already open.

   The file lists provide a tree-structured view of the hierarchical system of nested files and folders that comprise your web site. The file list in the Dreamweaver Site window will probably look familiar to anyone who has used the file management windows of the Windows or Macintosh operating systems. Icons identify folders and the various kinds of document files.

   Clicking the plus sign (+) (on Macs, it's an arrow) beside a folder icon expands the file list to show the contents of that folder. Clicking a minus sign (–) beside a folder collapses that branch of the tree and hides the contents of the folder. The various columns show details about the files such as file size and the date the file was last modified. In addition to the standard assortment of columns, the file lists in the Dreamweaver Site window have a couple of special-purpose columns— you'll learn what they're for in later chapters.

   In addition to the web site files in your local site, the Local Files list includes an icon for your computer desktop. (It's lurking at the bottom of the Local Files list.) This gives you access to any of the files on your computer or local network, just like in a Windows Explorer or Macintosh Finder window.

## Understand Site Map View

The Site Map view, shown in Figure 1-10, is a handy way to get an overview of your web site and the connections between the pages. The site map diagram appears in one pane of the Site window (usually the left) and the local file list (usually) appears on the right.

To select Site Map view click Site | Site Map or press ALT-F8. (These techniques work even if the Site window isn't open.) You can also click the Site Map button in the toolbar if the Site window is already open.

The Site Map diagram starts with the site's home page at the top and shows the pages linked directly to your home page in a row beneath it.

- Click the plus (+) box (on Macs, it's an arrow) next to a page icon to expand the diagram to show the pages linked to that page. You can keep expanding the site map diagram as needed to show the detail you need. Click the minus (–) box to collapse the diagram and hide the linked pages.

- Click the percent display in the left end of the Site window status bar and choose a new magnification to reduce the size of the icons in the site map diagram and make room for more detail.

- Right-click a linked page and choose View as Root from the context menu that appears to redraw the site map with the selected page as the root page at the top of the diagram. This hides other pages at the same level and above the selected page and makes more room available for a detailed examination of the pages below. The Site Navigation bar at the top of the site map pane shows the navigation links to the current root page.

- Click the leftmost page icon in the Site Navigation bar to return the site map to the original root homepage.

- Drag the border between the two panes left or right to resize the panes.

# Work with Panels

Dreamweaver keeps the main document window relatively clean by moving most all the tools and resources that you use as you design and edit web pages out of the Document window and into a collection of smaller satellite windows called *panels*. The panels—22 in all—are a diverse lot. They vary significantly in appearance depending on the content and how you use them to create web pages.

With so many panels available, they could easily consume the whole screen, leaving no room for document windows. So the default workspace arrangement starts out with just two individual panels open (the Insert Bar and the Property Inspector panel) and most others consolidated into the *panel dock*, a separate window where you organize a collection of panels for easy access.

You can open, close, and rearrange panels most any way you want. You can move the panels and panel dock around on the screen, resize them, show or hide individual panels in the panel dock, move panels in and out of the panel dock, and rearrange panel dock groups. The variations are almost endless.

# Insert Objects with the Insert Bar

The Insert Bar panel is basically a free-floating toolbar stocked with buttons that enable
you to insert objects into your web page. By default, the Insert bar starts out in the
upper-left corner of your screen, immediately to the left of the Document window. It's
the tall skinny panel filled with an assortment of colorful icons. (Interestingly, in the
alternate Dreamweaver workspaces, the Insert bar appears as a tabbed toolbar near the
top of the application window instead of as a separate panel.)

The objects you can insert from the Insert bar run the gamut from major page-
structure components, such as tables and forms, to images and multimedia objects
to special text characters.

There are far too many buttons in the Insert bar to show them all at once, so the
panel is divided into categories. The small arrow button at the top of the Insert bar is
the Category selector. Click the button, and then select a category from the menu,
which then appears to display the icons from that category. The default category list
includes the following items:

- **Common**   Commonly used objects such as images, links, anchors, horizontal
  rules, tables, and more
- **Text**   Text formatting tags
- **Tables**   Table tags such as row, cell, header, and caption
- **Frames**   Predefined framesets that you can create with a click of your mouse
- **Forms**   Forms and form components, such as text box, check box, and
  radio button
- **Templates**   Tools for creating templates, such as editable region, repeating
  region, and optional region
- **Characters**   Special text characters, such as copyright symbol (©), em dash (—),
  line break, and nonbreaking space
- **Media**   Multimedia objects, such as Flash and Shockwave files
- **Head**   Buttons for adding meta tags to the page header
- **Script**   Buttons for script, noscript, and server-side includes
- **ASP**   Buttons for inserting ASP programming codes
- **Application**   Buttons for creating database-driven pages such as recordset, dynamic
  text, dynamic table, and recordset insertion

In addition to the standard objects, you can download and install Dreamweaver extensions
that add objects and categories to the Insert bar. See Chapter 10 for more on extensions.

By default, the Insert bar buttons are labeled with graphic icons instead of text descriptions,
but it's relatively easy to decipher the meaning of most of the icons. If you're in doubt about
what kind of object a button represents, just point to the icon and let your pointer hover there
a moment—Dreamweaver pops open a tool-tip box with a text description of the object.

### Insert an Object from the Insert bar

To insert an object from the Insert bar, simply drag the Insert bar button for the kind of object you want and drop it onto your page in the desired location, or position the insertion point on the page first and then simply click the Insert bar button. Depending on the kind of object you are inserting, Dreamweaver may open a dialog box where you supply necessary information about the object (such as selecting a filename for an image file) before inserting the object into your page. Inserting objects from the Insert bar is really just an alternative to selecting a command from the Insert menu. But most users find the Insert bar a little faster and easier to use—especially when inserting several related objects, one after the other.

### Use the Layout View Buttons

The buttons at the bottom of the Insert bar provide easy access to the Layout view feature, which changes the way tables are shown in Design view. The bottom two buttons (labeled "View") enable you to switch between Standard Table view and Layout Table view. The Layout buttons, located just above the View buttons, are available only in Layout view. When they are active, you can click the left button to add a layout table to the current web page, or you can click the right button to insert a Layout Table cell. Chapter 6 explores tables in detail. (In the Integrated workspace, you'll find the counterparts to these buttons on the Layout tab of the Insert bar.)

## Work with the Property Inspector Panel

If there is one panel that you use more than any other in Dreamweaver, it's the Property Inspector panel. The Property Inspector is where you can view and edit the attributes of the object currently selected in the Document window. The Property Inspector is where you format text, define hyperlinks, and adjust image attributes.

The default location of the Property Inspector is at the bottom of the screen below the Document window. It's a little unusual in certain respects. It's the only panel with its title bar on the left side instead of across the top, and although you can move the Property Inspector around on your desktop, you can't resize the Property Inspector by dragging its border—you can only click an arrow button in the lower-right corner to show or hide the optional detail settings in the lower half of the panel.

When you select an object in the Dreamweaver Document window, the Property Inspector immediately displays the attributes of that object. If you select text, the Property Inspector displays the properties of a text object. Buttons and list boxes in the Property Inspector enable you to adjust the style, font, size, color, attributes such as bold and italics, paragraph alignment, and more. But if you select an image, you see an entirely different set of options in the Property Inspector. Image properties include height and width, vertical and horizontal space, border thickness, and alignment, among others.

You can change any of the selected object's attributes by editing the settings in the Property Inspector panel. When you do, Dreamweaver immediately updates the web page in the Document window. You can see the effect of your changes in Design view, and you can observe the code changes in Code view.

## Manage Panels with the Panel Dock

Each Dreamweaver panel is potentially a separate window that you can show, hide, move, and resize independently. However, the sheer number of panels available in Dreamweaver means that it's impractical to keep all of them open at once. And opening, closing, and rearranging separate individual panels as you perform various tasks can be a nuisance. So Macromedia bestowed upon Dreamweaver MX a new feature called the *panel dock*. It's a sort of super panel where you can store and manage a collection of individual panels, neatly organized into a series of collapsible *panel groups*. The panel dock is normally the home for all the panels except the Insert bar and Property Inspector (and a couple of other odd panels that aren't used frequently).

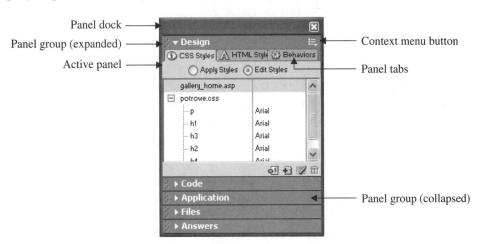

The default location of the panel dock is to the right of the Document window, along the right edge of the screen. The panel dock starts out with five panel groups (Design, Code, Application, Files, Answers), which each contain from one to four individual panels. You can expand or collapse a panel group to show or hide its component panels. Each panel in the group is represented by a tab, and as in a tabbed dialog box, only one tab at a time can be active in a given group. As you expand and collapse panel groups, the panel dock expands and contracts vertically to make room.

You can move panels from one panel group to another, and you can add, delete, and rearrange panel groups within the panel dock. You can also move individual panels and entire panel groups in and out of the panel dock, which is called *docking* (moving in) or *undocking* (moving out). Here's how to manipulate panels:

- To expand or collapse a panel group, click the group name.

- To access a panel within a group, click its tab.

- To rename a panel group, click its context menu button and choose Rename Panel Group.

- To undock a panel group, drag the textured area at the left end of the group title bar and drop it outside the panel dock. A new window border appears around the group, and you can move and resize it independently from the panel dock.

- To dock a panel group, drag the textured area at the left end of the group title bar and drop it on the panel dock.

- To undock a panel, right-click its tab and choose Group *Panel Name* with | New Panel Group. A new window border appears around the panel, and you can move and resize it independently from the panel dock.

- To dock a panel, right-click its title bar and choose Group *Panel Name* with | *Group Name*. The panel appears within the selected group.

- To remove a group from the panel dock, right-click the group name and choose Close Panel Group.

- To rename a panel group, right-click the group name and choose Rename Panel Group. Type a new name in the Rename Panel Group dialog box and click OK.

- To expand a panel group vertically to the maximum size, right-click the group name and choose Maximize Panel Group.

- Choose Window | *Panel Name* to open or close an individual panel in the panel dock.

- Choose Window | Others | *Panel Name* to open or close one of the less-used panels. (Some of these panels open in the panel dock by default, others open in their own separate panel windows.)

- Click a panel's icon in the Launcher to open or close the panel.

- Choose Window | Hide Panels (or press F4) to close the panel dock and all its panels.

- Choose Window | Arrange Panels to automatically position all open panels against the outer edges of your computer desktop.

## Know Your Panels

In addition to the Insert bar and the Property Inspector panel, Dreamweaver includes an assortment of other panels that provide tools for performing a variety of tasks. Here's a list of the Dreamweaver panels and a brief summary of their purpose, arranged according to their default grouping in the panel dock. Coverage of a couple of specific panels follows the list. (I'll cover the features of the other panels in more detail in context elsewhere in this book.)

**Design Panel Group**    This is a collection of panels that you're likely to use as you design web pages in Design view:

- **CSS Styles panel**    Provides a place to manage Cascading Style Sheet styles and apply them to your web page. See Chapter 11 for information on using style sheets.

- **HTML Styles panel**    Define custom styles in the HTML Styles panel and apply them to the text on your web page. Refer to Chapter 3 for information on using HTML styles.

- **Behaviors panel**    Enables you to attach Behaviors to HTML tags on your web page and to edit existing Behaviors. You can learn about Behaviors and using the Behaviors panel in Chapter 13.

**Code Panel Group**    You're more likely to use these panels as you edit code in Code view. You can find more information about all these panels in Chapter 5.

- **Tag Inspector panel**    A tree-structured display that shows how tags are nested in your document. You can also select any given tag and edit its attributes.

- **Snippets panel**    A collection of code blocks that you can paste into your web documents.

- **Reference panel**    Your access point for an online library of reference material about HTML, CSS styles, accessibility standards, and more.

**Application Panel Group**    You'll use these panels if you develop dynamic database-driven web pages. See Chapter 14 for a brief overview of Dreamweaver MX's tools for creating dynamic web pages and web applications.

- **Databases panel**    Shows the databases that are available for the current site and allows you to define new database connections.

- **Components panel**    Makes ColdFusion components available for editing and use in your ColdFusion-based web pages.

- **Bindings panel**    Shows the recordsets (query results) that are available for the current page and allows you to define new recordsets.

- **Server Behaviors panel**    Enables you to insert server behaviors into your web page to create and manipulate dynamic data.

**Files Panel Group**    These panels help you manage your site files:

- **Site panel**    In the Floating workspace, the Site window is a separate window. But in the other two Dreamweaver workspaces, the contents of the Site window appear in a panel, and by default it's docked in this group.

■ **Assets panel** Creates a master list of resources such as image files, templates, and Flash files located both in your current site and in a Favorites list. The Assets panel helps you to quickly find and reuse images and other resources that you've used on other pages in the site.

**Advanced Layout Panel Group** This panel group doesn't appear unless you open one of its component panels by choosing Window | Others | *Panel Name*. The group contains some of Dreamweaver's more specialized layout tools:

■ **Layers panel** This is where you keep track of layers on your web page. You can use the panel to select a layer for editing and to make layers visible or hidden. Chapter 12 explores some of the things you can do with layers.

■ **Frames panel** A handy reference showing the arrangement of the frames in a document. You use the Frames panel to select frames and framesets. You can find more information on frames and using the Frames panel in Chapter 7.

**History Panel Group** This is another optional panel group. It appears only if you open the History panel by choosing Window | Others | History. The History panel is where Dreamweaver keeps track of your recent actions as you create and edit your pages. You can select actions from the History panel and replay them to perform repetitive tasks.

**Answers Panel** This isn't really a panel group, although its title bar appears in the panel dock looking like a group. It's really a single panel that you can open by choosing Window | Others | Answers. The Answers panel contains links to Dreamweaver Help files and tutorials.

**Other Panels** These panels don't appear docked in the panel dock—at least, not by default. Instead, they appear as separate, floating panels with their own title bar and border. You can dock the Code Inspector and Timelines panels into the panel dock if you want, but their size would probably make that awkward.

■ **Code Inspector panel** Yet another place for you to view and edit the HTML code for your web page. It's exactly the same view you get in the Document window in Code view, but the Code Inspector panel gives you the option to work in a separate window if you prefer to use it. See Chapter 5 for more information.

■ **Sitespring panel** Provides access to a Sitespring server for web development teams using the Macromedia Sitespring collaboration software. The Sitespring panel is *not* dockable in the panel dock window. Choose Window | Others | Sitespring to open the panel.

■ **Timelines panel** The Timelines panel is the tool you use to create and edit animation effects. To open the Timelines panel, choose Window | Others | Timelines. To find out more about using Timelines, see Chapter 12.

**Results Panel** This panel shows the results of a search operation, report, or log. Unlike other panels that you open in order to access resources that you want to add to your web page, this panel normally appears to show the results of a task or command, such as running a site report or checking a page for compatibility with a target browser. The Results panel can show the results of several different operations and commands, each on separate tabs. Click a tab to view the related information. You can initiate most reports by clicking the green arrow at the upper-left corner of the tab.

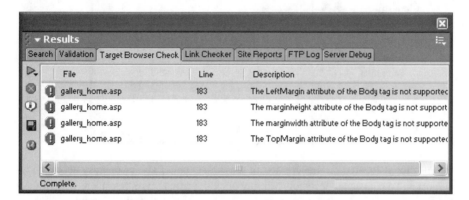

- **Search tab**   Shows the results of a Find and Replace operation (choose Edit | Find and Replace) where you click the Find All button instead of stepping through each item one at a time in the Find and Replace dialog box. (See Chapter 5.)

- **Validation tab**   Shows a list of errors found when validating code in one or more documents. (See Chapter 15.)

- **Target Browser Check tab**   Shows a list of browser incompatibilities found during a target browser check on one or more documents. (See Chapter 15.)

- **Link Checker tab**   Shows the results of a scan for broken links. The Show list box lets you choose to display a list of broken links, external links, or orphaned files. (See Chapter 16.)

- **Site Reports tab**   Shows the results of any of the reports you run from the Reports dialog box (choose Site | Reports). The site reports check your web pages for a variety of common errors. (See Chapter 15.)

- **FTP Log tab**   Shows a log of FTP activity resulting from transferring files between the local and remote sites in the Site window.

## Use the Assets Panel

The Assets panel is a convenient central access point for the various page elements you use to build your web site. Dreamweaver keeps track of just about everything you place on your pages throughout your entire site and arranges it all into categories. The Assets panel is the only panel in the Files panel group in the Floating workspace. Since no panel tab appears unless there is more than one panel in a group, you may not realize that the panel name is Assets rather than Files.

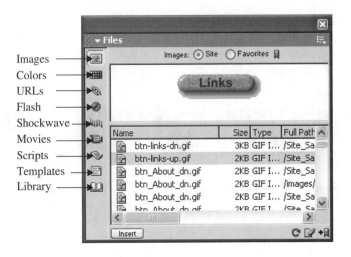

Images ——
Colors ——
URLs ——
Flash ——
Shockwave ——
Movies ——
Scripts ——
Templates ——
Library ——

A column of icons located on the left side of the Assets panel gives you easy access to the various categories. To choose any category, simply click the icon that represents it. Dreamweaver displays the inventory of items in that category in the main list. A thumbnail preview of the selected item appears above the list.

To add a particular asset from any category to your page, either drag it from the Assets panel into your web page or select the item and then click the button on the bottom left of that panel. The button changes from Insert to Apply, depending upon the type of asset. Images, for instance, are inserted, while colors are applied.

To edit an asset, click the Edit button. Dreamweaver opens items such as templates and library items in a Dreamweaver document window. For images and other external files, Dreamweaver launches the external editor associated with the file type to edit the item.

The problem with the Assets panel is that it lists every single asset in the entire site. This can be a huge amount of material to wade through. You may, for instance, use a color only once, yet it will show up in the Assets panel just as do colors you use a hundred times. The solution to this is to use Favorites to cull the list.

Favorites is a special subcategory containing only those assets you want to include. To make any asset into a favorite, simply select it; then click the Add to Favorites button. To view the favorites for a selected category, click the Favorites radio button at the top of the Assets panel.

You can also create special groupings of favorites. To do so, click the New Favorites Folder button. Dreamweaver adds an "untitled" folder to the folder list. Type a new name for the folder. After you create the folder, you simply drag any favorites into it. You can click the + to display the contents of the folder, or click again to hide the folder contents—just as you do when working with folders in the Site Files list.

## Use the History Panel

The History panel provides a supercharged way to undo and redo steps you have taken in Dreamweaver. Instead of relying on the old-fashioned method of using the Edit menu (or its shortcut key equivalents), the History panel displays the complete list of all your recent steps, which you can work with in unique ways.

Suppose, for example, that you need to undo several steps. Instead of choosing Edit | Undo repeatedly, you can simply push the slider button on the left side of the History panel as far up the list as you want to go. Everything in your path will be undone. You can redo steps by reversing direction with the slider. Just slide up for undo, down for redo.

Perhaps the best feature of the History panel, however, is its ability to redo only selected steps. By choosing certain steps and leaving out others, you can create a customized set of steps. Simply CTRL-click on the steps you want to redo; then click the Replay button.

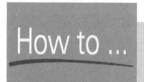

# How to ... **Record a Quick Command Macro**

You can quickly record and playback an unnamed command to automate a multi-step procedure. The effect is similar to creating a custom command from a series of History steps, but it creates a single, temporary command without going through the History panel.

- **Start Recording**   Choose Commands | Start Recording to start recording a series of steps and commands for reuse. Then, after you perform the steps you want to record, choose Commands | Stop Recording to end the recorded sequence. Dreamweaver records the series of steps as a temporary macro that you can use like a command.

- **Play Recorded Command**   Executes the temporary command created by Start Recording.

You can add a series of steps from the History panel to the Command menu for later replay as well. To do this, select the desired steps; then right-click one of them. Choose Save as Command from the pop-up menu that appears. Dreamweaver prompts you to give the new command a name. After you do so, Dreamweaver adds the command to the Commands menu. Then, to repeat the action, you can choose the new command just as you do any other command.

# Set Preferences

Dreamweaver is a highly customizable program. You can change and adjust many aspects of the program, from the layout of its user interface to the way you like code syntax colored in Code view. This section covers some of the more general preference settings. Others are covered in other chapters, in the context of the topics to which the preference settings relate.

The master control center for Dreamweaver customization is the Preferences dialog box, shown in Figure 1-11. From this one dialog box, you can make changes to almost every aspect of the program. Dreamweaver packs a lot of settings into this one dialog box. The secret to its versatility is the long list of categories on the left side. For each category, Dreamweaver displays a different set of preference settings in the body of the dialog box.

The basic process for changing any of the Dreamweaver preference settings is the same. The following steps summarize the procedure, and you can click the Help button to display a description of the options in each category.

1. Choose Edit | Preferences to open the Preferences dialog box (see Figure 1-11).

2. Select a category from the Category list. Dreamweaver displays the settings for that category.

3. Adjust the settings as needed. Most of the settings are check boxes that you click to enable or disable an option. But there are also text boxes, pop-up menus, color pickers, and so on, depending on the settings available in each category.

4. Repeat steps 2 and 3 as needed to change settings in other categories.

5. Click OK to close the Preferences dialog box and record your settings. Most settings take effect immediately. A few settings will become effective the next time you start Dreamweaver. All settings apply to the Dreamweaver program as a whole, not just to individual sites or documents.

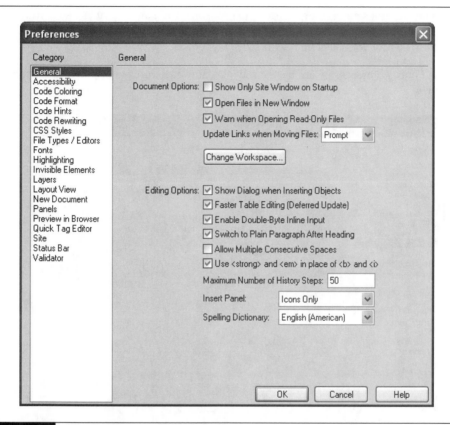

FIGURE 1-11    The Preferences dialog box

The following list provides a brief overview of some of the preference categories that aren't covered elsewhere in this book.

**General**   The General settings (see Figure 1-11) set some file-handling rules and editing preferences as well as telling Dreamweaver what to do every time you open the program. And of course, this is where you select your workspace layout.

**Fonts**   The Fonts preferences determine the fonts Dreamweaver uses to display your documents in Design view.

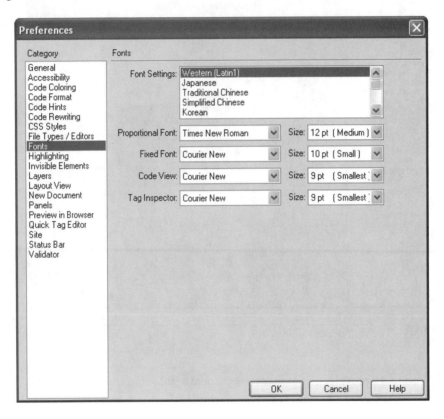

**Highlighting**   The Highlighting preferences tell Dreamweaver how to display highlighted elements, such as template regions when you're working in Design view. You can specify colors for editable regions and locked regions of templates, library items, third-party tags, and more. You can select a color using the color picker for each option, or type a hexadecimal value in the text box. Check or clear the Show check box to control whether Dreamweaver displays the associated highlight.

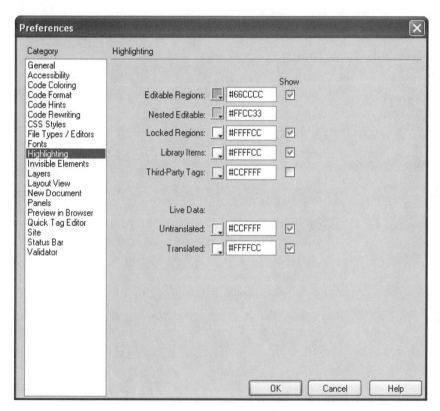

**Invisible Elements** *Invisible elements* are page elements that are normally invisible when you view the page in a web browser, but Dreamweaver can display icons in Design view to represent those elements so you can select and manipulate them. You toggle the Invisible Elements display on and off by choosing the View | Visual Aids | Invisible Elements command. The options in the Invisible Elements category determine which elements appear when the Invisible Elements display is enabled.

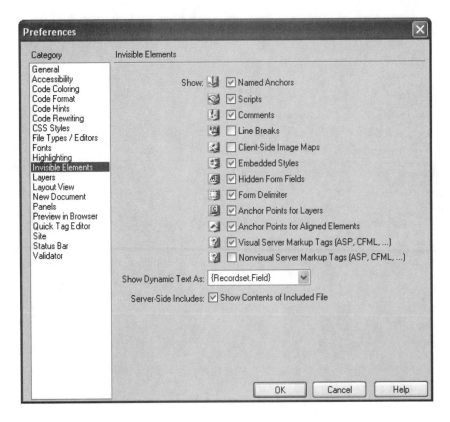

**New Document**   The New Document category is where you set the default document type and encoding for new documents you create in Dreamweaver. You can override these settings when you create an individual document file, but it's convenient to set the default for the document type you use the most.

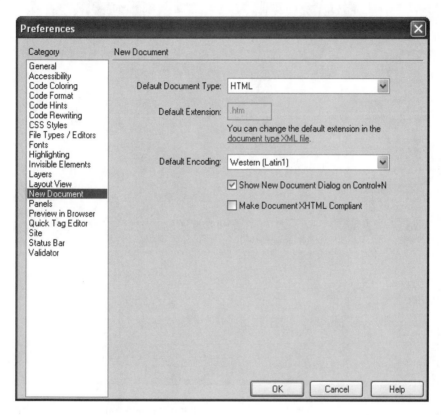

**Panels**   The Panels category is where you control which panels always remain in front of the Document window when they overlap and which panels are represented in the Launcher in the Design View status bar.

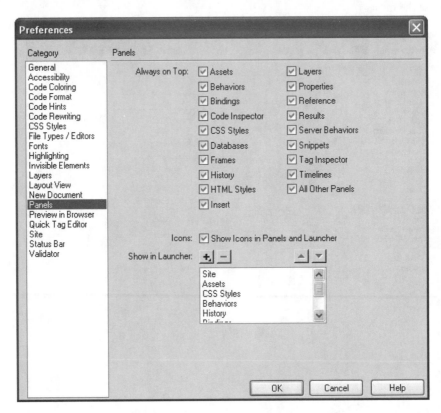

Click the check box beside a panel name to ensure that it stays on top of the Document window. The Show in Launcher list shows all the panels that appear in the Launcher. To add a panel to the Launcher, click the plus (+) button and choose the panel from the menu that appears.

To remove a panel from the Launcher, select the panel in the Show in Launcher list and then click the minus (–) button.

**Status Bar**   The Status Bar category enables you to configure options for the status bar that appears at the bottom of the Document window. You can adjust settings for the Window Sizes box and the Connection Speed calculation.

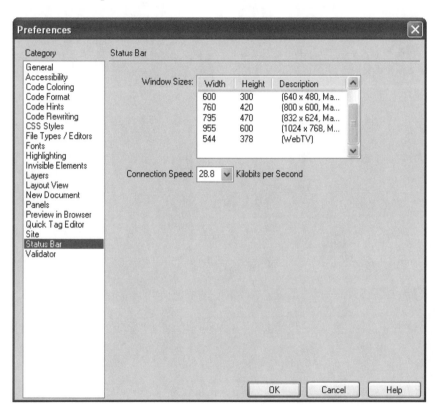

# Chapter 2

# Define a Site in Dreamweaver

## How to...

■ Define a site in Dreamweaver

■ Work with files in the Dreamweaver Site window

■ Create a site map and use it to develop the site structure

In the early days of the Web, people talked about having a Web *home page*. And frequently, that's all it was—a single web page. But the Web has grown since then, and so has the complexity of the typical web presence. Nowadays, the web home page is rarely a stand-alone entity—it has evolved into the entry point for a web site consisting of dozens, hundreds, or even thousands of interlinked pages. Managing all those web documents and related files can be a formidable task.

Dreamweaver is more than a web page creation and editing tool—it's a web *site* creation and maintenance tool. Dreamweaver provides the file management capabilities you need to keep track of all the web documents you create for a site, as well as all the supporting files required for graphics, media, and special effects on those pages. Dreamweaver also gives you the tools for publishing your site by copying web documents and supporting files from the computer where you created them to the web server that makes them accessible to viewers with browsers.

Having a file manager and a file-transfer utility built into Dreamweaver is convenient, but Dreamweaver's site-management capabilities don't stop there. Dreamweaver can compare files on a remote web server to local copies of those files and automatically update only the files that have changed. And Dreamweaver automatically handles the tedious chore of updating file references in your web documents.

If you use Dreamweaver only to create and edit individual web documents that consist entirely of simple text, then you can ignore the program's site-management features. However, as soon as you start creating multipage web sites and web pages with graphics and rich media features, you'll need to deal with file-management issues. When you do, you'll appreciate Dreamweaver's site-management tools. What's more, you'll find that the Dreamweaver features that help you publish your site when you finish it can also be invaluable aids in planning your site from the beginning.

# Everything Starts with the Site Definition

Before you create your first web page, you should have a plan for the web site that the page will be part of. After all, you wouldn't expect to build a house without a set of plans. And, just as carpenters and electricians need to know something about the house plans before they begin work, Dreamweaver needs to know something about your site before its site-management features will work. So the first step in using Dreamweaver on a web development project is to *define your site*, which simply means providing the program with some key information about the site, such as where the site files are (or will be) stored.

You can start from scratch and create an entire site with Dreamweaver. Or you can use Dreamweaver to edit and maintain an existing site—even if the site was not originally developed with Dreamweaver.

# The Relationship Between Local and Remote Sites

In Dreamweaver, the term *site* refers to a collection of related web documents along with their supporting files and folders. Note that, according to this definition, a web site does not necessarily have to be hosted on a web server and available to the public. A web site might be stored on an intranet, where it's available only to internal corporate users. A web site might reside on a network drive somewhere on a local network. Or a web site might be stored on your computer's local hard drive.

When you define a web site in Dreamweaver, you normally define two sets of site files, not just one:

- First, there is the *local folder,* where you create and edit working copies of the site files.
- Second, there is the *remote site*, where the final published files go.

**NOTE**   *In addition to the local and remote sites, Dreamweaver also lets you define a test site that you can use to test web applications during development. (See Chapter 14.) The test site is normally the same as the remote site, but you can define a separate test site when necessary.*

## The Local Folder

The local folder acts as a work area where you can begin building and testing pages without putting them out on the Web for all to see. Some people call this the *staging site, dummy site,* or *dev (development) site*. The local folder is usually a folder on your computer's local hard drive, but it can also be a network drive on a LAN.

**TIP**   *Storing local folder files on your local hard drive improves performance significantly by avoiding network delays when Dreamweaver reads and saves files.*

When the site is ready to publish, you copy the files from the local folder to the remote site. The remote site is often called the *live site*. After you publish the site, you can continue to add and edit pages in the local folder without disrupting the remote site. When the additions and changes are complete, Dreamweaver helps you automatically update the proper files on the remote site.

## The Remote Site

The remote site is usually a directory on a web server that is accessible via the Internet. If your remote site is an in-house web server, you may be able to transfer files to the remote site over a LAN connection. However, normally you need to use an FTP (file transfer protocol) utility to transfer files to the remote site over the Internet. Dreamweaver has its own built-in FTP utility, so you don't need to use a separate program. (Dreamweaver also supports accessing a remote site via RDS, SourceSafe, and WebDAV.)

Basically, the idea is to have two copies of your web site with duplicate sets of files. You create web documents in the local folder and then duplicate those files on the remote site. As you

# Folder versus Directory

The computer terms *folder* and *directory* are interchangeable. Both refer to groupings of files on a computer hard disk or other storage media. Historically, the term *directory* was used across almost all operating systems. However, as the manila file folder gained general acceptance as a visual metaphor (icon) for directories, the term *folder* has become an acceptable alternative for *directory*. Nowadays, *folder* is the term favored by typical Windows and Macintosh users, while *directory* remains the term preferred among UNIX users and many computer professionals. In this book, I use *folder* in context with the Dreamweaver program and your local computer, and I use *directory* when referring to remote servers, which are usually set up and administered by professional computer geeks.

continue to create and edit web documents in the local folder, the local files get out of sync with their counterparts on the remote site. But that's a temporary situation. Eventually, the additions and changes get published to the live remote site, and the two sites are again synchronized. And if you happen to make a mess of things as you edit the local copy of a web document, you can always replace the local file with a copy downloaded from the remote site.

## Duplicate the Site Structure

It's not enough to have duplicate sets of files in both the local folder and the remote site—you also need to duplicate the structure of the site with all the nested folders and subfolders, as shown in Figure 2-1. Dreamweaver doesn't impose a predefined folder structure on your site, but it does require that the same structure exist in both the local folder and the remote site. So if the web documents for the product pages in the remote site are stored in the \Products folder, and the images for those pages are in the \Products\Assets\Images folder, then those same folders must exist in the local folder to hold the local copies of the corresponding files.

Actually, you don't have to duplicate the entire directory structure of the remote web server on your local machine. The remote server may host several complete web sites, and the site you plan to edit with Dreamweaver might be in a directory nested several levels deep. You only need to identify the directory that contains your site and duplicate the files and subdirectories that you will be editing with Dreamweaver, along with any supporting files on which the web documents depend.

Dreamweaver is smart enough to keep track of file and folder locations relative to the site's root folder, which is the folder that contains your site's home page and all the other nested folders and files. For example, a web site with the address www.mysite.com might be located in the following directory on the web server:

D:\web\users\~mysite\webroot\

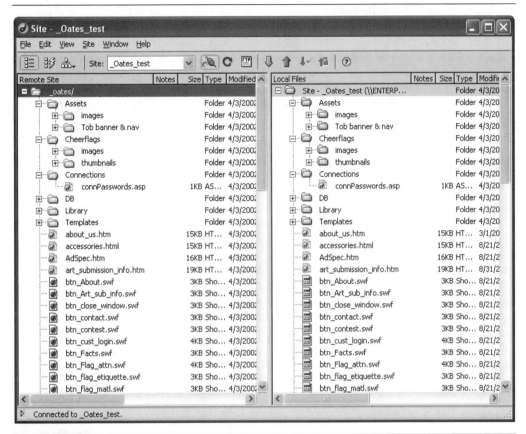

**FIGURE 2-1**    The structures of the local and remote sites must match.

This is the site's root folder on the remote site. You might access that location via FTP at the following address:

ftp://mysite.com/webroot/

You might want to store the site's files in the following location on your local hard drive:

C:\mysite\

This is the root folder for the local folder.

It isn't necessary for the root folders on the local site and the remote site to match. In other words, you don't need to create a bunch of nested folders on your hard drive to match the

\web\users\~mysite\webroot\ path of the remote site. In fact, you don't even have to know the actual location of the files on the remote server as long as you know the FTP address used to access them. Dreamweaver can keep track of the two different root folders provided that the files and subfolders within both sites have the same relationship to their respective roots.

For example, if image files are in D:\web\users\~mysite\webroot\**assets\images**\ on the remote site, they need to be in C:\mysite\**assets\images**\ on the local site. As long as the \*assets*\*images*\ portions of the path are the same on both sites, Dreamweaver can do its thing to keep the local and remote sites synchronized.

*Use folders and subfolders to separate supporting files (such as images) from the actual web document files. Folders help organize supporting files into logical groups, and separating the supporting files from the web documents makes it much easier to find the web document you want to edit.*

As a rule, you need to maintain duplicate structures of nesting folders below the root folder on the local and remote sites. However, there are a few exceptions. You don't need to duplicate any folder that doesn't contain either web documents that you will be editing with Dreamweaver or supporting files that are used by those web documents.

All this business of maintaining duplicate files and folder structures on two sites may sound complicated, but it's really not difficult at all—at least not with the tools that Dreamweaver places at your disposal. All you need to do is set up the local folder; Dreamweaver will take care of the details of duplicating the local site to the remote site. Or you can start with an existing remote site and let Dreamweaver automatically duplicate the entire remote site (or a selected portion) on your local hard drive. After you set up the local and remote sites, Dreamweaver automatically copies files to the correct folders when you synchronize the sites.

## Define a Site

Before you begin creating pages for a web site, you need to tell Dreamweaver a few basic facts about the site. Although it's possible to use Dreamweaver to create and edit individual web documents without first defining a site, doing so is awkward and doesn't use the program to its full potential.

Defining a site takes just a minute or so, and you'll reap a generous return on that time investment by being able to take advantage of Dreamweaver's site-management tools to help you manage all the web documents and supporting files that make up the site.

To define a site, you need to gather the following information:

- A name for the site. You can use any short name that is meaningful to you.

- The location of the local site files—usually a folder on your hard drive. If the folder doesn't exist, you can create it as you define the site.

- The location of the remote site. Usually that's an FTP address consisting of the FTP server name and the host directory for the site. However, Dreamweaver can also access remote sites on your LAN or through RDS, SourceSafe, or WebDAV.

- The user name and password you need to access the remote site.

2

If you plan on using a server technology such as ASP (Active Server Pages) or ColdFusion with your site, you can also identify that server technology and set up access to a test server during the initial site definition.

TIP    *Actually, you can define a local site with just the site name and the local root folder and then fill in all the other information later. However, you won't be able to use all of Dreamweaver's site-management features until you finish defining both the local and remote sites.*

 After you get your information together, you can define the site in Dreamweaver MX. The program includes a wizardlike interface to get you started quickly with a basic site definition. Here's how to use it to set up a simple Dreamweaver site (one that doesn't use server technologies):

**1.** Choose Site | New Site from the menu in either the Dreamweaver Document window or Site window. Dreamweaver opens the Site Definition dialog box, shown in Figure 2-2. (If the dialog box displays the Advanced options, just click the Basic tab to switch to the Site Definition wizard interface.)

**2.** Type a name for your site in the text box. This name identifies the site in the Dreamweaver menus and lists. Click the Next button to display the Editing Files, Part 2 options.

TIP    *It's best to keep site names short but descriptive. The client name or the domain name (mysite.com) is often a good choice. Try abbreviations for long client names; for instance, Smith, Jones, and Doe, Inc. becomes SJ&D.*

**3.** Click the button labeled "No, I do not want to use server technology" to indicate that your site will contain standard HTML web pages (without embedded programming code to access server technologies such as ASP or ColdFusion). Click Next to display the Editing Files, Part 3 options.

**4.** Select one of the options to indicate how you want to edit and test your files as you work with them in Dreamweaver. Normally, you'll want to go with the default selection, which is to edit your files locally and then upload them to the remote server for final publication, but you can elect to edit files directly on the server, if you insist. (Instructions throughout this book assume that you are editing files locally.)

**5.** Enter the path to the folder where you want to store local copies of the site files. You can type the path name into the Where on Your Computer box, or you can click the folder icon to open the Choose Local Root Folder for Site dialog box. Navigate to the folder where you want to store local site files. If the folder doesn't exist, you can create it by clicking the Create New Folder button in the Choose Local Folder dialog box. When you have the site's root folder open, click Select to close the Choose Local Folder dialog box and enter the information into the Site Definition dialog box. Click Next to move on to the next page.

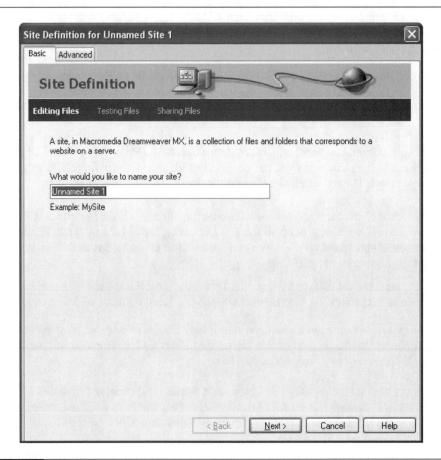

FIGURE 2-2 Defining the local site

**6.** Select an option from the How Do You Connect to Your Remote Server box to specify how you want to copy files to the remote server. Dreamweaver supports FTP, RDS, SourceSafe, WebDAV, and local network connections. (You can also select I'll Set This Up Later to skip the remote server settings for now.) Depending on the connection you select, Dreamweaver displays a different set of text boxes and buttons that enable you to define details such as the location of the remote server and your login ID and password. (Figure 2-3 shows the options for FTP access to a remote server, which is probably the most common scenario.) Fill in the appropriate information to define the remote server connection and then click Next. Dreamweaver displays a Summary page that recaps your settings.

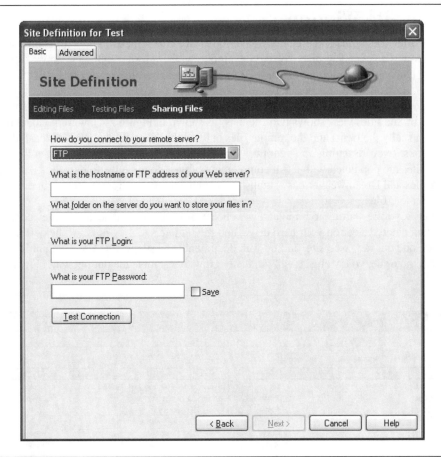

**FIGURE 2-3**    Setting up Dreamweaver to access the server for a remote site

TIP    *The options for setting up an FTP connection to the remote site include a Test Connection button, which you can click to confirm that Dreamweaver can successfully connect to the server using the settings you entered.*

**7.** Click Done to close the Site Definition dialog box. Dreamweaver displays a message box offering to create a site cache.

**8.** Click OK to create the cache. Dreamweaver displays your newly defined site in the Site window, ready for you to begin creating new web documents and building the site.

# Work in the Site Window

Immediately after you define a site Dreamweaver opens the Site window, and with good reason: the Site window is an excellent place to start developing your web site. In the Dreamweaver Site window, you can begin to build the structure of your site, even before you create the first web document.

If you specified both a local and a remote site when you defined your Dreamweaver site, the Site window in Site Files view shows two file lists (as shown in Figure 2-4), with the local files on one side (usually the right) and the remote files on the other (usually the left). At least, that's the way it looks if you're setting up Dreamweaver to access an existing site where both the local and remote sites are populated with a full complement of web documents, folders, and supporting files and Dreamweaver has established a connection to the remote server in order to display the remote files.

However, if you're starting to build a new web site from scratch, the local site may consist of nothing but an empty folder on your hard drive, and the remote site may not even be defined yet. As you work on your new web site, adding web documents and supporting files and publishing them to the remote site, your web site will gradually grow to resemble the one shown in Figure 2-4.

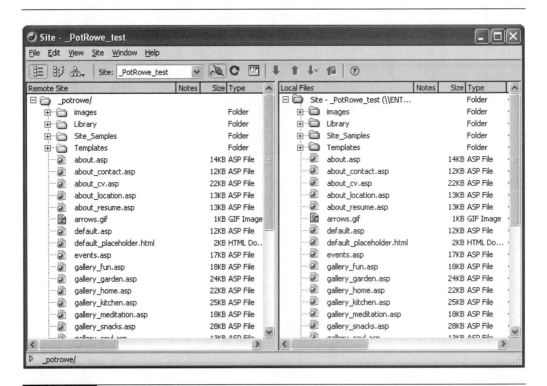

**FIGURE 2-4** The Site Files view shows the contents of the remote and local sites side by side.

The basic techniques for viewing files and folders in Site Files view are pretty standard. Icons beside each file or folder name in the file list enable you differentiate files and folders and identify the various file types.

- Click the plus sign (it's an arrow on the Mac) beside a folder icon to show the contents of the folder.
- Click the minus sign (an arrow on the Mac) to hide the folder contents.
- Click an item to select it.
- CTRL-click to select multiple items.
- Double-click a web document to open the document for editing in the Dreamweaver Document window.
- Double-click other file types to work with those files. This has the same effect as double-clicking the file in your system's file-management utility—it launches the associated program for editing that file type and opens the file for editing. You can override that association with a Dreamweaver preference setting, as described in Chapter 10.
- Double-click a folder to expand or collapse the view—to show or hide the contents of a folder.

Normally, you do all your file creation and maintenance in the Local Files list and manage the remote site by uploading files from the local folder. However, you can use the same techniques to work directly with files and folders in the remote site if the need arises.

# Create Files and Folders

Obviously, the Site window's file lists enable you to view the files and folders that make up your web site. What isn't so obvious at first glance is that you can also *create* both files and folders in the Dreamweaver Site window. In other words, this is where you can build the structure of your web site by adding folders, subfolders, and web document files.

## Create Folders

The procedure for creating new folders in the Local Files list is similar to creating folders in Windows Explorer. Just follow these steps:

1.  Select the folder in which you want to create the new subfolder.
2.  Choose File | New Folder or right-click anywhere within the parent folder and choose New Folder from the context menu that appears. Dreamweaver creates a new folder with the unimaginative name *untitled* and highlights the folder name, ready for editing.

SHORTCUT    *The keyboard shortcut for the New Folder command is* CTRL-ALT-SHIFT-N.

3.  Type in the name for the folder and press ENTER.

You can create as many folders and subfolders as you need to build a logical structure for your site. Web document files for the site's home page (and sometimes the first tier of general site pages) typically go in the site's root folder, but it's a good idea to store all other site files in subfolders to avoid cluttering the root folder. One common arrangement is to create an Assets folder that contains separate subfolders for images, Flash objects, audio files, and so on. And if you have more than a few web document files, you'll want to organize them in subfolders as well.

## Create Files

You can create web document files directly in the Site window without opening a Dreamweaver Document window. It might seem counterintuitive to create files in this way, but it's actually a fast and efficient way to build a web site. As you build the structure of your web site in the Local Files list, you can quickly and easily create blank web document files to populate the folders. After you create blank web document files in the Local Files list you can use the site map to build links between those files and visualize the way key documents relate to one another without getting bogged down in the details of creating content for each of those pages. (See "Link Pages in Site Map View," later in this chapter.) Then, when you're ready to add content to the blank documents you created in the Site window, the tedious first step of naming and saving a new document file is already done.

The procedure for creating a document file in the Local Files list is similar to the procedure for creating folders. Follow these steps:

1. Select the folder in which you want to create the new file.

2. Choose File | New File, or right-click anywhere within the parent folder and choose New File from the context menu that appears. Dreamweaver creates a new file named untitled.htm and highlights the name, ready for editing.

 *The keyboard shortcut for the New File command is* CTRL-SHIFT-N.

3. Type a name for the file and press ENTER.

## Other File-Maintenance Commands

In addition to creating folders and files, you can perform a number of other file-maintenance tasks in the Site window's file lists. In general, the techniques mirror those you use elsewhere in your computer system. Here is a quick summary of some common Windows commands:

■ **Rename** Select a file or folder and then choose File | Rename to change the name of the selected item. Dreamweaver highlights the item name. Type a new name (don't forget to include the appropriate file extension) and press ENTER. Dreamweaver automatically offers to update any web documents that contain references to the renamed file or folder.

■ **Delete** Select one or more files or folders in a Site window file list and then choose File | Delete to delete the selected items. Dreamweaver displays a dialog box requesting confirmation of the action. If you click Yes, Dreamweaver deletes the selected items from the site.

- **Move**   Select one or more files or folders, and then drag the selected items and drop them on a folder icon to move the items into the target folder. Dreamweaver automatically offers to update any web documents that contain references to the files or folders you just moved.

- **Access Your Desktop**   Expand the Desktop icon in the Local Files list to access resources elsewhere on your computer or local network. Drag and drop files and folders to move or copy them between your Dreamweaver site and other folders on your system.

Of course, you can perform the same file-maintenance tasks outside Dreamweaver, but if you do, you miss out on one very important advantage: When you move, rename, or delete files in the Dreamweaver Site window, Dreamweaver automatically checks all your web documents for any reference to the changed files and offers to update those documents to reflect the changes. If you move or rename a site file using some other utility outside Dreamweaver, you must manually locate and update the file references in all your web documents. And that can be quite a chore, even on a relatively small site.

# Connect to the Remote Site

If your remote site is accessible across your local network, Dreamweaver establishes and maintains a full-time connection to the remote site. However, if the remote site portion of your web site is located on a system requiring an FTP connection, Dreamweaver only connects to the remote server as needed to get updates and perform file transfers.

## Establish a Connection

Dreamweaver normally waits for you to initiate the connection to the remote server in order to work with the files and folders there. To trigger a connection to the remote server, choose Site | Connect or click the Connect button on the toolbar. Dreamweaver uses the settings you entered in the Site Definition dialog box to establish the required connection to the remote server. If it's successful, the button changes slightly (the gap between the plugs disappears) to indicate a successful connection, and the program displays a current list of the files on the remote site in the Remote Site pane.

 *If you need to manually establish a connection to the Internet before you use other programs, such as your web browser, you'll need to do so for Dreamweaver as well. Be sure to establish the Internet connection before attempting to connect to your remote site in Dreamweaver.*

You don't have to manually connect to the remote site every time you want to do something. Dreamweaver automatically initiates a connection to the remote server as needed, whether it's to transfer files or to update the remote file list. The manual connection is just an option that you can use to check or update the connection without actually doing something on the remote site.

## Refresh the File List

Sometimes, site files get changed outside Dreamweaver, and the changes aren't immediately reflected in the Site window's file lists. This can happen if you use another utility to make changes to the files and folders on your local or remote site, but it's more likely to occur when a team or workgroup collaborates on a site. Another team member might edit and update certain site files while you work on others. The Remote Site file list in your Dreamweaver Site window won't show any changes that were made since the last time you connected to the remote server from within Dreamweaver.

 To update the file list, simply click anywhere in the list and click the Refresh button on the toolbar.

 *The keyboard shortcut for refreshing the file list is* F5.

## Copy Files Between Local and Remote Sites

One of the primary functions of Dreamweaver's Site Files view is to enable you to conveniently copy files and folders between local and remote sites. After all, copying files from the local folder to the remote server is how you publish your site. And it's standard practice to copy files from the remote site to your local machine so you can edit the copies without disrupting the live site.

Dreamweaver uses different terms for the copy operation depending on whether you are copying files to or from the remote site:

- **put**  Copy files or folders from the local folder to the remote site.
- **get**  Copy files or folders from the remote site to the local folder.

The terms make a lot of sense if you remember that Dreamweaver always looks at the copy operation from the perspective of the local folder as home base. *Put* and *get* describe what the program needs to do to move files to and from the remote site—and the terms are much shorter than the alternatives: *upload* and *download*.

### Put Files

When you're ready to copy files and folders from the local folder to the remote site in Dreamweaver's Site Files view, follow these steps:

1. Select one or more files or folders in the local folder file list.

 *Selecting a folder automatically selects all the files and subfolders contained in that folder.*

 2. Click the Put File button on the toolbar or choose Site | Put. Dreamweaver displays the Dependent Files dialog box.

 Dependent files *are all the images, templates, library files, and other supporting files that the browser needs to render the selected web document(s). Dreamweaver automatically locates all the dependent files for any web document you copy with the Put or Get commands.*

3. Click Yes or No, depending on whether you want Dreamweaver to copy dependent files in addition to the selected files. Dreamweaver connects to the remote site (if it isn't already connected) and begins the copy process. The status bar at the bottom of the Site window shows the name of each file as it is copied to the remote site.

 *Drag a file or folder icon from one site pane and drop it on the other site pane to copy the file or folder to the target site.*

## Get Files

Getting files—downloading files from the remote site—is really the same as putting files, but in reverse. Here are the steps:

1. Select one or more files or folders in the Remote Site file list.

 2. Click the Get File button on the toolbar or choose Site | Put. Dreamweaver displays the Dependent Files dialog box.

3. Click Yes or No, depending on whether you want Dreamweaver to copy dependent files in addition to the selected files. Dreamweaver begins the copy process, and the status bar at the bottom of the Site window shows the name of each file as it is copied from the remote site.

# Download an Entire Remote Site

When you use Dreamweaver to edit and maintain an existing web site, you're usually faced with a scenario that is just the reverse of the normal workflow. Instead of creating web documents in a local folder and then publishing them to the remote web server, you start out with files that exist on the remote server. You need to create an exact copy of those files and folders on your local system for convenient editing. Fortunately, Dreamweaver makes it easy to copy an entire remote site to your local folder. Here's how:

1. If you haven't already done so, create a new site (see "Define a Site," earlier in this chapter) using the existing site specifications for the remote site and an empty folder on your hard drive as the location for local site.

2. Open the local site, and click the Connect button if necessary to establish a connection to the remote site.

3. Click the root folder at the top of the Remote Site file list. This selects the root folder and all the files and subfolders therein—in other words, the entire site.

4. Click the Get Files button to start the download. Dreamweaver displays a small dialog box asking you to confirm that you want to copy the entire site.

5. Click Yes to confirm getting the whole site. Dreamweaver begins copying files and folders from the remote site to the local folder.

That's all there is to it. Dreamweaver automatically replicates the remote site on your local system, duplicating the folder structure and copying all the files into the appropriate folders.

# Create a Site Map

The Dreamweaver Site Map view (see Figure 2-5) is a great tool for visualizing the way the documents in your site relate to one another. The site map diagrams the links between pages, so you can see a graphical representation of the navigational flow from one page to another. Chapter 1 introduced the site map and how to access it.

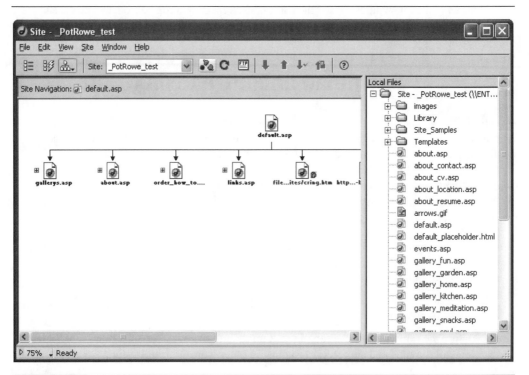

FIGURE 2-5   Site Map view

You can use the site map as a navigation tool to move through your site, locate web documents, and open them for editing by double-clicking the page icon in the site map. The site map's usefulness as a way to display the links between pages is obvious. As you create web documents in the Dreamweaver document window and add links from that document to others, the site map view reflects the growing complexity of the interconnected maze of your site.

> **TIP** *Dreamweaver can display either filenames or page titles to label the page icons in the site map—it's your choice. Choose View | Show Page Titles or press* CTRL-SHIFT-T *to switch between titles and filenames.*

What isn't as obvious is that you can use the site map to build those relationships very early in the site development process, even before you create content for any web documents. In fact, you can build a site map for your site using blank web document files that you created in Site Files view.

## Define the Home Page

The Dreamweaver site map starts with the site's home page and shows how the links to other pages flow from that starting page. Consequently, Dreamweaver can't draw the site map until you define a home page for the site. To define (or redefine) the home page, follow these steps:

**1.** Select a web document in the Local Files list that will become your site's home page.

**2.** Choose Site | Set as Home Page or right-click the document icon and choose Set as Home Page from the context menu that appears.

> **NOTE** *You can also set the home page when you define a site or edit a site definition. The Home Page setting is in the Site Map Layout category of the Advanced tab of the Site Definition dialog box.*

After you define the home page, Dreamweaver draws the site map in the Site Map pane of the Site window. The site map displays the home page at the top of the chart and diagrams the links to other pages from that home page in the next row of page icons. (Refer back to Figure 2-5.) If the document you selected as the home page contains no links to other pages, then the home page alone appears in the site map.

## Link Pages in Site Map View

Normally, you create most links between web pages as you work with the content on those pages. You select some text or graphic on a page and create a link from it to another document. Or you add a button graphic, image map, navigation bar, or other navigation device to the page that includes a link to another page. As you build links into your web documents, Dreamweaver updates the site map to show those links.

> **TIP** *Click the Refresh button to get the latest changes in an open document to show up in the site map.*

However, you can also initiate links between web documents from within the site map. This process is especially useful for planning a web site, before you get down to the detail work of building the content on individual pages. You can create the link between documents and Dreamweaver inserts the linked document's filename or other text into the source document to serve as the link text. You can use any of the following techniques to create a link:

- Drag a file from a Windows Explorer window and drop it on a page icon in the site map. Dreamweaver copies the file from Windows Explorer into your local site folder and adds to the file a link to the page you selected in the site map.

- Select a page in the site map and then choose Site | Link to Existing File to open the Select HTML Link dialog box. Browse to the file you want to link to, and then click Select to close the dialog box and add the link to the site map. (Windows only.)

- Select a page icon in the site map. Click and drag from the Point to File icon (the cross-hairs symbol that appears beside the page icon) to the link target, as shown in Figure 2-6. The target of the link can be any page in the site map or in the site files list.

- To create a link to a new file, select a page in the site map, then choose Site | Link to New File to open the Link to New File dialog box. Then enter a filename, title, and text of the link in the corresponding boxes, and click OK. Dreamweaver creates a new file with the filename and title you specified and adds a link to that file (using the Text of Link text) to the page selected in the site map.

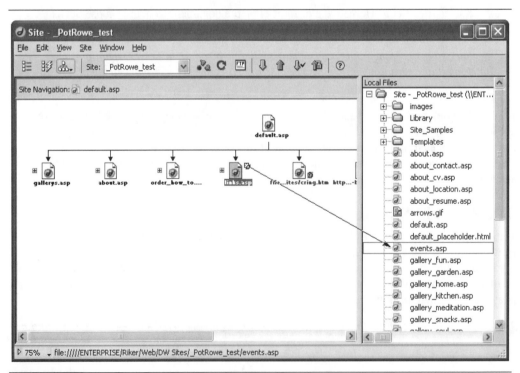

**FIGURE 2-6** Creating a link from the site map

# Part II

# Creating Basic Web Pages

# Chapter 3

# Create a Page with Text

## How to...

- Create a web document page
- Work with text on a web page
- Import text from text files and word processor documents
- Insert horizontal lines
- Work with fonts and character formatting
- Use paragraph formatting for headings and lists
- Create and use HTML styles
- Check your page for spelling errors

Hypertext Markup Language (HTML) and the World Wide Web were originally developed as a way for scientists and academics to share technical documents. Sometimes, when you look at all the eye-catching graphics and rich media content featured prominently on many of today's web pages, it's hard to believe that the Web has its roots in such a humble, and recent beginning.

Then again, when you look past the flashy introduction pages on many web sites, you see that, even today, the vast majority of web documents are composed primarily of text. Perhaps the text is embellished with graphics, but the bulk of the content on most web sites is still good old text. So it's entirely appropriate to start your exploration of Dreamweaver's page-creation capabilities with the program's text-handling features.

# Create a Web Document

Of course, before you can begin working with text or anything else on a web page, you need to create or open a web document in Dreamweaver. You have a choice of starting a new document or opening an existing document file. If you create a new document, Dreamweaver gives you several additional choices, which enable you to create different document types based on a variety of different templates.

When you start the Dreamweaver program, an untitled document window (see Figure 3-1) appears automatically—unless you start Dreamweaver by opening an existing document file or have the program configured to display the Site window on startup. If you open an existing document as you start the program, Dreamweaver displays that document instead of the blank untitled document. When you create or open a document from within Dreamweaver, the program

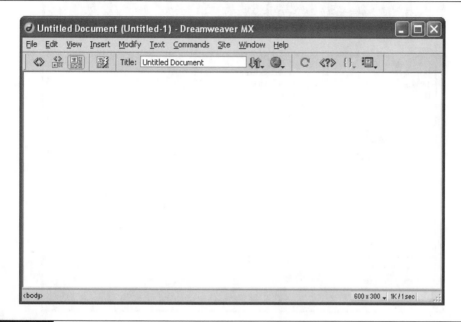

**FIGURE 3-1**    A new web document starts out completely blank.

normally displays a separate document window for each document—you can have several document windows open at once.

When a blank new page appears in a Dreamweaver document window, the very first thing you should do is save the document file. Dreamweaver doesn't force you to save the document immediately, but you should make it a habit to do so because working in an unsaved document can cause some annoying problems.

## Create a Blank Page

To create a new document in Dreamweaver, follow these steps:

**1.** Choose File | New from the menu in a Document window or File | New Window from the menu in the Site window. Dreamweaver opens the New Document dialog box.

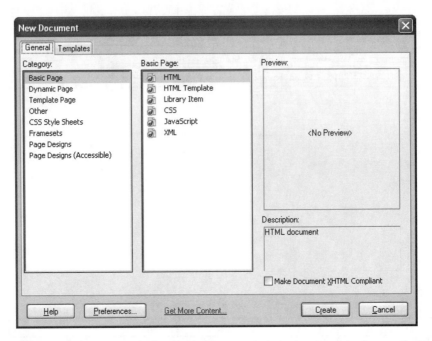

2. Select the kind of document you want to create by clicking items in the two list boxes. First, select an item from the Category list. Dreamweaver changes the list in the middle of the dialog box to show the document types available in that category. Then select the specific document type in the second list box.

*To create a simple web page, select Basic Page in the Category list and HTML in the Basic Page list.*

3. Optionally, click the Make Document XHTML Compliant check box if you want Dreamweaver to generate code that is compatible with the newer XHTML standard instead of the older plain HTML standard.

4. Click Create. Dreamweaver closes the New Document dialog box, opens a new document window, and labels it "Untitled" (see Figure 3-1).

The General tab of the New Document dialog box gives you access to an assortment of predefined document templates for a variety of different document types. But you're not restricted to the templates that come with Dreamweaver MX. The Templates tab of the same dialog box enables you to create new documents based on your own custom templates. These templates let you define common elements that will appear on multiple pages and place them on the page all at once. Chapter 9 covers creating and using templates.

## Open an Existing Page

To open an existing web document for editing in Dreamweaver, use one of the following techniques:

■ Choose File | Open from the menu in either the Document window or the Site window. The Open dialog box appears. Browse to the desired document file, click to select it, then click the Open button to close the dialog box and open the document.

**TIP** *For best results, always open and edit only pages within the current site.*

■ Locate the document file in the Site window and double-click the file's icon to open the document in the Document window.

**CAUTION** *When selecting a document from Site window, pay attention to whether the file is in the Local Files list or the Remote Site list. Dreamweaver lets you select and edit either one. Normally, you want to do all your editing on the local site, but there are times when editing the remote site files is appropriate. However, editing the live copy when you meant to work on the local one (or vice versa) can have unpleasant results.*

■ Double-click the page icon in the site map to open that document in the Document window for editing.

## Save the Document

The process of creating a new web page isn't complete until you save the document. Until then, it exists only in Dreamweaver's program memory and lacks the essential identifying elements of a filename and a location in your site. Dreamweaver keeps track of the location of links, image files, and other dependent files used on each page relative to the location of the page itself. Until you save the web page in a file, Dreamweaver can't keep track of the other file locations properly. To save a new web document, follow these steps:

**1.** Choose File | Save As to open the Save As dialog box.

**2.** Browse to the folder where you want to save the file.

**3.** Type a filename in the File Name text box. Pay particular attention to the extension to make sure it matches the type of document you are saving. Dreamweaver normally defaults to the correct extension for the document type you specified when you created the document. (For standard web pages, the extension should be .htm or .html.)

4. Click Save to close the dialog box and save the file. Dreamweaver changes the title bar of the document window to display the new filename in place of the temporary "Untitled" document name.

After the initial document save that gives your web document a filename, you can easily save updates to your web document using either of the following techniques:

- Choose File | Save from the menu.

- Press CTRL-S.

**TIP**

*Save your document frequently as you work. Unlike some word processors and other common programs that automatically save your document every few minutes, Dreamweaver leaves the decision of when to save your file entirely up to you. An asterisk (*) after the document name in the Document window's title bar is Dreamweaver's way of reminding you that the document contains unsaved changes.*

## Did you know?

# The Correct Extension Is Important

Most web document files carry the extension .html or .htm. The .html extension indicates a file containing HTML (Hypertext Markup Language) code, which is the standard language of the web. The .htm extension is simply an abbreviated three-letter version of .html, which was originally intended for use on older DOS-based systems that limited filenames to eight characters and extensions to three characters. Nowadays, the two extensions are used interchangeably.

In addition to standard HTML web documents, you can use Dreamweaver MX to create and edit a variety of other document types, and each of those document types is identified by its own extension. For example, documents that contain special programming code to access server technologies such as ASP (Active Server Pages) or ColdFusion Markup use the extensions .asp or .cfm, respectively. Similarly, XML (eXtended Markup Language) documents use the .xml extension.

Dreamweaver MX normally assigns the correct extension to a file to match the document type. (That's why you need to specify the document type when you create a new document.) Use caution when changing document types or extensions to make sure the extension matches the kind of information and code contained in the document.

# Set Page Properties

After you create and save a new web document, you'll probably want to set the page properties next. *Page properties* is the term Dreamweaver uses for a collection of general document attributes that apply to the page as a whole, such as the page title, margins, color scheme, and background image.

*All the page properties except the title are attributes of the `<body>` HTML tag that defines the beginning and end of the main web page. The title is a separate tag, `<title>`, contained in the document header.*

Actually, you can set (or change) the page properties at any time, or you can just leave the page properties at the default values. But you'll probably want to change at least the page title, and it's a good idea to take care of that detail immediately after you create the page. (It's too easy to forget about it later, and you wouldn't want to publish the site containing a bunch of pages labeled "Untitled Document.")

## Set the Page Title

The title of your web document is a handy bit of reference information that is stored in the document file and displayed in the browser's title bar while the page is on display. You can also configure the Dreamweaver site map to display page titles under each page icon in the map. In addition, web directories and search engines use the page title to index pages in their databases.

To change the title of your web page from the default, "Untitled," to something more appropriate, use either of the following techniques:

■ Edit the page title in the Title text box in the Document window toolbar.

■ Choose Modify | Page Properties to open the Page Properties dialog box, shown in Figure 3-2. Edit the contents of the Title text box, and then click Apply or OK.

*If you don't want to assign a unique name to each page in your web site, you can enter the web site's name as the page title. This ensures that something meaningful appears in browsers' title bars and search engines' indexes.*

## Set the Color Scheme

The color scheme settings enable you to specify the color of the page background, the default color for text, and the color of text links. You can determine whether your page has dark blue type on a white background, white type on a black background, or any other combination.

Dreamweaver lets you control five different color settings:

■ **Background** The page background. You'll probably want to select a background color (such as white, #FFFFFF) to keep your page from reverting to the old browser-default color scheme of a dull gray background.

■ **Text**   Sets the default color for body text. The most common text color is black (#000000). You can change the color of individual text passages with the Property Inspector to override the default color.

■ **Links**   The color of text hyperlinks. Dreamweaver leaves this setting blank when you create a new page, which means that the browser's default link color (usually blue) is used. Select a color to specify a different color for text links on your page.

■ **Active Links**   The color of text hyperlinks as they are clicked. Normally, the active links color appears only momentarily. As it does with the links color, Dreamweaver leaves this setting blank when you create a new page, which means that the browser's default active-links color (usually red) is used. Select a color to specify a different color for active links on your page.

■ **Visited Links**   The color of text hyperlinks the visitor has already viewed. Again, Dreamweaver leaves this setting blank when you create a new page, which allows the browser's default visited-link color (usually purple) to prevail. Select a color to specify a different color for visited links on your page.

To change the color settings for your page, follow these steps:

**1.** Choose Modify | Page Properties to open Page Properties dialog box (see Figure 3-2).

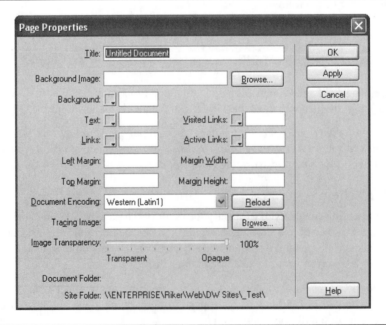

FIGURE 3-2   The Page Properties dialog box

**2.** Click the color picker button for each color setting, and select the desired color from the color picker box that appears (see Figure 3-3). You can select colors for background, text, links, active links, and visited links. (See the boxed text on using the color picker.)

**3.** Click Apply or OK to record your color scheme for the current page. Dreamweaver updates the Document window to reflect your color choices.

**3**

NOTE    *You don't have total control of the color scheme for your page. The popular browsers can all be configured to override the color scheme you specify in the web document. As a result, your page may not display as intended if a visitor elects to use this option.*

## How to ...  Use the Dreamweaver Color Picker

The Dreamweaver color picker is a handy tool that you'll see time and again throughout the program. It provides a fast, easy way to choose colors for objects on your web page. Using the color picker certainly beats specifying colors by typing hexadecimal codes representing the RGB (red, green, blue) values of the desired color. The color picker lets you select a color by clicking a sample of the color; then Dreamweaver takes care of entering the correct codes into the HTML code for your page.

The color picker button appears in many Dreamweaver dialog boxes and panels as a small square box that displays a sample of the currently selected color.

Click the button to expand the color picker and display its color palette (see Figure 3-3). The pointer changes to an eyedropper. As you move the pointer around, the color swatch in the upper-left corner of the color picker shows the color selection under the eyedropper pointer, and the corresponding color code appears at the top of the color picker box. An array of color swatches fills most of the color picker box.

In the upper-right corner of the color picker is a button labeled with an arrowhead. Click the arrow button to display a menu of different color palettes that you can display in the color picker box.

To select a color with the color picker, simply click the eyedropper on a sample of the color you want to use. The color sample can be in the color picker box or in any Dreamweaver window. The ability to select a color by clicking on objects in other Dreamweaver windows makes it easy to match colors you've used elsewhere.

The Default Color button (the first button to the right of the color number at the top of the color picker box) enables you to specify no color for an object, which means the browser displays the object using its default color.

When you click a color sample with the eyedropper, Dreamweaver closes the color picker box and records your color selection. To cancel a color selection and close the color picker, press ESC.

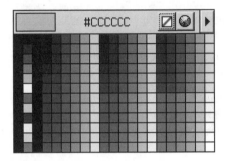

FIGURE 3-3    The Color Picker box

## Did you know?

# It's Best to Work with Web-Safe Colors

The hexadecimal color codes used for specifying colors in web documents can define 256 separate colors. Nearly all computer monitors can display that many colors—usually more. However, testing has shown that web browsers can *reliably* display only 216 of those colors properly. The 216 colors that web browsers display reliably are called *web-safe colors*.

Naturally, web page designers normally confine their color choices to the web-safe colors and avoid the 40 colors that don't display properly in one browser or another.

By default, the color picker box displays only web-safe colors and Dreamweaver automatically selects the nearest web-safe alternative if you click a non-web-safe color from outside the color picker box. However, you can disable this feature of the color picker by clearing the Snap to Web Safe option in the color palette menu.

On rare occasions, you might need to select a color from among the thousands of colors that a modern computer monitor can display, even though it may not be a web-safe selection. You can do so by following these steps:

1. Open the color picker box.

2. Click the System Colors button (the color wheel in the upper-right corner of the color picker box; see Figure 3-3). Dreamweaver closes the color picker box and opens the Color dialog box (or its equivalent on your operating system).

3. Click a color. In the Windows Color dialog box you can click one of the basic color boxes, select a hue from the large spectrum box, and then modify it with the intensity slider to the right, or type in numbers in the Hue, Saturation, Luminance or the Red, Green, Blue boxes.

4. Click OK to close the Color dialog box and record your color selection in Dreamweaver.

### Set Margins and Other Page Properties

Besides page title and colors, the other page properties you're most likely to use are the page margins. The page margin settings enable you to specify how close objects on your page can come to the top and left edge of the browser window. If you don't specify the page margins, each browser will use its own, slightly different, default margin settings.

Because the two leading browsers, Internet Explorer and Netscape Navigator, implement page margins by responding to different HTML code attributes, Dreamweaver's Page Properties dialog box includes two sets of margin settings:

■ **Left Margin** and **Top Margin**   Set the left and top page margins for Internet Explorer

■ **Margin Width** and **Margin Height**   Set the left and top page margins, respectively, for Netscape Navigator

Unless you know for sure that all your web site visitors will be using the same browser, you should specify both sets of margin settings. Enter the size of the desired margin in pixels, and make sure that the corresponding settings for the different browsers match.

TIP    *If you plan to place graphics at the top and left side of your page and want them to extend all the way to the edge of the browser window, set the page margins to zero (0).*

The Page Properties dialog box also gives you the option of specifying a background image, document encoding, and a tracing image. Unless you work with web pages in foreign languages, you'll rarely need to change the document encoding. Chapter 4 covers background and tracing images as well as other images on your web pages.

# Enter and Edit Text

The Dreamweaver document window in Design view (shown in Figure 3-4) looks and acts much like a typical word processor document window when it comes to basic text entry and editing. You can enter, select, and edit text in Dreamweaver using the same techniques that you use in most other programs.

Behind the scenes, an HTML document for a web page is distinctly different from a plain text file or a word processing document. But when you're working in Design view, Dreamweaver effectively masks those differences. The result is a program that handles text the way a typical computer user expects it to, with very few surprises.

Dreamweaver also gives you the option of entering text in Code view. Generally, only the most hardened hand-coders prefer that mode to the convenience and simplicity of Design view for routine text entry. Still, it's good to know that Code view is available as a text-entry option should you need it.

## Type in Regular Text

Entering regular text into a web document is easy—just start typing. The blinking vertical cursor marks the insertion point where new text is added to the page.

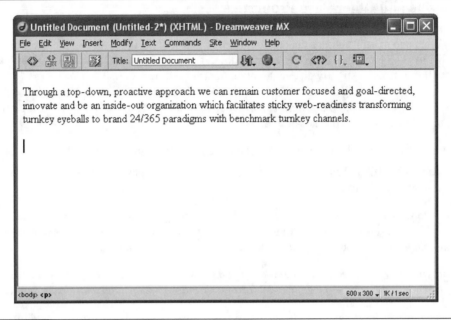

FIGURE 3-4    Entering text in Design view

Text entry starts at the upper-left corner of the document window and flows to the right and down the page. Text wraps to the next line automatically when the line reaches the right side of the document window. Dreamweaver rewraps the text automatically when you change the size of the document window. Pressing the ENTER key ends a paragraph—not every line.

Dreamweaver lets you enter any of the standard alphanumeric characters on the keyboard, including upper- and lowercase letters, numbers, and the standard punctuation characters. Dreamweaver also lets you enter any of the standard symbols (~ @ # $ % ^ & * _ + = < > \ |) available on a normal computer keyboard, even though many of those symbols must be represented by special code in an HTML file. You simply type the desired character on your keyboard, and Dreamweaver takes care of translating that character into the corresponding HTML code, if necessary.

*Don't attempt to enter the HTML codes for symbols, special characters, or HTML tags in Design view. Dreamweaver automatically converts angle brackets (< >) and other symbols into the coded representation of those symbols, so you would end up with a jumble that the browser can't interpret. If you want to enter HTML codes directly into your document, use Code view.*

## Select and Edit Text

Dreamweaver also follows common conventions for selecting and editing text. As you move the mouse pointer over a text paragraph, the pointer assumes the familiar I-beam shape, as shown in Figure 3-5.

Try these other common text selection and editing techniques:

■ Click to move the insertion point.

■ Double-click to select a word.

■ Drag the I-beam pointer across text to select it.

■ Drag and drop selected text to move it.

■ Press DELETE or BACKSPACE to delete selected text.

■ Type to replace selected text with the new text you enter.

■ Right-click and choose Copy or press CTRL-C to copy selected text.

■ Right-click and choose Paste or press CTRL-V to paste text into the document at the insertion point.

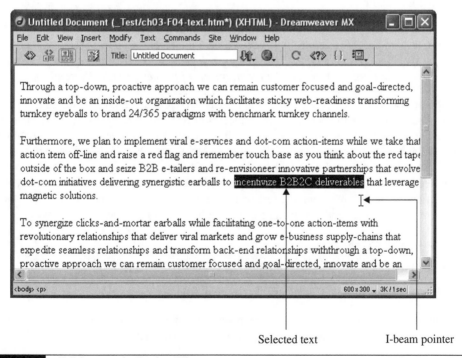

Selected text          I-beam pointer

**FIGURE 3-5**   Editing text in Design View

*To select an entire line of text, move the pointer to the left page margin beside the line you want to select. The pointer changes to an arrow that points to the right. Click to select the line the arrow is pointing to. Click and drag to select multiple lines.*

## Work with Paragraphs and Line Breaks

In a web document, pressing the ENTER key ends a paragraph, just as it does in most word processing programs. Paragraphs are significant in a web document because the entire paragraph of text gets treated as a unit for formatting, alignment, and text-flow purposes, and paragraphs are separated from other paragraphs by a line of blank space.

**NOTE** *The HTML tag for the beginning of a paragraph is <p>; for the end of a paragraph it's </p>. Although both paragraph tags aren't required for every paragraph in a web document, Dreamweaver follows the recommended practice of inserting beginning and ending tags for each paragraph.*

### Insert Line Breaks

You can use a separate line-break code to force a line of text within a paragraph to end before reaching the right side of the document window, where it would normally wrap to the next line. The line break enables you to create a series of short lines without extra space between the lines, such as in a postal address.

**NOTE** *The HTML tag for a line break is <br>. This is the tag that Dreamweaver normally inserts into the HTML code for your Document view when you press SHIFT-ENTER. If you specified XHTML compatibility for your document, Dreamweaver modifies the tag with a slash (<br />) to meet the requirements of the newer XHTML standard.*

Word processors often let you get by with pressing ENTER to end a line because the next paragraph usually starts on the very next line. A series of one-line paragraphs can look the same as a single paragraph with several lines ending in line breaks. However, standard web documents don't work that way—paragraphs are *always* separated by a blank line (unless you go to great lengths to override the standard rules with settings in a CSS style sheet). So when you press ENTER in Dreamweaver, the insertion point drops two lines down the page. If you want to enter a short line of text to be followed by more text on the next line without a blank line between them, you *must* use the line-break code. You can enter a line break in any of the following ways:

- Press SHIFT-ENTER.
- Click the Line Break button on the Insert bar's Character category
- Choose Insert | Special Characters | Line Break from the menu.

 Dreamweaver displays a special icon to represent each line break in Design view. The icon makes the normally invisible line break character visible so you can select and edit it easier.

TIP

*If the icon doesn't appear in Design view, choose View | Visual Aids | Invisible Elements to display icons for invisible elements. If the icon still doesn't appear, choose Edit | Preferences to open the Preferences dialog box, click Invisible Elements in the Category list, make sure the Line Breaks box is checked, then click OK to close the dialog box.*

## Add Empty Paragraphs

Another peculiarity of web documents is that browsers ignore multiple spaces. That means that you can't use a string of spaces to move text to the right. Consequently, Dreamweaver also simply ignores multiple presses of the spacebar.

TIP

*If you must create white space within a text paragraph, like what you would normally get by entering multiple spaces between words in a typical word processor, use the nonbreaking-space special character instead of the spacebar. You can insert a nonbreaking space by clicking the Non-Breaking Space button on the Character page of the Insert bar or by pressing* CTRL-SHIFT-SPACEBAR. *You can also set a Dreamweaver option so that the program automatically inserts nonbreaking-space characters when you type multiple consecutive spaces. The setting is in the General category of the Preferences dialog box.*

NOTE

*The nonbreaking-space character appears in the HTML code for your page as  .*

Similarly, web browsers ignore empty paragraphs, which means that you normally can't use a series of empty paragraphs to move text down the page in a web document. However, the technique of using the ENTER key to insert a line of white space and move the insertion point down the page is so ingrained in most users that Macromedia chose to support it in Dreamweaver. So if you press the ENTER key at the beginning of a paragraph, Dreamweaver assumes that you want to create an empty paragraph to act as a spacer and automatically enters an invisible character (a nonbreaking space) in addition to the paragraph marker. Since the paragraph isn't empty, the browser doesn't ignore it, and you get the result you expected (white space equal to a one-line paragraph).

NOTE

*The HTML code that Dreamweaver enters for an "empty" paragraph is* `<p> </p>`.

## Insert a Date

If you want to insert a date into your web document, you can always just type it in. But Dreamweaver also gives you the option of entering a preformatted day, date, and time with a menu command. You can even have Dreamweaver automatically update the date entry when you save your web document file; for example, to record the date on which the page was last updated.

To insert a date onto your web page, follow these steps:

**1.** Choose Insert | Date from the Document window menu. Dreamweaver opens the Insert Date dialog box.

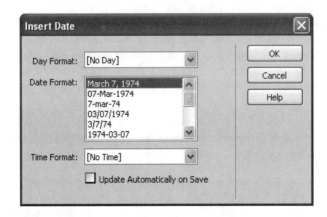

2. Select the Day Format, Date Format, and Time Format from the list boxes. If you don't want the time portion of the entry in your document, select No Time from the Time Format list. You can suppress the day and date portion of the entry the same way.

3. Check the Update Automatically on Save option at the bottom of the dialog box if you want Dreamweaver to automatically insert the current date when you save the web document file.

4. Click OK to close the Insert Date dialog box and enter the date into your document.

## Special Characters

Although the characters you need for normal text entry are on the keyboard, a few special characters that you may need from time to time aren't so readily available. The old way to enter special characters was to look up a special code for the character you needed and embed that code in the HTML document. Dreamweaver simplifies the process dramatically. You can insert special characters into your web document with either of the following techniques:

- Select the Character category in the Insert bar, and then click the button for the special character you want.

- Choose Insert | Special Character | *character*

Both these techniques enable you to select any of the following special characters:

| Character | Description | HTML code |
|-----------|-------------|-----------|
| © | Copyright | &copy; |
| ® | Registered trademark | &reg; |
| ™ | Trademark | &#153; |
| £ | Pound Sterling | &pound; |
| ¥ | Yen | &yen; |

| Character | Description | HTML code |
|---|---|---|
| € | Euro | &euro; |
| " | Opening quote | &#147; |
| " | Closing quote | &#148; |
| — | Em (long) dash | &#151; |
| | Line break | <br> or <br /> |
| | Nonbreaking space |   |

If you need a special character that isn't listed, click the Other Character button in the Insert bar or choose Insert | Special Character | Other to open the Insert Other Character dialog box. Click the character and then click OK. Dreamweaver closes the dialog box and inserts the selected character into your document at the insertion point.

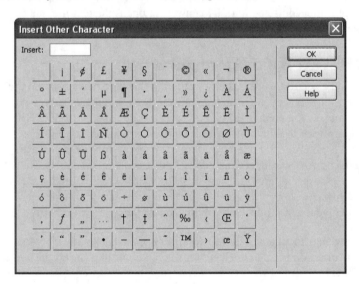

# Work with Text from Other Programs

If you have text in a document that was created by another program, and you want to use that text on your web page, there is an excellent chance that you will be able to do so without retyping the text in Dreamweaver.

## Open and Edit HTML Files

Dreamweaver can open and edit any standard HTML document. It doesn't matter whether the web document was originally created in another web design program or hand-coded in a text editor. As long as the web document contains text and standard HTML codes, Dreamweaver can open it. In other words, if your browser can read the web document, so can Dreamweaver.

To open an HTML file, choose File | Open, locate the file in the Open dialog box, and click Open. Or, if the file appears on the file list in the Dreamweaver Site window, simply double-click the file icon. Dreamweaver opens the selected file in a new Document window, and you can edit it just like any web document that you create in Dreamweaver.

## Open and Edit Text Files

Dreamweaver can not only open and edit standard HTML files, it can also open text files, XML files, Active Server Pages, ColdFusion document files, several kinds of script files, and a host of other related file formats. The ability to open and edit these files means that you can use Dreamweaver to edit plain text files, most kinds of program source files, and some e-mail messages.

You can open a text file in Dreamweaver using exactly the same technique you use to open a web document (see the preceding section). Dreamweaver opens the text file in a new document window and displays the text in Code view.

## Import HTML Text from Microsoft Word

Microsoft Word is very popular word processor program that enjoys widespread use. In addition to creating documents in its own .doc format, Word can save documents as web pages using the HTML format. Of course, you could use Dreamweaver to open and edit HTML files produced by Word by simply opening the file like any other web document.

However, Word is notorious for adding a lot of extraneous comments and extra code to the HTML files it produces. As a result, editing a Word-produced web document can be messy. So Dreamweaver includes a special import feature just for Word HTML files that cleans up the code and makes it more manageable.

To import a web document produced by Word, follow these steps:

1. Create a new web document in Dreamweaver or open an existing web document and position the insertion point at the location where you want to insert the contents of the Word HTML file.

2. Choose File | Import | Word HTML. Dreamweaver opens the Select Word HTML File to Import dialog box (it's a fairly standard file-selection dialog box).

3. Browse to the file you want to import, then click Open. Dreamweaver closes the Select Word HTML File to Import dialog box and opens the Clean Up Word HTML dialog box.

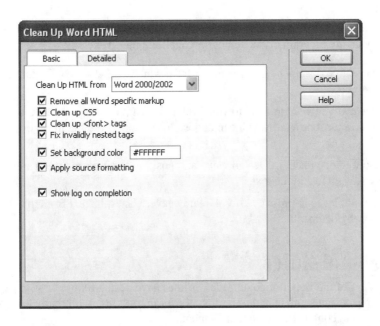

**4.** Select the version of Word that produced the file, and check the items you want Dreamweaver to clean up. (Dreamweaver can usually detect the Word version automatically, and you'll normally want to leave all the cleanup options checked.)

**5.** Click OK to close the dialog box and start importing the contents of the Word file.

Dreamweaver copies the contents of the Word HTML file and pastes them into the Dreamweaver web document, but not before it cleans up the HTML code considerably. Depending on the size of the Word HTML file, it might take a moment or so for the imported text to appear in the Dreamweaver Document window.

TIP    *Dreamweaver can also clean up a Word HTML document that you open in a Dreamweaver Document window without going through the import step. Choose Commands | Clean Up Word HTML to open the Clean Up Word HTML dialog box. Adjust the settings as needed, and click OK to start the cleanup procedure.*

## Cut and Paste Text from Anywhere

Text files and HTML files created in other programs account for a lot of the text you'll want to add to your web documents, but there are many other sources from which you can't import directly into Dreamweaver. Fortunately, you can use standard cut-and-paste techniques to copy text from just about any program or document on your computer. Here's how:

1. Open the source document (the document from which you want to copy text) in its native program.

2. Select the text you want to copy to your web page, and then copy the text to the system clipboard. In most programs, you can choose Edit | Copy from the menu or just press CTRL-C.

3. Open the web document in Design view, and position the insertion point at the location where you want to add the text.

4. Choose Edit | Paste or press CTRL-V. Dreamweaver pastes the text from the clipboard into the web document.

# Insert Horizontal Rules

Since the early days of the web, horizontal rules or lines have been a fixture on web pages, serving as a simple design element and as a separator for text. Rules aren't really text, but they are commonly used in conjunction with text elements.

Adding a horizontal rule to your web page is easy. Just position the insertion point where you want to insert the rule and then do one of the following:

■ Click the Horizontal Rule button in the Insert bar's Common category.

■ Choose Insert | Horizontal Rule from the menu.

Dreamweaver inserts a line into the document, as shown in Figure 3-6.

After you insert a horizontal rule into your document, you can modify its characteristics with the Property Inspector. There are just a few simple settings for this simple object:

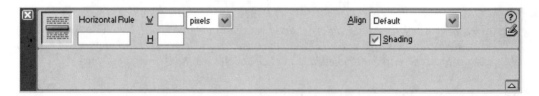

■ **W** Width (length) of the rule. You can specify the width in either pixels or as a percentage of the browser window's width.

■ **H** Height (thickness) of the rule. Enter a number of pixels.

■ **Alignment** The horizontal alignment. Choose left, center, right, or default (center).

■ **Shading** Clearing this box turns off the drop shadow effect that makes the rule look embossed.

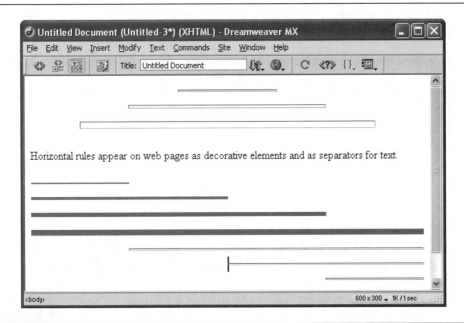

**FIGURE 3-6**    A sampling of horizontal rules.

# Apply Character Formatting

You can change the appearance of text on your web page by changing attributes such as font (type size and typeface), color, and formatting, such as bold and italic. Collectively, these text characteristics are called *character formatting,* because you can apply them to individual text characters. Other formatting attributes, such as alignment on the page and indentation, apply to whole paragraphs and are known as *paragraph formatting*.

Of course, you don't generally apply formatting to one character at a time. Usually you select words, phrases, sentences, or even whole paragraphs and apply character-formatting attributes to the selection.

When you type text on your web page, that text assumes the generic default character formatting until you change it. Default text formatting is a browser configuration setting that isn't controlled by Dreamweaver. However, the traditional default settings are fairly standard, and few users bother to change them. So the default text settings you see in Dreamweaver's Design view are a reasonable approximation of what most site visitors will see. These are the settings:

■ **Font**    Times Roman or an equivalent serif font

■ **Size**    3 (on a scale of 1–7)

■ **Color**    Black (uses the default text setting from the Page Properties)

- **Bold**    Off
- **Italic**   Off

The basic procedure for applying character formatting is always the same. Here are the steps:

1. Make sure the document window is open in Design view and the Property Inspector panel is accessible.

2. Select the text you want to format. You can select anything from a single character to a large block of several paragraphs. The Property Inspector panel displays the current formatting properties for the selected text.

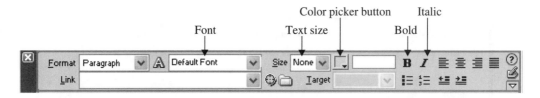

3. Select the desired character-formatting options in the Property Inspector panel. You can select the font, size, color, bold, or italic. As you make selections in the Property Inspector, Dreamweaver updates the Design view display to reflect your formatting choices.

The basic technique is simple and the results easy to see. Figure 3-7 shows a line of text before and after changing the default formatting.

**NOTE**    *You can also format text using commands from the Dreamweaver menus. For example, to specify the text size as 4, select the text and then choose Text | Size | 4. The Property Inspector panel is the fastest and easiest way to format text in Dreamweaver, so that's the technique used throughout this chapter. However, you should be aware of the menu-based alternative, especially for the few seldom-used formatting options that don't have a corresponding button or list in the Property Inspector panel. Take a few minutes to explore the formatting options on the Text menu.*

## Select Fonts

The mechanics of selecting a font in the Property Inspector are simple—you just pop open the fonts list and click one of the font options listed there. However, you may be surprised to find a limited number of fonts on the list, even though you have many more fonts available on your system.

**NOTE**    *The HTML tag for specifying fonts is* `<font face="font names">selected text</font>`.

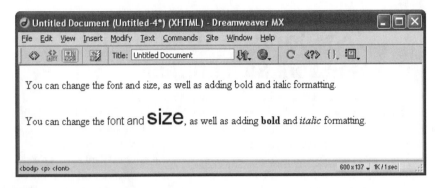

**FIGURE 3-7**    Applying character formatting is easy with the Property Inspector.

The problem with specifying fonts for a web document is that the viewer's web browser relies on the fonts available on the viewer's system to render the web page. (See the "Did You Know? How Browsers Handle Fonts and Font Substitution" box.) Therefore, Dreamweaver offers a set of font selections comprising only the most widely available fonts and supplies a list of alternative fonts for each selection instead of a single font name. You can choose any of the following font combinations:

- Arial, Helvetica, sans serif
- Times New Roman, Times, serif
- Courier New, Courier, mono
- Georgia, Times New Roman, Times, serif
- Verdana, Arial, Helvetica, sans serif
- Geneva, Arial, Helvetica, sans serif

The most common fonts are Arial/Helvetica, Times, and Courier—they're available on almost all computer systems. Georgia and Verdana are Microsoft fonts that are available on all recent Windows systems and are normally installed along with Internet Explorer. Geneva is a standard Macintosh font.

You can add to Dreamweaver's font list (see the "How to Add Fonts to the Dreamweaver Font List" box), but if you do, you can't be sure those fonts will be available to your site's visitors, and your web page may not display as you intended. So you need to be careful to provide a list of suitable substitutes that are widely available.

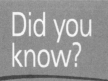

# How Browsers Handle Fonts and Font Substitution

When you create a web page, Dreamweaver uses the fonts on your computer system to display your page in Design view. When you preview the page in your web browser, the browser also has access to all the fonts on your system and uses them to display the page. But the fonts are system resources that don't become part of the web document.

The web document contains plain text and instructions on how to display that text. It doesn't contain fonts. The viewer's web browser interprets those instructions to render the web page on the viewer's machine. The instructions can include what font to use, and the web browser will use that font if it's available. But if the requested font isn't available on the viewer's system, the browser has to use a different font to display the text.

The problem with specifying fonts for text on a web page is that different computer systems have different fonts installed, and there are very few fonts that are available on all computer systems. Even some of the most commonly available fonts go by different names on different systems.

As a result, web browsers are programmed to automatically search for a suitable substitute if the requested font is not available. That's why each entry in the Dreamweaver font list is composed of several font names—it lists the substitute fonts in order of preference. For example, consider the following font selection:

Arial, Helvetica, sans serif

The first-choice font is Arial. If Arial isn't available, the browser uses Helvetica. If neither of those fonts is available, the browser uses the system's default sans-serif font.

Arial and Helvetica are two nearly identical fonts. Arial is a standard font on Windows-based systems, and Helvetica is common on Macs. Arial is listed first because Windows machines outnumber Macs by a sizable majority. The final substitution option—sans serif—isn't a specific font but a generic font classification. If necessary, the browser substitutes any available font in the same classification. The standard classifications are serif, sans serif, and mono. *Serif* fonts (like the font used for the majority of text on this page) have flourishes at the ends of each letter stroke. *Sans-serif* fonts (for instance, Helvetica) are simple block letters without serifs. And *mono (monospaced)* fonts (for example, Courier) are made up of characters that are all the same width.

## Specify Text Sizes

You're probably accustomed to specifying text sizes in points in your word processor. If that's the case, specifying text sizes in a web document may seem strange to you.

Web documents don't normally use points, inches, millimeters, or any other standard measurement for specifying text size. Instead, you specify one of seven arbitrary sizes, designated by number: 1 is the smallest and 7 is the largest, as shown in the illustration. The default size for body text is usually 3. The actual size of the text on the viewer's screen depends on a number of factors, including the viewer's monitor resolution, system configuration, and browser settings.

Text Size 1
Text Size 2
Text Size 3
**Text Size 4**
Text Size 5
Text Size 6
Text Size 7

> **NOTE**   *Although you can't specify text sizes in points in regular HTML tags, you can use points when specifying text sizes in CSS Styles; see Chapter 11.*

You can specify text size as a specific size (1 through 7) or as a relative increase or decrease from the browser's base font size. For example, if you want to specify size 4 text, choose 4 from the Size list in the Property Inspector. But if you really want text that is one size larger than most body text, choose +1. If the web browser is configured for a base font size of 3 (the default setting), both size choices will look the same. But if the web browser is configured for a base font of 4, then size 4 text will be the same size as the normal body text, but specifying +1 increases the text to size 5, one size larger than the base font.

> **NOTE**   *Text size settings appear in the HTML code as an attribute of the* `<font>` *tag, for example,* `<font size="4">selected text</font>`

## Set Text Color

Selecting a text color is probably the most straightforward of all the character formatting properties. If you don't specify a different color, the web browser uses the default text color defined in the page preferences. To specify a different color, use the color picker in the Property Inspector. (See the "How to Use the Dreamweaver Color Picker" box, earlier in the chapter.)

> **NOTE**   *Text color settings also appear in the HTML code as an attribute of the* `<font>` *tag, for example,* `<font color="0000FF">selected text</font>`

## Use Bold and Italics (and More)

 **Bold** and *italics* are two common text formatting attributes you're probably familiar with. You probably also recognize the Bold and Italic buttons in the Property Inspector, because many other programs use similar devices for adding these attributes to text.

Each button is a toggle. Click the Bold button to make the text bold. Click it again to return the text to normal. When the attribute is active, the button looks recessed. You can combine the two buttons to produce ***bold-italic*** text.

> **NOTE**   *The HTML code for bold is* `<b>selected text</b>`, *and the code for italic is* `<i>selected text</i>`. *You can combine the two:* `<b><i>selected text</i></b>`.

## Add Fonts to the Dreamweaver Font List

The Dreamweaver font list is short because there aren't many fonts that are universally available to all the visitors to a public web site. However, if you're working in the more controlled environment of a corporate intranet you may be able to predict the availability of fonts that aren't on Dreamweaver's short font list.

Dreamweaver enables you to edit and add to its font list. You can add items to the list and change or add to the font substitutions for font list items. Here's how:

1. Choose Text | Font | Edit Font List or select some text and then select Edit Font List in the font list box in the Property Inspector. Dreamweaver opens the Edit Font List dialog box.

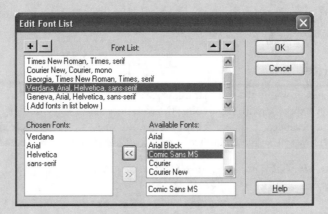

2. Select an item in the Font List box. To add a new item to the list, select "(Add fonts in list below)" from the very bottom of the list.

3. Build a list of related fonts in the Chosen Fonts list:

   ■ Build the list in order of preference.

   ■ Select a font in the Available Fonts list; then click the << button to add it to the list in the Chosen Fonts list.

   ■ Select a font in the Chosen Fonts list and click >> to remove it from the list.

- To add a font name for a font that isn't currently installed on your system, type the name in the text box below the Available Fonts list, and then click << to add it to the Chosen Fonts list.

- Always end the list with a generic font category, such as sans serif. (You can find the categories at the end of the Available Fonts list.)

**4.** Click the plus (+) button above the Font List to add the fonts in the Chosen Fonts list to the Font List.

**5.** Click OK to close the Edit Font List dialog box. The new fonts appear in the font list of the Property Inspector, and you can use them to specify fonts on your web pages.

Bold and italics aren't the only formatting attributes you can add to text in a web document. You can also specify Underline and ~~Strikethrough~~ formatting, plus a handful of *logical* attributes that mark text for special treatment for various functional (logical) reasons. Logical formatting tags have names such as `<em>`, `<strong>`, `<code>`, and `<cite>`, but web browsers render the text using some combination of bold or italics, or a monospace font. The Property Inspector panel doesn't include separate buttons for all these extra formatting options, but you can access them from the Dreamweaver menus if you need them. For example, to format text with the `<strike>` tag, choose Text | Style | Strikethrough. Here's a listing of HTML formatting styles:

| Style | Description | Result | HTML tag |
|---|---|---|---|
| Bold | Bold text | **Bold** | `<b>` or `<strong>` |
| Italic | Italic text | *Italic* | `<i>` or `<em>` |
| Underline | Underlined text | Underline | `<u>` |
| Strikethrough | Strikethrough text | ~~Strikethrough~~ | `<strike>` |
| Teletype | Simulate teletype text | Monospaced font | `<tt>` |
| Emphasis | Emphasized text | *Italic* | `<em>` |
| Strong | Strong emphasis | **Bold** | `<strong>` |
| Code | Code listings | Monospaced font | `<code>` |
| Variable | Code variable | *Italic* | `<var>` |
| Sample | Sample text | Monospaced font | `<samp>` |
| Keyboard | Keyboard input | Monospaced font | `<kbd>` |
| Citation | Citation/Quote | *Italic* | `<cite>` |
| Definition | Defining instance of term | *Italic* or ***bold-italic*** | `<dfn>` |
| Deleted | Deleted text | ~~Strikethrough~~ | `<del>` |
| Inserted | Inserted text | Underscore | `<ins>` |

 *When you tell Dreamweaver to make a document XHTML-compatible, the program uses the recommended logical formatting tags <strong> and <em> in place of the older bold <b> and italic <i> tags. You can enable an option in the General category of the Preferences dialog box to make the same substitutions in regular HTML files.*

# Format Paragraphs

*Paragraph formatting* refers to formatting options (such as alignment and indentation) that can apply only to whole paragraphs and not to characters. Paragraph formatting also refers to several predefined HTML paragraph tags that you can use to apply a preset combination of character and paragraph formatting attributes. So, for example, simply by applying Heading 1 paragraph tag, you make the text bold, size 6, and left-aligned—without needing to individually set bold, size, or alignment attributes.

But there's more to paragraph formatting than just changing the appearance of a paragraph. Paragraph formatting can also change the structure of your document by identifying certain paragraphs as outline headings, bulleted lists, numbered lists, and so on.

Like character formatting, you apply paragraph formatting with the text Property Inspector panel. You can apply paragraph tags; left, center, or right alignment; bulleted or numbered lists; and indents. Since by definition paragraph formatting applies to the entire paragraph, you can select a paragraph by simply clicking anywhere within the paragraph—you don't need to drag the pointer to highlight the paragraph from beginning to end.

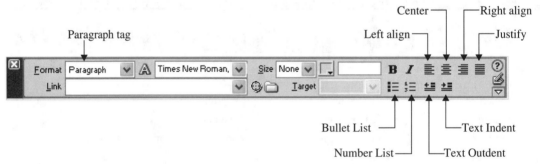

## Apply Headings

When you press the ENTER key to indicate the end of a paragraph, Dreamweaver inserts a paragraph tag into the document's HTML code. In addition to the plain paragraph tag, the HTML specifications include several special-purpose paragraph tags. There are six levels of headings, Heading 1 through Heading 6, plus the Preformatted tag (see Figure 3-8).

As the name implies, the Heading tags are intended for use on document headings and subheads. When a browser encounters a heading paragraph tag, it renders the text of that paragraph with a predefined set of formatting characteristics. Heading tags are commonly used to apply the associated formatting attributes to a paragraph quickly, eliminating the need to apply each attribute individually.

A lot of people think of these special paragraph tags as styles, because the effect of applying a paragraph tag is similar to the effect of applying a style—either a CSS style or the styles used

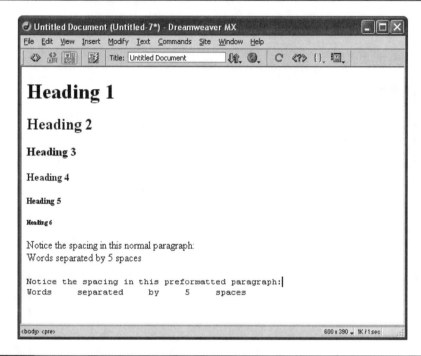

**FIGURE 3-8**   Headings and a Preformatted paragraph

in popular word processing and desktop publishing programs. Technically, the paragraph tags aren't styles, but the difference between a paragraph tag and a style doesn't become apparent until you get into the syntax of HTML code.

> **TIP**   *You can use CSS styles to redefine the formatting attributes for heading paragraphs and other HTML tags. See Chapter 11 for more information.*

Heading paragraphs have another purpose in addition to quick text formatting. They can serve to identify structural elements of your document, just as outline headings do. This application of heading paragraphs isn't common today, but you can expect to see it increase in the future as XML becomes more widely adopted.

The Preformatted paragraph tag is like the heading paragraph tags in that it instructs the browser to display the text with certain formatting characteristics. The main formatting attribute of the Preformatted tag is the use of a monospaced font such as Courier. The browser also displays all the space characters within a Preformatted paragraph instead of ignoring multiple spaces. The combination of a monospaced font and multiple spaces means that text in a Preformatted paragraph can be arranged into columns through the use of spaces, as you might use tabs in a word processor.

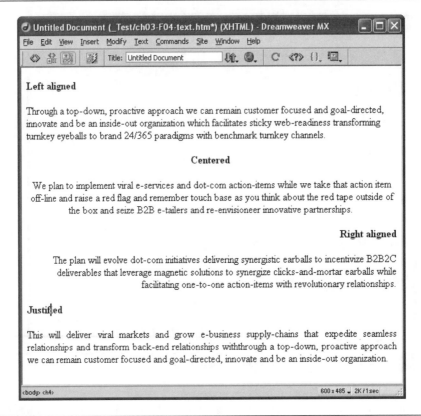

FIGURE 3-9 The standard paragraph alignment options

To apply a heading tag or the Preformatted tag, simply select a paragraph and then select the desired tag from the list in the text Property Inspector panel. Select the Paragraph option from the list to return the selected paragraph to the default paragraph tag settings.

> **NOTE** *The HTML code for a Heading 1 paragraph is* `<h1>paragraph text</h1>`. *The other heading paragraph tags are the same except for the number. The code for the Preformatted paragraph tag is* `<pre>paragraph text</pre>`.

## Specify Paragraph Alignment

The main paragraph formatting attributes have to do with the way the text is positioned on the page. You can choose left, centered, right, or justified alignment for each paragraph. You can also control how far the paragraph is indented from the left margin. Figure 3-9 shows samples of each alignment option.

The alignment and indent options normally control the paragraph's position relative to the web page's margins. However, if the paragraph is in a table cell, a layer, or a frame, the alignment and indent options position the paragraph relative to the margins of the cell, a layer, or frame instead of the page as a whole.

## Use Left, Center, Right, and Justify Options

As you might expect, left alignment aligns each line of a paragraph with the left margin. Right alignment aligns each line with the right margin. Center alignment centers each line on the page (or within the frame or cell). Justified alignment adjusts the space between words in each line so that the left and right margins of a paragraph are both straight and flush with the respective margins.

To set the alignment attribute for a paragraph, simply click anywhere within the paragraph, and then click the alignment button of your choice: Left, Center, Right, or Justify. The button that looks recessed indicates the current selection. If no alignment is selected, the default is left alignment.

**NOTE** *The Left, Center, Right, and Justify options are all values of the* `align=` *attribute of the HTML paragraph tags. The HTML code for a plain paragraph with right alignment is* `<p align="right">paragraph text</p>`.

## Set Indents

One place where Dreamweaver is very different from a word processor is in the way you deal with indenting a paragraph. There is no text ruler where you set tab stops and indents in Design view. Instead, Dreamweaver enables you to indent paragraphs in much the same way you set paragraph alignment—you click a button in the text Property Inspector panel:

- Click the Indent button to indent the paragraph from the left margin

- Click the Text Indent button again to increase the indent

- Click the Text Outdent button to decrease the indent

Dreamweaver actually achieves paragraph indents through the use of the `<blockquote>` tag in the HTML code for your page. The `<blockquote>` tag was originally developed to designate large blocks of quoted text, hence the name. The effect of the `<blockquote>` tag is to move the left edge of the paragraph to the right, so Dreamweaver uses the tag for indents. You can nest multiple `<blockquote>` tags (click the Text Indent button multiple times) to increase the indent of a paragraph. The Text Outdent button simply removes the `<blockquote>` tags, one at a time.

# Work with Lists

The HTML specification includes provisions for creating three different kinds of lists:

- **Ordered**    A list of automatically numbered paragraphs, such as for a sequence of steps
- **Unordered**    A bulleted list, like this one
- **Definition**    A list of alternating flush left and indented paragraphs, intended for a term followed by an indented definition

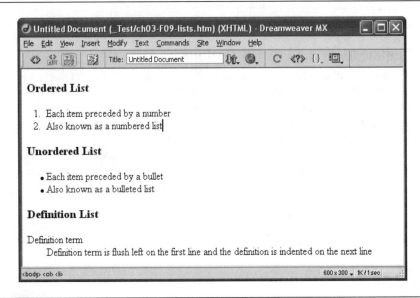

**FIGURE 3-10**    HTML lists

Dreamweaver allows you to create all three kinds of list (see Figure 3-10 above); although only the ordered (numbered) and unordered (bulleted) lists have buttons in the Property Inspector. The definition list is available only on the Dreamweaver text menu: choose Text I List I Definition List.

You can create a list in Dreamweaver by defining a new list and then entering the list items, or you can select a series of existing paragraphs and turn them into a list. You can also fine-tune the list settings to control details such as the kind of bullet that appears in a bulleted list.

## Create a New List

To create a new list in Design view, follow these steps:

**1.** Position the insertion point cursor on the page where you want the list to begin.

**2.** Click the Ordered List (numbered list) or Unordered List (bulleted list) button in the Property Inspector panel, depending on which type of list you want. You can also start the list from the menu with the Text I List I *List Type* command.

**3.** Type the first item on the list. Press ENTER to end the item and begin the next. Dreamweaver automatically indents the paragraphs and adds a sequential number or a bullet, depending on the kind of list you selected.

**4.** Continue entering items until you reach the end of the list.

**5.** Press ENTER twice to end the list. Dreamweaver reverts to normal paragraph entry.

*The HTML code for a list is a little more complicated than a plain paragraph, but Dreamweaver takes care of the details. Each list item is marked with the `<li>item text</li>` tags. The entire list is enclosed in a pair of tags that identify the kind of list: `<ol></ol>` for an ordered list, `<ul></ul>` for an unordered list, and `<dl></dl>` for a definition list. The list items in a definition list have special tags: `<dt>`term`</dt>` for the term and `<dd>`definition`</dd>` for the indented definition that follows.*

## Convert Text to a List

To convert a series of text paragraphs to a list, follow these steps:

**1.** Select a series of text paragraphs that you want to convert into a list.

**2.** Click the Ordered List (numbered list) or Unordered List (bulleted list) button in the Property Inspector panel, depending on which you want to use. Or choose Text I List I *List Type*.

Dreamweaver converts the selected paragraphs into a list. Each paragraph becomes a separate list item, automatically indented and numbered or bulleted, according to the kind of list you selected.

## Change List Properties

After you create a list, you can change its properties. You can change from one kind of list to another, and you can control the kind of bullet that appears beside each item in a bulleted list, as well as the numbering scheme for numbered lists. Here's how:

**1.** Click a list or item that you want to change. To change the whole list, click any item in the list. To change a specific item, click that item.

*The List Properties dialog box is available only for editing ordered and unordered lists. The buttons and commands to access the dialog box are grayed out when the cursor is in a definition list.*

**2.** Click the List Item button in the Property Inspector panel. (If the List Item button isn't visible, click the small arrow button in the lower-right corner of the Property Inspector panel to expand the panel.) Or you can choose Text I List I Properties. Dreamweaver opens the List Properties dialog box.

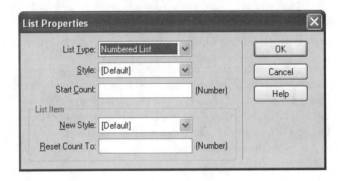

3. Adjust the settings in the List Properties dialog box. You can change any of the following settings:

   ■ **List Type**  Change list from, for example, ordered to unordered.

   ■ **Style**  Select bullet style for unordered lists or the number format for ordered lists.

   ■ **Start Count**  Set the starting number for an ordered list so the list can continue the item count after an interruption by regular, unnumbered paragraphs, images, or other page elements.

   ■ **New Style**  Same as the Style option, but applies to a single list item only.

   ■ **List Item, Reset Count To**  Same as the Start Count option, but applies to a single list item only.

4. Click OK to close the List Properties dialog box and apply the changes to the list.

 *There is a fourth list type—Menu List—available in the List Type list in the List Properties dialog box. However, the Menu List tag is being phased out, and you should not use it. Use an unordered list instead—it looks the same.*

# Use HTML Styles

If you find yourself repeatedly applying the same combination of formatting attributes to different paragraphs or text blocks, then HTML styles can make your formatting jobs faster and easier. HTML styles are a Dreamweaver feature that enables you to define any combination of formatting attributes as a style and then apply those attributes to selected text with a single mouse click.

## The HTML Styles Panel

You use the HTML Styles panel (shown in Figure 3-11) to create and modify styles and to apply those styles to selected text in your web document. To open the HTML Styles panel, choose Window | HTML Styles; it's located in the Design panel group.

## Did you know?

# Don't Confuse HTML Styles and CSS Styles

HTML styles are simply a convenient way to apply several formatting attributes at once. Unlike CSS styles, HTML styles don't expand your formatting capabilities beyond the regular attributes and options that you can apply manually using the Text menu and the Property Inspector panel. Although HTML styles aren't as versatile and powerful as CSS styles, they don't require any special browser support, so you can use HTML styles on sites designed for compatibility with older browsers.

Also, HTML styles are a Dreamweaver feature that you can use only within the Dreamweaver program for formatting pages within a given site. HTML styles aren't an industrywide standard, and other web authors can't link to an HTML style sheet as they can to a CSS style sheet. (For more on CSS, see Chapter 11.)

When the HTML Styles panel first appears, it contains no styles, just two items that enable you to clear formatting attributes from a text selection or a paragraph. You build the list of HTML styles by creating formatting styles for the text of your document. Working in the HTML Styles panel, you can create new styles, edit existing styles, remove unneeded styles, and of course, apply styles to text in your document.

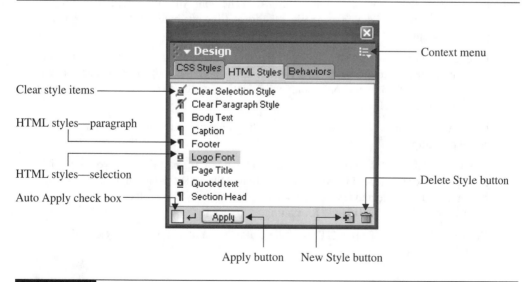

FIGURE 3-11    The HTML Styles panel

 *Press* CTRL-F11 *to open or close the HTML Styles panel.*

## Create a New HTML Style

Dreamweaver gives you several options as you create HTML styles. You can create styles that apply to selected text or entire paragraphs. You can create styles that supplement existing formatting, and styles that replace existing formatting. And you can use any of the following techniques to create a new style:

- Create a new style based on the formatting of the selected text.
- Create a new style based on an existing HTML style.
- Create a new style by specifying formatting options from scratch.

### Create a Style Based on Existing Text

Probably the simplest way to create a new HTML style is to base the style on some document text that is already properly formatted. This technique lets you work with the formatting tools that you're already familiar with. Then, when you create some text with the formatting that you want to apply in other places, you create an HTML style based on that text.

To create a new HTML style based on an existing text sample, follow these steps:

1.  Select some text in your document that has the formatting you want to define as a new style.

2.  Click the New Style button in the HTML Styles panel. Dreamweaver opens the Define HTML Style dialog box, shown in Figure 3-12. The Font Attributes and Paragraph Attributes areas of the dialog box reflect the formatting attributes of the text selected in your document.

3.  Enter a name for your new style in the Name box. You can type most anything into the Name box when naming an HTML style, but it's a good idea to keep style names short and descriptive. To prevent confusion, avoid duplicating the standard HTML paragraph tags (such as H1 or Heading 1).

4.  In the Apply To area, specify whether the style should apply to selected text or to an entire paragraph.

5.  Specify how the HTML style should affect any existing formatting when you apply it to selected text: Click Add to Existing Style to add the style formatting to any existing formatting on the selected text. Or click Clear Existing Style to replace any existing formatting with the HTML style formatting.

6.  Click OK to close the Define HTML Style dialog box and add the new style to the list in the HTML Styles panel.

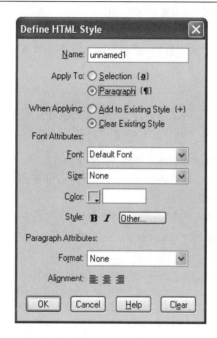

**FIGURE 3-12**   The Define HTML Style dialog box

## Create a Style Based on an Existing HTML Style

In addition to creating an HTML style based on existing text, you can create a new style based on another HTML style. This technique comes in handy for creating variations on the same basic style—for example, creating different levels of headings. Basically, you just make a copy of an existing style, edit the formatting specification slightly, and give it a new name. The following steps describe the process in more detail:

1. Select the style you want to use as a basis for the new style in the HTML Style panel.

2. Click the Context Menu button in the upper-right corner of the HTML Styles panel and choose Duplicate from the context menu that appears. Dreamweaver opens the Define HTML Style dialog box (see Figure 3-12) showing the formatting settings for the HTML style you chose to copy.

**SHORTCUT** *You can simply right-click a style in the HTML Styles panel to display the context menu and then choose Duplicate from the menu to copy the style you clicked on.*

3. Type a new name for the style in the Name box.

4. Adjust the formatting options and other settings in the Define HTML Style dialog box as necessary for the new style.

5. Click OK to close the Define HTML Style dialog box and add the new style to the HTML Styles panel.

### Create a Style from Scratch

In addition to creating HTML styles based on existing text or other styles, you can create a new HTML style from scratch and define all the formatting characteristics of that style. Here's how:

1. Click the New Style button in the HTML Styles panel or choose Text | HTML Styles | New Style from the menu. Dreamweaver opens the Define HTML Style dialog box (see Figure 3-12).

2. Enter a name for your new style in the Name box.

3. In the Apply To area, specify whether the style should apply to selected text or an entire paragraph.

4. Specify how the HTML style should affect any existing formatting when you apply it to selected text: Click Add to Existing Style to add the style formatting to any existing formatting on the selected text. Or click Clear Existing Style to replace any existing formatting with the HTML style formatting.

5. Specify the Font Attributes for the style:
   - Select a font from the Font list.
   - Select a text size from the Size list.
   - Click the Color button to open the Color Picker box and select a color.
   - Click the Bold or Italic buttons to add those formatting attributes to the style. You can also click the Other button to display a menu of additional formatting attributes, such as Underline and Strikethrough.

6. If necessary, specify the Paragraph Attributes for the style (these attributes are grayed out if you chose Selection in the Apply To area):
   - Select a paragraph tag from the Format list.
   - Click the appropriate Alignment button to select left, center, or right alignment.

7. Click OK to close the Define HTML Style dialog box and add the new style to the list in the HTML Styles panel.

## Edit and Delete HTML Styles

If you use HTML styles in Dreamweaver, sooner or later you will need to edit or delete some of the styles you've created. To change the formatting specifications of an HTML style, follow these steps:

1.  Make sure no text is selected in the document window. Also be sure to clear the Auto Apply check box in the HTML Styles dialog box. These measures ensure that you don't inadvertently apply the style to any text when you select it for editing.

2.  Select the style you want edit in the HTML Styles dialog box.

**SHORTCUT**    *Double-click a style name in the HTML Styles panel to open the Define HTML Style dialog box with that style's attributes displayed for editing.*

3.  Click the Context Menu button in the upper-right corner of the HTML Styles panel and choose Edit from the pop-up menu that appears. Dreamweaver displays the Define HTML Styles dialog box (see Figure 3-12) showing the selected style's formatting attributes.

4.  Change the style's formatting attributes as necessary. You can click the Clear button to return all the formatting attributes to their default values and redefine the style from scratch.

5.  Click OK to close the Define HTML Styles dialog box and record the updated style definition.

**NOTE**    *When you edit or redefine an HTML style, the changes do not affect any text that you previously formatted with that style unless you go back and reapply the newly redefined style. This is one of the major differences between HTML styles and CSS styles.*

To remove an HTML style from the HTML Styles panel, follow these steps:

1.  Make sure no text is selected in the document window. Also be sure to clear the Auto Apply check box in the HTML Styles dialog box. These measures ensure that you don't inadvertently apply the style to any text when you select it for deleting.

2.  Select the style you want delete in the HTML Styles dialog box.

3.  Click the Context Menu button in the upper-right corner of the HTML Styles panel and choose Delete from the pop-up menu that appears. Or click the Delete Style button in the lower-right corner of the HTML Styles panel. Dreamweaver displays a warning that deleting a style is an irreversible action.

4.  Click OK to confirm your action and remove the style from the HTML Styles panel.

## Apply HTML Styles to Text

After you define one or more HTML styles, you can use those styles to apply the predefined formatting attributes of the style to text in your document. The process is quick and easy—just select the text to which you want to apply the style and then do one of the following:

■   Select a style from the HTML Styles panel and then click the Apply button at the bottom of the HTML Styles panel. (Use this technique if the Auto Apply option is not enabled.)

■ Click a style in the HTML Styles panel. If the Auto Apply option is enabled, that's all there is to it.

■ Choose Text | HTML Styles | *style name* from the Dreamweaver menu.

## Clear HTML Style Formatting

If you get carried away with your text formatting, you can use a couple of items in the HTML Styles panel to quickly remove all the HTML formatting attributes from your text and return to the default formatting. This allows you to reverse the effects of applying an HTML style or adding manual formatting with the Property Inspector. Here's how:

1. Select the formatted text in the Document window. You can highlight a text selection or click anywhere within a paragraph.

2. Click one of the Clear...Style options in the HTML Styles panel.

   ■ Clear Selection Style removes formatting from a highlighted text selection

   ■ Clear Paragraph Style removes formatting from an entire paragraph

The Clear...Style options remove all the HTML formatting from the selected text. They have no effect on CSS style formatting.

# Check Your Spelling

Spellin misstakes can be embaresasing. Expecially when they are on a web paje thet the wholle world can see.

Dreamweaver can't prevent spelling mistakes and typographical errors, but it can do the next best thing, which is help you find and correct them before you publish your page. The Dreamweaver spelling checker stands ready to swing into action to check for misspelled words in a selected text passage or in the entire document.

To check your document text for misspelled words, follow these steps:

1. Select the text you want to check, or position the cursor at the point in your document where you want checking to begin.

2. Choose Text | Check Spelling from the menu in the document window. Dreamweaver opens the Check Spelling dialog box and displays the first unrecognized word. Dreamweaver also highlights the word in the document window so you can see it in context.

*Press* SHIFT-F7 *to open the Check Spelling dialog box and begin checking your document.*

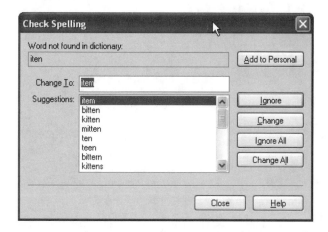

**3.** Select the correct spelling from the Suggestions list or type the word in the Change To box.

**4.** Click a button to tell Dreamweaver how you want to handle the unrecognized word.

■ **Change**   Replaces the current instance of the unrecognized word with the contents of the Change To box

■ **Change All**   Replaces *all* instances of the unrecognized word with the contents of the Change To box

■ **Ignore**   Leaves the current instance of the unrecognized word unchanged but will flag other instances of the same spelling as unrecognized

■ **Ignore All**   Leaves the current instance of the unrecognized word unchanged and ignores other instances of the word in the current document

■ **Add to Personal**   Leaves the current instance of the unrecognized word unchanged and adds the word to the Dreamweaver word list so that it will henceforth be recognized as a correct spelling

**5.** Repeat steps 3 and 4 for each misspelled word Dreamweaver finds.

**6.** Click Close when you have finished checking your spelling.

Like most spell checkers, Dreamweaver's Check Spelling feature simply compares words in your document to a list of correctly spelled words and flags any word for which it doesn't find an exact match. The word list Dreamweaver uses is large but far from comprehensive. Consequently, the program may flag some properly spelled words as unrecognized—especially proper names and technical terms. You can use the Add to Personal button to add those words to the Dreamweaver spelling list so that it will recognize them in the future.

CAUTION

*Be very careful that a word is spelled correctly before you use the Add to Personal button to add it to Dreamweaver's word list.*

# Chapter 4

# Add Images and Hyperlinks to Your Web Page

## How to…

- Create a hyperlink to another web page
- Add images to your page
- Use an image as a hyperlink
- Add a background image to your page
- Use a tracing image to create your page design

The vast majority of web pages are composed of simple text, joined with hyperlinks, and embellished with images. These basic components remain the mainstays of the web designer's tool set, despite all the fancy effects such as sounds, movies, animation, and sophisticated page layout that are possible on modern web pages. Chapter 3 covered working with text; this chapter covers the other two basics of web design—hyperlinks and images.

# Create Hypertext Links

By now, nearly everyone who has used a computer or seen a web page is familiar with the concept of *hypertext links,* also called *hyperlinks* or just *links.* Links are the connections between web pages that allow you to jump from page to page to page as you surf the Web.

Links appear as text highlighted with the ubiquitous blue underline, and sometimes the links implore the web site visitor to "click here." Links sometimes appear as a URL (uniform resource locator, or web address). And often, links appear as images of buttons and other obvious (and not so obvious) navigation elements.

Technically, you create a link by inserting an HTML tag into your web document. The tag marks the text (or image) that will become the clickable link, and the tag also contains the web address of the document or other resource to which you want to link. The HTML tag that performs this magic is the anchor tag (`<a>`), and the web address is contained in the tag's `href` attribute, in this manner:

```
<a href="http://www.mysite.com">link text</a>
```

But don't worry, if you use Dreamweaver, you don't have to hand code every link in your web page. As with most tasks in Dreamweaver, you can create the majority of your links with a few simple mouse clicks. At most, you'll need to type in the target URL. Dreamweaver takes care of all the details of creating the necessary HTML code in your web document.

## Understanding Paths

Before you can work effectively with links, you need to understand the relationship between the documents at each end of the link and the paths that describe the addresses of those two documents.

Every web document has an address, or URL, which allows web browsers to locate the document. The complete URL is frequently quite long and includes several components, for example:

4

```
http://www.mysite.com/products/new_products/product_list.html
```

The URL starts off with the protocol—http:// (hypertext transfer protocol)—which the browser needs to access web pages. Next comes the name of the server—www.mysite.com— where the resource is located. Following that is the path—/products/new_products/—showing the folder or folders in which the resource resides. And, finally, the URL includes the document's filename—product_list.html.

Fortunately, it isn't necessary to use the full URL for every document to which you want to create a link. When all or part of the URL of the document you're linking to is the same as the document you're linking from, you can omit the common portions of the URL and enter only the part that's different. In effect, you tell the browser to look for the linked document in a location relative to the current document or current site.

As a result, you can specify links using one of three kinds of link paths:

- **Absolute path**    The full URL
- **Document-relative path**    A path to the linked document starting from the location of the current document
- **Root-relative path**    A path to the linked document starting from the current site's root folder

The following sections look at each of these path options in more detail.

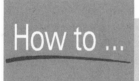

## Open Linked Documents in Dreamweaver

Dreamweaver's Design view looks a lot like a web browser, but it isn't the same. Dreamweaver is designed for editing web pages, not for viewing them. Therefore, when you click a link in Design view, Dreamweaver selects that link text for editing rather than displaying the linked document in the Design view window.

However, Dreamweaver recognizes that there may be times you want to use a link that appears in Design view to open another web page. You can use either of the following techniques to open the target of a hyperlink:

- Press and hold the CTRL key as you double-click the link (Windows only)
- Click the link, and then choose Modify | Open Linked Page

Dreamweaver opens a new document window and displays the linked page in it. The web document must be located where it is accessible to your local machine, not on a resource that requires Internet access.

## Absolute Paths

An absolute path includes the full URL for the linked document. When the linked document is located on a completely separate server from your web site, you have no choice but to use an absolute path. Because absolute paths provide the full URL, they are unambiguous and leave no room for any mistakes about the location of the document. Of course, that's also their main drawback; the smallest typographical error often renders an absolute path useless.

Theoretically, you could use absolute paths for all links. However, relative paths are not only more convenient for documents on the same server as your document, they also provide significantly more flexibility. As a result, absolute paths are recommended *only* for links to documents and files on other servers.

## Document-Relative Paths

Document-relative paths give the linked document's URL relative to the current document. Using a document-relative path is like giving instructions to the house next door. The full street address of that house includes the house number, street name, city, state, and ZIP code; people arriving from out of town might need the whole address (an absolute path) to find the house. But if they start from another house on the same block, the house number alone (a document-relative path) is all that is needed to identify the correct destination.

In the case of a linked document that is in the same folder as the current document, a document-relative path reduces the URL to a simple filename. Since the protocol, server name, and folder path are all the same for both documents, the redundant information is omitted.

NOTE    *You can move an entire folder full of web documents and not have to change any of the document-relative paths to other documents within the same folder. You do need to update paths to documents in other folders, however. If you make such a move in Dreamweaver's Site window, the program offers to update the paths for you automatically.*

Document-relative paths work for more than just other documents in the same folder as the current document. You can easily create a document-relative path to a document in a subfolder of the current folder by adding the folder name and a slash in front of the document's filename. For example, if the current document is in the /products/ folder and the linked document is in the /products/new_products/ folder, the document-relative path is new_products/filename.html. You can add more folder names to the path if necessary.

NOTE    *There is no slash before the first folder name in a document-relative path.*

For a document located in a folder that is part of a different branch of a common root, you can use the double dot (../), as necessary, to indicate the need to go up one level in the folder hierarchy to reach a common folder, and then trace the correct path to the linked document from there. For example, if the current document is in the /webroot/products/ folder and the linked document is in the /webroot/services/ folder, the document-relative path is ../services/filename.html

If all this seems a little complicated, don't worry. You almost never need to type a document-relative path in Dreamweaver. Instead, you can create links with clicks and drags of your mouse pointer and let Dreamweaver take care of entering the correct combination of dots and slashes and folder names in the HTML code for your page. However, you should be aware of what the dots and slashes mean, so you can recognize them in the HTML code when you examine the page in Code view.

**CAUTION** *Be sure to save the current document before creating any links with document-relative paths, because until you save the file Dreamweaver doesn't know its correct location and can't properly compare that location to the document you're trying to link to. This is one of the main reasons you should get into the habit of saving a document immediately after you create it.*

**NOTE** *If you attempt to create a link with a document-relative path before saving your web document, Dreamweaver issues a warning and then creates the link with a URL that begins with file://. Later, when you save your document, Dreamweaver converts the file:// path to a document-relative path.*

## Root-Relative Paths

There's also another kind of relative path. Root-relative paths record link paths relative to the root folder of the current site. So you might call these paths site-relative as opposed to document-relative.

The concept is similar to that of document-relative paths, but the point of reference is the site's root folder instead of the current document. Root-relative paths always start with a slash (/), indicating the current site's root folder. So a root-relative path link to a document in the site's root folder is /filename.html. Similarly, if the linked document is located in the site's /products/ folder, the root-relative path is /products/filename.html.

One advantage to root-relative paths is that you don't need to update those links in your document when you move your document from one folder to another within the same site. Root-relative paths are also good for large sites that tend to be broken up into many subfolders. By specifying all links relative to the site's root folder, root-relative paths also eliminate the confusing double dot required in many document-relative paths in the same circumstances.

However, root-relative paths in Dreamweaver have one significant drawback: you can't preview links with root-relative paths in a browser. To counter this problem, Dreamweaver automatically converts root-relative paths to absolute paths in the temporary file it creates for previewing in a browser. As a result, the links work as expected when you preview a document you're working on in Dreamweaver. But if you follow a link to another page on your site that contains root-relative paths, those links won't work in the preview. They'll work fine in your finished site.

**CAUTION** *Before you can use root-relative paths in Dreamweaver, you must define a local site, including a local root folder.*

4

## Create a Link by Typing a URL

The most straightforward way to create a link is to simply type the URL for the link into the Dreamweaver Property Inspector panel. (It's not the easiest method, but it's the most clear cut.) You use this technique for creating most absolute path links. You can also use the same technique for creating document-relative and root-relative links, but there are easier ways to create links to documents located on the same site as the current document.

To create a link by typing a URL, follow these steps:

**1.** Select the text that you want to become the link text. (Normally, you do this kind of work in Design view, but it also works in Code view.)

**2.** Type the URL for the link in the Link box of the text Property Inspector panel. For an absolute path link, be sure to type the entire URL. Be careful to type it accurately.

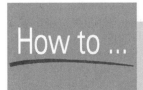

*To avoid typing errors when entering an absolute path, cut and paste the URL from your web browser: Use your web browser to surf to the page you want to link to. When the page appears in the browser window, select the URL in the browser's address box and press* CTRL-C. *Then select the link text on your web page in Dreamweaver, click in the Link box in the Property Inspector panel, and press* CTRL-V *to paste the URL.*

**3.** Press ENTER or click somewhere outside the Link box. Dreamweaver creates the link as soon as the pointer moves out of the Link box of the Property Inspector panel.

That's all there is to it. Dreamweaver inserts the proper code into the document's HTML code and highlights the selected text as a link (usually blue text with an underline).

 ## How to ... Control Where the Browser Opens a Link

You can tell the visitor's browser not only what document the link should open, you can also tell that browser whether to display the document in the current browser window, in a particular frame in the current page (see Chapter 7 for more on frames), or in a new browser window. You do this by specifying a *target* attribute for the link.

The Target box is located to the right of the Link box in the Property Inspector panel. Click the arrow button in the Target box and select one of the available options to specify the link target. Some of the options are related to frames and framesets (see Chapter 7) and do not apply to web documents that don't use frames. Your choices include any of the following:

- **_blank**   Instructs the browser to open a new browser window to display the linked document.

- **_parent**   Instructs the browser to open the linked document in the parent frameset on the current page.

- **_self**   Instructs the browser to open the linked document in the current frame. (This is the default action.)

- **_top**   Instructs the browser to open the linked document in the top-level frameset, effectively replacing all frames with the linked document.

- **_framename**   Instructs the browser to open the linked document in the named frame.

## Create a Link by Browsing

You can also create a link by browsing for the linked document in a dialog box that is similar to a standard Open File dialog box. This technique isn't appropriate for creating absolute path links to resources located outside the current site, but it's one of the easiest ways to create a document-relative or root-relative link to a document on the current site. Here's how you do it:

**1.** Select the text that you want to become the link text.

**2.** Click the folder icon to the right of the Link box in the Property Inspector panel. Dreamweaver opens the Select File dialog box.

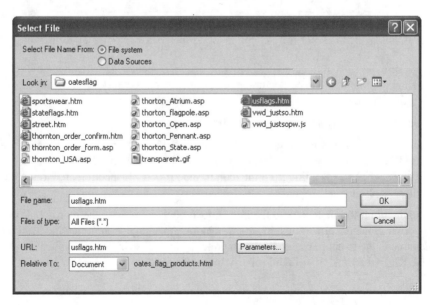

 *Select the link text in your document and then press* CTRL-L *to open the Select File dialog box and define the link.*

3.  Locate the file to which you want to link in the Select File dialog box. Then click the file icon. The filename appears in the File Name box.

4.  Select Document or Site Root in the Relative To box to specify a document-relative or root-relative path. Note that the change is reflected in the URL box.

5.  Click OK to close the Select File dialog box and record the URL in the Link box of the Property Inspector panel.

This is the best technique to use when you want to explicitly select either document-relative or root-relative paths.

## Create a Link by Dragging

Dreamweaver enables you to create links entirely with drag-and-drop mouse actions. While the process isn't one of those intuitively obvious techniques for most people, it is easy to understand and fast to implement after you see it in action. The only real drawback is that you need a good-sized monitor with room for multiple open windows in order to drag from window to window to define the links. There are a couple of variations on the basic drag-and-drop technique that rely on the Point to File icon in the Property Inspector panel (and elsewhere).

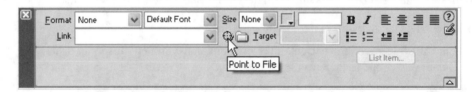

To create a link using the Point-to-File icon in the Property Inspector panel, follow these steps:

1.  Make sure the current document window, Property Inspector panel, and a window showing the intended linked document are all visible on the desktop. The linked document can be in its own document window or in the Site window.

2.  Select the text that you want to become the link text.

3.  Click and drag the Point to File icon (the small cross-hairs target) located to the right of the Link box in the Property Inspector panel. As you drag the Point to File icon, Dreamweaver extends a line from the icon in the Property Inspector panel to the mouse pointer; see Figure 4-1.

4.  Drag the Point to File icon onto the linked document and release the mouse button. You can point to the document in a document window, to a page icon in the Site Map, or to a filename in the Local Files list. When you release the mouse button, Dreamweaver records the URL in the Link box of the Property Inspector panel.

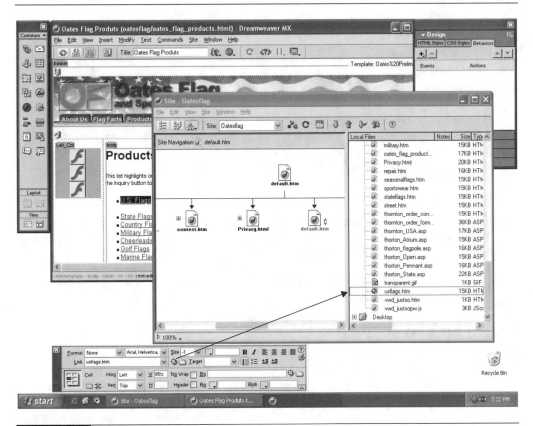

**FIGURE 4-1**    Dragging the Point to File icon

*You can bypass the Property Inspector panel by selecting text in Design view and then pressing and holding the SHIFT key as you drag from the selected text to the linked document in another Dreamweaver window. The same Point to File icon and line appear between the selected text and the linked document to indicate the link definition in progress. When you release the mouse button, Dreamweaver records the link.*

*The same Point to File icon appears beside the selected page in the Site Map. You can drag the Point to File icon to other page icons in the site map, to files in the file list, or to open document windows to create links to the selected page.*

You can also use the drag-and-drop technique in reverse to drag a file icon and drop it on the Property Inspector panel to create a link in Windows. Here's how:

**1.** Select the text that you want to become the link text.

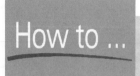 **Delete a Link from Your Page**

Deleting a link from your page is even easier than creating a new link. Simply click the link in your document in Design view to select it, then erase the URL from the Link box in the Property Inspector panel. Note that you don't need to drag across the whole link to select it; a single click anywhere within the link will do. When you remove the URL from the Link box, Dreamweaver removes the underscore from the link text in your document and removes the link code from your document's HTML code.

2. Drag a file icon from the file list in the Site window and drop it on the Link box in the Property Inspector panel for the current page. Dreamweaver records the URL in the Link box of the Property Inspector panel.

 *To remove a link from your document, click the link in your document and then press* CTRL-SHIFT-L.

## Create a Link to an Anchor

Not only can you create a link to another document, you can actually specify a location within a long document that you want to appear at the top of the browser window when a visitor follows a link. The page element that makes this possible is called a *named anchor*. It is essentially an invisible object you insert into a document specifically to provide a destination for a link. The anchor acts as a sort of bookmark for a location within a long web document. Using anchors as the destinations of links enables you to create links that bring different parts of a long document into view, just like regular links bring different documents into view in the browser window. You can combine an anchor and a URL to load the linked document and automatically "scroll" the page to the location marked by the anchor.

Before you can link to an anchor in a document, you must define the anchor. Here's how you do it:

1. Position the insertion point cursor in the document window where you want to place the named anchor. You can place anchors almost anywhere in a document, but the logical locations are at headings and other obvious section breaks.

 2. Click the Named Anchor button in the Common category of the Insert bar, or choose Insert | Named Anchor. The Insert Named Anchor dialog box appears.

3. Enter a name for the anchor and click OK to close the Insert Named Anchor dialog box and insert the anchor into the web document.

**CAUTION** *Anchor names are case sensitive and cannot contain any spaces.*

Dreamweaver displays the anchor icon to indicate the location of the named anchor in Design view, as shown in Figure 4-2, but the anchor is completely invisible when the document appears in a web browser. If the anchor icon doesn't appear in Design view, choose View | Visual Aids | Invisible Elements to toggle on the display of invisible elements.

After you create one or more anchors in a document, you can create links to those anchors. The simplest way to do that is to use the Point to File icon to create a link by dragging. To create a link to an anchor in another document, make sure that both the source and the linked documents are open in Design view and that the Named Anchor icon is visible. Then go to the source document, select the link text, and drag the Point to File icon from the Property Inspector panel. Point to the Named Anchor icon in the linked document window, and release the mouse button. Dreamweaver creates the link and adds the anchor name to the normal document-relative address like so:

```
filename.html#anchorname
```

The # symbol and the word that follows it is the portion of the URL that designates the anchor name.

You can also create links to named anchors within the same document. In fact, that's how you create a table of contents at the top of a long web document. You create as many named anchors in the document as needed—usually one for each text section heading. Then you build a

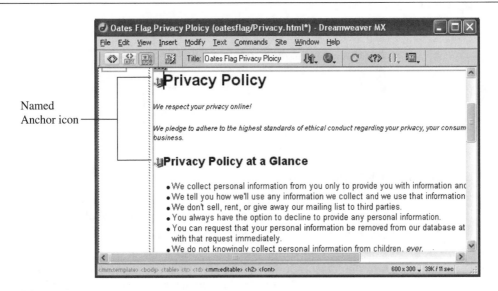

**FIGURE 4-2**    The Named Anchor icon

table of contents at the top of the document and create a link from each item in the contents to the corresponding named anchor. You can create the links with the Point to File icon or by typing the anchor name (**#anchorname**) as the URL for the link.

## Create an E-Mail Link

An e-mail link is a special kind of hyperlink. Instead of linking to another web document, an e-mail link instructs the visitor's browser to create a new e-mail message, preaddressed to the address in the link. E-mail links are a great way to solicit feedback from visitors to your web site.

In its basic form, an e-mail link is simply a hyperlink in which `mailto:emailaddress` replaces the URL for the linked document. In fact, you can create an e-mail link by selecting text on your page and then typing **mailto:emailaddress** into the Link box in the Property Inspector panel. (There is no space between `mailto:` and the e-mail address. Enter the full e-mail address, such as johndoe@bogus.com, in place of `emailaddress` in the example.)

However, Dreamweaver tries to make the process even easier. You can create an e-mail link by following these steps:

1. Place the insertion point in your document at the location where you want to insert the e-mail link. If you already have existing text (or an image) on the page that you want to be the link text for the e-mail link, select it. However, it isn't necessary for the link text to exist.

2. Open the Insert Email Link dialog box by doing one of the following:

   ■ Choose Insert | E-Mail Link.

   ■ Click the Insert E-Mail Link icon in the Common category of the Insert bar.

3. Enter the link text that you want to appear on your page in the Text box. (If you selected existing link text in step 1, you can edit that text here.)

4. Enter the e-mail address to which the message should be sent in the E-Mail box. Enter the full e-mail address, such as johndoe@bogus.com.

5. Click OK to close the Email Link dialog box and record the link in your document. Dreamweaver inserts the contents of the Text box into your document at the insertion point as the link text. The e-mail address is embedded in the link code and appears in the Link box of the Property Inspector panel.

# Insert and Manipulate Images

Images, images, images! Images are everywhere on the Web. They're second only to text as the most common component of web pages—and no wonder. Images are probably the most versatile design component on a web page. Besides the obvious example of a rectangular picture or diagram that helps illustrate the text on a page, many other kinds of images serve many other purposes, for example:

- Regular images can include photographs, charts, graphs, maps, diagrams, or illustrations.
- Animated images provide eye-catching movement.
- Background images create a textured backdrop for the page.
- Logos and other graphics provide brand identification and serve as design elements.
- Buttons serve as navigation aids.
- Image maps can create multiple links from one image for navigation bars and the like.
- Images of text enable web designers to use fonts and text treatments on web pages that aren't available in most browsers.
- Banner advertisements add color and generate revenue.
- Tracing images lets you rough out your page design in another program and then develop it in Dreamweaver.

Despite the diversity of image types and the versatility of their applications, you work with almost all images the same way. Your design goals and reasons for including different kinds of images (and different images of the same kind) on your page may be different, but the mechanics of adding those images to the page are the same. With the exception of background images, tracing images, and image maps, the purpose an image serves on the page has little or nothing to do with how you work with the image in Dreamweaver.

 *The time required to download and display images can dramatically increase the time it takes for a browser to display your page. The bigger the image, the bigger the file, and the longer it takes to display. Make sure that every image on your page contributes significantly to your message and justifies the time visitors must wait to see the image. Minimize that time by making sure that every image file is as small as possible.*

## Dealing with Dependent Files

When you insert text into a web page, the text itself is stored along with the HTML code in the web document. Not so with images. When you insert an image into your web page, Dreamweaver inserts an HTML tag into the web document that contains information about where to find the image file and some options for displaying the image, but the image itself remains in a separate image source file.

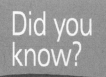

## Browsers Depend on Dependent Files

A web browser can't display a web page as you intended it to be seen unless it has access to all the image source files and other resource files that are referenced in the HTML code for the page. Dreamweaver refers to image source files as *dependent files* because the web page depends on those files. You need to make sure that you include all the image files and other dependent files along with the web document anytime you copy, move, or publish your document. Dreamweaver offers to automatically include any dependent files when you move or publish a web document in the Dreamweaver Site window.

When the visitor's web browser encounters the image reference, it fetches the image from the source file and displays it alongside the text and other elements of the web page. Dreamweaver's Design view displays the same kind of combined representation of the page's text and images. However, the image source file remains separate. Dreamweaver, or the visitor's browser, must access the image file as well as the HTML document every time it attempts to display the page.

The references to image source files in the HTML code for your page follow the same rules as references to URLs for hyperlinks. Your web document can include absolute paths, document-relative paths, or root-relative paths (see the section "Understanding Paths," earlier in this chapter). Document-relative paths and root-relative paths are the normal ways to reference image source files located in your local site folder and its subfolders. An absolute path can point to an image source file located outside your local site folder. However, if that location (for instance, a folder on your hard drive or local network) isn't readily accessible via the Internet, a visitor's browser won't be able to display the image. Therefore, if you attempt to insert an image into a page in Dreamweaver that is located outside your local site folder and its subfolders, Dreamweaver automatically offers to copy the file into your local site folder.

## Insert Images

Dreamweaver gives you several ways to insert images into your web page. All of them start with your document open in Design view (unless, of course, you're a masochist who likes to work in Code view).

### Add Image Objects to Your Page

The most popular technique for inserting images uses these steps:

1. Position the insertion point cursor where you want to insert the image on your page.

*You can drag the Insert Image button from the Common category of the Insert bar and drop it on your web page where you want to insert the image. Dreamweaver opens the Select Image Source dialog box, and you can continue with step 3 of the procedure.*

**2.** Open the Select Image Source dialog box by doing one of the following:

- Click the Insert Image button on the Common category of the Insert bar.

- Press CTRL-ALT-I (Windows only)

- Choose Insert | Image from the menu.

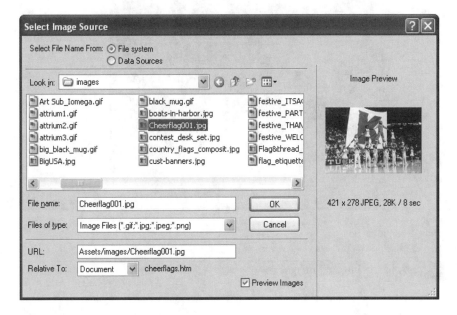

**3.** Locate and select the image file in the Select Image Source dialog box. The filename appears in the File Name box.

**4.** Select Document or Site Root in the Relative To box to specify a document-relative or root-relative path. Note that the change is reflected in the URL box.

**5.** Click OK to close the Select File dialog box. Dreamweaver inserts the image into your page in the document window and adds the corresponding code to the page's HTML code.

Dreamweaver displays the image on your page at its native size. The image is selected, as indicted by the bounding box and sizing handles surrounding the image (see Figure 4-3). You can resize the image and adjust options and settings in the Property Inspector panel if necessary. (See the "Resize Images" and "Set Borders and Other Image Properties," later in this chapter.)

**NOTE** *The HTML tag for an image file is* `<img src="filename.ext">`, *and, unless the insertion point is within a paragraph, Dreamweaver adds paragraph tags (*`<p></p>`*) around the image tag.*

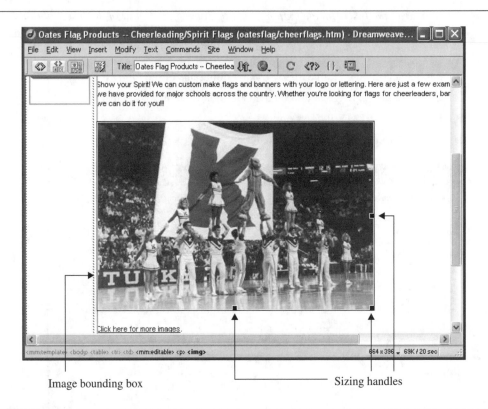

Image bounding box                                    Sizing handles

FIGURE 4-3    A newly inserted image

## Drag and Drop an Image

You can also use drag-and-drop techniques to insert images into your web page. Here's how:

1. Make sure the current document window and a window showing the desired image file are visible on the desktop. The image file can be on your desktop, in a Windows Explorer window, in the Site window, or in the Assets panel.

2. Drag the image file icon from the file list in the Site window and drop it on your web page at the location where you want to insert the image. Dreamweaver inserts the image into your page in the document window and adds the corresponding code to the page's HTML code.

TIP    *You can also insert images from the Assets panel by selecting an image and then clicking the Insert button at the bottom of the Assets panel.*

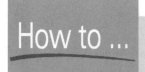

## Create an Image Placeholder

4

Ideally, you would have all the text, images, and other elements of a web page on hand before you start creating that page document in Dreamweaver. However, in the real world, images are often unavailable, so you must proceed with the rest of the page design and fill in the images later. Since image placement often has a major impact on page layout, that could be a problem. Fortunately, Dreamweaver includes a feature that lets you create a placeholder box for the missing image so that the page layout works as it should. Then you can plug the image into the placeholder when the image file becomes available. To create a placeholder image, follow these steps:

1. Position the insertion point where you want to insert the placeholder image on your page.

2. Choose Insert | Image Placeholder from the menu. Dreamweaver opens the Image Placeholder dialog box.

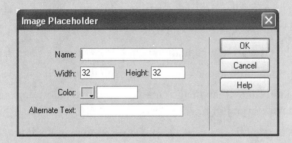

3. Enter a title for the image in the Name box. (The name can't begin with a number or contain spaces.) You can also set the size and color of the placeholder box and enter alternate text if desired.

4. Click OK to close the Image Placeholder dialog box. Dreamweaver adds a corresponding image tag to the HTML code for your page.

In Design view, Dreamweaver displays the placeholder image as a colored rectangle with the name and size superimposed in bold type. You can select and manipulate the placeholder image just like any other image in Design view.

When it's time to replace the placeholder with a real image, simply select the placeholder image box in Design view, click the Src box in the Property Inspector panel, and enter the appropriate image filename. You can type the path and filename, use the Point to File icon to make a drag-and-drop selection, or click the folder icon to open the Select Image Source dialog box and make your selection there.

## Control Image Position

The HTML standard provides several alignment options for images and similar objects, and Dreamweaver's image Property Inspector panel (shown in Figure 4-4) gives you ready access to all of them. However, remember that the original HTML specifications were conceived for publishing academic research papers and other technical documents, so the image alignment options are tailored to those limited needs. They work pretty well for positioning an image against the right or left margin and allowing text to flow around the rectangular image outline. But if your needs are more sophisticated than that, you'll probably want to look into using tables (see Chapter 6) or layers (see Chapter 12) to control image placement with more precision and flexibility.

There are actually two sets of image-alignment controls. First, since each image is contained within a text paragraph, you can use the standard paragraph-alignment options to control the horizontal position on the page.

Second, you can select one of ten alignment attributes to control how the image aligns with the surrounding text. These alignment options have essentially no effect on an image that sits alone in a paragraph that contains no text, but they have a significant effect on the relationship of text and images in the same paragraph. Remember that the image tag is embedded in the text of a paragraph. The alignment options tell the browser how to display the image in relation to the line of text in which the image tag resides. You can choose any of the following image-alignment options from the Align list box in the Property Inspector panel:

- **Default**    Uses the browser's default alignment setting, usually Baseline
- **Baseline**    Aligns the bottom edge of the image with the baseline of the text
- **Top**    Aligns the top edge of the image with the top of the tallest object in the line (text or another image or object)
- **Middle**    Aligns the middle of the image with the baseline of the text
- **Bottom**    Same as Baseline

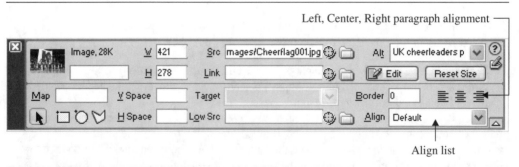

Left, Center, Right paragraph alignment

Align list

| FIGURE 4-4 | The Image Property Inspector panel expanded to show all the options. (Click the small arrow in the lower-right corner to expand the panel.) |

- **Text Top**   Aligns the top edge of the image with the top of the text
- **Absolute Middle**   Aligns the middle of the image with the middle of the text
- **Absolute Bottom**   Aligns the bottom edge of the image with the lowest extent of the current line of the text, including the descenders (the tails of characters such as *g*)
- **Left**   Aligns the image on the left margin and wraps text around it on the right
- **Right**   Aligns the image on the right margin and wraps text around it on the left

> **TIP**   *Use the paragraph-alignment buttons to set horizontal alignment and the Align options to set vertical alignment.*

## Resize Images

When you insert an image into your page, it appears in the document window at its original size. Often, that's not the size that works best in your page layout, and you'll need to resize the image to fit.

The mechanics of resizing an image in Dreamweaver are simple. You can either drag the resizing handles to resize the image visually or adjust the height and width settings in the Property Inspector panel.

To resize the image visually, click on the image to select it (see Figure 4-3), then do one of the following:

- Drag the sizing handle on the right side to make the image wider or narrower.
- Drag the sizing handle on the bottom to make the image taller or shorter.
- Drag the sizing handle in the lower-right corner to change height and width simultaneously.
- Press and hold the SHIFT key as you drag the lower-right sizing handle to maintain the image proportions as you make it larger or smaller.

> **NOTE**   *The smallest you can make an image by dragging resizing handles is 8×8 pixels. To make an image smaller, enter height and width values in the Property Inspector panel.*

As you change the image size by dragging the sizing handles, the numbers in the Height and Width boxes in the Property Inspector panel change to reflect the changes in image size. Also, the height and width numbers appear in bold to indicate that the image is no longer its original size.

To use the Property Inspector panel to control image size, try these techniques:

- Type new dimensions directly into the Height and Width boxes in the Property Inspector panel to resize the image "by the numbers." The image dimensions appear in pixels.
- Click Reset Size to instantly restore the image to its original size.

# Optimizing Image Files

One of the key considerations in adding any image to a web page is the size of the image file and how long it takes to download. Visitors to your web site tend to be an impatient lot and may not be willing to wait for a page with numerous large images to load. For this reason, it's imperative that you make every image file as small and fast to load as possible.

You should consider resizing an image in Dreamweaver as a temporary measure—something you do as you experiment with your page layout to determine what size the image should be. After you determine the correct size, go back to your image-editing program and generate a new image file to that exact size, and then reinsert it into your page. The goal is to have an image file that is the precise size needed for display—no more and no less. Relying on the browser to resize images as it displays them is inefficient and often produces an inferior display.

*The close integration of Dreamweaver and Fireworks dramatically simplifies the process of generating optimized image files after resizing an image in Dreamweaver; see Chapter 10 for details.*

## Set Borders and Other Image Properties

Image size and alignment aren't the only attributes you can adjust in the Property Inspector panel. You can also add a border around the image, set padding space, and more. Here's a rundown of the image properties and what they do:

*If all the options don't appear in the Property Inspector panel, click the small arrow in the lower-right corner to expand the panel.*

- **Image name** (unlabeled box under the thumbnail image)   An optional name for easy reference.
- **W**   Image width in pixels.
- **H**   Image height in pixels.

- ■ **Src**   Source file for the image.
- ■ **Link**   Create a hyperlink to another document or file.
- ■ **Alt**   Text to display in place of the image (see the box "How to Add Alt Text for Images").
- ■ **Edit button**   Click to open the image file in the associated image-editing program (usually Fireworks).
- ■ **Reset Size button**   Click to reset the image to its original size.
- ■ **Map**   Create client-side image maps (see "Create an Image Map," later in this chapter).
- ■ **V Space**   Specify the minimum amount of white space around the outer edges of the image at the top and bottom.
- ■ **H Space**   Specify the minimum amount of white space around the outer edges of the image at the sides.
- ■ **Target**   Specify the target browser window or frame for a hyperlink.
- ■ **Low Src**   An alternate image file that is loaded before the main image. This gives the visitor a preview of the image while waiting for the main image to load. It's usually a copy of the main image but with fewer colors and lower resolution so that it downloads much faster.
- ■ **Border**   Specify the thickness of the border around the image. The default is 0, no visible border.
- ■ **Left, center, right buttons**   Paragraph alignment buttons control horizontal placement.
- ■ **Align**   Alignment options controlling how the image aligns with text in the paragraph.

## How to ... Add Alt Text for Images

Alt text (alternate text) is an important attribute for images on your web page. It's one of the key factors in making your site accessible to visitors whose web browsing experience doesn't include images.

The average site visitor will probably only glimpse the alt text for an image in the seconds between the time the page begins to load and when the image appears in all its glory. But other visitors may be using a text-only browser or have their browser set to display images manually, in order to compensate for a slow Internet connection. Or they may be visually impaired and use screen reader software. All these visitors rely on the alt text for information about the image and its purpose on the page. Otherwise, the image appears as an empty rectangle.

Simply identifying an image as "Photo" or "Logo graphic" gives the visitor more information than an empty rectangle, but to be truly useful the alt text should be "functionally equivalent" to the image it's substituting for. So, if the image is a button linked to the Products page, the alt text should be something like "link to Products." If the image conveys information, the alt text should state that information. If the image is purely decorative, a simpler alt text entry is adequate.

You can add an alt text attribute to your image by simply typing the text in the Alt box in the Property Inspector panel. You can also have Dreamweaver display a dialog box that prompts you for alt text every time you insert an image. To enable this option, open the Preferences dialog box (choose Edit | Preferences), and select Accessibility in the Category list. Make sure the Images option is checked, and then click OK to close the Preferences dialog box.

# Use Images as Links

An image can serve as the anchor for a hyperlink, just as text does. When the site visitor moves the mouse pointer over an image that is a link, the pointer changes from the arrow to the familiar pointing finger, and when the visitor clicks on the image, the browser follows the link and displays the linked document. In short, an image link works just as a text link does.

The process for creating an image link in Dreamweaver is also the same as the process for creating a text link. In fact, you can use any of the techniques for creating links described earlier in this chapter. The only adjustment you need to make is to select an image instead of text in the document window to serve as the anchor for the link. The details of selecting the linked document file and dealing with paths and targets for the link are exactly the same for an image link and a text link.

## Create Buttons

One of the leading uses of linked images is as navigation buttons. Graphic images that resemble onscreen buttons lead site visitors to intuit that the image is something they can click on to make something happen.

Simple buttons are nothing more than a small image, usually a small GIF file, with an attached link. For example, in Figure 4-5, the Gallery button is an image file (btn_Gallery.gif) linked to the site's Gallery page (gallery.html). While it's possible to get fancy with a rollover effects (see Chapter 13), Flash buttons (see Chapter 10), and other special effects, the vast majority of buttons on the Web today are just the kind of simple image link illustrated in Figure 4-5.

4

**FIGURE 4-5**   Most buttons are simple image links.

## Create an Image Map

An image map takes the idea of a simple image link one step further. In an image map, instead of defining one link for the entire image, you can define multiple *hotspots* (subsections of the image) and create a separate link for each one. That means one image can anchor several links, and site visitors can go to different destination links depending on what portion of the image they click on.

One example of this concept would be a map of the United States with hotspot areas defined to match state borders. Each state hotspot could be linked to documents for that state. Figure 4-6 shows a similar use of an image map. More often, however, image maps are used to join several navigation buttons together to give them a seamless graphic treatment.

In the early days of the Web, image maps were created on the web server using some fairly complicated programming. Nowadays, most image maps are *client-side image maps*; all the programming code is contained in the web document and executed by the browser.

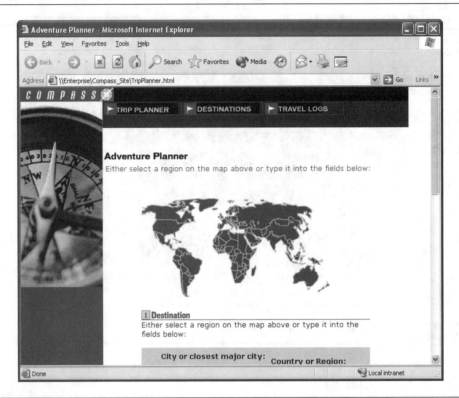

FIGURE 4-6    Image maps enable you to link one image to multiple destination pages.

Dreamweaver enables you to create client-side image maps without resorting to hand coding. Here's how:

1.  Insert the image that you want to use as an image map into your document, or select an existing image. Make sure the image Property Inspector panel is visible. (In Windows, you can press CTRL-F3 to open the panel if it isn't already open.)

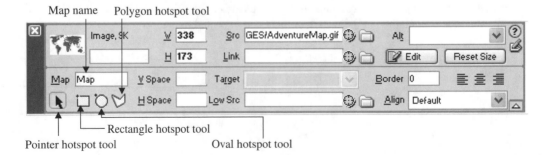

TIP *If the Map box and hotspot tools aren't visible in the Property Inspector panel, click the arrow button in the lower-right corner to expand the panel.*

**2.** Enter a name for your image map in the Map box of the Property Inspector panel.

**3.** Click one of the hotspot drawing tools, and then click and drag on the image to define a hotspot.

   ■ To create a rectangular hotspot, click the Rectangle hotspot tool then drag the pointer diagonally on the image to define the hotspot.

   ■ To create a circular hotspot, click the Oval hotspot tool then drag the pointer on the image to define the hotspot.

   ■ To create an irregularly shaped hotspot, click the Polygon hotspot tool, then click on the image to define the first point of the perimeter of the hotspot. Add points to the polygon by clicking as you work your way around the perimeter of the hotspot shape. Click the Pointer hotspot tool in the Property Inspector panel to close the polygon.

The hotspot Property Inspector panel appears when you create the hotspot.

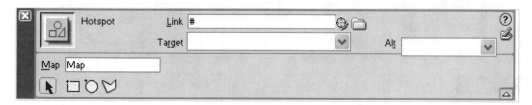

**4.** Click the Link box in the Property Inspector panel and define the link using your favorite technique. (Type a filename in the Link box, drag the Point to File icon to a file icon, or click the folder icon to open the Select Link File dialog box.)

**5.** Select an optional target for the link, and enter alt text for the hotspot in the Property Inspector panel.

**6.** Click the image outside the current hotspot to go back to the Property Inspector panel for the main image. Then repeat steps 3 through 5, as needed, to define additional hotspots and links.

Dreamweaver's Design view displays hotspots as translucent cyan (blue-green) overlays on image map images, as shown in Figure 4-7. This feature makes it easy for you to see and select the hotspots as you develop your page, but it doesn't affect how the image map appears to the visitor viewing your page in a web browser. In the browser, the hotspots are invisible. Only the ability to jump to different locations by clicking different areas of the image distinguishes the image map from a normal image.

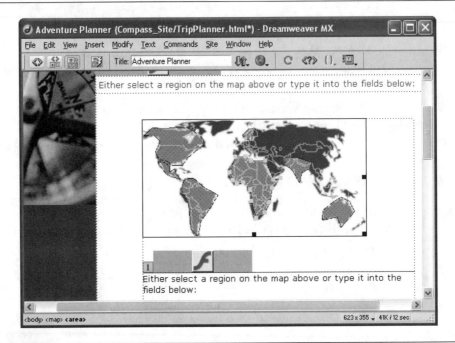

**FIGURE 4-7**     Hotspots appear as light shapes superimposed on your image in Design view.

After you create an image map, you can use the following techniques to edit the image map.

- Click a hotspot in Design view to select it. The hotspot Property Inspector panel appears, and you can change the link or any of the other settings.
- To move a hotspot, click the hotspot and drag it to the new location.
- To delete a hotspot, click the hotspot and press the DELETE key.
- Right-click a hotspot and choose Bring To Front or Send To Back to control which hotspot takes precedence (is in front) where hotspots overlap.
- To reshape a hotspot, select the hotspot with the pointer tool, and then drag any of the handles located on the edge.

# Work with Background Images

A *background image,* as its name implies, is an image that serves as a background for your web page (see Figure 4-8). You can create some interesting effects with background images, but you need to choose the image carefully to avoid conflicts that make the text and other foreground elements on your page hard to read.

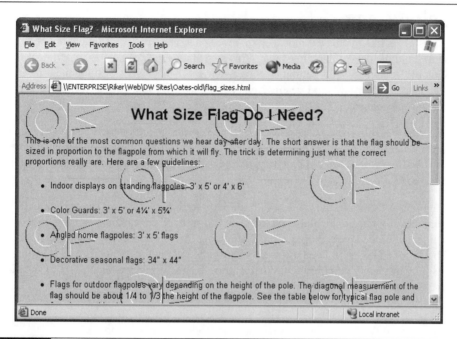

4

**FIGURE 4-8** A background image is tiled to fill the page.

An image large enough to fill the entire background of a web page, even when viewed on a large monitor, would require a large image file, and the time to download and display the image would probably be unacceptable. Therefore, background images are normally small images that can be downloaded quickly and then *tiled* (repeated in rows and columns) to fill the browser window. Dreamweaver tiles background images the same way web browsers do, so you can preview the effect in the Design view window.

To add a background image to your page, follow these steps:

**1.** Choose Modify | Page Properties to open the Page Properties dialog box.

**2.** Enter the image filename in the Background Image box. Alternatively, you can click the Browse button to open the Select Image Source dialog box, locate and select the file, and click OK to close the dialog box and enter the selected file into the Background Image box.

**3.** Click OK to close the Page Properties dialog box and apply the background image to your page.

**TIP** *The trick to successfully using background images is in image selection. Look for a low-contrast image that will tile without showing obvious seams. A subtle texture is usually better than an eye-catching pattern.*

# Use a Tracing Image

Some web designers like to create a mock-up of a web page in a graphics application before attempting to build the page in Dreamweaver. This step allows the designer to experiment freely with the look of the page without getting bogged down in the mechanics of implementing the design. Later, the designer turns to Dreamweaver for the task of producing a working web page based on the design concept.

*If you're the retro type, you can sketch your page layout with pencil and paper; then scan your sketch to create an image you can use as a tracing image in Dreamweaver. Just be sure to save the scanner output in (or convert it to) a web-friendly file format such as GIF or PNG.*

A tracing image facilitates the process of building a web page to match a preexisting design created in another program by enabling you to create and position page elements in Dreamweaver on top of an image of the mocked-up design. The tracing image replaces the page's background color and background image in Dreamweaver's Design view, but the tracing image is visible only in Design view, never in a browser. You can turn the tracing image on and off, change its opacity, and change its position.

To add a tracing image to a page, follow these steps:

**1.** Choose Modify | Page Properties to open the Page Properties dialog box.

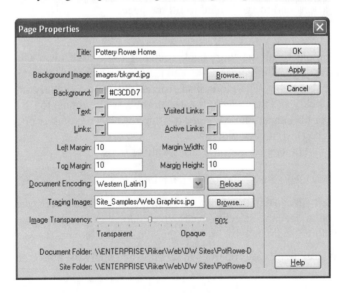

**2.** Enter the filename of the image in the Tracing Image box, or click the Browse button to open the Select Image Source dialog box, locate and select the file, and click Select.

**3.** Drag the Image Transparency slider to set the level of transparency for the tracing image.

**4.** Click OK to close the Page Properties dialog box and add the tracing image to your page, as shown in Figure 4-9.

After you add a tracing image to your page, you can manipulate it with the following techniques:

■ To specify the position of the tracing image, choose View | Tracing Image | Adjust Position to open the Adjust Tracing Image Position dialog box. Enter coordinates into the X and Y boxes, and then click OK to close the dialog box and move the tracing image.

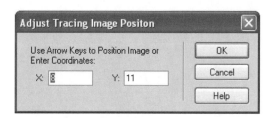

TIP · *While the Adjust Tracing Image Position dialog box is open, you can tap an arrow key (up, down, right, or left) to move the tracing image a pixel at a time. Press* SHIFT-*arrow key to move the tracing image 5 pixels at a time.*

■ To align the top-left corner of the tracing image with the currently selected object, choose View | Tracing Image | Align With Selection.

■ To turn the tracing image on or off, choose View | Tracing Image | Show.

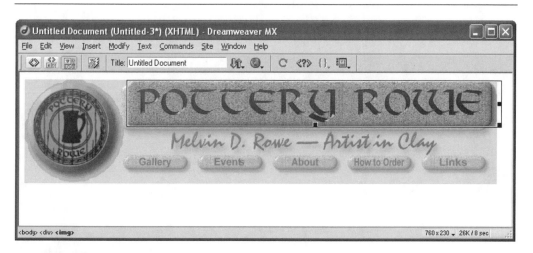

**FIGURE 4-9** A tracing image makes it easier to match a page mock-up created in another program.

# Chapter 5

# Edit HTML Code in Dreamweaver

# How to...

■  Use Dreamweaver's various code viewing windows and panels

■  Work with code in Design view

■  Use Dreamweaver's code-editing helpers

■  Clean up your code

■  Find and replace text and code

■  Work with code from other programs

When you view a web page in a browser, you see nicely formatted text and images, and perhaps animation, movies, and other special effects. But behind the pretty face you see in the browser, the web document is actually a plain text file containing unformatted text plus the HTML tags and other codes that tell the browser how to format and display the text, images, and other elements on the page.

Although it's convenient to think of a web page as the finished image you see in a browser, the reality is that a web document is composed of plain text interspersed with HTML tags and other codes. That's what is in the file stored on the web server; that's what gets downloaded to the browser; and that's what you create and edit in Dreamweaver.

Normally, you can click and drag and select objects and options to design web pages in Design view without being too concerned about the underlying HTML codes that Dreamweaver manipulates to achieve the desired effect. Of course, if you have a programming background, you may actually prefer to work directly with the HTML code for your web page. And Dreamweaver gives you that option with several ways to access and edit HTML code within the program. Dreamweaver also cooperates nicely with external programs, so you can continue to use your favorite text editor or programming environment.

Even if you're not a programmer, you'll undoubtedly need to work with HTML code from time to time. Sometimes working with code is the best, if not the only, way to troubleshoot a problem or achieve a certain effect. At the very least, you need to gain a general understanding of the real web documents you're creating with Dreamweaver—the HTML code. As a result, every Dreamweaver user needs to know at least the basics of how to access and manipulate HTML code. Fortunately, Dreamweaver creates an environment in which you can quickly and easily switch back and forth between a graphical representation of your web page and the underlying HTML code. You can even view the visual design and the code simultaneously, which is a tremendous advantage.

NOTE  *This chapter covers the various tools Dreamweaver provides for working directly with the HTML tags and other programming code in your web documents. However, explaining the proper use of that code is beyond the scope of this book. You can find some information on HTML tags and syntax in Dreamweaver's Reference panel. McGraw-Hill/Osborne also publishes some good books on the subject. Check out* HTML: A Beginner's Guide, *by Wendy Willard (2001), and* HTML: The Complete Reference, *by Thomas A. Powell (2001). Refer to the Osborne web site (http://www.osborne.com) for more books on XML, ASP, ColdFusion, and the other programming technologies Dreamweaver supports.*

# View and Edit Code in Dreamweaver

Like so many other things in Dreamweaver, when it comes to working with HTML code, Dreamweaver gives you options. There's not just one way to access and edit the code for your web document; you have your choice of multiple windows and techniques:

- **Code view**   Shows the HTML code for your web document in the Dreamweaver Document window.

- **Code and Design view**   Shows a split screen view of your web document in the Dreamweaver Document window. This allows you to see simultaneously a visual representation of a portion of your web page and the underlying HTML code.

- **Code Inspector panel**   Shows the HTML code for your document in a panel, separate from the main Document window.

You use different commands to open Code view, Code and Design view, and the Code Inspector panel, but otherwise you work with them in the same way.

Working in Code view or in the Code Inspector panel is very different from working in Design view, where you manipulate objects in a WYSIWYG environment while Dreamweaver automatically generates the code necessary to implement your vision. In Code view, you enter or edit the raw text for the codes yourself, using the same text-editing techniques you use for the text portions of the web document. You have complete control over every detail of the code for your web document, but along with that control comes the sole responsibility for entering the correct codes using the proper syntax.

Dreamweaver's Code view enables you to work directly with the raw text of your web document, but that doesn't mean that it's nothing more than a plain text editor like Windows Notepad. Dreamweaver includes numerous features to make editing code easier and more productive, including automatic code coloring, indents, line numbering, code hints, code snippets, and invalid HTML highlighting. Macromedia borrowed many of these code manipulation features from HomeSite, the advanced code editing environment that it acquired in a merger with Allaire, the developers of HomeSite and ColdFusion.

## Code View

Code view displays your document's HTML code in the Dreamweaver Document window (see Figure 5-1). This puts the code up front and in your face, so if you like working directly with the HTML source code for your web pages, this view is for you. In Code view, the Dreamweaver Document window functions as a text editor, allowing you to manipulate the text and code directly by typing in the Document window.

To view your document in Code view, click the Show Code View button on the Document window toolbar or choose View | Code from the menu.

Code view automatically displays the HTML code for the portion of the document you were working on in Design view. If you select an object or text passage in Design view, Dreamweaver selects the corresponding code in Code view. Otherwise, the insertion point cursor appears in the position in the code corresponding to its position on the page in Design view.

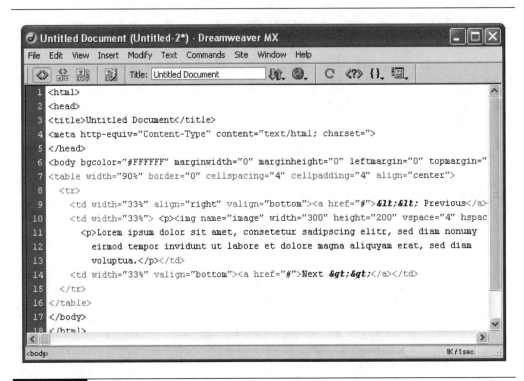

FIGURE 5-1    A web document in Code view

## Code and Design View

In addition to the full-fledged Code view, which devotes the entire Document window to displaying the web page's HTML code, Dreamweaver offers another option—Code and Design view—which splits the Document window into two panes, one showing HTML code and the other showing a visual representation of the page. At first glance, this hybrid view (shown in Figure 5-2) may seem strange, because neither the Code view pane nor the Design view pane is large enough to provide a good overview of the document. However, Code and Design view is an excellent way to examine the code for an element on your page while simultaneously viewing the graphical rendering of that same element in the Design view pane.

 To view your document in Code and Design view, click the Show Code and Design Views button on the Document window toolbar, or choose View | Code and Design from the menu. As with the full-sized Code View window, the Code View pane automatically displays the HTML code for the selected object in Design view, and vice versa. If you scroll one pane with its scroll bar, the other pane doesn't scroll simultaneously to match the portion of the document that is in view, but if you select an object or position the insertion point cursor in either pane, the other pane jumps to the corresponding place automatically.

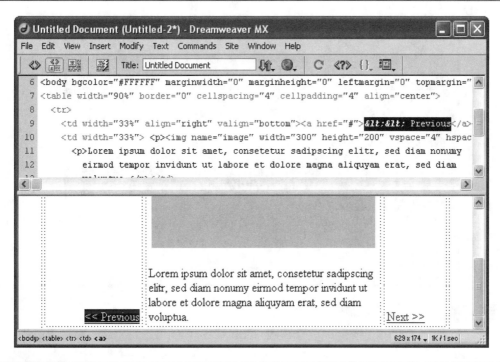

```
 6  <body bgcolor="#FFFFFF" marginwidth="0" marginheight="0" leftmargin="0" topmargin="
 7  <table width="90%" border="0" cellspacing="4" cellpadding="4" align="center">
 8   <tr>
 9     <td width="33%" align="right" valign="bottom"><a href="#">&lt;&lt; Previous</a>
10     <td width="33%"> <p><img name="image" width="300" height="200" vspace="4" hspac
11       <p>Lorem ipsum dolor sit amet, consetetur sadipscing elitr, sed diam nonumy
12         eirmod tempor invidunt ut labore et dolore magna aliquyam erat, sed diam
```

Lorem ipsum dolor sit amet, consetetur sadipscing
elitr, sed diam nonumy eirmod tempor invidunt ut
labore et dolore magna aliquyam erat, sed diam
<< Previous | voluptua. | Next >>

`<body> <table> <tr> <td> <a>`   629 x 174   1K / 1 sec

**FIGURE 5-2**  A document in Code and Design view

*By default, the Code View pane is on the top and the Design View pane is on the bottom in Code and Design view. But you can swap the panes by choosing View | Design View on Top. You can also resize the panes by dragging the border separating the two panes up or down.*

Code and Design view lets you switch back and forth between the two panes at will. You can make changes in the Design View pane and watch the HTML code change in the Code View pane. Edits in the Code View pane aren't instantly reflected in Design view, but you need only click in the Design View pane, click the Refresh button in the Property Inspector panel, or press F5, to see the results of your code edits.

## Code Inspector Panel

Unlike Code view, the Code Inspector panel displays your document's HTML code in a separate panel (see Figure 5-3) instead of in the main Document window. To view the HTML code for your document in the Code Inspector panel, choose Window | Others | Code Inspector or press F10. The Code Inspector panel functions exactly the same as Code view, except that it appears in a separate panel. The Code Inspector panel is a little unusual in that it isn't docked into the panel dock by default, but otherwise it's similar to other panels.

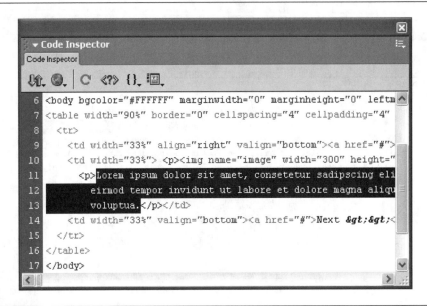

**FIGURE 5-3**    Code Inspector panel

## Set Code-Viewing Options

Dreamweaver lets you exercise control over several aspects of the appearance of your document's source code in Code view and the Code Inspector panel. You can easily enable or disable several code viewing options, and you can set detailed preferences for colors and formatting, as well as control whether and how much Dreamweaver rewrites imported code to match your Dreamweaver specifications.

Many of the code-viewing options are readily accessible, as is appropriate for options that you might want to change as you work. To access these options, just click the View Options button on the toolbar in the Code view or Code Inspector panel windows.

Clicking the View Options button opens a pop-up menu where you can enable and disable options. (The same options are available on the View | Code View Options menu.) A check mark designates an active option. Click an option to enable or disable it. You can choose any combination of the following code-viewing options:

- **Word Wrap**    Wraps lines of code so that the entire line is visible within the Code View window without scrolling horizontally.

- **Line Numbers**    Adds line numbers along the left side of the window to aid in identifying and navigating to specific parts of your code.

- **Highlight Invalid HTML**    Marks invalid HTML tags with a bright yellow highlight. (See the "Locate and Correct Code Errors," later in this chapter.)

- **Syntax Coloring**   Uses color to mark different codes and code elements to make it easier to identify those elements in the Code View window. You can adjust the specific colors Dreamweaver uses and the codes to which the colors apply in the Code Colors category of the Preferences dialog box.

- **Auto Indent**   Automatically indents the code. You can specify which tags indent and the indent spacing in the Code Format category of the Preferences dialog box.

All the code-viewing options affect only the way the code displays in the Code view or Code Inspector panel window. None of the code-viewing options changes the source code itself.

For more detailed control over the code-viewing options and other code-handling options, you can adjust the settings in the Preferences dialog box (choose Edit | Preferences to open the dialog box). You can set preferences in the following categories:

- **Code Coloring**   Set overall background color for the Code view window and also colors for use by the Syntax Coloring view option. Select a document type and click the Edit Coloring Scheme button to open a dialog box where you can specify colors for the various kinds of code in that document type.

- **Code Format**   Set formatting options, such as line length, case, and indenting.

- **Code Hints**   Enable Dreamweaver's Code Hint feature and set the time delay before the hints appear. Also select which menus of hints you want to display.

- **Code Rewriting**   Control whether and what kind of changes Dreamweaver makes to the code when you open a web document in Dreamweaver.

- **Fonts**   Select the font Dreamweaver uses to display code in Code view, the Code Inspector panel, and the Tag Inspector panel.

## Edit Code in Code View

Basically, when you edit code in Dreamweaver, you use the program as a fancy text editor. You can type HTML codes in Code view, just as you would any other text. And you can select, move, insert, delete, and edit HTML codes just as you would any other text.

 *Don't attempt to type HTML code directly into a document in Design view. The text characters that make up the code will look correct onscreen, but that's an illusion— they won't have the desired effect. The special formatting that Dreamweaver applies to angle brackets and other special characters so they are displayed as visible characters in Design view prevents those characters from working properly as code. If you need to enter HTML codes, switch to Code view or use the Quick Tag Editor.*

However, if you're like most Dreamweaver users, you'll rarely, if ever, enter HTML code from scratch. Instead, you'll probably let Dreamweaver build the code for the pages you create in Design view and then use Code view to examine that code and make occasional minor edits.

In addition to its basic text-editing capabilities, Dreamweaver provides some special features just to make life easier when you work with HTML code. Check out these tips and techniques for manipulating code:

- To indent a line of code in Code view, select the line(s) of code and choose Edit | Indent Code or press CTRL-SHIFT+>. Choosing Edit | Outdent Code or pressing CTRL-SHIFT-< moves the selected line(s) to the left.

- To check for balanced tags, click the content inside the tag you want to check, then choose Edit | Select Parent Tag or press CTRL-[. Dreamweaver highlights the tags enclosing the selected content. Choose Edit | Select Parent Tag again to highlight the next level of nested tags.

- To insert a comment in your code, place the insertion point at the location where you want to add the comment and click the Comment button in the Common category of the Insert bar, or choose Insert | Text Objects | Comment. Dreamweaver inserts a comment tag (`<!--- --->`) into your source code and positions the insertion point in the middle awaiting your typed comment. (If you're in Design view, Dreamweaver opens the Comment dialog box, where you can type the comment text to be inserted into the web document.)

> **TIP**
>
> *Scrolling through a long document in Code view looking for a particular code can be tedious. It's usually easier to find what you're looking for in Design view. You can click the object on the page and then use the Tag Selector in the Design view status bar to select the tag. When you return to Code view (or the Code Inspector panel), the tag you selected in Design view is highlighted in Code view, too.*

## How to ...    Use Code Hints to Enter Code

Dreamweaver's Code Hints feature can help you generate code faster and easier when you're Code Hints category of the Preferences dialog box) and you type an aworking in Code view. When Code Hints and Auto Tag Completion are enabled (see thengle bracket to open a tag, Dreamweaver presents a pop-up menu of options from which you can select the tag you want to enter. As you continue to build the tag by adding attributes to it, Code Hints pops up to offer its list of suggestions at each step along the way. Using Code Hints, you can enter a complete HTML tag in Code view with almost no typing—and you're assured that the code syntax is correct. However, using Code Hints is always optional. If you just keep typing, the pop-up Code Hints menu disappears and you can enter the code or text manually.

# Work with Code in Design View

Working with HTML code in Design view is a little different from editing code in Code view. Normally, you don't see any HTML code in Design view. You click, drag, and otherwise manipulate text and objects visually, not by editing HTML tags. To change the attributes of an object, you select options from the Property Inspector panel. Dreamweaver takes care of the HTML for you, creating and editing the source code to reflect the changes you make in the Design View window.

However, there are times when the best way to get something done is to enter or edit HTML code directly. For any substantial changes to the HTML source code you'll want to use Code view or the Code Inspector panel, but for quick edits and additions, the Quick Tag Editor is a handy tool. You can use it to insert an HTML code or to inspect and edit a tag without having to switch to Code view or open the Code Inspector panel. Dreamweaver also includes features that enable you to access header content and to edit scripts from Design view.

5

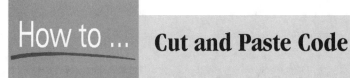

## How to ...    Cut and Paste Code

Copying and pasting HTML code from one location to another in a web document or from one document to another works just as you would expect it to—as long as both the source and destination documents are in a Code view Document window (or the Code Inspector panel or the Code view portion of Code and Design view).

1. Select the code and/or text you want to copy.

2. Press CTRL-C or choose Edit | Copy to copy the selected text.

3. Position the insertion point cursor where you want to insert the code and press CTRL-V or choose Edit | Paste.

You can even copy HTML code from an external text/programming editor such as HomeSite+ and paste it into Code view using the same technique.

If you attempt to use the same technique to paste HTML code into a document in Design view, the code will appear in the page as text instead of being inserted into the document as HTML code. This is a handy way to create a web page that describes HTML code without actually executing that code. If you want the HTML code to function as code, paste it into your document using the Edit | Paste as HTML command.

A companion command, Edit | Copy as HTML, enables you to copy text and codes from Design view as code instead of as visible text, so that you can subsequently paste it into Code view.

## Quick Tag Editor

To insert an HTML tag using the Quick Tag Editor, follow these steps:

1. Place the insertion point cursor in the document where you want to insert the code.

2. Press CTRL-T or click the Quick Tag Editor button in the Property Inspector panel. Dreamweaver opens the Quick Tag Editor in Insert HTML mode. After a short pause, a drop-down list of HTML tags appears.

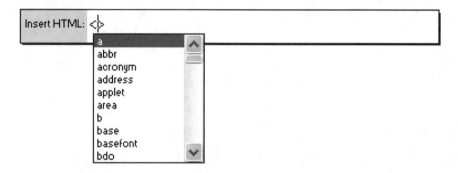

3. Type an HTML tag into the Quick Tag Editor between the angle brackets, or select one from the drop-down list.

4. Edit the tag by adding attributes or other options as needed.

5. Press ENTER to close the Quick Tag Editor and insert the tag into the HTML source code for your page. Press the ESC key to close the Quick Tag Editor without entering the code into your document.

You can also use the Quick Tag Editor to edit existing HTML tags. The process is basically the same as for inserting an HTML code in Design view, except that, instead of positioning the insertion point, you select a tag by selecting the text or object to which the tag applies and/or by using the Tag Selector in the status bar. When you open the Quick Tag Editor with an existing tag selected, it opens in Edit mode. You can edit the tag, add and edit attributes, and so on. After editing the tag, press ENTER to close the Quick Tag Editor and record your changes to the web document.

If you select some unformatted text or an object that isn't currently enclosed by an HTML tag and then open the Quick Tag Editor, the Quick Tag Editor opens in Wrap Tag mode. Wrap Tag mode is the same as the Insert HTML mode described previously, except that Dreamweaver will insert both the opening and closing tags so that they enclose the selected text or object.

TIP    *To remove a tag while keeping the content, right-click the content in Design view, and then choose Remove Tag from the context menu.*

## View and Edit Head Content in Design View

Naturally, the visible portion of a web page—the section marked by the `<body>` tag and displayed in the web browser—gets most of the attention. But the other required section of an HTML document—the head, marked by the `<head>` tag—contains some important information as well. The document title, meta tags, and scripts are just some of the contents of the document header. Except for the title, these elements are invisible, but their effects aren't.

You can view and edit the contents of the document header in Code view or in the Code Inspector panel by simply scrolling up to the top of the HTML source code and working with the code between the `<head>` and `</head>` tags.

To access head content in Design view you need to first display the Head Content pane in the Document window by choosing View | Head Content. The head content appears as a row of icons in a pane across the top of the document in Design view, as shown in Figure 5-4.

To view or edit the contents of any of the head content, click an icon in the Head Content pane. Dreamweaver displays the head content in the Property Inspector panel. To insert new head tags, choose Insert | Head Tags | *tag*. The available head tags include:

- **Meta**   Define generic meta tags.
- **Keywords**   Enter keywords for search engines to use for indexing your page.
- **Description**   Enter a description for your page—another bit of information used by search engines.
- **Refresh**   Instruct the browser to automatically reload the current page or go to another URL after a specified delay.
- **Base**   Set a base URL for all relative links in the document.
- **Link**   Define a link between the document and another document.
- **Script**   Access scripts (JavaScript or VBScript) embedded in the document header. Dreamweaver displays information about the scripts in the Property Inspector panel. Click the Edit button in the Property Inspector to edit a script.

When you choose one of the Insert | Head Tag commands, Dreamweaver opens a small dialog box where you can enter or select attributes and values for the tag. Enter the tag options, and then click OK to close the dialog box and add the tag to your document.

# Use Dreamweaver's Code-Editing Helpers

Dreamweaver doesn't leave you entirely on your own working with code—you don't have to type every character of every HTML tag and attribute entirely from memory. The program includes several features to make entering and editing code faster and easier.

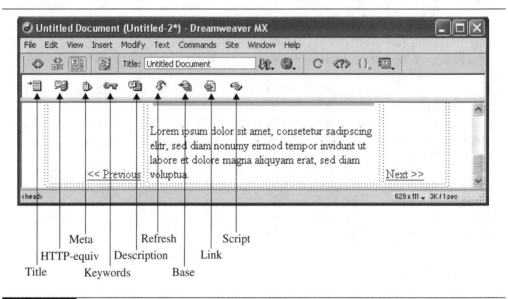

Meta

HTTP-equiv   Description

Title   Keywords   Base   Link   Script   Refresh

FIGURE 5-4   The Head Content pane

## Use the Tag Editor

Dreamweaver's Tag Editor (shown in Figure 5-5) enables you to view and edit all the available attributes for a selected HTML tag in a convenient and easy-to-use dialog box. The Tag Editor gives you access to options and settings that aren't available in the Property Inspector panel, and it does so without requiring you to memorize and type arcane attribute settings in Code view. The Tag Editor, which is a new feature of Dreamweaver MX, is available in both Design view and Code view. Here's how it works:

1. Select an object in Design view or highlight a tag in Code view.

2. Choose Modify | Edit Tag or right-click and choose Edit Tag from the context menu that appears. Dreamweaver displays the Tag Editor dialog box. The specific options and settings available in the dialog box vary depending on the selected HTML tag, but the settings shown in Figure 5-5 are fairly typical.

3. Click the Tag Info button to show or hide the tag reference information that appears across the bottom of the dialog box.

4. Select a category from the list on the left to display the associated settings in the right side of the dialog box.

5. View and/or edit the attribute settings as needed. If you don't need a particular setting, just leave it blank.

6. Click OK to close the dialog box and update your document's code.

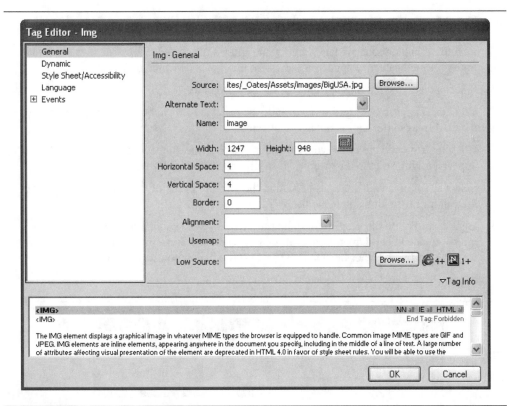

**FIGURE 5-5**    The Tag Editor dialog box

## Use the Tag Chooser

The Tag Chooser (shown in Figure 5-6) is another new feature of Dreamweaver MX. It enables you to select an HTML tag (or tags for ColdFusion, ASP, and other languages) from a dialog box and enter the code for that tag into your document without typing. You get point-and-click access to a comprehensive library of tags and codes to use in your web documents. You can use the Tag Chooser in both Design view and Code view. Here's how:

1. Position the insertion point at the location where you want to insert a tag, or select the text or other object to which the tag will apply.

2. Click the Tag Chooser button in the Common category of the Insert bar or choose Insert | Tag from the menu. (In Code view, you can also right-click and choose Insert Tag from the context menu that appears.) Dreamweaver opens the Tag Chooser dialog box, shown in Figure 5-6.

3.  Select a tag category in the list on the left side of the Tag Chooser dialog box. The tag categories are arranged in a tree structure. Click the plus or minus button beside a folder icon to expand or collapse the category and show any subcategories. The tags available in the selected category appear in the list on the right side of the dialog box.

4.  Select a tag in the list on the right side of the dialog box.

5.  Click the Tag Info button to show or hide the panel across the bottom of the dialog box, which displays information about the selected tag.

6.  Click Insert to add the tag to your document. In most cases, the Tag Editor dialog box appears, giving you the opportunity to specify attributes for the selected tag.

7.  Select or fill in tag attributes as needed in the Tag Editor dialog box. (See the preceding section for instructions on using the Tag Editor.)

8.  Click OK to close the Tag Editor dialog box and insert the code for the selected tag into your web document. Dreamweaver inserts the code at the insertion point or surrounding the selected text or other object. The Tag Chooser dialog box stays open for further use.

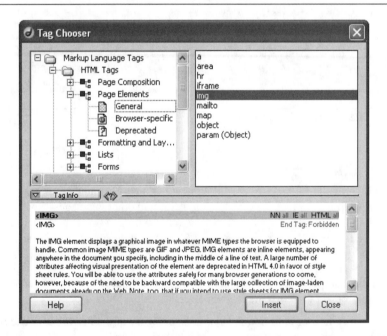

**FIGURE 5-6**    The Tag Chooser dialog box

## Use the Tag Inspector Panel

NEW IN
MX

The Tag Inspector panel is yet another new feature of Dreamweaver MX. It provides a unique perspective on your document by displaying the tags in a tree view, which enables you to see how tags are nested within other tags. The Tag Inspector panel also gives you ready access to all the attributes for any tag you select in the tree view.

5

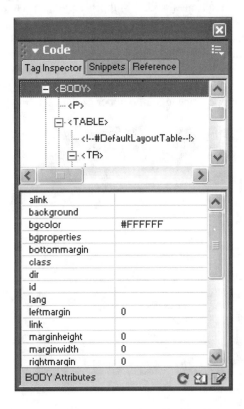

Choose Window | Tag Inspector or press F9 to open the Tag Inspector panel, which is located in the Code panel group by default. The Tag Inspector panel is divided into two panes. The top pane contains the tree view of your document's tags. Click the plus or minus button beside a tag name to expand or collapse the display (to show or hide the nested tags).

When you select a tag in the tree view, the lower pane of the Tag Inspector panel displays a list of all the available attributes for the selected tag. The attributes appear in the left column, and the associated values for each attribute appear in the right column. Click an attribute value field to select or enter a value.

## Work with Code Snippets

Why build the code for a page footer or other common document feature manually on each page when you can cut and paste code from another page and edit it to fit your needs? Why indeed? Code Snippets is a new feature of Dreamweaver MX that enables you to organize and store blocks of code and insert them into your documents with a couple of mouse clicks. The Snippets panel comes stocked with a generous assortment of code snippets and you can add to or edit the snippets to build your own library of reusable code.

Choose Window | Snippets or press SHIFT-F9 to open the Snippets panel. By default, the panel appears in the Code panel group. The Snippets panel is divided into two panes. The lower pane shows a tree-type list of folders and snippet icons. Use the usual plus and minus buttons to expand or collapse folders and the scroll bars to navigate the list. When you select a snippet icon in the list, a preview of that snippet appears in the upper pane of the Snippets panel.

The buttons along the bottom of the Snippets panel enable you to edit and use the snippets:

■ Select a snippet and click the Insert button to insert the snippet code into your document at the current insertion point. You can insert snippets into your document in Design view or Code view.

■ Click the New Snippet Folder button to add a new folder to the list in the Snippets panel. Type a name for the new folder and press Enter.

■ Select a portion of a web page in Design view or a block of code in Code view, and then click the New Snippet button to open the Snippets dialog box with the selected code displayed. Edit the contents of the dialog box as needed, and then click OK to add the snippet to the Snippets panel.

■ Select a snippet in the Snippets panel and click the Edit Snippet button to open the Snippets dialog box with the code for the selected snippet displayed. Edit the contents of the dialog box as needed, and then click OK to record your changes.

■ Select a snippet in the Snippets panel and click the Remove button to delete the snippet from the list.

■ Click and drag a folder or snippet icon to another location in the list to rearrange the snippet list.

5

# Produce Clean Code

A clean web document is one that is uncluttered by redundant tags, extraneous fragments of code, and other debris that accumulates so easily in the source code for many pages. Documents that aren't bloated by unnecessary garbage lurking in the code not only download and display faster and more predictably, they're just plain easier to work with. Dreamweaver includes a number of features to help you keep your web documents clean and tidy.

## Clean Up Your Code

Dreamweaver performs a basic code cleanup every time you open a web document. You can configure the automatic cleanup options using the settings in the Code Rewriting category of the Preferences dialog box.

When you want to do a more thorough code cleanup on a web document than Dreamweaver does automatically, the Clean Up HTML command will get the job done. You might use this command when editing an older web document or after opening a document produced in another program. You can also use this command to remove Dreamweaver-specific comments (such as template areas and library items) from a web document before sending it to someone who doesn't have Dreamweaver. This feature is similar to the Clean Up Word HTML command, described in Chapter 3.

To clean up the HTML source code in a web document, follow these steps:

**1.** Open the document you want to clean up.

**2.** Choose Commands | Clean Up HTML. Dreamweaver opens the Clean Up HTML dialog box.

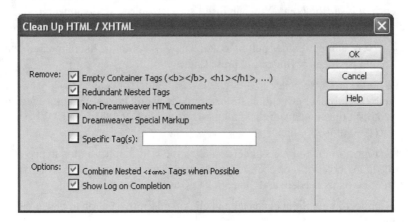

**3.** Select the cleanup options by clicking the check boxes in the dialog box. You can select any combination of the following:

■ **Remove Empty Container Tags**    Removes any pair of opening and closing tags that don't enclose any content. This cleans up any unneeded tags that were left behind after you deleted the content to which they applied.

■ **Remove Redundant Nested Tags**    Removes nested copies of the same tag, such as removing the bold (<b>) tag around a word within a sentence that is also tagged as bold.

■ **Remove Non-Dreamweaver HTML Comments**    Removes any comments that were inserted into the code by other programs (or programmers).

■ **Remove Dreamweaver Special Markup**    Removes any comments inserted into the source code by Dreamweaver. This includes comments that mark template areas and library items.

CAUTION    *Removing Dreamweaver HTML comments converts Dreamweaver templates and library items in the document to plain HTML, thus breaking the connection to the master template and library items for the site. After removing the Dreamweaver HTML comments, template and library items in this document won't update automatically when you change the site's master template and library.*

■ **Remove Specific Tag(s)**    Removes any tags identified in the text box to the right of the option. Use this option to remove valid but unwanted HTML tags, such as the obnoxious <blink> tag.

- ■ **Combine Nested `<font>` Tags When Possible**   Consolidates nested `<font>` tags that apply to the same text into a single pair of opening and closing tags with multiple attributes.
- ■ **Show Log on Completion**   Displays an optional alert box on completion of the cleanup process. It shows statistics on how many changes were made to the code.

**4.** Click OK to close the Clean Up HTML dialog box and begin the cleanup. Dreamweaver rewrites the HTML code, correcting the errors as specified. The process takes a few moments to complete—how long depends on the size of the web document and the speed of your computer.

## Locate and Correct Code Errors

Dreamweaver helps you locate and correct code errors by highlighting invalid tags in bright yellow. The program highlights HTML tags that it doesn't support and common errors such as extra closing tags left in the code after you delete the corresponding opening tag.

In Design view, the invalid HTML tags appear as bold text with a bright yellow highlight. It really stands out, because no other code is normally visible in Design view. When you click a highlighted code, Dreamweaver displays information in the Property Inspector panel describing why the code is highlighted and suggesting corrective action.

Invalid HTML highlighting is a little more subtle in Code view (or the Code Inspector panel). Dreamweaver highlights the tag with the same bright yellow, but it isn't bold and it remains in context with the rest of the source code. Again, when you click the highlighted tag, Dreamweaver displays information in the Property Inspector panel.

# Find and Replace Text and Code

Find and Replace is one of those features that you expect to find in any program that deals with handling text. Dreamweaver doesn't disappoint. The program includes a Find and Replace feature (choose Edit | Find and Replace) that works just the way you expect it to.

However, in addition to the obvious and expected ability to search for and replace plain text, Dreamweaver's Find and Replace command includes special features for working with code and for expanding Find and Replace operations beyond the current document to encompass selected documents or the entire site.

## Set the Scope of a Search

Whether you're just searching for text or digging down into the details of HTML codes and attributes, you can control the scope of a search in Dreamweaver. The primary tool for determining how narrow or broad the search will be is the Find In list in the Find and Replace dialog box (see Figure 5-7). Here's a rundown of your options:

- To search a single document only, open the document and choose Edit | Find and Replace from the Document window's menu. In the Find and Replace dialog box, select Current Document from the Find In list box. Dreamweaver displays the document name to the right of the Find In box.

- To search selected files, first select the files in the Site window's Local Files list, and then choose Edit | Find and Replace from the Site window's menu. In the Find and Replace dialog box, click the Selected Files in Site option in the Find In list box. Dreamweaver displays the path to the folder containing the selected files to the right of the Find In box.

- To search all the web document files in a particular folder, choose Edit | Find and Replace from the menu in either a document window or the Site window. In the Find and Replace dialog box, select Folder in the Find In list box. Then click the folder icon that appears to the right of the Find In box to open the Choose Search Folder dialog box. Locate and select the folder you want to search, and click the Select button to close the dialog box and record the folder in the Find and Replace dialog box.

- To search all web documents in the entire site, choose Edit | Find and Replace from the menu in either a document window or the Site window. In the Find and Replace dialog box, select Entire Local Site in the Find In list box. Dreamweaver displays the site name to the right of the Find In box.

After you set the scope of the search, you can define the other search parameters and proceed with the search.

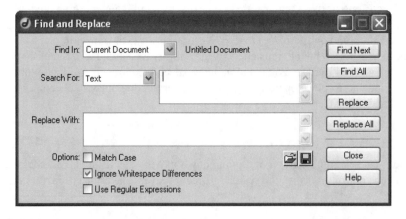

FIGURE 5-7   The Find and Replace dialog box

## Search for Text

The simplest find-and-replace operation is a simple text search. When you search for text, Dreamweaver does just that—it searches the document text for a match to the text you enter in the Find and Replace dialog box. Dreamweaver ignores HTML codes when conducting a plain text search. When Dreamweaver finds a match, it selects the matching text, and you have the option to replace it with the text you enter in the Replace With box in the Find and Replace dialog box. Here's the step-by-step procedure:

1. Choose Edit | Find and Replace to open the Find and Replace dialog box.

SHORTCUT    *Press* CTRL-F *to open the Find and Replace dialog box.*

2. Select an option from the Find In list box to define the scope of the search.

3. Select Text in the Search For list box. Dreamweaver displays the text search options in the Find and Replace dialog box as shown in Figure 5-7.

4. Enter the text you want to search for in the box to the right of the Search For box.

5. In the Replace With box, enter the text you want to insert in place of the search text.

6. Click the Find Next button. Dreamweaver locates the first instance of the text you specified and highlights it in the Document window.

7. To replace the selected text in the Document window with the text in the Replace With box, click the Replace button. To leave the selected text unchanged and continue the search, click Find Next. To automatically replace all instances of the search text, click the Replace All button.

8. Repeat step 7 until you reach the end of the document(s). Then click the Close button to close the Find and Replace dialog box.

TIP    *Press* F3 *or choose Edit | Find Next to open the Find Next dialog box, which is an abbreviated version of the Find and Replace dialog box that includes only the Find options—no Replace options. Use the Find Next command to search for something that you don't necessarily want to change.*

## Search Source Code

A source code search takes a simple text search one step further by expanding the search to include HTML code as well as page text. So, for example, a search for the word "sailboat" might find the word in the text on the web page and also in the filename sailboat.gif in an image tag and in the alt text attribute for that image.

Searching source code is an option if you start the Find and Replace operation from Design view. It's the default if you start the operation from Code view. The procedure for conducting a source code search is the same as for a simple text search (as described in the preceding section) except that in step 3, you select Source Code in the Search For box.

## Advanced Text Search

An advanced text search takes Dreamweaver's Find and Replace command to the next level of sophistication above text and source code searches. Not only does an advanced text search find text in source code as well as page text, the option lets you confine the search to specific tags and/or attributes or exclude specific tags or attributes.

When you select Text (Advanced) in the Search For list box, Dreamweaver displays the advanced text search options in the Find and Replace dialog box.

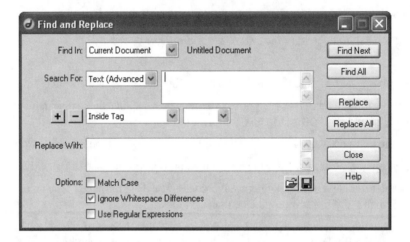

Enter the text you want to search for in the box to the right of the Search For box, select Inside Tag or Not Inside Tag in the list box below the Search For box, and select the tag in the list box to the right. To refine the search, click the plus (+) button to add another row of list boxes for selecting attributes, contents, and tags as needed.

## Search Specific Tags

A specific tag search does away with the text part of a find-and-replace operation and searches your document's HTML code for a specific tag. You can refine the search by specifying attributes, contents, and nested tags.

You also have several options for the action Dreamweaver can perform on the found tag. You can change attributes, insert and delete contents, and more.

To conduct a specific tag search, you follow the same basic procedure as for any other search, but you select Specific Tag in the Search For list box. Dreamweaver displays the specific tag options in the Find and Replace dialog box.

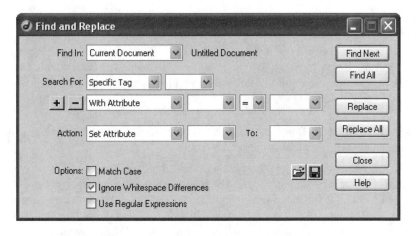

Select the tag you want to search for in the box to the right of the Search For box and then select the options and settings to refine the search in the row of list boxes below the Search For box. Continue to refine the search in subsequent rows.

After you set the search parameters, you can select options and enter or select values in the Action row of list boxes to define what Dreamweaver does when you click the Replace or Replace All button. You can select any of the following actions and then specify a value to add or replace.

- Replace Tag & Contents
- Replace Contents Only
- Remove Tag and Contents
- Strip Tag
- Change Tag
- Set Attribute
- Remove Attribute
- Add Before Start Tag
- Add After End Tag
- Add After Start Tag
- Add Before End Tag

**TIP** *Clicking the Find All button in the Find and Replace dialog box generates a list of all instances of the search text in the current document or, in a search of multiple documents, a list of all documents containing the search text.*

## Other Search Options

As if all the text, tag, and attribute options weren't enough—there are three check boxes at the bottom of the Find and Replace dialog box that enable you to expand or limit your searches. Click the check boxes to enable or disable each search option. The options are as follows:

- **Match Case**   Check this option to cause the search to be case sensitive.
- **Ignore Whitespace Differences**   Check this option to ignore spaces, paragraph breaks, and line breaks when matching the search text.
- **Use Regular Expressions**   When checked, this option enables you to use special wildcard characters in the search text. The list of regular expressions you can use is long; you can find it in Dreamweaver's online Help. Choose Help | Using Dreamweaver to open the Help file in a browser window. Click Index, click R, and then click Regular Expressions to display the complete list of expressions and their meanings.

# Work with Code from Other Programs

Dreamweaver MX provides a fairly complete web site development environment, so in theory you could create and edit web pages and maintain web sites using just Dreamweaver and its companion programs, such as Fireworks—you wouldn't need to use any other programs. However, the reality is that most Dreamweaver users must work with web documents from a variety of sources and often use several different tools over the course of developing a single HTML document. So Macromedia wisely designed Dreamweaver to cooperate nicely with other programs that may manipulate the HTML source code for a web document.

## Use External HTML Editors

Although Dreamweaver offers built-in code-editing capabilities, Macromedia realizes that true code warriors may prefer to use their favorite editor when editing HTML source code. Dreamweaver is designed to enable you to switch easily to and from an external editor. As a result, it's easy to use Dreamweaver for visual editing in Design view and your favorite text-based editor for working with HTML source code.

When you want to use the external editor, Dreamweaver automatically saves the current document and launches your preferred external editor with instructions to open the current document. When you return to Dreamweaver, the program automatically checks the status of the document file and prompts you to refresh the Document window if it detects any changes made by the external editor.

Dreamweaver ships with a full copy of HomeSite+ (Windows) or BBEdit (Macintosh) on the program CD. If you install one of these text-based editors along with Dreamweaver, the installation routine automatically configures Dreamweaver to use it as your external editor for HTML files. If you want to set up another program as your external editor, you can do so using the File Types/ Editors category of the Preferences dialog box.

# Part III

# Going Beyond the Basics

# Chapter 6

## Create and Edit Tables

## How to...

- Insert a table into your document
- Work with table rows, columns, and cells
- Format tables
- Add content to tables
- Create nested tables
- Use tables as a layout tool
- Use Dreamweaver's Layout view
- Draw Layout Tables and Layout Cells
- Create Layout Tables that shrink and stretch with changes in the browser window
- Create nested Layout Tables

Everyone knows how to build a table. You start with a large flat top, add four legs, and...
Oops, wrong table!

The tables that appear on web pages aren't the top-and-four-legs kind; they're the columns-and-rows kind—the same kind of table that gives spreadsheets their structure and is the basis for invoices, airline schedules, price lists, and most anything else that arranges blocks of text into columns and rows.

Undoubtedly, you've seen many examples of tabular matter on various web sites. But the obvious examples of tabular matter are just the tip of the iceberg. HTML tables are so versatile that web designers use them as general-purpose positioning tools to control web page layout. After all, tables are just a way to provide structure for content by defining horizontal and vertical spacing and position. What makes tables so versatile is the fact that each table *cell* (the space defined by the intersection of a row and a column) is a container that can hold just about anything you can place on a web page, including text, images, media objects—and even smaller tables.

So HTML tables have two applications on the Web. First, they provide the means for presenting traditional tabular matter in neatly arranged columns and rows. Second, and even more important, tables are the leading page-layout tool.

Dreamweaver has always had the ability to create and manipulate HTML tables visually in Design view. However, because tables are so widely used as a layout tool, Macromedia added a special feature to Dreamweaver called *Layout Tables*. This feature is really just a special way of representing HTML tables in Design view, which makes it easier to work with tables and table cells as layout elements rather than just as tabular matter.

This chapter covers working with tables in Dreamweaver MX. It starts with the basics of HTML tables and how to work with tables in Dreamweaver's Standard Table view. Then the second half of the chapter explores how to create and edit tables in Layout Table view.

# Insert a Table

The HTML code for a table can be complicated. There are separate tags for the table, for each row within the table, and for each column within the row. All those codes must be properly nested within one another, and the content and the tags marking the content must be nested within the table tags. Fortunately, you don't have to mess with the intricacies of the HTML source code unless you really want to—you can create, edit, format, and fill your tables entirely in the visual editing environment of Dreamweaver's Design view.

To add a table to your web page, follow these steps:

**1.** Position the insertion point cursor at the location in the document where you want to place the table.

**2.** Click the Table button in the Common category of the Insert bar or choose Insert I Table from the menu. Dreamweaver opens the Insert Table dialog box.

6

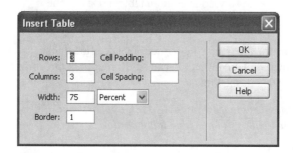

**3.** Enter the appropriate settings in the dialog box to specify the initial table configuration. You can edit all these values later. You may enter the following settings:

- **Rows**   Specify the number of table rows.

- **Columns**   Specify the number of table columns.

- **Width**   Enter a number, and then select Percent or Pixels to specify the width of the table.

- **Border**   Enter the thickness of the table border (in pixels).

- **Cell Padding**   Enter the number of pixels of space between the edge of a cell and the contents of the cell.

- **Cell Spacing**   Enter the number of pixels of space between adjacent cells.

**4.** Click OK to close the Insert Table dialog box. Dreamweaver enters the HTML code for the table into your web document and displays the empty table in Design view, as shown in Figure 6-1.

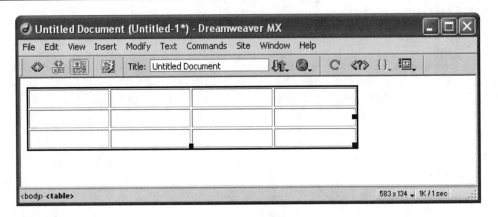

**FIGURE 6-1** An empty three-row, four-column table in Design view

If you defined borders for the table, one border of a specified thickness surrounds the table and each cell is outlined with a 1-pixel line. If you set Border to 0, Dreamweaver shows the table and cells outlined with a dashed line.

 *If the dashed lines designating the table don't appear, choose View | Visual Aids | Table Borders to display the invisible table borders.*

Just for grins, here's the HTML code for the top row of the simple table shown in Figure 6-1. Note the table tags (<table>), the row tags (<tr>), and the cell tags (<td>). Each cell contains a single nonbreaking space character ( ) as a placeholder.

```
<table width="75%" border="1" cellspacing="2" cellpadding="1">
  <tr>
    <td> </td>
    <td> </td>
    <td> </td>
    <td> </td>
  </tr>
  ...
</table>
```

## How to ...   **Make Your Table Accessible**

One of Dreamweaver's many customizable preferences allows you to instruct the program to prompt you for additional table settings when you insert a new table into a web document. The settings are called *accessibility options* because they are particularly useful for visitors who access your web site with alternative technologies such as screen readers.

To activate the accessibility options prompts for tables, open the Preferences dialog box (choose Edit | Preferences) and select the Accessibility category. Make sure the Tables check box is checked, and then click OK to close the dialog box.

With the accessibility options enabled, Dreamweaver adds a step to the process of inserting a table into your document. When you close the Insert Table dialog box, Dreamweaver opens the Accessibility Options for Tables dialog box instead of generating the table immediately.

You can set the following attributes:

- **Caption**   Enter a title for the table. This text will be visible above the table.
- **Align Caption**   Set the alignment for the caption.
- **Summary**   Enter a short description of the table contents. Like the alt text for an image, this hidden alternative text describes the table for people who access your site with screen readers.
- **Header**   Mark the first column, the first row, or both as headers or labels for the table data. Again, this helps people who access the table with screen readers.

Click OK to close the Accessibility Options for Tables dialog box and create the table. Dreamweaver enters the HTML code for the table into your web document and displays the empty table in Design view. Dreamweaver modifies the plain table by adding a caption, summary, and header row or column according to the settings you entered in the dialog box.

# Select and Edit Tables and Cells

After you create a table, you have a lot of flexibility and control over the shape and the configuration of the table. You can change every aspect of the table arrangement. You can select and manipulate the table as a whole, one or more rows or columns, or one or more individual cells. You can resize the table; add, delete, and resize rows and columns; and merge cells so they span multiple rows or columns.

## Select Table Cells, Rows, and Columns

Of course, before you can effectively manipulate a table, you must be able to select the table, or the portion of the table, that you want to change.

### Select the Entire Table

To select the entire table, use any of the following techniques:

- Click anywhere within the table; then click the `<table>` tag in the Tag Selector in the status bar.
- Click the bottom or right border of the table.
- Right-click anywhere within the table and choose Table I Select Table from the context menu that appears.
- Click anywhere within the table and choose Modify I Table I Select Table.

Dreamweaver highlights the selection with a bold line surrounding the table and sizing handles (small black squares) on the bottom and right edges (see Figure 6-1).

### Select Table Rows or Columns

You can use Dreamweaver's special selection pointer to select one or more rows or columns in a table:

- To select a row, move the mouse pointer to the left border of the table, beside the row you want to select. After a brief pause, the pointer changes to a small, solid black arrow pointing to the right.

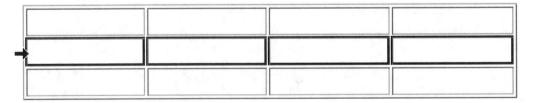

Click to select the row the pointer is on, or drag to select multiple rows.

■ To select a column, move the mouse pointer to the top border of the table to activate the column selection pointer, which points down instead of to the right.

*You can verify that you have selected a table, row, column, or cell by checking the Property Inspector panel (see Figure 6-2). Make sure the Property Inspector panel is expanded to show all the options (click the arrowhead button in the lower-right corner); then check the table icon and label at the left end of the Property Inspector panel.*

## Select Individual Table Cells

To select an individual cell, CTRL-click within the cell. Dreamweaver highlights the selected cell with a bold outline around the cell border. For many operations, it's sufficient to simply click within the cell, since Dreamweaver displays the cell properties in the Property Inspector panel along with the properties of text and other contents of the cell.

To select multiple cells, click and drag across the cells you want to select. You can also select multiple cells by selecting the first cell and then CTRL-clicking additional cells. If you select one cell and then SHIFT-click another cell, Dreamweaver selects both cells along with any cells located between the two.

# Add and Delete Table Rows and Columns

You can quickly expand or reduce the size of your table by adding or deleting columns or rows. The process for adding rows and columns is essentially the same, the only difference being that you choose the Insert Row command for one and Insert Column for the other. Whether you're adding rows or columns, you can use any of the following techniques:

■ Click a row (or column) in the table and choose Modify | Table | Insert Row (or Insert Column). Dreamweaver inserts a blank row (or column) into the table immediately below (or to the right of) the selected row.

■ Right-click a cell in the table and choose Table | Insert Row (or Insert Column) from the context menu that appears. Again, Dreamweaver inserts a blank row (or column) into the table immediately below (or to the right of) the selected cell.

Table icon    Split Cell button

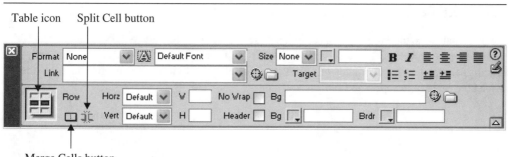

Merge Cells button

**FIGURE 6-2**   Property Inspector panel for a table row

■ To insert multiple rows or columns, select a cell in the table and choose Modify | Table | Insert Rows or Columns (or right-click a cell and choose Table | Insert Rows or Columns from the context menu). Dreamweaver opens the Insert Rows or Columns dialog box.

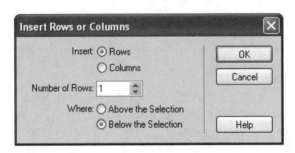

In the dialog box, select Rows (or Columns) to insert, specify the Number of Rows (or Number of Columns), and choose where to insert the new rows (either Above... or Below... for rows or Left... or Right... for columns). Then click OK to close the dialog box and insert the rows or columns into your table.

TIP    *As you enter content into the table, Dreamweaver automatically adds rows to the table to accommodate additional content. Simply position the insertion point cursor in the rightmost cell of the bottom row of the table and press* TAB *to move the insertion point to the next cell. Dreamweaver adds a new row to the bottom of the table and moves the insertion point to the first cell in the row.*

You can use similar techniques to delete rows or columns from your table:

■ Click anywhere in the row or column you want to delete and choose Modify | Table | Delete Row (or Delete Column). Dreamweaver removes the selected row or column from the table.

■ Right-click anywhere in the row or column you want to delete and choose Table | Delete Row (or Delete Column) from the context menu. Dreamweaver removes the selected row or column from the table.

■ Select an entire row or column and press the DELETE key.

You can also use the Property Inspector panel (see Figure 6-3) to change the size of your table. Select the entire table and then change the number in the Rows or Cols boxes in the Property Inspector panel. Dreamweaver adds or removes rows on the bottom or columns on the right side to adjust the table to the specified size.

# Resize Tables, Rows, and Columns

In addition to adding and removing rows and columns of cells in your table, you can adjust the size of the table as a whole and also control the height of individual rows and the width of individual columns in the Property Inspector panel (see Figure 6-3).

- To adjust the table size visually, select the table and drag the sizing handles to resize the table. Drag the sizing handle on the right border to adjust table width. Drag the sizing handle on the bottom border to adjust table height. Drag the sizing handle in the lower-right corner to adjust both height and width simultaneously.

- Select the table and adjust the values in the W and H boxes in the Property Inspector panel (Figure 6-3). You can set table size in pixels or as a percentage (%) of the browser window.

**NOTE**
*When you resize the whole table, Dreamweaver resizes all table cells proportionally, unless you previously specified a fixed size for one or more cells. In that case, those cells retain their fixed size and the remaining cells resize along with the table.*

- To adjust the width of a column visually, drag the right side of the column left or right. Dreamweaver adjusts the widths of all the cells in the column.

- To adjust the height of a row visually, drag the bottom of the row up or down. Dreamweaver adjusts the height of all the cells in the row.

- To set column width, select a column and enter a width in the W box in the Property Inspector panel (see Figure 6-2). You can enter a number to set the width in pixels or a number followed by the percent sign (%) to specify the column width as a percentage of the table width.

**TIP**
*Leave the height and width settings for columns, rows, and cells blank in the Property Inspector panel to allow the browser to dynamically resize table cells as needed to fit table content.*

6

Convert Table Widths to Pixels button

Clear Column Widths button          Convert Table Widths to Percents button

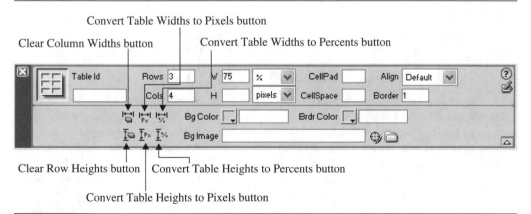

Clear Row Heights button │ Convert Table Heights to Percents button

Convert Table Heights to Pixels button

**FIGURE 6-3**   The Property Inspector Panel for a table

■ To set row height, select a row and enter a height in the H box in the Property Inspector panel (see Figure 6-2). You can enter a number to set the height in pixels or a number followed by the percent sign (%) to specify the row height as a percentage of the table height.

## Make Cells Span Columns and Rows

Sometimes you need to create a table that includes a cell that spreads out over more than one column or row. Or perhaps you need to divide one cell into two while the remaining cells in that column or row remain unaffected. Well, HTML tables can do that, and Dreamweaver makes this task easy.

The HTML term for joining one or more cells is *span*, but Dreamweaver uses the more descriptive term *merge*. The Dreamweaver term for dividing one cell into multiple cells is *split*.

To merge two or more adjacent cells, follow these steps:

1. Click and drag to select the cells you want to merge. The cells to be merged must be adjacent to each other and form a single rectangular shape.

2. Click the Merge Cells button in the Property Inspector panel, or choose Modify | Table | Merge Cells.

Dreamweaver combines the selected cells into a single cell and inserts all the necessary code in your web document.

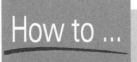

## Convert Height and Width from Pixels to Percent

As you make adjustments to the height and width of a table, you may find it easier to work in pixels even though you want to set the finished table sizes in percentages, or vice versa. Go ahead and use the measurement that is most comfortable or convenient. Dreamweaver can convert the measurements for you later. When you get the table the way you want it, select the table and then choose Modify | Table | Convert Widths to Percent (or Convert Widths to Pixels, or Convert Heights to Pixels, or Convert Heights to Percents). Dreamweaver converts the column widths or row heights to percent or pixel measurements as requested.

To split a single cell into multiple cells, follow these steps:

1. Select the cell you want to split.

2. Click the Split Cell button in the Property Inspector panel, or choose Modify | Table | Split Cell. Dreamweaver opens the Split Cell dialog box.

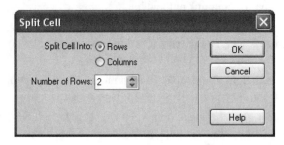

3. Select Rows or Columns to instruct Dreamweaver to split the cell horizontally or vertically.

4. Enter the number of cells to make out of the selected cell.

5. Click OK to close the Split Cell dialog box and split the selected cell. Dreamweaver displays the result in Design view and inserts the necessary code in your web document to create the additional cells.

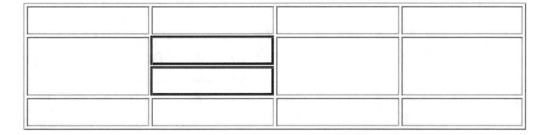

# Format Tables

There's more to formatting tables than just setting the number of rows and columns, the width of the columns, and the height of the rows. You can customize the appearance of your tables with background and border colors, cell spacing, cell padding, border thickness, and alignment on the page. You can also exercise similar control over each row, column, and cell in the table.

## Set Table Properties

To control the formatting for a table, select the table and adjust the settings in the Property Inspector panel (see Figure 6-3). When working with table properties, be sure to click the expander button in the lower-right corner of the Property Inspector panel to display all the table properties. Here's a rundown on the table-formatting attributes:

- **Table ID**   Enter a short name for the table. It's optional and only for your reference.
- **Rows**   Set the number of rows in the table.
- **Cols**   Set the number of columns in the table.
- **W (width)**   Set the width of the table. Enter a number, and select pixels or % (percent). Percent measurements specify a percentage of the browser window or, in the case of nested tables, a percentage of the parent table cell.
- **H (height)**   Set the height of the table. Enter a number, and select pixels or % (percent). Percent measurements specify a percentage of the browser window.
- **CellPad (cell padding)**   The space (in pixels) between the cell border and the cell content. Enter 0 to specify no cell padding. If you leave this blank, the browser displays the table with cell padding of 2 pixels.
- **CellSpace (cell spacing)**   The space (in pixels) between cells. Enter 0 to specify no cell spacing. If you leave this blank, the browser displays the table with cell spacing of 1 pixel.
- **Align**   Horizontal alignment of the table within a paragraph on the web page. Select Left, Center, Right, or Default (which is usually the same as left alignment).
- **Border**   Set the thickness of the outer border around the table. Enter 0 to specify no border. If you leave this blank, the web browser will probably display the table with a 3-pixel border.
- **Clear Column Widths**   Click to remove column width settings throughout the table.
- **Clear Row Heights**   Click to remove row height settings throughout the table.

TIP   *Use the Clear Row Height and Clear Column Width buttons to erase existing height and width settings. Doing so lets the table automatically size itself to the content, or you can start over fresh after trying some resizing experiments.*

- **Convert Table Widths to Pixels**   Click to convert all table and cell width settings to fixed pixel measurements.
- **Convert Table Widths to Percents**   Click to convert all table and cell width settings to percent measurements.
- **Convert Table Heights to Pixels**   Click to convert all table and cell height settings to fixed pixel measurements.
- **Convert Table Heights to Percents**   Click to convert all table and cell width settings to percent measurements.
- **Bg Color (background color)**   Select a color from the color picker or enter a hexadecimal value to specify the background color for the cells and the spaces between the cells.
- **Brdr Color (border color)**   Select a color from the color picker or enter a hexadecimal value to specify the color of the border around the outside of the table.

- **Bg Image (background image)**    Specify an image to appear as the background for the entire table (supercedes the background color). You can enter the path and filename, click the folder icon and browse for the image file in the dialog box that appears, or drag the point-to-file icon to the file in the Dreamweaver Site window.

## Set Column, Row, and Cell Properties

Just as you can control the formatting for a table with the Property Inspector panel, you can set similar formatting attributes for rows, columns, and cells in your table. The row, column, and cell properties are in the lower portion of the Property Inspector panel (cell content properties are in the upper portion), so be sure to click the expander button in the lower-right corner of the Property Inspector panel to display all the table properties. The formatting options are identical for rows, columns, and cells. Here's a rundown on the available formatting attributes (see Figure 6-2):

- **Table icon**    This icon and the legend beside it indicate whether a row, a column, or individual cells are selected.

- **Merge Cells**    Click to merge the selected cells into one cell spanning multiple columns or rows. This button is grayed out if it isn't available.

- **Split Cell**    Click to split the selected cell into two or more cells. Clicking the button opens a dialog box where you can specify whether to split the cell into multiple rows or multiple columns and how many cells to create.

- **Horz (horizontal alignment)**    Select the horizontal alignment for the content within the selected cells. You can choose Left, Center, Right, or Default (usually the same as left alignment).

- **Vert (vertical alignment)**    Select the vertical alignment for the content within the selected cells. You can choose Top, Middle, Bottom, Baseline, or Default (usually the same as middle).

- **W (width)**    Set the width of the cell(s). Enter a number and select pixels or % (percent). Percent measurements specify a percentage of the table, not the page.

- **H (height)**    Set the height of the cell(s). Enter a number and select pixels or % (percent). Percent measurements specify a percentage of the table, not the page.

- **No Wrap**    Check this option to disable word wrapping within the cell.

- **Header**    Check this option to mark the selected cells as header cells, which causes the browser to display the cell contents centered and in bold (unless you override those settings).

- **Bg (background image)**    Specify an image to appear as the background for the selected cell(s). You can enter the path and the filename, click the folder icon and browse for the image file in the dialog box that appears, or drag the point-to-file icon to the file in the Dreamweaver Site window. This image appears behind any text or other content in the cell(s). It works like the background image for a page, including the way a small image tiles to fill the space with multiple copies. It's not the same as adding an image to the cell as foreground content.

- ■ **Bg (background color)**   Select a color from the color picker, or enter a hexadecimal value to specify the background color for the cell(s).
- ■ **Brdr (Border Color)**   Select a color from the color picker or enter a hexadecimal value to specify the color of the border around the cell(s).

## Apply a Design Scheme to a Table

By adding borders, background colors, and other formatting to the table and the various rows and cells within the table, you can create an almost infinite variety of table treatments. For example, you can assign different colors to alternating rows in the table to make it easier for the viewer to read across each row. You can make these changes by selecting each row in turn and adjusting the settings in the Property Inspector panel. Or you could make all the changes at once with just a few mouse clicks by applying one of Dreamweaver's preformatted design schemes. Figure 6-4 shows one such design scheme applied to a simple table. You can apply this scheme and others to your tables by following these steps:

**1.**   Select the table to which you want to apply a design scheme.

   *You can't apply design schemes to tables with captions.*

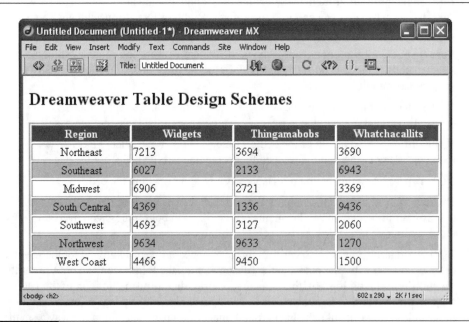

**FIGURE 6-4**    A table formatted with a Dreamweaver design scheme

**2.** Choose Commands | Format Table. The Format Table dialog box appears.

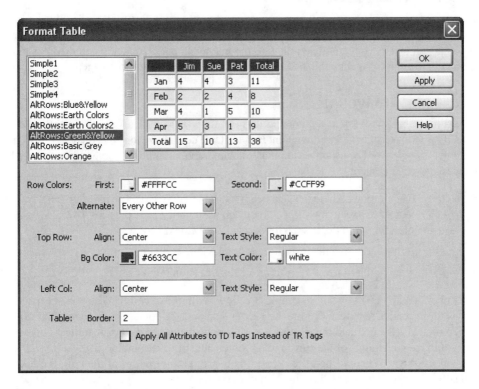

**3.** Select a design scheme from the list box in the upper-left corner of the dialog box. A preview of the selected scheme appears to the right of the list.

**4.** Fine-tune the scheme by adjusting the settings for Row Colors, Top Row, and Left Col.

**5.** Adjust the border thickness by entering a number in the Border box.

**6.** Check or clear the Options check box. Leaving this option unchecked causes the command to apply formatting to entire table rows instead of cells, which makes the HTML more compact but may fail to format some table cells that were previously formatted. Checking the option applies all formatting attributes to the <td> tags for the individual table cells, which is sure to override any existing formatting, at the expense of bulkier code.

**7.** Click OK to close the dialog box and apply the design scheme to the selected table. Dreamweaver modifies the HTML source code for the table and displays the formatting in Design view.

The design scheme is just a fast way to apply multiple formatting attributes all at once. You're not limited by the design scheme at all. After applying a design scheme, you can edit and refine your table formatting and content anyway you like.

# Add Content to a Table Cell

Adding content to a table cell is actually the easiest part of working with tables. Basically, you just click a cell to position the insertion point cursor in the cell and then add text, images, and other content to the cell just as you would add them to the main web page. In fact, when it comes to adding content to a table, you can think of each table cell as a miniature web page.

## Use Text and Images in Tables

Adding text to a table is as easy as adding text to the main web page. The only thing you need to do differently is to make sure the insertion point is in the table cell where you want the text to appear. You can enter a single word or a number, a phrase, a paragraph, or multiple paragraphs combined with images and other content.

- To move the insertion point to the next cell in the table, press TAB. The insertion point moves from left to right across a row. When you reach the end of a row, pressing TAB moves the insertion point down to the first (leftmost) cell in the next row.
- Press SHIFT-TAB to move the insertion point back one cell to the left.
- Press the right and left arrow keys to move the insertion point right or left one cell.

Remember that any text you add to a table cell flows within that cell. Unless you set specific dimensions for the cell, Dreamweaver (and the viewer's browser) automatically expands the table cell to accommodate the text and other content within it, provided, of course, that there is room to do so within the constraints of the surrounding table cells, the overall table size, and the other elements on the page. When a line of text exceeds the maximum width of the cell, the text automatically wraps to form a new line, just as it does on the main web page—unless you activate the No Wrap option for the cell in the Property Inspector panel.

You can format text in a table cell using any of the normal text formatting attributes, such as fonts, sizes, paragraph and heading tags, bold, italics, and so on (see Chapter 3 for the details). Alignment attributes align text relative to the borders and cell padding of the cell instead of relative to the page margins, but otherwise all text formatting works the same within a table cell.

Table cells can contain more than just text. You can also insert images into a table cell—as well as just about any other media object you can insert into a normal web page.

The techniques for inserting an image into a table cell are the same as for inserting an image anywhere else on your web page. See Chapter 4 for details on working with images.

## Copy and Paste Table Cells

Dreamweaver provides you with considerable versatility in the way you cut, copy, and paste table cells to rearrange content within the table. You can copy multiple cells, including both the cell content and the properties of the cell itself, or you can copy and paste just the cell content. You can paste cells and cell content into another location in the same table or into another table, or you can use the copied cells to create an entirely new table elsewhere on your page.

Use the same cut, copy, and paste commands in tables that you use when editing other parts of your web document. You can use the commands on the Edit menu or shortcut keys (such as CTRL-C and CTRL-V). The key to controlling the copy and paste operations in a table is in selection—selecting what to copy and selecting where to paste. Here's a rundown of common copy and paste operations:

- To copy only the contents of a cell, select the contents of a single cell and choose Edit | Copy. Before you copy, check the Tag Selector in the Design view status bar to make sure you select only the content of the cell and not the cell tag (`<td>` or `<th>`).

- To paste content into a cell, position the insertion point cursor in the cell and choose Edit | Paste. Select the existing content of the cell before issuing the paste command if you want the pasted content to *replace* the existing content.

- To copy one or more cells *and* their contents, select the cells you wish to copy and choose Edit | Copy. If you select multiple cells, you automatically get the cells as well as their content. If you select a single cell, check the Tag Selector in the Design view status bar to make sure you select the cell tag (`<td>` or `<th>`) and not just the content.

- To insert the copied cells and their content into a table, position the insertion point cursor at the location in the table where you want to add the cells, and choose Edit | Paste. Dreamweaver adds the cells and their content to the table and moves the existing cells and content down and to the right to make room.

- To replace existing table cells with the copied cells and their content, select the range of cells to be replaced and choose Edit | Paste. Note that the number of cells copied and the number of cells replaced must match in number and configuration. For example, if you copy two rows of three cells each, you must select six cells in the same two-row configuration in order to complete the paste operation.

- To create a new table composed of the copied cells, position the insertion point cursor anywhere on your page outside an existing table and choose Edit | Paste. Dreamweaver automatically creates a new table to enclose the pasted table cells.

- To remove content from one or more cells, select the cells (less than a full row or column) and press DELETE. Dreamweaver deletes the content of the cells but leaves the cells themselves intact.

- To remove a row or column of cells from the table, select the row or column and press DELETE. If you select one or more entire rows or columns, Dreamweaver deletes the cells as well as their content from the table.

## Sort Table Contents

If you've done much work with tables in a spreadsheet program or a recent word processing program, you're probably accustomed to being able to sort a table—rearrange the rows to put them in alphabetical or numerical order. Dreamweaver also provides a basic table sorting capability.

You can sort on one or two columns, and you can sort alphabetically or numerically in ascending or descending order. Here's how:

1. Select the table.

2. Choose Commands I Sort Table to open the Sort Table dialog box.

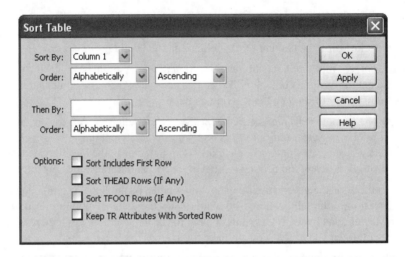

3. Select a column in the Sort By list box. This is the column containing the primary sort criteria.

4. Select Alphabetically or Numerically in the Order list box and then select Ascending or Descending.

5. To specify a secondary sort criteria, select a column in the Then By list box and select the kind of sort and direction in the Order list boxes below. Leave the Then By box blank to perform a simple, one-column sort.

6. Select one or more of the following options, as appropriate:

   ■ **Sort Includes First Row**    Dreamweaver normally excludes the first row of the table from the sort because the first row frequently contains column headers. Check this option if the first row of your table contains data that you want to include in the sort.

   ■ **Sort THEAD Rows (If Any)**    Sorts the header rows if they exist. Header rows remain at the top of the table but are sorted according to the same criteria as the rest of the table.

   ■ **Sort TFOOT Rows (If Any)**    Sorts the footer rows if they exist. Footer rows remain at the bottom of the table but are sorted according to the same criteria as the rest of the table.

   ■ **Keep TR Attributes With Sorted Row**    Check this option if your table includes rows highlighted with color or some other formatting attribute associated with the content of the row. Leave this option unchecked if your table includes formatting, such as alternating row colors, that will be disturbed if the row formatting moves along with the content.

**7.** Click OK to close the Sort Table dialog box. Dreamweaver sorts the table and rearranges the rows according to the sort criteria you specified.

CAUTION    *You can't use the Sort Table command on a table that contains merged cells.*

## Import Table Data

If you have tabular data created in another application that you want to use in your web page, you don't have to reenter all the data in Dreamweaver or copy and paste it one cell at a time. If you can export that tabular data into a delimited text file, you can import the data from the file and use it to create a new table in Dreamweaver.

Of course, a necessary prerequisite is creating a delimited text file (a text file that uses a standard character, such as a tab or a comma, to separate the data fields). Follow the instructions for creating such a file from the data in the source application. After you create the delimited file, follow these steps to import the data into Dreamweaver:

**1.** Position the insertion point cursor where you want to create the new table on your page.

**2.** Choose Insert | Tabular Data to open the Insert Tabular Data dialog box.

**3.** Enter the path and the filename for the delimited file in the Data File box, or click the Browse button to open a dialog box where you can locate and select the file.

**4.** Select the delimiter character used in the file from the Delimiter box. You must specify the correct delimiter character, or the tabular data won't import correctly.

**5.** Set the Table Width. Click the Fit to Data option to allow Dreamweaver to automatically size the table to accommodate the data. Click Set and enter a number, then select Percent or Pixels to specify the table width as a percentage of the page size or as a fixed width.

**6.** Set the other options as appropriate:

- **Cell Padding**    Specify the number of pixels between the cell border and the cell content. Enter 0 for no padding; otherwise, Dreamweaver and the browsers default to 1-pixel padding.

- **Cell Spacing**    Specify the number of pixels of space between cells. Enter 0 for no cell spacing; otherwise, Dreamweaver and the browsers default to 3-pixel spacing.

- **Format Top Row**    Select character formatting to be applied to the contents of the cells on the top row of the table. You can choose from Bold, Italic, Bold-Italic, or No Formatting.

- **Border**    Enter a border thickness in pixels. Enter 0 for no border.

**7.** Click OK to close the Insert Tabular Data dialog box and import the data into your web document. Dreamweaver creates a new table, adds the appropriate number of rows and columns, and enters the data into the cells of the table.

# Create Nesting Tables

Table cells can contain other tables.

This simple statement has profound consequences for what you can do with tables. *Nesting tables*—placing one table within another—dramatically increases the versatility of tables, especially in their application as page layout tools. Just as you can use a table to divide a web page into rectangular cells to position content on the page, you can further subdivide a cell by inserting a table into that cell, as shown in Figure 6-5.

The concept of nesting tables is simple enough—a table cell can contain almost anything you can place on a regular web page, *including other tables*. Implementing this concept in the HTML code can get a little messy when you nest tables several layers deep, but Dreamweaver's Design view insulates you from the complexities of the source code and makes nested tables manageable for most web authors.

You create a nested table just as you create any other table in Dreamweaver. The only difference is that you start with the insertion point in a cell of another table. After you create the nested table, you can add and delete rows and columns; adjust table, row, and column sizes; and apply formatting to the table and its rows, columns, and cells just as you would with any other table. The only difference is that the size of the table is constrained by the size of the table cell in which it resides.

# Why Use Tables as a Layout Tool?

It's fair to say that tables are an essential component of the majority of pages on the Web today. And it's not because there is an overabundance of tabular matter on most web sites. Sure, you'll see something you'd instantly recognize as a table on a web page here and there. But the tables on most web pages are invisible.

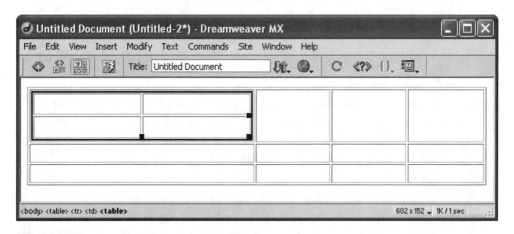

FIGURE 6-5    A nested table within a table cell

The same HTML tags that arrange tabular matter into neat columns and rows in a traditional table can also provide horizontal and vertical spacing and positioning for the text, images, and other elements of the web page. In other words, HTML tables function as a layout grid for many web pages.

Web designers often fill the page with one large table that breaks the page into columns (see Figure 6-6). Text, images, and other content placed in the table cells flow within the table instead of across and down the page as a whole, thus giving the designer more control over the position of those elements on the finished page. Adjusting the width of the table columns adjusts the page layout horizontally. Similarly, table rows enable the designer to control the vertical positioning of elements on the page. In effect, HTML tables and cells take on the role of the columns and text boxes that are the primary page layout tools in desktop publishing programs.

Tables do a good job of positioning elements on a web page, but working with those tables can be a challenge. The ability to work with tables visually in Dreamweaver's Design view goes a long way toward addressing the difficulties of working with HTML source code for tables, but Dreamweaver's traditional table-manipulation tools still are not the optimum solution for using tables as a layout tool.

6

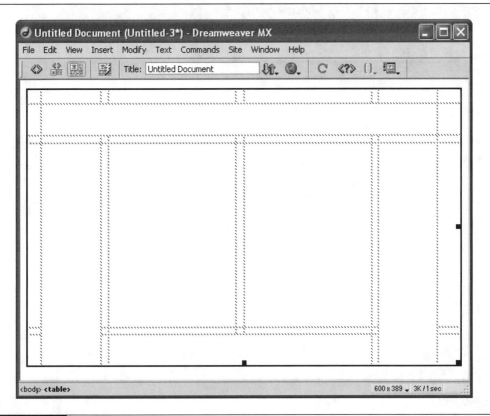

**FIGURE 6-6**   A table set up for use as a page layout tool

In many ways, layers are easier to use as a layout tool, especially in Dreamweaver's Design view (see Chapter 12). If you need to position an object at a particular location on the page, you just click the Insert Layer icon in the Insert bar and drag the pointer on the page to create a layer in that location; then you insert your object into the layer. With layers, you don't have to define a whole table to create that one cell that you need as a container for the object, and you don't have to manipulate row and column sizes to position or move the cell.

The problem with layers is that they suffer from browser compatibility issues, so they're not suitable for web sites that must be accessible to the greatest possible number of visitors. Tables, however, are compatible with all browsers, old and new. Also, tables can do some things layers can't do, such as automatically shrink and expand cells to fit different browser window sizes.

Starting with Dreamweaver 4, Macromedia added a new way of creating and manipulating tables in Design view that makes them easier to use for page layout. As a result, table cells can be almost as easy and intuitive to use for page layout as layers. Layout view doesn't actually change anything about the underlying HTML code for tables. Instead, Layout view is a new way of rendering tables and table cells in Design view (see Figure 6-7).

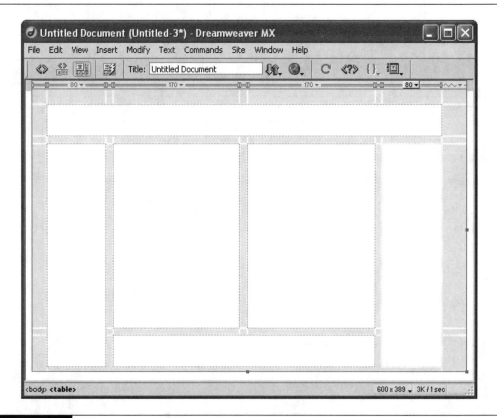

**FIGURE 6-7**     Dreamweaver in Layout view

When you're working in Layout view, you can create a table cell anywhere on the web page with a click and a drag—like creating a layer. You don't have to define a table and specify a bunch of parameters. Dreamweaver does all that for you automatically. If you want a Layout Table cell positioned in a particular place, you draw it there. Dreamweaver creates a table, with all the rows and columns sized as necessary to place the cell right where you indicated, ready to accept your content. If you want to move a Layout Cell, just drag it to a new position. Dreamweaver "automagically" adds, deletes, merges, splits, and resizes rows, columns, and cells in the table as needed to accommodate the new cell position.

# Work in Layout View

Layout view provides an alternative way of rendering and working with tables and table cells in Dreamweaver's Design view document window. The traditional table rendering in Design view is still available; it's now called *Standard view*. Layout view works best for creating and manipulating tables for page layout. Standard view, in contrast, remains the best way to work with tables that contain traditional tabular matter. You can switch back and forth between the two views at will.

■  To select Layout view, click the Layout View button at the bottom of the Insert bar, or choose View | Table View | Layout View.

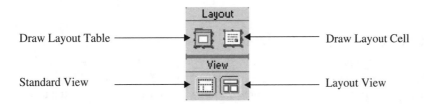

Draw Layout Table ———————→   Draw Layout Cell

Standard View ———————→   Layout View

■  To select Standard view, click the Standard View button at the bottom of the Insert bar, or choose View | Table View | Standard View.

*The keyboard shortcut for Layout view is* CTRL-F6. *The shortcut for Standard view is* CTRL-SHIFT-F6.

When you're in Layout view, Dreamweaver uses a different system for rendering tables. The View | Visual Aids | Table Borders command is inactive, and the dashed lines designating table and cell borders that are set to zero disappear and are replaced by colored lines—green for table borders and blue for cell borders. A tab at the top of each table shows column divisions and sizes and provides easy access to a menu of table options. Compare Figure 6-7, showing Layout view, to Figure 6-6, which shows the same table in Standard view.

**NOTE**   *The colored outlines and white or gray backgrounds you see in Layout view are simply visual aids that Dreamweaver uses to make the tables and cells easy for you to see and work with. They don't appear on the finished web page as seen in a browser.*

Note that some of the cells in Layout view have a white background and blue border and others have a gray background and white border. The white cells are Layout Cells as defined in Layout view. (The next section of this chapter shows you how to create Layout Cells and Layout Tables.) The gray cells are the extra placeholder cells Dreamweaver created to fill in around and between the Layout Cells. When working with Layout Tables, you manipulate the Layout Cells and let Dreamweaver manipulate the gray placeholder cells surrounding the Layout Cells.

Also note that the Layout Table is composed of columns and rows, just like a normal table. Many of the cells in the table span multiple columns and rows, which makes the table structure less obvious than it would be if all the cells were normal size, but the column and row structure remains the basis for the table. As you work with Layout Tables in Layout view, you don't need to be concerned about merging and splitting cells to achieve the proper effect, but that's what Dreamweaver is doing behind the scenes.

When working in Layout view, you can insert content into the white Layout Cells but not into the gray placeholder cells. If you move or resize a Layout Cell, Dreamweaver automatically adds, deletes, and resizes the gray placeholder cells as necessary to accommodate the changes in the Layout Cell. Dreamweaver doesn't automatically resize Layout Cells.

*When you first enter Layout view, Dreamweaver displays a large dialog box describing Layout view and how to use it. Check the "Don't show me this message again" box and click OK to make the annoying dialog box go away and not return.*

# Draw Layout Cells and Tables

When you work in Layout view, Dreamweaver enables you to create a table cell almost anywhere on the web page without first creating a table. Of course, an HTML table cell can't exist outside a table, so Dreamweaver automatically creates the table for you and configures the table with the rows and columns necessary to create a cell in the location you specify. You can also create a table yourself and then draw cells in that table, but it isn't necessary to do so.

To facilitate this new way of working with tables in Layout view, Dreamweaver provides special Layout Cell and Layout Table buttons on the Insert bar that you use for creating cells and tables. The normal Insert I Table command and the corresponding button in the Insert panel are unavailable in Layout view. If you want to work with tables using those commands and techniques, switch back to Standard view.

*Creating a Layout Table works best when you start with a blank document and create the basic layout for the page before adding any content. If there is existing content on the web page, you can create a Layout Table only below the existing content.*

## Draw Layout Cells

When you are working in Layout view, the normal sequence of actions for creating a table is reversed. In Standard view, you start by defining a table, setting the table size and the number of rows and columns, and then manipulating the row and column settings to create table cells where you need them. In Layout view, you start by defining where you want a table cell, and then you let Dreamweaver do the work of creating a table around that cell.

You can draw a *Layout Cell* (a table cell created in Layout view) almost anywhere on the current web page. The only restrictions are these:

- The cell must start below any existing content on the page.

- The cell must not overlap any existing Layout Cell.

- The cell must not overlap the border of an existing Layout Table. You can create new Layout Cells inside or outside an existing Layout Table; you just can't draw the cell over the table border.

Here's the technique for drawing a Layout Cell:

1. Click the Draw Layout Cell button at the bottom of the Insert bar. The mouse pointer changes from the normal arrow to a cross-hairs pointer (+).

2. Position the pointer where you want to place one corner of the Layout Cell, and then click and drag diagonally to the location of the opposite corner. Dreamweaver displays a box shape as you drag. When the box is the proper size for the new Layout Cell, release the mouse button.

> **TIP**
> *To make it easier to align Layout Cells, Dreamweaver snaps the new Layout Cell to the edge of any other Layout Cell, Layout Table, or page border that you get close to (within about 8 pixels). Press* ALT *to disable snapping.*

> **NOTE**
> *Don't worry about getting the Layout Cell perfectly sized or positioned. You can easily resize and move the cell after you create it.*

When you finish drawing the Layout Cell, Dreamweaver automatically creates a Layout Table to surround the cell (unless you draw the cell within an existing table), as shown in Figure 6-8. The table extends the full width of the page and includes as many rows and columns of cells as necessary to create a cell at the location you specified. The Layout Cell appears with a blue outline and a white background. The other cells that Dreamweaver creates for positioning the Layout Cell appear in gray.

The Layout Table and all the cells within it are constructed with normal HTML table tags. The table and individual cells are all set for no border or background so they are invisible on the finished web page. The default formatting for a Layout Table also includes no cell padding or cell spacing. You can change these settings later if you want (see "Format Layout Tables and Cells," later in this chapter), but these settings are the ones commonly used for tables that serve as page layout tools.

The insertion point automatically appears inside the newly created Layout Cell, ready for you to begin inserting content into the cell. However, you'll probably want to finish creating the Layout Cells you'll need to define your page layout before you start filling the cells with text, images, and other content.

> **TIP**
> *To draw several Layout Cells without having to click the Layout Cell button in the Insert bar each time, press and hold the* CTRL *key as you begin drawing the first cell. Hold the* CTRL *key down until you finish drawing all the cells.*

6

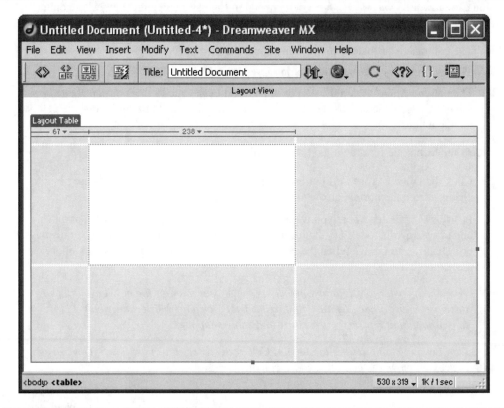

FIGURE 6-8 A newly created Layout Cell surrounded by the Layout Table Dreamweaver created

## Draw a Layout Table

Dreamweaver automatically creates a Layout Table for you when you draw a Layout Cell on the page in Layout view—there's no need to draw the Layout Table first. However, there are times when you may want to draw the table yourself instead of accepting Dreamweaver's default table configuration, or you may want to draw a Layout Table to create nested tables. Here's how you do it:

1. Click the Draw Layout Table button at the bottom of the Insert bar. The mouse pointer changes from the normal arrow to a cross-hairs pointer (+).

2. Position the pointer on the page and drag diagonally to define the size of the Layout Table. The upper-left corner of the Layout Table automatically snaps to the upper-left corner of the page (if this is the first table on an empty page) or to the lower-left corner of the bottom Layout Table or other content. Dreamweaver displays a box shape as you drag. When the box is the proper size for the new Layout Table, release the mouse button.

Dreamweaver creates the Layout Table according to your specifications, as shown in Figure 6-9. The Layout Table appears with a bar across the top that shows the dimensions of the table column(s). The Layout Table tab at the upper-left corner of the table serves as a selection handle. Sizing handles (small boxes) appear on the bottom and right borders of the table. A newly created layout table starts out with just one cell—a gray placeholder cell. You can create one or more Layout Cells within the new Layout Table.

## Create a Nested Layout Table

One of the features of Layout view enables you to quickly and easily create *nested tables*—tables contained within other tables (see Figure 6-10). There are several reasons why you might want to create nested Layout Tables, but one of the most common is to gain better control over the way Layout Cells automatically expand and contract to accommodate the content you place in them. For example, a Layout Cell that is set to Autostretch (discussed in detail shortly) can encroach on the space occupied by an adjacent empty Layout Cell but not on the space occupied by a nested Layout Table. So, nested Layout Tables are a kind of super Layout Cells.

Layout Table tab                    Column size bar

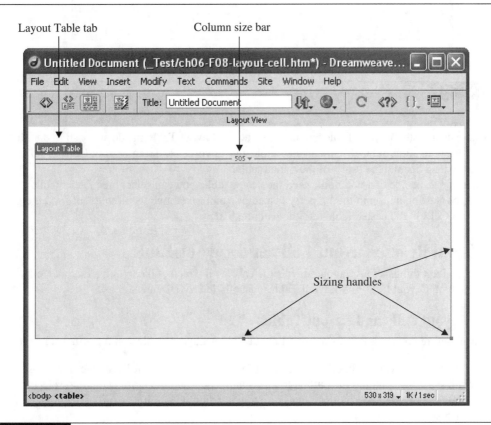

**FIGURE 6-9**    An empty Layout Table

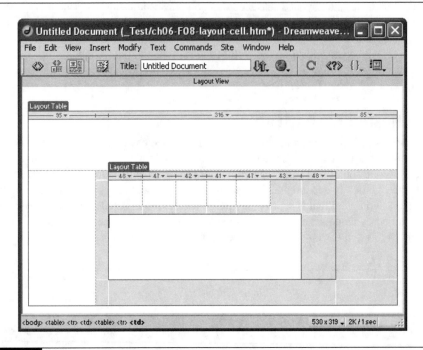

FIGURE 6-10    Nested Layout Tables

To create a nested Layout Table, simply draw a new Layout Table inside an existing one. It's just like drawing a Layout Cell—the nested table can't overlap existing Layout Cells or tables and can't extend beyond the limits of the parent table.

 Later, if you decide that you don't need the nested table, you can select the table and click the Remove Nesting button in the Property Inspector panel to remove the nested table and merge any Layout Cells in the nested table into the parent table.

# Move and Resize Layout Cells and Layout Tables

One of the nicest things about Layout view is the ease with which you can move Layout Cells and resize both Layout Cells and Layout Tables visually in Layout view.

## Select Layout Cells and Layout Tables

Of course, before you can move or resize a Layout Cell or Layout Table you must first select it:

■ To select a Layout Cell, click the cell outline. It's a thin line, but Dreamweaver helps you see it by changing the outline to red when your pointer is close enough to select the cell. The selected cell outline displays sizing handles at the corners and in the middle of each side.

TIP *You can* CTRL-*click anywhere in a cell to select it.*

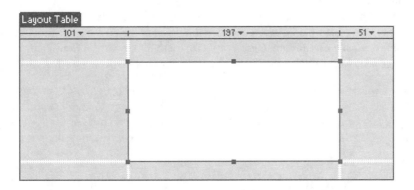

- To select a Layout Table, click the table outline or the green tab at the upper-left corner of the table, or click anywhere on a gray placeholder cell in the table. The selected table displays sizing handles in the lower-right corner and on the bottom and right sides. A column size bar also appears across the top, as shown in Figure 6-9.

TIP *You can suppress the display of the Layout Table tab and column size bar across the top of the Layout Table. Choose View | Table View | Show Layout Table Tab to toggle the display on and off.*

## Move or Resize a Layout Cell

You can freely move or resize a Layout Cell within a Layout Table. The only restrictions are that you can't move the cell beyond the edge of the table, and the cell can't overlap other Layout Cells. The gray placeholder cells, however, are not an obstacle.

To move or resize a Layout Cell, select the cell and then use one of the following techniques:

- Click and drag the cell outline to move the cell. Click anywhere on the outline except at a sizing handle. As you drag, Dreamweaver displays a dotted-line rectangle showing the new position. Release the mouse button to drop the cell in the new position.
- Press the arrow keys to move the cell up, down, left, or right one pixel at a time. Press SHIFT along with an arrow key to move the cell 10 pixels.
- Drag any of the sizing handles on the cell outline to resize the layout cell. Drag one of the handles in the middle of a side to move that side. Drag one of the corner handles to move the two adjacent sides simultaneously.

TIP *Press and hold the* SHIFT *key as you drag a corner sizing handle to maintain the cell's proportions as you resize it.*

### Resize a Layout Table

Just as you can resize a Layout Cell, you can also resize a Layout Table. The technique is essentially the same—you select the table and then drag one of the sizing handles. The biggest difference is that a Layout Table has sizing handles only on the bottom and right side.

The restrictions on resizing a Layout Table are simple and logical. You can't reduce the size of a Layout Table beyond the minimum required to make room for the Layout Cells it contains. And you can't enlarge a Layout Table so that it overlaps another Layout Table or other page content.

*Dreamweaver won't let you visually resize the height of a Layout Table that has another Layout Table immediately below it. To work around the limitation, you can temporarily insert a text paragraph to separate the two Layout Tables and then resize the upper table visually. Or you can resize the table by adjusting the height setting in the Property Inspector panel.*

## Format Layout Tables and Cells

Formatting tables and cells in Layout view is essentially the same as formatting tables and cells in Standard view. When you select a Layout Table or a Layout Cell, the Property Inspector panel displays the attribute settings and options for the selected object. And of course, you can edit those settings in the Property Inspector panel.

Most of the formatting attributes and options are the same as those for tables and cells in Standard view—after all, you're working with the same HTML tags. However, there are a few options (such as border color and background images) that Macromedia chose not to display, presumably because the options are irrelevant when you are using tables as layout tools. And there are a few options—such as Autostretch—that are specific to Layout view. (For more on the Autostretch option, see "Create Layout Tables That Resize in the Browser," later in this chapter.)

### Format Layout Tables

To adjust the formatting attributes of a Layout Table, select the table and then adjust the settings in the Property Inspector panel.

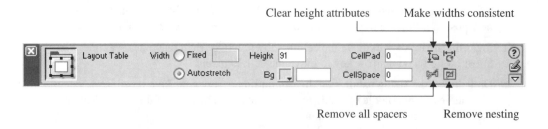

Most of the settings mirror their counterparts in a standard table. The following list describes the ones that are different:

■ **Clear Row Heights**   Click to delete fixed height settings for layout table cells, thus allowing the cell heights to expand and contract to fit the content.

- **Make widths consistent**    Click to set the width of all fixed-width cells in the table to match the width to which they expanded to accommodate the content you entered. (See "Work with Fixed-Width Columns" later in this chapter.)

- **Remove all spacers**    Click to remove spacer images from the table. (See "Create Layout Tables That Resize in the Browser," later in the chapter for more information on spacer images.)

- **Remove nesting**    Click to remove the selected table and make its cells part of the parent table.

### Format Layout Cells

To adjust the formatting attributes of a Layout Cell, select the cell and then adjust the settings in the Property Inspector panel. The settings have the same effect as their counterparts in a standard table.

# Add Content to Layout Table Cells

Adding content to a Layout Cell is essentially the same as adding content to a regular table cell in Standard view—which is to say it's the same as adding content anywhere else on your page.

To add text to a Layout Cell, just click the cell and begin typing. You can also cut and paste or import text into the cell. You can use all the normal text-formatting options to control the appearance of the text in a Layout Cell. (See Chapter 3 for details.)

Likewise, you can add an image or other object to a Layout Cell using the same techniques you use to insert the same object elsewhere on the page. (See Chapter 4 for details on adding images.)

Layout view does add a couple of restrictions on what you can place in a table cell:

- You can't insert a table into a Layout Cell in Layout view—you can nest tables within Layout Tables, but not within Layout Cells

- You can't insert a layer into your web page while you are working in Layout view

# Create Layout Tables That Resize in the Browser

One of the most challenging aspects of page layout design for the Web is that the viewer's browser window isn't a predictable size. As a result, if you design your web page to have the desired layout at one window size, visitors viewing the page in browser windows of different sizes see a less-than-optimum version of the page. Either the page content fails to fill the viewer's window or it's too big and the viewer must scroll left and right as well as up and down to see the entire page.

One way to address this problem is to take advantage of the ability of HTML tables to automatically scale to fit the browser window. Dreamweaver does this in Layout view with a feature called Autostretch. Autostretch makes the Layout Table elastic, so it can shrink and expand to fit different size browser windows. You can assign the Autostretch feature to the Layout Table itself and to one column of cells within the table. The other columns of a Layout Table remain fixed widths.

## Work with Fixed-Width Columns

When you draw a Layout Cell, the default setting is for fixed width, and the cell is exactly the size you draw. When you draw a Layout Cell and let Dreamweaver create a Layout Table around it, that table is also a fixed width, sized to fit the full width of the current Design view window. So you don't usually need to specify fixed width for a column unless you previously changed it to Autostretch.

Later, if you need to convert an Autostretch column back to fixed width, you can use either of the following techniques:

- Select a cell in the column and select the Fixed option in the Property Inspector panel. A number appears in the Fixed box to show the column width Dreamweaver calculated for the column. Enter a new number to adjust the column width.

- Click the column-width indicator at the top of the layout table and choose Make Column Fixed Width from the menu that appears. Dreamweaver sets the column width to accommodate the content in that column.

 As you enter text and other content into a Layout Cell, Dreamweaver sometimes adjusts the cell width to accommodate wider content, even though the cell supposedly has a fixed width. When this happens, the column-width indicator at the top of the table (see Figure 6-10) displays two numbers—the original column-width setting and the adjusted width. To eliminate the double numbers, click the column-width indicator and choose Make Cell Widths Consistent from the menu that appears, or click the Make Cell Widths Consistent button in the Property Inspector panel.

## Use Autostretch Columns

When you draw a Layout Table or a Layout Cell, the default width setting is Fixed, so if you want to use Autostretch columns, you need to explicitly select that option by specifying which column should expand and contract to fit different browser window widths. Remember that only one column in a Layout Table can be Autostretch.

To specify an Autostretch column, do one of the following:

- Click the column-width indicator at the top of the layout table, and choose Make Column Autostretch from the menu that appears.

- Select a cell in the column that you want to be Autostretch, and click the Autostretch option in the Property Inspector panel.

When you designate an Autostretch column, Dreamweaver converts any existing Autostretch column in the table to fixed width and changes the HTML code for the selected column so it will automatically expand horizontally to fill any space not occupied by other cells. To keep the Autostretch column from spanning the entire width of the page, Dreamweaver also inserts spacer images in the other columns to maintain their designated widths.

# Use Spacer Images

A *spacer image* is a transparent image that Dreamweaver uses as a placeholder to control column widths in a Layout Table. Since the image is transparent, it's invisible in the browser window, but its presence in a table cell means that the cell (and the column) isn't empty. This is important because an Autostretch column automatically expands horizontally to fill any and all empty space. The spacer image puts a "no trespassing" sign on adjacent columns so those fixed-width columns retain their specified widths. Without the spacer images, empty Layout Cells and placeholder cells alike would disappear from view as the Autostretch column expands to fill the void.

Dreamweaver automatically inserts spacer images in all the fixed-width columns of a Layout Table when you designate one column as an Autostretch column. You can also insert spacer images manually into fixed-width columns by clicking the column-width indicator at the top of the layout table and choosing Add Spacer Image from the menu that appears. A double line over a column indicates a column that contains a spacer image.

When you (or Dreamweaver) insert a spacer image into a Layout Table for the first time in a given site, Dreamweaver opens the Choose Spacer Image dialog box, giving you the option to create a new spacer image file for the site, select an existing spacer image, or decline to use spacer images with Autosize columns.

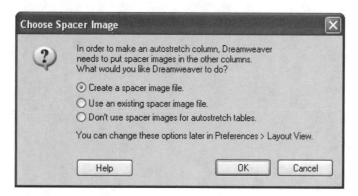

Depending on your choice in this dialog box, you see either another dialog box, in which you can tell Dreamweaver where to save a new spacer image file, or a dialog box in which you can locate and select an existing spacer image.

Just as you can add spacer images, you can also remove them. As you develop your page and add content to cells, you may want to delete spacer images from columns that are no longer empty, thus allowing the column widths to automatically adjust to fit the content.

- To remove the spacer image from a single column, click the column-width indicator at the top of the layout table and choose Remove Spacer Image.

- To remove all the spacer images from the table, click any column-width indicator at the top of the layout table and choose Remove All Spacer Images, or click the Remove All Spacers button in the Property Inspector panel.

 *Removing all spacer images will almost surely cause your page layout to change. The change can be drastic if there are numerous (or large) empty columns in Layout Tables on the page.*

# Chapter 7

# Use Frames and Framesets

## How to...

- Decide when and when not to use frames
- Create frames and framesets
- Set frame properties
- Build a navigation bar with frames
- Create alternate pages for non-frames-capable browsers

Frames were introduced by Netscape several years ago, and since then they have become a widely used web design feature. Because the vast majority of today's web browsers are capable of displaying frames, there are few compatibility issues to worry about. So frames have become a common feature of every web designer's toolkit. Though creating frames-based layouts is more complicated and involved than creating frameless pages, Dreamweaver MX offers some great tools to simplify the process. In addition, Dreamweaver makes it easy to create alternative content for non-frames-capable browsers, allowing you to reach 100 percent of your audience with a minimum of effort.

# How Frames Work

The concept behind frames is simple: instead of using one HTML page to display your content, you can use frames to divide the browser window into multiple rectangular areas, each of which displays a separate web page. If used correctly, frames both allow designers more control over layout and make their sites easier to navigate. With a properly designed frameset you can, for instance, place a navigation menu in a frame that always remains in view while serving content pages in other frames that scroll or update as needed. This setup saves users time because they don't have to keep loading the same navigation menu information over and over. Lots of "cutting-edge" designers have also used frames to create all sorts of artistic and innovative implementations. However, you need to be careful with frames because they can just as easily detract from the user experience.

Building frames with Dreamweaver isn't difficult, but it can be a little bit confusing since there are some fundamental differences between building pages with frames and building pages without frames. If you are new to frames, you need to remember that a frames-based web page has three components:

- The frameset
- The frames inside the frameset
- The separate web page documents displayed in each frame

A *frameset* is a web document that contains the frame structure—the code that divides the browser window into rectangular sections. Each section of a frameset is called a *frame*. And each frame contains a link to a separate web document, which the browser displays within the frame. The result is a composite page with two or more component web documents displayed together in frames within the same browser window, according to the layout defined in the frameset document.

Although the frameset is the page people use to access your frames content, the frameset itself never appears in the browser. Instead, it divides the page up and displays whatever URLs are assigned to each individual frame. A frameset page is distinguished from other web pages by <frameset> tags, which take the place of the <body> tags and any other HTML code that normally resides within the <body> tags. For example, a two-frame frameset might look like this:

```
<frameset rows="80,*">
  <frame src="top.html">
  <frame src="bottom.html">
</frameset>
```

7

In this case, the top frame measures 80 pixels high, and the bottom frame is set to expand automatically depending on the size of the browser window.

As you can see, this page references two other pages: top.html and bottom.html. Even though the browser accesses the frameset document, the frameset itself is not what people visiting the site see, because the frameset contains only code pointing to other web pages. The visitor sees the content of top.html and bottom.html.

# Create a Frameset

The first step in creating a page using frames is to build a frameset. Usually this begins with opening up a new blank page (you can also start with an existing page) and using Dreamweaver's frame creation tools to divide the page into individual frames. You can divide a page into two, three, or more frames, and you can size them as needed to customize the layout.

Designing frames with Dreamweaver MX is dramatically simplified compared to the old days of calculating and coding numerical values for the rows and columns needed to create the layout. You can easily drag predefined framesets onto your page and modify them by clicking and dragging; or you can insert frames one by one onto the page with a menu command. You can modify frame properties with the Property Inspector panel and preview the layout in Dreamweaver's Design view without having to launch an external web browser. What's more, Dreamweaver enables you to view and edit the frameset and its component web documents in the same Document window.

## Insert Predefined Framesets

To make designing with frames easier, Dreamweaver MX includes 13 predefined frameset layouts accessible from the Frames category of the Insert bar. These framesets provide some of the more commonly used page layouts, including two- and three-frame layouts that you can further customize after you insert them onto a page. Using these predefined framesets makes designing frame layouts as easy as clicking a single button.

1. Click anywhere inside the Document window to place the insertion point in your document.

2. Click a frameset icon in the Frames category of the Insert bar. Pick a frameset that looks more or less like the frame layout you want to create. When you click the icon, Dreamweaver creates a frameset with that layout, dividing the page into frames using dashed lines to indicate the frame boundaries, as shown in Figure 7-1.

*If the frame borders don't appear in your document, choose View | Visual Aids | Frame Borders to make the frame borders visible.*

3. Drag the dividing lines between frames to alter the size of the frames. Reposition them by clicking and dragging them to a new position.

You can also insert another frameset inside a frame by clicking inside the frame in the Document window and then clicking a frameset icon in the Insert bar. This enables you to build more complex, nested framesets. Using the 13 predefined framesets in the Frames category of the Insert bar as a starting point, and then adjusting the size of the frames and adding additional framesets, you can create almost any kind of frame layout.

*Each of the frameset icons in the Insert bar's Frames category displays one of its frames with blue shading. The blue-shaded frame represents the location of the current page in the frameset. When you are working with existing web pages, this feature tells you where the content on that page will appear within the frameset.*

## Insert Frames and Split Frames

Another way to insert frames into a page is to use either the Insert Frame command or the Split Frame command.

The Insert Frame command inserts a new frameset into the current document or frame, depending on which is selected. To use this command, choose Insert | Frames | Left (or any choice). The item you choose will decide which way the new frame or frames appear. You can choose between Left, Right, Top, Bottom, Bottom Nested Left, Bottom Nested Right,

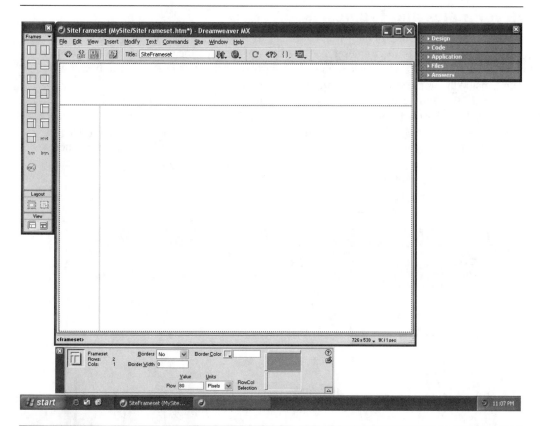

**FIGURE 7-1**   Inserting a predefined frameset

Left Nested Top, Left Nested Bottom, Right Nested Bottom, Right Nested Top, Top and Bottom, Top Nested Left, or Top Nested Right. These choices mirror the frameset buttons on the Insert bar's Frames category.

You can achieve similar results using the Split Frame command. Choose Modify | Frameset | Split Frame Left—or Right, Up, or Down. The direction you pick depends on whether you want to split the frame into columns or rows. When you select this command, the page or frame is divided into two equal-sized frames, with the new, empty frame added in the direction selected. Because you can perform this command on either a blank page or an existing frame, you can use it to build any kind of frameset you want by splitting and resizing frames until you have achieved the desired layout.

*Don't go overboard with the frames on a page. Very few effective examples of framed sites use more than three or four frames in their layout.*

## Select Frames and Framesets

As you work with a frameset document, you'll need to be able to select each of the individual frames in the document or the frameset itself so that you can alter the content in each of them. You can't just select a frame in Design view by simply clicking anywhere inside it, because clicking inside the frame selects the frame content instead of the frame.

The easiest way to select frames is to use the Frames panel (shown in Figure 7-2). The Frames panel mimics the layout of your frameset, displaying each frame along with its name in miniature view. (Setting the frame name and other properties in the Property Inspector panel is covered in "Modify Frame Settings," later in this chapter.) By clicking a frame in the Frames panel, you automatically select the frame associated with it. To display the Frames panel, choose Window | Others | Frames from the Document window menu.

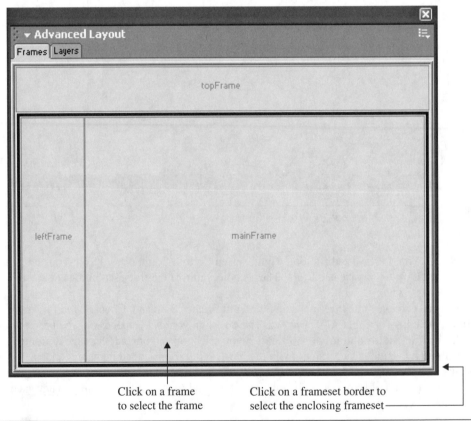

Click on a frame
to select the frame

Click on a frameset border to
select the enclosing frameset

**FIGURE 7-2**    Use the Frames panel to select frames and framesets in a document.

Selecting framesets works the same way but requires a bit more manual dexterity, since you have to click on the frameset border. Framesets are represented in the Frames panel by thick gray borders (see Figure 7-2). To select a frameset, click on the border in the Frames panel. The border is only a few pixels wide, so you've got a small target, but it isn't too difficult. You can tell the difference between selecting a frame and a frameset by looking at the Property Inspector panel. When a frame is selected, the Property Inspector panel displays the properties of the frame; the properties of the frameset display when you select a frameset.

You can also select and edit the content inside a frame, but you must remember that when you do so you are actually editing the web page that is displaying inside the frame, not the web page used to create the frameset. This can be confusing because Dreamweaver allows you to edit other web pages in a frameset without ever opening those document files in a separate Document window. Make sure you are aware of this when you work with framesets—you can easily lose track of which page you are editing.

## Adjust the Layout of a Frameset

7

You can drag the frame borders to resize frames in the frameset or use the frameset Property Inspector panel to define more precise measurements and options. Because visitors to your web site will be using different size monitors and can resize their browser windows, you'll never know exactly what size window your page will be viewed in. The way to address this with frames is to make one or more of your frames a fixed size and the remaining frame or frames relative sizes. Relative-size frames resize as the browser window resizes; fixed-size frames always stay the same. To set the size for each frame in the frameset, select the frameset by clicking on its border in the Frames panel. This displays the frameset Property Inspector panel, shown in Figure 7-3.

The frameset Property Inspector panel enables you to customize the way the selected frame appears in the frameset. In any frameset there are two or more frames, arranged in either rows or columns. The frameset Property Inspector panel displays either rows or columns in the RowCol Selection indicator on the right side of the panel, depending on how the frameset is divided. You can click on either a row or a column to view and edit the properties for each frame. Figure 7-3 shows the properties for a row that's set to a fixed size of 80 pixels tall. To set the other row to resize automatically, select that row and leave the Row Value blank. You don't need to enter an absolute measurement for a relative-size frame. However, if you want both frames to resize with the browser, you can enter a percentage value for each frame. For example, 25 percent for the top and 75 percent for the bottom. That way when the user resizes the browser window, both frames resize but keep their relative proportions.

## Insert Content into Frames

Whenever you add frames to a page, you are actually dividing the page into different regions, each of which will display a separate web page. For each frame you create, you can have it display an existing web page or you can create new content for the frame and save it as a new web page. To complete the frameset page, each frame needs to contain a linked web page.

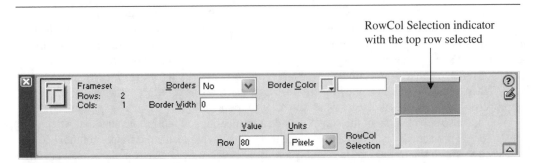

RowCol Selection indicator
with the top row selected

| FIGURE 7-3 | The RowCol Selection indicator allows you to select a row or a column in the frameset in order to modify its properties. |

## Add Existing Pages to a Frameset

Once you create your frameset, you have the option of either populating the frames with existing pages or creating new ones. When you add an existing page, you'll want to make sure that it fits into the context and space provided by the frame you are adding it to. To add an existing page to a frame:

1.  With the frameset selected, save your frameset by choosing File | Save Frameset. Enter a name for the file in the Save As dialog box, and click Save.

2.  Choose Window | Others | Frames to display the Frames panel. The Frames panel displays a miniature rendition of the layout of your frameset.

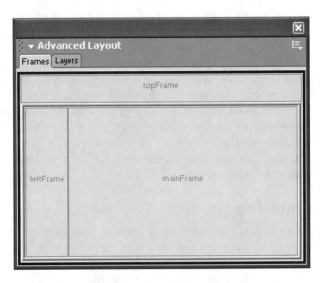

3.  In the Frames panel, click inside the frame where you want to add the page. When you select the frame, its properties appear in the Property Inspector panel (see Figure 7-4).

| FIGURE 7-4 | Property Inspector panel showing Frame options |

4. In the Src field, enter the URL of the page to which you want to create a link. As in creating hyperlinks, you can type the path and filename, or you can click the folder icon next to the Src field to open the Select HTML File dialog box. Use this dialog box to locate and select the web document file you want to display in the frame; then click Select to close the dialog box. You can also drag and drop the Point to File icon to select the page. The web page you inserted appears inside the frame in the Dreamweaver Document window.

The great thing about editing framesets in Dreamweaver is that once you insert existing pages into a frame you can edit those pages in the frameset document without opening them separately. Simply click anywhere inside the frame, and then edit the page just as you would if it were displayed in a separate Document window.

Of course, you can also open the page separately if you prefer to edit it that way. The only disadvantage to editing the page in its own Document window is that you won't be able to see how the page looks in the context of the frameset without previewing it in a browser.

## Create New Frame Pages

Many times, instead of inserting existing pages into your frames, you'll want to start from scratch and create the web pages for each new frame as you go along. To do this, simply insert your cursor anywhere in a newly created frame and choose File | Save Frame As. Dreamweaver prompts you to name the document file for the frame and save it onto your hard drive. Whether the page is saved or not, you can start typing or inserting content the way you normally would with any web document. To save other frames on the frameset page, you need to select each frame in turn and choose File | Save Frame As to save the frame contents. To save the frameset itself, select it by clicking on the frameset border in either the Document window or the Frames panel. Then choose File | Save Frameset As.

## Save Frames and Framesets

Perhaps the thing that most confuses people about using frames in Dreamweaver is saving them. With normal Dreamweaver documents, you usually work on only one document at a time. Even if you have several documents open in separate Document windows, only one document is active, so when you choose File | Save, the currently active document is saved. However, using frames in Dreamweaver is a bit different because the current document actually contains other documents.

When you work with frames documents, Dreamweaver's save commands become contextual, changing their appearance depending on whether you are editing a frameset or a frame. If you look in the File menu when you have a frameset document open and the frameset is selected, you'll notice that File | Save is not available—instead there are several alternate save options: Save Frameset, Save Frameset As, and Save All. The File menu changes again when you select a frame. It displays Save Frame, Save Frame As, Save Frame as Template, and Save all Frames.

This is very important to remember because when you choose any of these save commands (except Save All Frames) only the currently selected frame or frameset file is saved. You can also press CTRL-S on the keyboard to save a file, but that too saves only the currently selected file—it's the equivalent of choosing File | Save Frame or File | Save Frameset, depending on whether you have an individual frame or the master frameset page selected. On the other hand, the Save All Frames command saves the frameset file and the contents of all the individual frames in one operation. To avoid confusion and the possibility of lost data, it's a good practice to use the File | Save All Frames command when working with frames.

# Modify Frame Settings

The settings in the Property Inspector panel (see Figure 7-4) control the way that frames look and behave on your pages. For example, you can change frame borders, margins, scrolling status, and more. It's even possible to create a page that most visitors can't tell is made with frames.

## Name That Frame

You need to assign each frame a name in order to able to specify it as a target for links in other frames. Dreamweaver sometimes names frames when you create them, but it's usually better to replace the names Dreamweaver devises with your own, more descriptive names. To add or change the name of a frame, select the frame and enter a new name into the Frame Name field in the Property Inspector panel. Descriptive names such as Top, Left, Bottom, and Content help you remember which names correspond to which frames.

## Set Page Properties

Because every page in a frame is its own web document, each frame can have independent properties, such as title, background color, link color, and so forth. Setting titles for web pages within frames isn't really necessary, since the only title that appears in the browser is the title used in the frameset document. Still, you may want to set some of the other page properties for frames. The technique is the same as for setting page properties for normal documents. The only difference is that you have to make sure you first select the correct frame so that you can edit it. To do this you can either click on a frame in the Frames panel or click within a frame in the

Document window so that the blinking insertion point cursor appears. When the frame is selected, choose Modify | Page Properties or use the CTRL-J keyboard shortcut to open the Page Properties dialog box and enter the appropriate settings.

# Set Frame Borders

When you create a frames page in Dreamweaver, you can decide between colorful three-dimensional borders, flat gray borders, or no borders at all. Most web designers tend to avoid displaying frame borders since it often detracts from the overall page design. However, should you decide to use them, you have a lot of flexibility in customizing the way that they appear. Here's how it works:

1. Select a frameset by clicking the frameset border in the Frames panel. The Property Inspector panel displays the settings for the frameset (see Figure 7-3).

2. Specify any of the following options in the frameset Property Inspector panel:

   - **Borders**   Select Yes to display borders in three-dimensional color. Select No to display borders as flat gray. Select Default to allow the user's browser to determine how the borders are displayed. Most browsers default to Yes.

   - **Border Color**   Select a color using the pop-up color picker. This sets the border color for all the frames in the frameset.

   - **Border Width**   Specify the width in pixels of the borders for all frames in the frameset. To make borders invisible, specify a border width of 0 (Dreamweaver's default setting).

Border settings applied to a frameset affect all the frames within the frameset unless you override those setting with different settings for individual frames.

To set individual frame borders:

1. Select the frame by clicking inside it or by clicking the frame in the Frames panel. The Property Inspector panel displays the settings for the frameset (see Figure 7-4).

2. Specify any of the following options in the frame Property Inspector panel:

   - **Borders**   Select Yes to display borders in three-dimensional color. Select No to display borders as flat gray. Select Default to allow the user's browser to determine how the borders are displayed. Most browsers default to Yes.

   - **Border Color**   Select a color using the pop-up color picker. This sets the border color for the currently selected frame and any frames directly adjacent to that frame.

## Set Margins, Scrolling, and Resizing Properties for Frames

In addition to setting border properties, you can also set the size of the frame's margins, determine whether or not frame content is scrollable, and specify whether or not frames can be resized in the browser. All these properties are accessible through the Property Inspector panel when a frame is selected (see Figure 7-4).

- **Scroll**  Use this option to specify whether or not scroll bars appear in the frame: Yes displays scroll bars regardless of whether they are needed or not. No turns off scroll bars. Auto displays scroll bars only if the content in the frame exceeds the size of the window. Default lets the browser decide, which in most cases is the same as Auto.

- **No Resize**  Select this option to restrict the size of the frame and prevent users from dragging the frame borders to resize them.

- **Margin Width**  Specify the distance in pixels between the left and right borders of a frame and its content.

- **Margin Height**  Specify the distance in pixels between the top and bottom borders of a frame and its content.

# Use Links with Frames

A web page document that is displayed inside a frame can contain hypertext links to other documents, just as any other web document can. Clicking a link in a frame causes the linked document to appear in the browser window, just like clicking a link in a normal web page. The difference is that the page designer has more control over where the linked page appears in a frameset. The default action is for the linked document to replace the previous content in the same frame. However, you can also elect to have the linked document appear in a different frame, if you want. In fact, it's this feature of frames that makes it possible for a navigation bar that appears in one frame to control what appears in other frames.

Creating a link from one frame to another frame (referred to as *targeting* a frame) simply involves adding a target attribute to the link in the Property Inspector panel. However, before you add a target attribute to a link, you need to know the name of the frame you want to target. The target attribute uses the frame's name to identify which frame to create the target for. For example, if you click a link in a frame named Left and you want the linked page to display in the frame named Center, use Center as your target. You set the target in the Property Inspector panel's Target field, just to the right of the Link field (see Figure 7-5). When you access the pop-up menu in the Target field, it displays a list of named frames in the current document as well as four standard targets: _blank, _parent, _self, _top. To create a target to an existing frame, select the frame's name from this menu. The other four targets function as follows:

- **_blank**  Opens the link in a new page while keeping the current page open in the background.

- **_parent**  Opens the link in the page's parent frameset. This is the innermost frameset directly above the frame containing the link.

- **_self**    Opens the link in the current frame, replacing its contents (the default).
- **_top**    Opens the link in the page's outermost frameset, replacing all the contents.

# Create Alternative Content for Browsers That Don't Support Frames

When frames first came out, web designers had no choice but to create alternative frameless content, since so many people still used browsers that weren't capable of displaying frames. Although the vast majority of today's web browsers support frames, there is a growing assortment of new devices accessing the Web—cell phones, PDAs, and other handheld devices—many of which don't support frames. There's also the issue of visually impaired users and others using screen readers and other assistive technologies that may have problems with frames. So there's still a need for a frameless alternative to any web page that includes frames. Fortunately, Dreamweaver makes it relatively easy to create a no-frames alternate for a frameset page.

The HTML frames specification includes a mechanism for supporting non-frames-capable browsers by including the `<noframes>` tag in a frameset document. Whenever you build a frameset page, Dreamweaver includes a set of empty opening and closing `<noframes>` tags in the document's HTML code. These tags are located just after the `<frameset>` tags. Included inside the `<noframes>` opening and closing tags are a pair of `<body>` tags, which provide viewable content to non-frames-capable browsers. Frame-enabled browsers ignore any content inside the `<noframes>` tag, but content within the `<body>` tags inside those `<noframes>` tags will display in a non-frames-capable browser.

Although Dreamweaver automatically creates the `<noframes>` and `<body>` tags, the program doesn't automatically place any content there. As a result, any non-frames-capable browser that visits the frameset page on your site will see a blank page until you place content inside the `<body>` tags.

To edit the content in the `<noframes>` section of a frameset document, choose Modify | Frameset | Edit No Frames Content. This opens up a new Document window in Dreamweaver

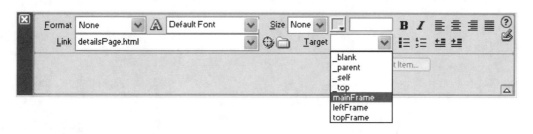

**FIGURE 7-5**    Using the Property Inspector panel to select a frame target

that enables you to edit the page as if it were a regular web page instead of a frameset page. All the normal tools and objects you are accustomed to using in Dreamweaver are available to edit this page; the only difference is that all the content you create will be placed inside the `<noframes>` tags. After editing the no-frames version of the page, choose Modify | Frameset | Edit No Frames Content once again to return to the frameset.

# Chapter 8

# Work with Forms

## How to...

- Add a form to your web page
- Add elements to your form
- Label and format forms
- Submit form data

Since the early days of the Web, forms have been an important part of many web sites. Forms enable you to gather information from visitors to your web site. You can use forms to solicit feedback from site visitors or to set up a guest book. A form can be as simple as a login screen or as sophisticated as the ordering mechanism for an online purchasing system.

Using Dreamweaver MX, you can create most any kind of onscreen form you can envision. Dreamweaver makes all the HTML form tags accessible and easy to use in the familiar Design View document window. However, Dreamweaver can't help you with one important part of any form—the form processing. For that, you must rely on scripts or applications running on the web server that hosts your site.

# What Are HTML Forms?

Because of the very nature of the Web, every web page includes the possibility of some interaction with the viewer. The web browser detects the location of the mouse pointer on the web page and sends a request to the web server if the viewer clicks on a hyperlink. The server responds by sending a new page to the browser. That sets the precedent for a two-way exchange of information between the viewer's browser and the web server. Once the communication channel is open, there's no reason it can't be used to send more than a simple mouse click—for instance, text characters or the status of a check box.

The HTML form tags provide the means for creating various user input areas on a web page. You can create text boxes, radio buttons, check boxes, list boxes, and more. The web browser displays these onscreen objects to solicit user input, as shown in Figure 8-1. The visitor types in a text box or selects an item from a list box to fill out the form. Then, when the visitor clicks a Submit button, the browser sends that information back to the web server.

What the web server does with the information received from the form depends on what kind of processing script or application is running on the server and how the information is submitted from the form to the script. Some form-processing scripts can send the contents of a form in an e-mail message to a specified e-mail address; others enter the information into a database or transfer it to another program.

The server-side scripting required to process form submissions is beyond the scope of this chapter. But you rarely need to delve into server-side scripting unless you're attempting to do something elaborate with your form data. Most web host servers have simple form mailers and other standard scripts available. To use these ready-made form-processing facilities, all you need to do is check with the webmaster or system administrator to find out the name and location of the script and how to submit your form data to it. You enter this information in your Dreamweaver form, and you're in business.

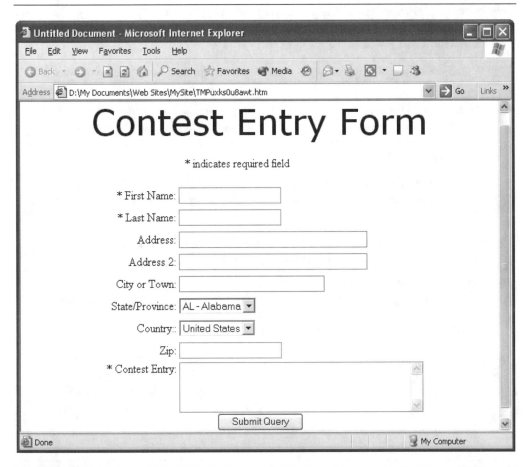

**FIGURE 8-1**   An HTML form

If you do need to delve into the server-side scripting needed to handle form submissions, Dreamweaver MX can help you do it. You can find an overview of scripting and related issues in Chapter 14.

# Create a Form

Before you begin placing text boxes and other form elements on your web page, you need to tell Dreamweaver (and the visitor's browser) that those elements are part of a form. You do so by inserting a form into your web page. Dreamweaver inserts the `<form>` tags into the source code for your page and draws a rectangle in Design view with a red dotted line to represent the form. The form tag contains essential information that tells the browser how to submit data from the form. That information includes the address of the script that will process the form data and the method by which the data is sent to the server. After you insert the form into your page, you can use the Property Inspector panel to set form attributes such as the submission method.

To insert a form into your web page, follow these steps:

1. Position the insertion point cursor at the location in your document where you want to insert the form.

2. Choose Insert | Form or go to the Forms category of the Insert bar and click the Insert Form button. Dreamweaver inserts a form into your document. The form appears as a short, wide rectangle drawn with a red dotted line, as shown in Figure 8-2. The insertion point appears inside the form rectangle.

*If the form rectangle does not appear in Design view, choose View | Visual Aids | Invisible Elements to activate Dreamweaver's display of forms and other invisible portions of your web page.*

3. Select the form by clicking inside the form rectangle and then clicking the `<form>` tag in the Tag Selector located in the Design view status bar.

4. In the Property Inspector panel, type a name for the form in the Form Name box. Every form must have a unique form name, which is necessary to reference the form with a scripting language. Dreamweaver supplies a default name such as "form1," but a more meaningful name will be easier to work with.

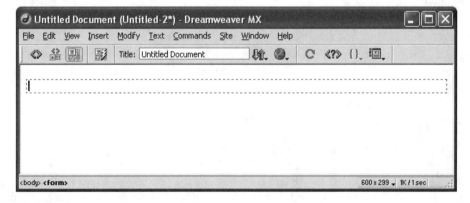

FIGURE 8-2    A newly created form in Design view

**5.** Enter the URL for the form processing script or application in the Action box. You can type in the complete path and filename or click the folder icon to open a dialog box that you can use to locate and select the script if it is located on a locally accessible drive.

**6.** Select the data submission method in the Method list box.

■ **Post**   Submits form data in blocks suitable for use in an e-mail message or similar application

■ **Get**   Submits form data by adding it onto the end of a URL

■ **Default**   Submits form data according to the default settings of the visitor's browser (usually the Get method)

You can simply insert a form into your web page and then immediately start adding form elements without first defining the action and method for the form in the Property Inspector panel. The form won't work until you define those essential attributes, but you can always add or modify them at a later time.

> NOTE   *The HTML code for a form looks something like this:* `<form name="form1" method="post" action="\cgi-bin\mailform.cgi"> </form>`

8

# Add Form Elements

After you add a form to your web page, you can begin building the visible portions of the form by adding form elements. The form elements are those components that the site visitor sees and interacts with to enter or select information. As with general page design, the choice of form elements to use is up to you. Dreamweaver offers the following objects that you can use to build your form:

■ **Text Field**   Solicits text input from the visitor. Dreamweaver's TextField object is primarily used to add single-line text boxes.

■ **Textarea**   Another kind of text input box. This one makes multiline text boxes.

■ **Check Box**   Presents the visitor with a yes-or-no choice.

■ **Radio Button**   Like the check box, a radio button presents the visitor with a yes-or-no choice, with the added restriction that only one item in a group of buttons can be answered yes.

■ **Radio Group**   A group of two or more radio buttons that are automatically grouped together.

■ **List/Menu**   List boxes and pop-up menus present a list of items from which one or more items can be chosen. You can create both scrolling lists and pop-up list boxes.

■ **Jump Menu**   A special form of pop-up list box that lists a series of links. This option is normally used as a navigation tool instead of a component of a typical form.

■ **File Field**   Enables the user to submit a file to the server.

- **Button**   The standard Submit and Reset buttons that send the form data to the server and clear the form fields.

- **Image Field**   Enables you to create custom, graphical buttons.

- **Hidden Field**   Enables you to insert information into the form that the visitor doesn't see. For example, you might need to use a hidden field to specify the e-mail address to which the form processor sends the submitted form data.

 - **Label**   Text that is linked to the form element it describes instead of being just plain text placed in the general proximity of a form field.

 - **Fieldset**   A box that surrounds and labels multiple form elements to help organize your form into logical subdivisions.

 *Form elements can be placed only into a form. If you attempt to place a form element on a page outside a preexisting form, Dreamweaver automatically prompts you to create the form.*

## Use Text Boxes

Text boxes in a form can range from short, single-line boxes for a user ID or e-mail address to large multiline text areas in which the visitor can type paragraphs of text. To protect passwords from prying eyes, you can configure a text box to display asterisks onscreen instead of text. Figure 8-3 shows the three kinds of text boxes.

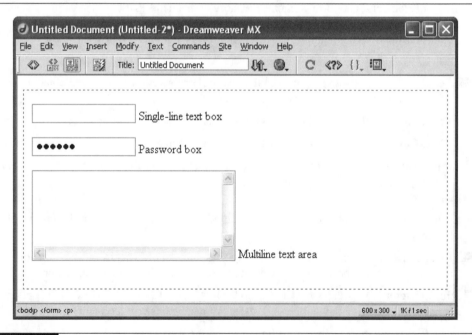

**FIGURE 8-3**   Text boxes in a form

No matter which kind of text box you want to place into your form, you start out the same way—by inserting a generic text box into the form. Then you use the Property Inspector panel to give the text box the characteristics you need.

## Single-Line Text Box

To create a single-line text box, follow these steps:

**1.** Position the insertion point cursor on the page at the location where you want to insert a text box. Make sure it is inside the red dotted outline of the form.

**2.** Click the Text Field button in the Forms category of the Insert bar, or choose Insert I Form Object I Text Field. Dreamweaver inserts a small, single-line text field into the form. A dotted line surrounding the text box indicates that it's selected.

**3.** In the Property Inspector panel, enter a unique name for the text field in the TextField box. Each text field must have a unique name to identify its contents. Dreamweaver assigns default names such as "textfield3," but it'll be much easier to work with the form data if you replace that with a meaningful name.

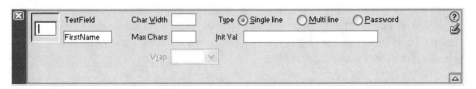

**4.** Select Single Line in the Type area to designate this as a single-line text box.

**5.** Enter a number in the Char Width box to set the width (in characters) of the text box in the form. This setting determines the size of the text box, not the maximum number of characters the visitor can type. The text box will automatically scroll horizontally to accommodate longer text entries. If you leave the Char Width box blank, the text box uses the browser's default size, which is usually about 26 characters.

**6.** Enter a number in the Max Chars box to set the maximum number of text characters the visitor can enter, or leave the box blank to allow the visitor to enter unlimited text. Use this setting to restrict fixed-length data, such as ZIP codes and passwords to the appropriate length.

**7.** If you want text to appear in the text box when the form first appears in the visitor's browser window, type that text in the Init Val box in the Property Inspector panel. Normally, you leave this box blank, but it can be useful for inserting default values into forms or for giving the visitor instructions (such as "Type your full name here").

**8.** Back in the Document window, click beside the text box and type a label or instructions for filling in the form. Or you can create a label with the Label form element.

NOTE *The HTML code for a single-line text box looks like this:* `<input type="text" name="textfield" size="30">`

8

## Password Text Box

A password text box is a single-line text box with a special characteristic that causes the browser to display asterisks or dots in the box in place of the characters the visitors type. This is a common practice intended to protect the visitors' passwords from prying eyes, while still allowing them to see how many characters they've typed.

To create a password text box in your form, follow the previous instructions for creating a single-line text box, but in step 4, select Password instead of Single Line as the text box type. Since passwords are normally limited to a fixed number of characters, you'll probably want to set that number in the Char Width box in step 5 and in the Max Chars box in step 6.

> **NOTE** *The HTML code for a password text box looks like this:* `<input type="password" name="textfield2" size="8" maxlength="8">`

## Multiple-Line Text Area

To create a multiline text area, follow these steps:

1.  Follow steps 1–3 from the instructions for creating a single-line text box, only in step 2, click the Textarea button (instead of the Text Field button) in the Forms category of the Insert bar, or choose Insert | Form Objects | Textarea to insert a text field that is preconfigured as a multiline text box.

2.  In the Type area of the Property Inspector panel, make sure Multi Line is selected to designate this as a multiple-line text area.

3.  Enter a number in the Char Width box to set the width (in characters) of the text area in the form. Again, this setting determines the size of the text box, not the maximum number of characters the visitor can type.

4.  Enter a number in the Num Lines (number of lines) box to set the height of the text area. Like the Char Width value, this setting determines the visible size of the text area in the browser window, not the maximum number of lines of text the visitor can enter into the text box.

5.  Select a setting in the Wrap list box to determine what happens if the visitor enters more text than will display in the text box. You can choose one of the following:

    ■ **Off**  Disables word wrapping. The text box scrolls horizontally to accommodate longer lines of text. The visitor must press ENTER to move down to the next line.

    ■ **Virtual**  Text wraps to the next line automatically to remain visible in the text area in the browser window, but the text is submitted for processing as one long line of text (unless the visitor presses ENTER to create line breaks).

    ■ **Physical**  Text wraps to the next line automatically, and corresponding line breaks are inserted in the text when it is submitted.

    ■ **Default**  The same as Off.

6.  If you want text to appear in the text box when the form first appears in the visitor's browser window, type that text in the Init Val box in the Property Inspector panel. Normally, you leave this box blank.

7.  Back in the Document window, click beside the text area and type a label or instructions for filling in the form. Or you can use the Label form element to create a label.

*The HTML code for a multi-line text area looks like this:* `<textarea name="textfield" cols="50" rows="6">initial value</textarea>`

## Use Check Boxes

Check boxes are a way to present the visitor with a predefined choice, to which the visitor responds with a yes/no or on/off kind of choice. Check boxes work equally well for single items that need a yes/no response (such as, "Would you like to be added to our mailing list?") or for a list of items from which the visitor can select one or more items (such as a list of interests: sailboat racing, weekend cruises, vacation charters). Figure 8-4 shows both applications of check boxes.

8

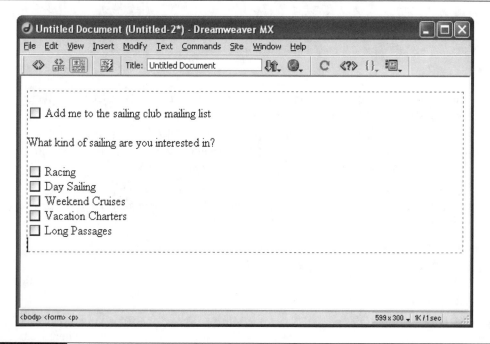

**FIGURE 8-4**   Check boxes in a form

To add a check box to your form, follow these steps:

**1.** Position the insertion point cursor on the page at the location where you want to insert a check box. Make sure it is inside the red dotted outline of the form.

**2.** Click the Insert Checkbox button in the Forms category of the Insert bar, or choose Insert | Form Object | Check Box. Dreamweaver MX inserts a small check box into the form as shown. The dotted line surrounding the box indicates that it's selected.

**3.** In the Property Inspector panel, enter a unique name in the CheckBox box. Like text boxes, each check box must have a unique name to identify its contents. Replace the Dreamweaver-assigned name with a meaningful name of your own.

**4.** Enter a descriptive identifier in the Checked Value box. This is the value that will be submitted as part of the form data, as in *checkedvalue=yes*.

**5.** Select Checked or Unchecked in the Initial State area. This setting controls whether the check box is checked or unchecked by default when the form first loads in the visitor's browser. In other words, it sets the default state of the check box.

**6.** Return to the Document window, click beside the check box, and type a label, or use the Label form element to create a label for the check box. Without a label, the visitor won't know what the check box represents.

> **NOTE** *The HTML code for a check box looks like this:* `<input type="checkbox" name="checkbox1" value="box1">`

## Use Radio Buttons

Like check boxes, radio buttons present the visitor with a yes/no or on/off kind of choice. The difference is that radio buttons appear in a group, and the visitor can select only one item from the group. Selecting one radio button automatically clears any other selection in the group. In other words, radio buttons force the user to choose only one of two or more choices.

Because of the exclusive choice characteristic of radio buttons, it's important to pay attention to how the radio buttons are grouped. In Dreamweaver, you can insert radio buttons one by one and assign each one to a group manually, or you can use the Radio Group form element to enter a group of radio buttons all at once. All the radio buttons you enter individually are in the same group by default. You assign radio buttons to different groups with the RadioButton name setting in the Property Inspector panel.

To add an individual radio button to your form, follow these steps:

**1.** Position the insertion point cursor on the page at the location where you want to insert a radio button. Make sure it is inside the red dotted outline of the form.

**2.** Click the Radio Button icon in the Forms category of the Insert bar, or choose Insert | Form Object | Radio Button. Dreamweaver inserts a small round radio button into the form as shown here. The dotted line surrounding the button indicates that it's selected.

**3.** In the Property Inspector panel, enter the name of the radio button group in the RadioButton box. Unlike many other form elements, this is not a unique name for the individual button but a name for the group of buttons in which the exclusive-choice rule will be enforced. As always, it's a good idea to replace the Dreamweaver-assigned name with a meaningful name of your own.

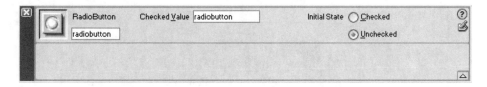

**4.** Enter a descriptive identifier in the Checked Value box. This is the value that will be submitted as part of the form data, as in `checkedvalue=yes`.

**5.** Select Checked or Unchecked in the Initial State area. This setting controls whether the radio button is checked or unchecked by default when the form first loads in the visitor's browser. Remember that only one button in a group can be checked.

**6.** Back in the Document window, click beside the radio button and type a label, or use the Label form element to create a label. As with check boxes, it's essential to provide a label on the form because there is nothing in the radio button to tell the visitor what it represents.

8

 The HTML code for a radio button looks like this: `<input type="radio"`
`name="radiobutton" value="button1">`

## Define Radio Groups

 You can create a radio button group by inserting each button individually and giving all of your radio buttons the same name. But it can seem pretty repetitive to have to type the same information in several times. Dreamweaver has a better way—using the Radio Group icon on the Insert Bar, you can define all the radio buttons in a group at once in a convenient dialog box. The result is the same as adding a series of radio buttons individually and assigning them to the same group. The Radio Group form element just makes it a little easier to do.

To add a radio button group to your form, follow these steps:

1. Position the insertion point cursor on the page at the location where you want to insert a radio button group. Make sure it is inside the red dotted outline of the form.

 2. Click the Radio Group icon in the Forms category of the Insert bar, or choose Insert | Form Object | Radio Group. Dreamweaver activates the Radio Group dialog box as shown.

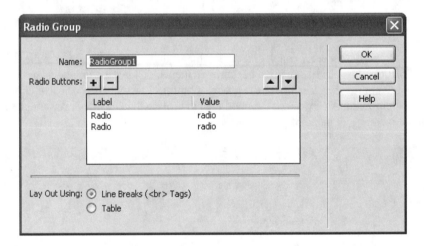

3. Enter a name for the radio button group in the Name box. Dreamweaver supplies a default name, but you'll want to replace it with something more appropriate.

4. Click on one of the two supplied radio button labels in the list, and edit it as needed. This is the text that will be displayed next to the radio button on the page. Once you have edited the label, press TAB to move the insertion point to the Value column, or click on the value text.

5. Type the value that you want to submit as form data when the visitor clicks on the radio button. This is a description of the button that is submitted with the form when the radio button is checked.

**6.** Click the plus (+) button to add another item to the list, and repeat steps 4 and 5 to define the label and value for each new button. Continue adding buttons until your group is complete.

**7.** Rearrange the order of the radio buttons by selecting one from the list and clicking the up and down arrow buttons to move it up or down in the list. To remove a button, select it and click the minus (–) button.

**8.** Select Line Breaks or Table in the Lay Out Using area at the bottom of the dialog box. The Line Breaks option instructs Dreamweaver to place each radio button (with its text label) on a separate line that ends with a line break. The Table option creates a table to hold the radio button group with each button in a separate table cell.

**9.** Click OK to close the Radio Group dialog box and add the buttons to your form. Dreamweaver adds the items to the source code, and the list box expands horizontally in Design view to accommodate the longest item label in the list. The list items also appear in the Initially Selected list in the Property Inspector panel.

To modify the buttons after they have been added to the form, simply click on one of them and edit the attributes in the Property Inspector as you would any other radio button.

8

# Build Selection Lists

As the name implies, a selection list presents a list of items from which the visitor can choose one or more items. You could theoretically accomplish the same thing with check boxes or radio buttons, but a selection list is much more compact and efficient.

Just as you can have multiline text areas and single-line text boxes, you can have multiline selection lists and single-line lists (which Dreamweaver calls *menus*). A multiline selection list is larger, with room for several items to be displayed in the list box, as shown in Figure 8-5. If there are more items in the list than there is room for, a scroll bar appears on the right side of the list to enable the visitor to scroll up and down through list to see all list items—hence the name *scrolling list*. You have the option of allowing the visitor to choose more than one item from a scrolling list.

A single-line list—called a *pop-up menu* or *drop-down list box*—is the most compact way to present multiple choices because it occupies only a single line of vertical space in the form. An arrow button at the right side of the list box gives the visitor access to the complete list. The visitor clicks the arrow to display the list items in a pop-up menu, then clicks one of the items in the menu to make the choice. The selected item appears in the list box.

Although the results look quite different, the procedures for creating both lists and menus are basically the same. The only difference is that, for a list, you need to specify the list height and you have the option of allowing multiple selections. To add a list or a menu to your form, follow these steps:

**1.** Position the insertion point cursor on the page at the location where you want to insert a selection list. Make sure it is inside the red dotted outline of the form.

**2.** Click the List/Menu button in the Forms category of the Insert bar, or choose Insert | Form Object | List/Menu. Dreamweaver inserts a small pop-up menu box into the form. A dotted line surrounding the list box indicates that it's selected.

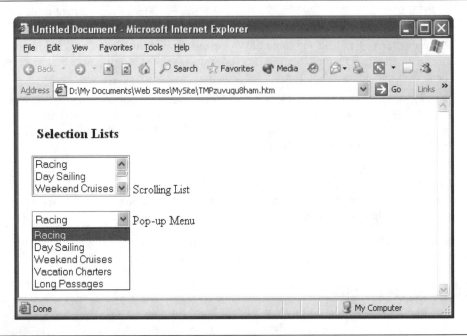

FIGURE 8-5     Single- and multiline selection lists

**3.** In the Property Inspector panel, enter a unique name for the selection list in the List/Menu box. You can accept the default name that Dreamweaver MX assigns, but a name that describes the list will be more useful.

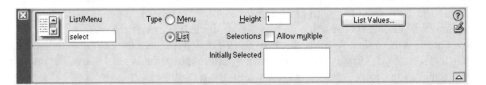

**4.** Select Menu or List in the Type area to designate this selection list as a scrolling list or a pop-up menu.

**5.** Enter a number in the Height box to designate how many lines the scrolling list will display. This option applies only to scrolling lists. The option is grayed out for menus.

**6.** Check the Selections, Allow Multiple option if you want to allow the visitor to select more than one item from the list. Again, this option applies only to scrolling lists; it's grayed out for menus.

**7.** Click the List Values button to open the List Values dialog box. The insertion point starts out in the Item Label column.

**8.** Type a label for a list item. This is the text that will appear as an item in the selection list. Press TAB to move the insertion point to the Value column.

**9.** Type the text that you want to submit as form data when the visitor chooses the corresponding list item. Often this value is the same as the Item Label, but it could also be a catalog number, filename, or other data that corresponds to the descriptive item label.

**10.** Click the plus (+) button to add another item to the list, and repeat steps 8 and 9 to define the label and value for the new item. Continue adding items until the list is complete.

**11.** Rearrange the list order by selecting an item from the list and clicking the up and down arrow buttons to move it up or down in the list. To remove an item from the list, select it and then click the minus (–) button.

**12.** Click OK to close the List Values dialog box and add the list items to the selection list in your form. Dreamweaver adds the items to the source code, and the list box expands horizontally in Design view to accommodate the longest item label in the list. The list items also appear in the Initially Selected list in the Property Inspector panel.

**13.** Select one item from the Initially Selected list if you want to designate a default selection to appear when the form loads in the visitor's browser. To deselect an item in the Initially Selected list, CTRL-click.

**14.** Click beside the selection list in the Document window and type a label or other instructions. Or use the Label form element to add a label to the list or menu.

NOTE

*The HTML code for a selection list looks something like this:*

```
<select name="select" size="3" multiple>
<option value="1">Item 1</option>
<option value="2">Item 2</option>
<option value="3">Item 3</option>
</select>
```

## Create a Jump Menu

In addition to the standard selection lists, Dreamweaver includes a separate command for creating a special kind of menu called a *jump menu*. A jump menu is a menu-style selection list that contains a list of URLs, like hyperlinks. What makes the jump menu special is that Dreamweaver automatically adds a bit of JavaScript code to your page that enables the browser to process the list selection immediately. As a result, when the visitor makes a selection from the jump menu, the browser goes to the associated URL just as if the visitor had clicked a normal hyperlink elsewhere on the page. The jump menu is really intended to be used by itself as a navigation tool rather than as a component of a larger form.

 *You can also create a jump menu using a Dreamweaver behavior. See Chapter 13 for the details on behaviors.*

To create a jump menu, follow these steps.

1. Position the insertion point cursor on the page at the location where you want to insert a jump menu. The jump menu must be located in a form, but Dreamweaver MX automatically creates a form to surround the jump menu if you don't place it in a preexisting form.

 2. Click the Jump Menu button in the Forms category of the Insert bar, or choose Insert | Form Object | Jump Menu. Dreamweaver opens the Insert Jump Menu dialog box.

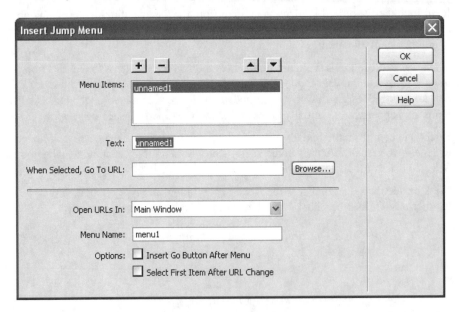

3. Type a list item in the Text box. This is the text that will appear as an item in the jump menu.

4. Enter a URL for the link in the When Selected, Go To URL box. You can type in the full URL or click the Browse button to open a Select File dialog box where you can locate and select a file on your system.

5. Click the plus (+) button to add another item to the list, and repeat steps 3 and 4 to define the text and URL for the next item. Continue adding items until the list is complete.

6. Rearrange the list order by selecting an item from the list and clicking the up and down arrow buttons to move it up or down in the list. To remove an item from the list, select it and then click the minus (–) button.

7. If your page uses frames, select a target frame in the Open URLs In box. Otherwise, accept the default of Main Window.

8. Enter a name for the jump menu in the Menu Name box.

9. You can select one or both of the following options, as appropriate:

   ■ **Insert Go Button After Menu**   Adds a Go button to the right of the menu box. Instead of the browser jumping to the URL as soon as the visitor clicks an item in the list, the visitor selects an item and then clicks the Go button to load the linked URL.

   ■ **Select First Item After URL Change**   Displays the first menu item as the default selection.

10. Click OK to close the Insert Jump Menu dialog box and add the jump menu to your page. Dreamweaver inserts a form into your page and creates a pop-up menu box within that form, as shown. A dotted line surrounding the list box indicates that it's selected.

NOTE *The HTML code for a jump menu looks something like this:*

```
<select name="menu1" onChange="MM_jumpMenu('parent',this,0)">
 <option value="TravelDetail_surf.html"
selected>Surf</option>
  <option value="TravelDetail_rockClimb.html">Rock
Climb</option>
  <option value="TravelDetail_mtnBike.html">Bike</option>
</select>
```

*In addition, Dreamweaver inserts some script code in the document header to process this special form.*

A jump menu is really just a pop-up menu tied to a bit of JavaScript. After you create the jump menu, if you need to edit the menu items or links, you do so by editing the contents of the List Values in the Property Inspector panel, just as you would any other pop-up menu.

## Insert a File Field

When combined with the appropriate server scripts, a file field enables your site visitors to upload files to your site. A file field looks like a single-line text box, but the file field is distinguished by a Browse button to the right of the text box, as shown in Figure 8-6.

To use the file field, the site visitor either types a path and filename into the text box portion of the file field or clicks the Browse button to open a dialog box where they can locate and select a file from their system. Closing the dialog box enters the path and filename for the selected file into the file field. Then, when the visitor clicks the form's Submit button, the browser sends the selected file to the server along with any other file data.

 *Before attempting to create a form with a file field, check with the webmaster or the server's system administrator to make sure file uploads are allowed on the server.*

To add a file field to a form on your web page, follow these steps:

**1.** Position the insertion point cursor on the page at the location where you want to insert a file field. Make sure it is inside the red dotted outline of the form.

 *File fields work only in forms that use the post method. The form's Action setting needs to specify the upload address.*

 **2.** Click the File Field button in the Forms category of the Insert panel, or choose Insert | Form Object | File Field. Dreamweaver inserts a file field and its accompanying Browse button into the form. A dotted line surrounding the text box indicates that it's selected.

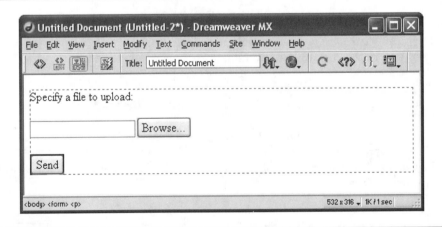

**FIGURE 8-6** A file field

3.  In the Property Inspector panel, enter a unique name for the file field in the FileField Name box. Replace the Dreamweaver default name with something more meaningful.

4.  Enter a number in the Char Width box to set the width (in characters) of the file field in the form. As with a single-line text box, this setting determines the size of the text box, not the maximum number of characters the visitor can type. The file field automatically scrolls horizontally to accommodate longer text entries. If you leave the Char Width box blank, the text box uses the browser's default size, which is usually about 26 characters.

5.  Enter a number in the Max Chars box to set the maximum number of text characters the visitor can enter, or leave the box blank to allow the visitor to enter unlimited text.

6.  Click beside the file field in the Document window and type a label or instructions for submitting the file. Alternately, use the Label form element to create a label for the file field.

**NOTE**  *The HTML code for a file field box looks like this:* `<input type="file" name="file2">`

## Create Submit and Reset Buttons

Submit and Reset buttons are standard features of almost every form. The visitor signals the browser to send the form data to the server by clicking the Submit button; clicking the Reset button is a quick way to clear the form contents and start over.

The procedure for adding these essential elements to your form is similar to adding other form elements. Here's how:

1.  Position the insertion point cursor on the page at the location where you want to insert a button. As always, make sure it is inside the red dotted outline of the form.

2.  Click Button in the Forms category of the Insert bar, or choose Insert | Form Object | Button. Dreamweaver inserts a button into the form as shown here. The default is a Submit button, but you can change that. The dotted line surrounding the box indicates that it's selected.

3.  In the Property Inspector panel, enter a unique name for the button in the Button Name box. Every button needs its own name, so give it something appropriate.

4.  Click Submit Form or Reset Form in the Action area. This setting specifies what happens when the visitor clicks the button. Dreamweaver automatically changes the Label setting to match your selection. There is also a third selection—None—that creates a button that doesn't have a predefined action. You can use Behaviors (see Chapter 13) to define a custom action for the button.

5.  Enter a label for the face of the button in the Label box. You can substitute something like Clear Form for the reset button or Send File for a submit button accompanying a File field.

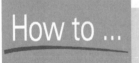 *The HTML code for a button looks like this:* `<input type="reset" name="Clear" value="Clear Form">`

## How to ... Create a Graphical Submit Button

You aren't stuck with the plain gray Submit and Reset buttons. You can substitute a graphical button of your own design if you prefer. The trick is to use the Image Field form object and use one of the reserved names, Submit or Reset, to tell the browser what the image is supposed to represent.

Of course, the first step is to create an image to use as the button. You can use Fireworks or your favorite image editor for that. Then you add the image to your form and identify it as a Submit or Reset button. Here's how to do it:

1.  Position the insertion point at the location in the form where you want to place the button.

2.  Click the Image Field button in the Forms category of the Insert bar, or choose Insert | Form Object | Image Field. Dreamweaver opens the Select Image Source dialog box, the same dialog box you use to insert regular images into your document.

3. Locate and select the image file in the dialog box. Click Select to close the dialog box and add the image to your form. The image appears with the dotted outline surrounding it indicating that it is selected. Note that the selection box identifies the image as a form element rather than a standard image.

4. In the Property Inspector panel, type **Submit** (or **Reset**) in the ImageField box. Changing the image name to one of these reserved names is what tells the browser to treat the image as the specified form button.

## Use Hidden Fields

A hidden field is one of those objects whose name describes what it does. It's a form field that is hidden from view in the visitor's browser, but it's part of the form nonetheless, and the contents of that field are submitted for processing along with the rest of the form.

Hidden fields give you the opportunity to insert information into the form that the visitor doesn't need to see. You can use hidden fields to identify the form and to pass information to the processing script. For example, a form mailer script might rely on hidden fields to provide the e-mail address to which to send the form contents and the mail server to use to post that message.

Although hidden fields aren't visible in the visitor's browser, Dreamweaver adds a marker icon to Design view to indicate the presence of a hidden field so you can select and manipulate it. (Make sure the View | Visual Aids | Invisible Elements option is enabled to view hidden fields and other invisible page elements.) Figure 8-7 shows a form with hidden field markers visible near the top of the form.

To add a hidden field to your form, follow these steps:

1. Position the insertion point cursor at the location inside the form rectangle where you want to insert the hidden field. Hidden fields are usually placed at the top of the form, but you're not forced to place them there.

2. Click the Hidden Field button in the Forms tab of the Insert bar, or choose Insert | Form Objects | Hidden Field. Dreamweaver inserts a hidden field marker in the form and selects it.

3. In the Property Inspector panel, enter a name for the hidden field in the HiddenField box.

 *If you're creating a hidden field to pass information to a script, be sure to enter the field name exactly as specified for the script. Spelling and capitalization count.*

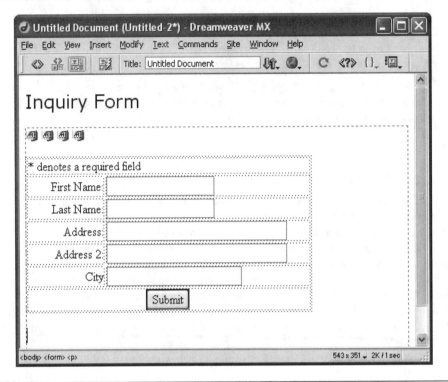

FIGURE 8-7    Hidden field markers in a form

4. Enter the field value in the Value box. This is the information you want the hidden field to submit for processing along with the rest of the form.

*The HTML code for a hidden field looks something like this:* `<input type="hidden" name="sendto" value="name@bogus.com">`

## Label Form Objects with the `<label>` Tag

The instructions for using most of the form elements covered in this chapter include entering text on the web page before or after the element to identify the form element to site visitors. Traditionally, that's the way web authors labeled form elements. However, the current HTML specification provides the `<label>` tag specifically for this purpose.

*The `<label>` tag is not supported by many older browsers. The tag is supported by Internet Explorer 4+ and Netscape 6. If you're at all concerned about browser compatibility, you should probably wait for the state of the art to mature before using the `<label>` tag in your forms.*

This tag also adds functionality to the form element by associating the descriptive text for the form element directly with that element. This can be useful for speech-based browsers, so that the form elements can have spoken text associated with them.

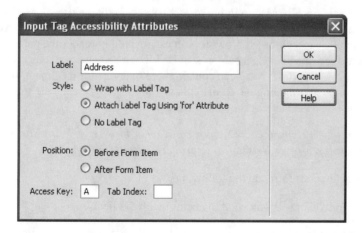

Dreamweaver MX provides an icon in the Forms category of the Insert bar to add a label to a form element. To add the label, select the form element that you want the label to be associated with. Then click the Label button or choose Insert | Form Objects | Label. The selected form element is wrapped with a label tag. Dreamweaver switches to Code and Design view and highlights the label tag for editing. After completing your edits, click the Refresh button in the Property Inspector panel to display the results in Design view.

*Because there is no Property Inspector for labels, in order to modify any of the attributes of the `<label>` tag you will need to do so in Code view.*

NEW IN MX

Manual editing of the label tags may seem onerous, but Dreamweaver MX comes to the rescue with the Accessibility options. Activating the Accessibility options for form objects causes Dreamweaver to display a dialog box prompting you for settings such as alt text for images and labels for form elements when you insert those objects into your web page. To turn on accessibility options for form elements, do the following.

**1.** Choose Edit | Preferences, and click on the Accessibility category.

**2.** Make sure Form Objects is checked in the Show Attributes when Inserting list.

**3.** Click OK to apply the changes.

Now, when you add a visible form input element—text fields, text areas, buttons, and so on—Dreamweaver displays the Input Tag Accessibility Attributes dialog box.

This dialog box offers the following options:

■ **Label**   Enter the text to be displayed for the label here. This is the descriptive text that identifies your form element on the page.

- **Style**   The style lets you choose one of three options for the label:
  - Wrap with Label Tag adds the label tag with the form element contained in it.
  - Attach Label Using 'for' Attribute uses the label tag's `for` attribute to identify the form element by name. This allows for more creative label placement. In other words, the label doesn't have to be adjacent to the form element if you use the `for` attribute to explicitly name the element it's labeling.
  - No Label adds the form element with no label, as if the accessibility option were turned off.
- **Position**   Choose Before Form Item or After Form Item. This determines the placement of the label text relative to the form element.
- **Access Key**   This item lets you specify a keyboard shortcut key to use to access the form element. This key, in conjunction with the CTRL key (in Windows) can be used to access the item when viewing the form in the browser. For example, if you assign the X key to a label, it can be accessed by pressing CTRL-X in the browser.
- **Tab Index**   The tab index allows you to specify the order that form elements will be cycled through when pressing the TAB key in the browser. The tab order goes from low to higher numbers.

*The HTML code for a label using the* `for` *attribute looks like this when associated with an input element:* `<label for="text1">Text1</label><input type="text" name="text1" value="text1" id="text1">`

## Define Fieldsets

NEW IN
**MX**

Another form element typically used to improve accessibility is the fieldset. This element is used to group related form fields together, which can make the user interface more intuitive, as well as provide information that speech-based browsers can use to audibly render the page.

A fieldset works very much like a label—it's an HTML tag that encloses a form element. The difference is that the `<fieldset>` tag can contain more than one form element. It is typically displayed with a border surrounding the form elements. If you supply a legend, that text appears above the bounding box on the left, as shown in Figure 8-8.

*The fieldset form element is not supported by older browsers. Your visitors will need Internet Explorer 4+ or Netscape 6 to properly display fieldsets.*

To add a fieldset to your form, do the following.

**1.**   Select the form elements you want to enclose with the fieldset.

*Pay attention to which form elements are highlighted as you insert a fieldset into your form. Dreamweaver sometimes expands the selection automatically to include additional form elements—or even the entire form—leading to unexpected results. If this happens, try reselecting the form elements (and any related text and paragraph tags) that you want to enclose in the fieldset in Code view instead of Design view.*

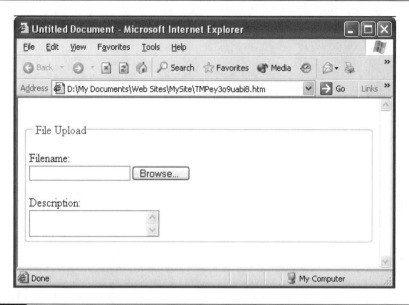

FIGURE 8-8    A fieldset grouping form elements together

**2.** Click the Fieldset button in the Forms category of the Insert bar, or choose Insert | Form Objects | Fieldset. Dreamweaver displays the Fieldset dialog box, shown here.

**3.** In the Label box, enter the text to use for the fieldset's `<legend>` tag. This is the text that will be displayed at the top left, above the fieldset's bounding box. Leave this blank to create the fieldset box without a text label.

**4.** Click OK to close the dialog box and insert the `<fieldset>` and `<legend>` tags into the HTML code for your page. Dreamweaver switches to Code and Design view for further editing if needed. Click the Refresh button in the Property Inspector panel to update the Design view display.

*The HTML code for a fieldset looks like this:*

```
<fieldset><legend>File
Upload</legend>
<p><label>Filename:<br>
  <input type="file" name="file1">
  </label>
</p>
<p><label>Description:<br>
  <textarea name="textarea"></textarea>
  </label>
</p></fieldset>
```

**CAUTION** *The bounding box that appears around a fieldset in Internet Explorer does not appear in Dreamweaver's Design view. You'll need to preview your page in a browser window to see the full effect.*

## Finish the Form

In addition to the form elements themselves, your form can include regular text, images, and anything else you can place on a web page. In particular, forms usually include text as labels for the various form elements and to provide instructions for the form. The `<label>` tag is now the recommended way to label your form elements, but that still leaves lots of need for text in forms as descriptions, instructions, headings, and so on. You enter text into a form just as you enter it anywhere else.

Tables provide an important tool for controlling the form layout. You can insert tables (preferably Layout Tables; see Chapter 6) into a form and use the table cells to arrange form elements on the page and align them both horizontally and vertically. Without tables, it's hard to create a form that isn't just a bunch of form fields stacked along the left page margin. With tables, you can create a form with logically grouped form elements neatly aligned and arrayed across the page. When using tables with a form, just make sure the entire table is within the `<form>` tags, which means within the bounds of the red dotted form rectangle in Design view.

# Submit the Information Gathered in a Form

Every web page depends on a web server to be the host for the site and respond to requests from the browser for the files required to display each page. Generally, you don't have to be too concerned about the particular web server software that hosts a site as long as it conforms to the prevailing standards (and all the web servers do). The web server and the platform it runs on become a concern only if you start working with database connectivity and advanced scripting applications.

You can get into just such issues when working with forms. You can design a form in Dreamweaver MX and the visitor can fill it out in the browser window, but nothing happens when the visitor clicks the Submit button unless there is a script or application on the server to process the form submission. Dealing with the requirements for submitting form data for processing can be fairly simple or quite complex, depending on what you want to do with the information you gather from the visitor with the form.

For example, if the form is designed to gather credit card information as part of an online shopping system, you need to submit the information to online financial service companies for credit card verification, authorization, and payment processing. That involves special accounts with the credit card processing companies and elaborate interconnections between your form and their payment processing systems. For security reasons, the data traveling between the various computers must be encrypted. Obviously, that kind of form processing is beyond the scope of this book.

On the other hand, if you just want to forward the contents of a customer feedback form to your e-mail address, that kind of form processing is much simpler. It involves submitting the form to a script or an application running on the server for processing, but the basic procedure isn't difficult to understand or implement. The only problem is that, although most web servers have such scripts available, there is no real standardization among those scripts and programs.

Because of the lack of standardization among form processing scripts, I can't provide you with step-by-step instructions for configuring your form for processing. Your best bet is to contact the webmaster or system administrator for the web server hosting your site and ask what form processing scripts are available and how to submit form data to them. You'll need to get the following information and incorporate it into your form:

- **Form submission method**   Select either Post or Get in the Method box in the form Property Inspector panel. Post is the most common method.

- **URL of the script or application**   Enter this URL into the Action box in the form Property Inspector panel.

- **Any parameters that must be submitted as form data**   This includes information such as the e-mail address the form data should be mailed to. It's normally inserted into hidden fields at the top of the form. The system administrator may supply sample code that you can paste into your page in Code view.

# Chapter 9

## Create and Use Dreamweaver Templates and Libraries

## How to...

- Create a Dreamweaver template
- Apply and edit templates
- Revise templates and template-based sites
- Work with Dreamweaver Library items

A well-designed web site uses a design scheme to give all the pages in the site a unified look. All (or most) pages in a site share certain elements, such as consistent background and text colors, as well as a standard layout that might include a logo graphic at the top of the page and perhaps a navigation bar on the left side. The rest of the page content may vary dramatically, but the common page elements remain consistent to give the site its visual identity.

In the past, the web designer had to carefully duplicate the layout and all other common elements from one page to the next. If the layout or one of the common elements changed, the designer had to painstakingly update each and every page on which it was used. Now, Dreamweaver's template and library features greatly simplify the process of creating—and maintaining—the common layout and design elements that appear on every page in your web site.

# Understand Dreamweaver Templates

A simple solution to the challenge of setting up a web site with a common design scheme is to create a master web document containing the common elements that you want to repeat on every page. You can then use that document (usually called a *template*) as the basis of the other pages you create for the site. When you work with a manually created template, you can either copy and paste HTML code from the master template page to each new page or simply make a copy of the template page and then customize the copy to create each individual page.

Dreamweaver takes this concept of a template document and improves upon it by automating the process of creating web documents based on a template. Furthermore, you can lock some portions of Dreamweaver templates to protect them from accidental change.

But the most important feature of Dreamweaver templates is the way Dreamweaver automatically updates template-based pages. When you make a change to the original (master) template file, Dreamweaver scans all the web documents in your site and automatically updates any document based on the template. This means that you can update dozens of pages that are based on a template in a matter of minutes—a chore that would take hours to do manually.

Dreamweaver templates are normal HTML files, just like any other web document. You edit page properties, layout, tables, text, graphics, and other elements in a template just as you edit them in any other web document. What distinguishes Dreamweaver templates from other documents is the ability to designate certain areas of the template as editable to control what portions of each template-based page can change and what portions must duplicate the template exactly.

When you create a template, Dreamweaver gives the template file a distinctive extension—.dwt—and stores it in the Templates subfolder in your site. However, despite the extension, the template file is still a standard HTML file. As you define editable and locked areas of the template, Dreamweaver inserts comment codes (<!--     -->) into the HTML source code for the template. Dreamweaver can interpret the contents of these comment codes and use that information to display the boundaries of editable and locked areas of the template in Design view and to deliver the other features of templates in Dreamweaver. Web browsers and other HTML editors simply ignore the contents of an HTML comment, so Dreamweaver's templates and template-based pages remain fully compatible with other programs—no proprietary codes are involved.

When you create a web page based on the template, Dreamweaver copies the relevant HTML code from the template to the new web page—effectively replicating the page properties, layout, and content of the template in the new page. That includes the information that designates portions of the document as editable. Dreamweaver allows you to freely edit the content of the editable areas but locks the rest of the document to protect it from change. This ensures that all the template-based pages in a site remain consistent with the master template.

Dreamweaver keeps track of the connection between a web document and the template on which it is based. If you make any change to the template, Dreamweaver offers to update the pages based on that template automatically. As a result, you can edit the template file to change a common design element that appears on every page in your site and quickly see that change reflected in all the pages, without having to open each web document individually to make the change.

# Create Templates

The mechanics of creating a template in Dreamweaver aren't difficult to master. A single command creates the template file. Dreamweaver takes care of the details of giving that file a special extension (.dwt) and creating the Templates subfolder in the root folder of your local site to store your template files. Menu commands enable you to define areas of the template as editable, optional, or repeating—Dreamweaver generates the comment codes needed to identify those regions in the template file. All the other page elements that appear in the template are the same as in any other web document—you create and work with them in exactly the same way you do on any other web page.

## Save an Existing Page as a Template

Perhaps the most common technique for creating a template is to start with an existing web document and save a copy of that document as a template. You can easily visualize how the template-based documents will look, because the template itself starts out as a completed web document. The existing document serves as a prototype for the documents created from the template.

To create a template based on an existing web document, follow these steps:

**1.** Select or create a web document to serve as the prototype for the template. Open that web page in Dreamweaver's Design View window.

**2.** Click the Make Template button in the Template category of the Insert bar or choose File | Save as Template. Dreamweaver opens the Save As Template dialog box.

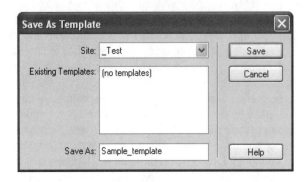

**3.** Select the site in the Site box and enter a name for the template in the Save As box.

**4.** Click Save to close the Save As Template dialog box and create the template file. Dreamweaver saves a copy of the web document with the .dwt extension. The file is saved in the Templates folder of the local root folder for the site you selected. If the Templates folder does not already exist, Dreamweaver creates it.

The newly created template file remains open in the Design View window, ready for editing. To make the template functional, you need to define editable areas of the template. (See the section "Define Locked and Editable Areas of a Template," later in this chapter.)

## Create a Template from Scratch

Templates don't have to be based on an existing web page. You can create a template from scratch. You typically use this technique when you're building a new web site from scratch and you have a well-defined page layout worked out in advance.

The simplest way to create a template from scratch is to create a new document and select HTML Template as the document type in the New Document dialog box. (Select Basic Page or Template Page in the Category list and HTML Template in the list in the middle of the dialog box.) When you click Create, Dreamweaver closes the New Document dialog box and opens your new template file in a Design View window, ready for editing.

To create the template, insert the page elements that you want to pass along to the template-based documents. After you edit your template file, choose File | Save or File | Save As Template to save it. Dreamweaver opens the Save As Template dialog box, where you select the site and enter the filename for the template. Click Save to close the dialog box and save the template in you site's Templates folder.

*Dreamweaver expects to find template files in a specific location in your site. Do not move the Templates folder. Do not move template files to another folder. And do not place nontemplate files in the Templates folder. Otherwise, the paths to files referenced in the template may not work properly.*

# Define Locked and Editable Areas of a Template

Templates exist to impose a degree of conformity on all the template-based pages. You define regions within the template to allow or restrict the changes that are possible in any document that's based on the template. When you create a new template, it starts out with the entire page locked. You must define one or more editable areas in the template in order to make the template useful. In Dreamweaver 4, templates could contain only one kind of editable area. Dreamweaver MX expands your options with multiple template regions, each of which has different characteristics.

Dreamweaver templates are composed of the following regions:

- **Locked region**    Any portion of the template that isn't specifically marked as editable is automatically locked and can't be changed in any documents based on the template unless you first break the link between the document and the template.

- **Editable region**    An area of the template that is unlocked so that you can freely edit that portion of a document based on the template.

- **Repeating region**    A portion of the template that you can duplicate as often as needed in a document based on the template. A repeating region can contain both locked and editable regions.

- **Repeating table**    A special form of repeating region composed of a table in which one or more rows of table cells are set up as editable regions that you can duplicate as needed to expand the table.

- **Optional region**    A portion of the template that can be configured to appear or not appear in the template-based document. You can elect to show or hide the optional region in each template-based document. The optional region can contain both locked and editable regions.

- **Editable optional region**    An optional region that is set to allow you to edit its content as well as control whether or not the region appears in the template-based document.

9

You can exercise fairly precise control over what portions of the template-based page are editable by careful selection of the editable areas. For example, if you want the template to control most of the formatting of a text block but allow the text itself to be editable, you define an editable region for the text but keep the surrounding paragraph tags (`<p></p>`) locked. Conversely, if you include the paragraph tags in the editable region, you can change the paragraph format, alignment, and so on when you edit the template-based document.

## Create an Editable Region

When you create an editable region of a template, that region can be an empty box into which you insert page content when you edit the template-based document, or it can include page content from the template. If the editable region contains content from the template, you can edit that content freely in the template-based document. Your template can contain multiple editable regions.

Here's how to mark existing page content as editable:

1. Select the text or other content that you want to be able to change in the template-based pages. You can select an individual paragraph of text, an image, or other individual page element, or you can select a large area of the page containing several page elements.

2. Click the Editable Region button in the Templates category of the Insert bar, choose Insert | Template Objects | Editable Region, or right-click the selection and choose Templates | New Editable Region from the context menu. Dreamweaver displays the New Editable Region dialog box.

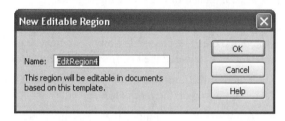

3. Enter a name for the editable region in the Name box. The editable region name must be unique within the current template and the name can't include special characters such as angle brackets (<>), quotation marks (" '), or the ampersand (&) character.

4. Click OK to close the New Editable Region dialog box. Dreamweaver marks the editable region of the template with a blue-green outline and labels it with a small tab at the upper-left corner, as shown in Figure 9-1.

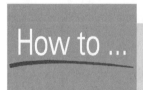 **Make Tables and Layers Editable**

When you work with tables and layers in Dreamweaver templates, you need to pay particular attention to how you select editable regions. Otherwise, you may not get the desired results in the template-based documents.

- You can select an individual table cell or an entire table as an editable region, but you can't select multiple table cells and mark them as one editable region. If you must make multiple cells editable, create a separate editable region for each cell.

- To mark the contents of a table cell as editable without making the cell itself editable, create a text paragraph in the cell and carefully select the paragraph and not the cell (check the Tag Selector to confirm that the <p> tag is selected but not the <td> tag).

- If you mark a layer as editable, both the layer position and contents are editable. If you mark the layer contents as editable, only the content is editable, not the layer itself.

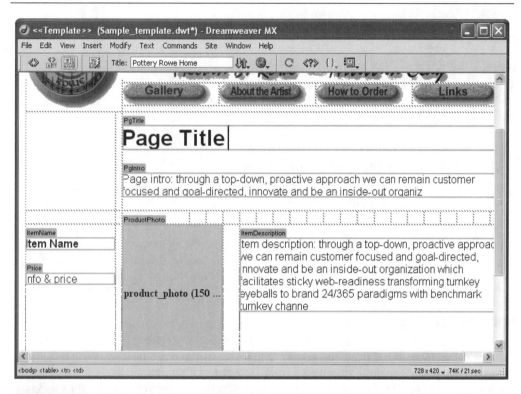

**FIGURE 9-1**    Editable regions in a template

To create an editable region that doesn't contain existing content, you follow the same basic procedure but position the insertion point where you want to create a new editable region, instead of selecting content as described in step 1. Dreamweaver inserts the name of the editable region into the template to act as a placeholder and surrounds it with the blue-green box.

TIP    *You can replace the text Dreamweaver places in the new editable region with a prompt or instructions.*

TIP    *Dreamweaver generally does a good job of keeping track of paths to links, image files, and other content in templates and adjusting those paths for the new locations of the pages based on the template. However, you can reduce the chances of broken links if you use root-relative paths instead of document-relative paths for all links and file references in a template.*

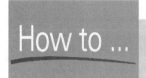 **Lock an Editable Region**

Occasionally, you may change your mind about the status of an editable region of a template and decide that it shouldn't be editable after all. To lock an editable region of a template, follow these steps:

1. Open the template file in the Design view window (if it isn't already open).
2. Select the editable area that you want to lock.
3. Choose Modify | Templates | Remove Template Markup, or right-click and choose Remove Template Markup. Dreamweaver removes the blue-green outline and name from the selected region.

You can use the same technique to remove the template region markings from optional regions, repeating regions, and repeating tables as well as editable regions. In each case, the selected content reverts to normal (locked) page content in the template.

## Create a Repeating Region

A *repeating region* in a template is a block of content that you can duplicate as many times as needed on the template-based page, like adding items to a list. The repeating region can include both locked and editable regions, making it a sort of template within a template.

For example, in the template for a news site, you might set up a repeating region for a news article. The repeating region might include editable regions for the text of the headline and article body but keep the formatting for those elements locked. Then, when you create a web document based on that template, you can use the repeating region to add multiple news articles to the page. The text of each news article varies but the formatting remains the same, and the page can contain two, five, or ten articles without requiring changes to the template.

To create a repeating region, follow these steps:

1. Select the page content in the template that you want to include in the repeating region, or position the insertion point where you want to create a new blank repeating region.

 2. Click the Repeating Region button in the Templates category of the Insert bar or choose Insert | Template Objects | Repeating Region. Dreamweaver displays the New Repeating Region dialog box.

| New Repeating Region | |
| --- | --- |
| Name: RepeatRegion1 | OK |
| This region will appear multiple times in documents based on this template. | Cancel |
| | Help |

3. Enter a name for the repeating region. The name must be unique to the current template and can't include special characters.

4. Click OK. Dreamweaver closes the dialog box and surrounds the selected portion of the template with a colored box and a tab labeling it as a repeating region. If you selected existing text and other content in step 1, that content appears inside the repeating region box. Otherwise, Dreamweaver inserts the region name as a placeholder.

After you create the repeating region, you can add to or edit its contents. Remember that, like the template itself, the contents of the repeating region remain locked unless you unlock portions of it by creating one or more editable regions within the repeating region—and a repeating region that doesn't contain at least one editable region is pretty useless. You use exactly the same technique to create an editable region inside a repeating region as you do elsewhere in the template.

## Create a Repeating Table

A repeating table is really just a convenient shortcut that automates the process of creating a table, defining one or more rows as a repeating region and making each of the cells in those table rows editable regions. The result is a table that you can format in the template and then expand as needed by adding rows in the template-based document.

**9**

NOTE    *Only selected rows of a repeating table become a repeating region, not the entire table.*

1. Position the insertion point where you want to insert a new repeating table into the template.

2. Click the Repeating Table button in the Templates category of the Insert bar or choose Insert | Template Objects | Repeating Table. Dreamweaver opens the Insert Repeating Table dialog box.

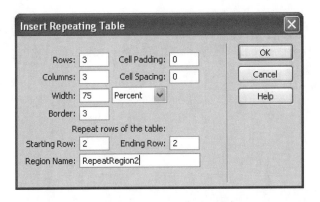

3. Enter the appropriate settings for Rows, Columns, Cell Padding, Cell Spacing, Width, and Border to define your table.

4. Set up the repeating region portion of the table by entering the Starting Row and Ending Row values and entering a name for the region.

5. Click OK to close the Insert Repeating Table dialog box and create the table in your template. Dreamweaver marks the specified rows as a repeating region and automatically makes each cell in those rows an editable region.

After you create the repeating table, you can edit and embellish it as needed using normal table-editing techniques (see Chapter 6).

## Insert an Optional Region

An *optional region* in a template marks content that you can choose to display or not display in the template-based document. Like a repeating region or the template itself, an optional region can contain locked content, editable regions, or both.

Optional regions enable you to create page "building blocks" that you can optionally include or omit from the template-based pages as needed. You can use this feature to avoid needing to create multiple versions of a template in order to accommodate variations in template content for different sections of the site. For example, a corporate site might have a master template for the entire site with optional regions for each department or branch office. As you work on a template-based page, you could turn on the optional region for the relevant department and hide the optional regions for the others. You don't need to create and maintain a separate template for each department.

To create an optional region in your template, follow these steps:

1. Select the page content in the template that you want to include in the optional region, or position the insertion point where you want to create a new blank optional region.

2. Click the Optional Region button in the Templates category of the Insert bar, or choose Insert | Template Objects | Optional Region. Dreamweaver displays the New Optional Region dialog box.

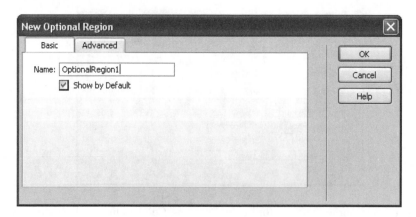

3. Enter a name for the optional region. As with all template regions, the name must be unique to the current template and it can't include special characters. Check or clear the Show by Default check box to determine whether the optional region starts out visible or hidden in template-based pages.

4. Click OK. Dreamweaver closes the dialog box and surrounds the selected portion of the template with a colored box and a tab labeling it as an optional region. If you selected existing text and other content in step 1, that content appears inside the optional region box. Otherwise, Dreamweaver inserts the region name as a placeholder.

You can include preexisting content when you create an optional region, and you can add to or edit content in an optional region of the template after you create it. You can make some, or all, of the optional region editable by creating one or more editable regions within the optional region.

However, if you want to make the entire contents of the optional region editable, you can save a step by using the Editable Optional Region button in the Templates category of the Insert bar or by choosing Insert | Template Objects | Editable Optional Region when you create the region. After you enter the region name in the New Optional Region dialog box and click OK, Dreamweaver simultaneously creates the optional region and an editable region within it.

9

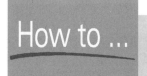 **Create Nested Templates**

Dreamweaver allows you to create nested templates to deal with the demands of sites with complex design needs. This allows you to set up a master template that contains the elements that are common to the entire site and use it as the basis for nested templates that add template elements for pages in a particular sections of the site. For example, the master template could establish the page background and the corporate header; and you could create several nested templates that add a different footer for each department or branch office.

To create a nested template, start by creating the base template. Include the content and regions that are common to the entire site. Don't forget to include one or more editable regions that will be controlled by the nested template. Next, create a new document based on the base template, and then save it as a template. This is the nested template. Add content, editable regions, and so on as needed to refine the template. Then you can create pages for that portion of your site based on the nested template, which includes elements from both the base template and the nested template.

The advantage of using nested templates is that you can make changes to the base template and Dreamweaver will automatically propagate those changes to all the nested templates and to all the documents based on those templates.

# Work with Templates

Creating a template is just the beginning. To use templates effectively, you need to be able to apply the template to the pages in your web site. Then you need to be able to work with those template-based pages, which means knowing how to select and edit content in the editable areas, as well as knowing how to identify the locked areas so you don't waste time trying to edit them.

The most common way to apply a template to a web document is to create a new document based on the template. You can also apply a template to an existing web page.

## Create a Page Based on a Site Template

Dreamweaver MX gives you the option of applying a template to every new document you create. To create a new template-based document, follow these steps:

1. Choose File | New from the menu in the Document window or File | New Window in the Site window. Dreamweaver opens the New Document dialog box.

2. Click the Templates tab to display the New from Template options.

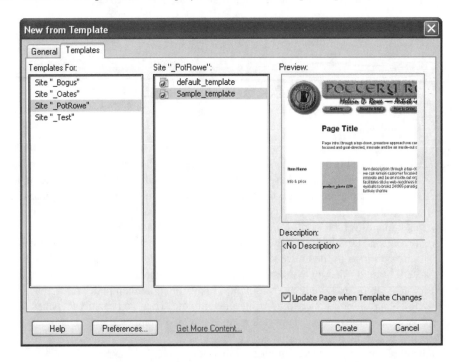

3. Select the site from the Templates For list box. Dreamweaver lists the templates available in the selected site in the Site list box.

4. Select a template from the Site list. Dreamweaver displays a preview of the selected template in the Preview box.

5. Make sure the Update Page When Template Changes option is checked.

**NOTE** *If you clear the Update Page When Template Changes option in the New from Template dialog box, Dreamweaver creates a new web document and copies the template content into that document, then disconnects the document from the template. As a result, everything in the new document is editable—there are no locked or protected areas— and Dreamweaver can't update the document to reflect changes in the template.*

6. Click Create to close the dialog box and create the new template-based page. Dreamweaver opens a Design View window containing the newly created web document with the template applied.

## Apply a Template to an Existing Page

You can also apply a template to the page you are editing in Design view. When you do, Dreamweaver scoops up the content on the existing page and pours it into the editable areas of the template. You can use this technique when you need to go ahead and create the body content for some of the pages on your site before the page design is finalized. Later, you can create a template to control page layout and background graphics and apply the template to the pages containing the body content to quickly create the finished pages.

**9**

**TIP** *Applying a template to an existing web page works best when there is just one large editable area in the template. If there are several editable areas, you may need to go through an additional step to tell Dreamweaver where to place the existing page content.*

1. Click the Template button in the Assets panel to display the list of available templates on the site.

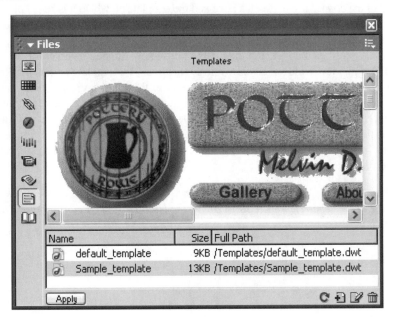

2. Select a template from the list and click the Apply button, or simply drag the selected template from the Assets panel and drop it on the page in the Design View window. Dreamweaver applies the selected template to the document.

TIP    *You can also apply a template to a page using a menu command. Choose Modify | Templates | Apply Template to Page to open the Select Template dialog box. Select a site and a template; then click Select to close the dialog box and apply the template.*

Here are a few things you should know about what happens when you apply a template to an existing document.

■ If no template had previously been applied to the document, Dreamweaver copies the template settings and content to the document and places the existing document content into the editable area of the template.

■ If there are multiple editable areas in the template and multiple blocks of content on the page, Dreamweaver displays a dialog box where you can select the editable area into which the content is placed.

■ If the document was based on another template, Dreamweaver replaces the old template content with the new template settings and content and tries to match the content of editable areas based on their names. For example, the content of the "Middle Column" editable area in the old template will be transferred to the "Middle Column" editable area of the new template, assuming that such an area exists.

## Edit a Template-Based Page

The very nature of the connection between a page and the template on which it is based places some constraints on editing a template-based page. Only the portions of the page that are designated as editable in the template are accessible for editing in Design view. Everything else is locked.

Dreamweaver identifies the locked and editable portions of the page with color-coded outlines in the Design view window, as shown in Figure 9-2. The template area is marked with a yellow outline that extends around the entire perimeter of the Design View window and it's labeled with a tab in the upper-right corner that bears the name of the template. The template content is all locked except for the designated editable areas, which are marked with blue-green outlines and labeled with the name of the editable region in a tab in the upper-left corner. Similarly, repeating regions and the repeating rows of repeating tables are marked with lighter blue-green outlines.

TIP    *You can customize the colors Dreamweaver uses for the outlines marking locked and editable areas. The relevant settings are in the Highlighting category of the Preferences dialog box.*

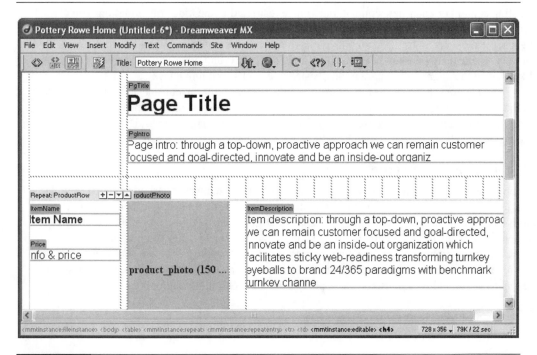

**FIGURE 9-2**    Colored outlines mark the locked and editable areas of a template-based page.

 As you move the mouse pointer over locked areas of the page, the pointer takes on the shape of the universal "do not" symbol to indicate that you can't select or edit content in that area. The pointer returns to normal in the editable regions, indicating that you can use normal editing techniques in those areas.

 *If the locked and editable region outlines don't appear in Design view, choose View |*
*Visual Aids | Invisible Elements to display Dreamweaver's clues to the existence of*
*elements that don't show up in the browser window.*

## Edit an Editable Region

The editable regions of a template-based page can be separate or enclosed within an optional region, a repeating region, or a repeating table. The extent of the editing you can do within an editable area depends on how that editable area is defined in the template. If the editable area includes only the text, image, or other content, without any surrounding tags, you can edit the existing content or enter new content, but you're restricted in the kinds of formatting you can apply to that content. On the other hand, if the editable area includes the surrounding paragraph tags, table cell tags, layers, and so on, you have much more freedom to manipulate the contents of the editable area. In addition to inserting and editing text and other content, you can do things like change the alignment of paragraphs, resize table cells, and move layers.

To edit a template-based document, you can simply click inside an editable area and then use any of the normal editing techniques to select, insert, delete, and modify the page content. To go directly to a specific editable region, choose Modify | Templates | *editable region name*. Dreamweaver selects the region and all its contents. To replace the contents with text, just start typing.

## Edit a Repeating Region

A repeating region enables you to select a block of content that was inherited from the template and make multiple copies of it on the template-based page. The repeating region may contain both locked content and editable regions. The editable regions within a repeating region are no different from any other editable region on a template-based page, and you edit them the same way. The only thing that is different about working with repeating regions is that you can expand the repeating region by adding copies of it to itself. You can add, delete, and move entries in a repeating region with the buttons that appear in the tab labeling the region.

Repeat: ProductRow    + − ▼ ▲

- To add another copy of a repeating region to the page, click the Add (+) button.
- To cut a repeating region entry from the page, click the editable portion of the entry and then click the Delete (−) button.
- To move a repeating region entry up or down, click the editable portion of the entry and then click the up or down arrow button.

You can also use menu commands to insert, delete, and rearrange entries in a repeating region. Choose Modify | Templates | Repeating Entries | *command*. The menus are a bit more cumbersome to use than the buttons on the repeating region tab, but they offer more options, such as the ability to insert a new entry before or after the current entry or at the beginning or end of the list.

TIP    *If the tabs for the editable regions in the table cells of a repeating table obscure the tab for the repeating table, thus making the buttons in the repeating table tab inaccessible, just use the menu commands to add, delete, and move entries in the repeating table.*

## Show or Hide an Optional Region

The main decision you need to make about an optional region is whether or not to show it on the template-based page. Here's how to define that property:

1. Choose Modify | Template Properties to open the Template Properties dialog box. The dialog box lists all the optional regions available in the template.

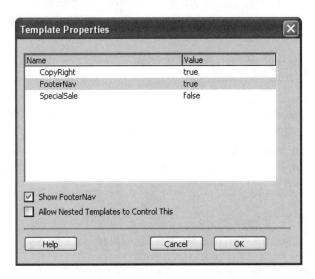

2. Select an optional region name from the list and click the Show... check box to change the selected region's status to show (true) or hide (false). Repeat as needed to show or hide other optional regions.

3. Click OK to close the dialog box and show or hide the content of optional regions from the template on the current page, according to the settings in the Template Properties dialog box.

Unlike other template regions, the content of an optional region isn't surrounded by a colored outline in Design view. If the optional region contains an editable region, the editable region is outlined, but there is no separate outline to mark the optional region. It's either visible on the page or it isn't. An optional region that is hidden is completely invisible in Design view and in the web browser—as if it doesn't exist.

# Update Template-Based Pages

One of the most powerful aspects of Dreamweaver's template feature is the program's ability to automatically update template-based pages throughout the site to reflect changes in the template. This means that you can make a change in one place—in the template file—and Dreamweaver automatically makes that change in all the web documents based on the template. You avoid the mind-numbing tedium of opening file after file and repeating the same edit on each one— Dreamweaver does the job for you, and does it faster and more accurately.

## Open a Template to Make Changes

When you need to edit a template, you can use one of the following techniques to open the template file. Regardless of the technique you choose, you end up with the template file open in a Dreamweaver Design view window.

- Double-click the template file's icon in the Site window. You'll find template files in the Template folder in the Local Files list.

- Click the Templates button in the Assets panel to display the list of templates in your site. Select the template you want to edit from the list in the Assets panel and click the Edit Template button.

- If you're working with a template-based page and you discover that you need to edit the template, you can just choose Modify | Templates | Open Attached Template to open the template on which the page is based.

## Edit a Template

Editing a template is a straightforward process. You can edit all the text, images, tables, and other page elements using any normal editing technique.

The editable regions of the template are clearly marked, but, unlike when you are editing template-based pages, no restrictions are imposed by the editable and locked regions of the template. Everything is fully editable on the template itself. You can edit the content of locked regions, repeating regions, and optional regions just as you can the content in editable regions. You can even change the various regions themselves.

Even though you can edit anything on the template page, you need to pay attention to whether or not your edits fall within an editable region because that determines how Dreamweaver updates template-based pages in your site.

If you edit a locked region (anything outside the editable regions), Dreamweaver offers to update all the web documents based on the template with the latest changes. If you edit the content of an editable region, Dreamweaver does *not* automatically copy the changes to any existing documents based on the template. The newly edited content will be copied to any new documents that you subsequently create based on the template, but editable content in existing pages isn't updated.

 *To make sure the current document is updated with the latest edits from the template, choose Modify | Templates | Update Current Page. To manually update all the pages in your site, choose Modify | Templates | Update Pages.*

## Disconnect a Page from a Template

When you're editing a template-based page, Dreamweaver won't let you make any changes to a locked region of the page. Normally, you must make the changes on the template and then update the template-based pages. However, there may be times when you need to change something in a locked region of one page without affecting all the other template-based pages in the site. To do so, you must first break the connection between the page and the template and thereby remove the lock on the previously locked regions.

To disconnect a document from its template, simply choose Modify | Templates | Detach from Template. The editable and locked region outlines disappear from Design view, and all areas of the page become editable. Any content or settings that the document inherited from the template remain, but the link to the template is broken. Of course, the trade-off is that once you break the link to the template, Dreamweaver can no longer update the page to reflect any changes in the template.

# Use the Repeating Elements Library

Dreamweaver includes another feature, Library items, that are similar to templates in some ways. You can use Library items to make it easy to reuse the same elements over and over on multiple pages throughout your site and to update them automatically. A Library item can consist of anything from a line of text to a major portion of your page design, such as a layout table or a complex image map.

As with a template, you create a Library item and save it in a separate file. Then you add the Library item to several different web pages. A Library item added to a web page is like a locked area of a template—you can't edit the Library content on the page unless you first disconnect it from the Library. If you need to make changes to the contents of a Library item, you make the changes just once, to the Library file, and Dreamweaver automatically updates all the web documents in your site that contain that Library item.

In this sense, a Library item is the same as a template. The difference is that Library items are used for small entities, such as a corporate logo and address text, a copyright notice (the information that normally appears at the bottom of each page), a set of buttons that you use together, or anything else that could change from time to time and would need to be updated across the site. Here are a few guidelines for choosing when to use Templates and when to use Library items.

- Use templates for standardizing page property settings and content that remain the same for all the pages in a site or in a section of a site.

- Use Library items for content that you use frequently throughout a site but don't want to place on the template because it doesn't appear on every page.

- Also use Library items for content that occurs in just a few locations in your site but needs to be updated frequently (for example, a weekly special or a news teaser).

- Use Library items or Snippets (see Chapter 5) for blocks of page content and code that you want to reuse in several locations in your site and don't expect to change.

- Use Snippets (not Library items) for blocks of page content and code that you want to reuse on several pages and need to edit slightly for each page.

- Don't bother creating a Library item for a single graphics file or other similar resources; that's what the Assets panel is for.

Library items appear in the Assets panel, and you can add them to your page with a couple of mouse clicks. Instead of being a simple listing of existing assets, such as the colors used in a site, Library items are something that you must define before you can use. You create and control Library items via the Assets panel.

## Create a Library Item

A Library item can be most anything you place on a web page—a paragraph of text, a table and its contents, an image and some accompanying text. The only limitation is that you must be able to select the Library item as a solid block without including any unwanted elements. So, for example, you could select the contents of a table cell and save it as a Library item, and you could select an entire table and all its contents, but you couldn't select a table and exclude its contents from the Library item.

To create a Library item, start with existing elements on a web page that you want to reuse on other pages. You can start with elements of an existing page or create a new page from scratch. To transform anything on a web page into a Library item, simply choose the Library category in the Assets panel; then select the page elements that you want to include in the Library item and drag the selection into the bottom of the Assets panel. Dreamweaver creates a new Library item called "Untitled" and highlights it. Type your own descriptive name and press ENTER. From here on in, anytime you want to add that Library item to a web page, all you have to do is to drag it from the Assets panel onto that page.

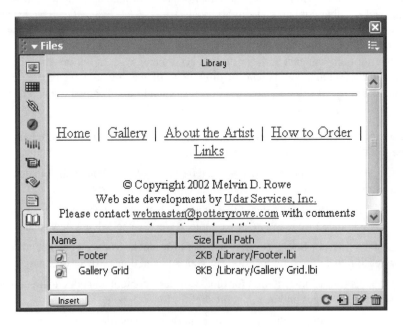

## Edit and Update a Library Item

To edit a Library item, select it and then click the Edit button at the bottom of the Assets panel. Dreamweaver opens the library item in its own document window, and you can work with it just as any web page. Then, when you save your changes (choose File | Save), Dreamweaver automatically applies the changes to every instance of the Library item throughout your site.

## Break the Connection to a Library Item

Dreamweaver prevents you from editing the contents of a Library item on the individual web pages where it is used. The library item is protected from local changes in order to preserve the ability to make changes to the master Library item in the Assets panel and have them automatically reflected in pages throughout the site. However, if you find it necessary to change the content of a library item on an individual page, you can do so.

Start by selecting the Library item, and then click the Detach from Original button in the Property Inspector panel. This action breaks the connection to the Library item file and transforms the former Library item content into plain, editable HTML code—just remember that Dreamweaver won't be able to perform automatic updates on the detached Library items when it updates other pages.

9

# Chapter 10

# Extend Dreamweaver's Capabilities

## How to...

- Add media files to your Dreamweaver documents
- Set parameters for media objects
- Use external editors for images and media objects
- Take advantage of close connections between Dreamweaver and Fireworks
- Enhance Dreamweaver with extensions

You can do a lot with creative combinations of text, images, and HTML code. But web designers are always looking for ways to enhance the visitor's web experience even further by incorporating into their web pages multimedia objects such as sound, movies, animations, and interactive features. Even though you can't edit media objects directly in Dreamweaver, the program makes it easy to insert them into your Dreamweaver documents. Then, when it's time to edit external files, whether they are images or other media objects, Dreamweaver gives you convenient access to your favorite media editor programs. For editing images, Dreamweaver offers especially tight integration with its Macromedia stablemate, Fireworks.

Just as you can use external media objects to enhance your web site and external editors to expand your file-editing capabilities, you can use Dreamweaver Extensions to enhance and extend Dreamweaver's features with customized commands and objects.

# Add Media Objects to Dreamweaver Documents

With the recent surge in popularity of digital video, MP3 audio, and web animation, more people than ever are incorporating some kind of media into their sites. Because there are so many different media formats and standards for displaying these objects in a browser, it can get very complicated trying to track down all the necessary code required to embed them into an HTML page. Dreamweaver, however, makes it easy to add these media components without doing any hand-coding. Adding sound, video, or other media objects is simply a matter of clicking a few buttons. Dreamweaver even allows you to edit some of the media file's playback parameters without ever leaving the program.

Remember, however, that you don't *create* sound, video, and other multimedia files using Dreamweaver. Instead, you create these files with *external media editors* and later *import* them into Dreamweaver. So, using such multimedia files involves either creating them in another application or using files created by someone else.

 *Most of the sounds, movies, and other multimedia files on the Web are copyrighted. Be sure any files you download from the Web for reuse on your site are not copyrighted and are intended for public use before you display them on your site. Otherwise, apply for reuse permission from the copyright holder.*

In Dreamweaver, you can work with five main kinds of external media objects: Flash, Shockwave, Java, ActiveX, and Netscape plug-ins. Each of these different file types has its own special button in the Media Category or the Insert bar that lets you add a component with just a mouse click. Even if you don't have the Macromedia Flash program, you can add Flash text and button treatments to your web pages using Dreamweaver's built-in Flash Text and Flash Button features.

Here's an overview of the media types Dreamweaver supports:

**Flash**    Macromedia Flash is a popular program for creating vector-based animations for display on the Web. Flash files (.swf) display within a browser with the help of the Flash plug-in, which is included with many browsers (though you'll still need to visit the Macromedia web site periodically to update the plug-in). Besides providing animation effects and interactivity, the big benefit of Flash is that it uses vector graphics. Often, vector graphics files are significantly smaller than similar bit-map graphics created in programs such as Photoshop or Fireworks. Moreover, Flash files can be scaled up or down in size without affecting the image quality. Since Flash is also a Macromedia product, it's especially easy to incorporate Flash files into Dreamweaver documents.

**Shockwave**    Shockwave is a compressed file format that allows you to deploy interactive multimedia files created with Macromedia Director. Shockwave uses bitmap graphics, so the file sizes are generally larger than those of Flash files, but Director allows much more complicated programming and interactive features. Like Flash, Shockwave files require a separate plug-in to display in a browser. The Shockwave plug-in is included as part of the default installation of recent versions of the popular browsers, and it's also available free from the Macromedia web site. Shockwave movies are normally a bit complicated to insert into raw HTML because Netscape and Internet Explorer (IE) browsers require different code. To code for both browsers, you need to include two different kinds of HTML tags and accompanying code. Fortunately, Dreamweaver takes care of all this behind the scenes, so inserting and editing Shockwave movies involves only a few clicks of the mouse.

**ActiveX Controls**    An ActiveX control is a kind of miniprogram that can function like a browser plug-in. However, ActiveX controls run only in Internet Explorer on Windows computers. Dreamweaver allows you to add ActiveX controls as well as access some of the properties of ActiveX objects through the Property Inspector.

**Java Applets**    Java applets are miniprograms created in the Java programming language that you can run on your web page. Java applets can run on any computer platform with Java Virtual machine software installed.

**Netscape Plug-Ins**    A long time ago, when Netscape Navigator was the dominant browser on the Web, Netscape invented a method of extending a browser's display capabilities with a plug-in architecture. Third-party companies could extend the capabilities of Netscape's browser by developing new plug-ins that conformed to the standard. Users then had only to download the new plug-in and install it to enjoy all sorts of new viewing possibilities with their browser. Today the generic plug-in standard developed by Netscape still exists and is used by other browser makers as well. In fact, Navigator plug-ins are used to provide playback capabilities for most media formats, including audio, video, 3D, and many others. Any format that uses the `<embed>` tag, employs a plug-in for browser display. The kind of media file you embed into your page determines which plug-in Dreamweaver and the visitor's browser will call upon to play or display the media file. Table 10-1 lists some of the more common media file formats and their corresponding plug-ins.

| Format | Plug-in | Description |
|---|---|---|
| .midi or .mid (Musical Instrument Digital Interface) | Windows Media Player (IE), Live Audio (Netscape), both built into the browser. | Instrumental-music-only format. Good sound quality (varies depending on the computer's sound card). Small file sizes. |
| .wav (Waveform Extension) | Windows Media Player (IE), LiveAudio (Netscape), both built into the browser. | One of the most common file formats for sound. Good sound quality but very large file size as sound-clip length increases. |
| .aiff, .aif (Audio Interchange File Format) | Windows Media Player (IE), Live Audio (Netscape), both built into the browser. | Similar to .wav. Good sound quality and large file size. |
| .mp3 (Motion Picture Experts Group Audio or MPEG-Audio Layer-3) | Windows Media Player (IE), QuickTime, Winamp, RealAudio (older computers may need to download plug-in) | Very high sound quality with relatively small file sizes. |
| .ra, .ram, .rpm (RealAudio) | RealAudio (requires plug-in) | High compression resulting in considerably smaller file sizes. Streaming technology allows sound to start playing before file is completely downloaded. Lower, but still acceptable sound quality. |
| .mov | QuickTime (standard on Macs, optional on Windows) | Popular format for video and audio content. Can be made to stream. |
| .mpg, .mpeg, .mpe (Motion Picture Experts Group video format) | Windows Media Player (older computers may need to download plug-in) | Compressed format keeps files smaller than noncompressed Quicktime and .avi movies while maintaining good quality. |
| .avi | QuickTime or Windows Media Player (older computers may need to download plug-in) | Older but still popular video format. |

**TABLE 10-1**    Common Audio and Video File Formats and the Browser Plug-ins Needed to Play Them

## Did you know?

## Dreamweaver Uses Plug-Ins, Too

Dreamweaver uses the same plug-ins to display files in the document window that your browser uses for display. In fact, when Dreamweaver first starts up, it searches your computer for all the installed plug-ins so that it can display the plug-in content when you click the Play button in the Property Inspector.

## Insert a Media Object

Inserting a media object into your Dreamweaver document is similar to inserting an image into your document. Like an image, the media content doesn't actually become part of the web page—the contents of the media file aren't copied into the document file. Instead, the HTML code for your web page contains a link to the media file and some attributes that tell the browser what to do with it. The browser downloads the media file along with the images and other page components and then calls on the appropriate plug-in to display the media object in the browser window. So the biggest difference between a media object and an image is that modern browsers don't need the help of a plug-in to display most images.

### Add a Media Object to Your Document

The procedure for inserting a media object into your Dreamweaver document is basically the same regardless of the type of media object you're working with. The following example describes the steps for inserting a Flash animation file:

1.  In Design view, place your cursor at the location on the page where you want the Flash movie to appear.

2.  Choose Insert | Media | Flash or click the Flash button in the Media category of the Insert bar. Dreamweaver opens the Select File dialog box.

3.  Locate and select the file you want to insert, then click OK to close the dialog box and add the Flash file to your document. Dreamweaver displays a placeholder icon on the page in Design view (see Figure 10-1). The icon is sized to the native dimensions of the Flash animation. (You can resize the Flash movie by typing in a new size in the height and width fields in the Property Inspector panel.)

**TIP** *You can resize a Flash object as you can an image—by dragging the sizing handles in Design view. Resizing doesn't affect the quality of most Flash animations.*

10

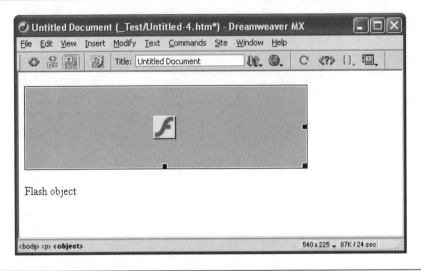

**FIGURE 10-1** Inserting a Flash object

4. Adjust the object's properties in the Property Inspector panel as needed. You can adjust any of the following:

- **Name** An optional name to identify the Flash object for use with scripting.
- **W** and **H** The width and height of the Flash movie.
- **File** The path to the Flash animation. You can also click the Browse button to locate the file.
- **Src** The path to the Flash source file that Flash MX can use to edit the animation. (Available only when both Flash MX and Dreamweaver MX are installed.)
- **Edit** Opens the Flash Text or the Button object dialog box or launches Flash (if available) to edit other Flash movies.
- **Reset Size** Resets the Flash object to its original size.
- **Loop** Replays the movie indefinitely.
- **Autoplay** Plays the movie automatically when the page loads.

- **V Space/H Space**   Specifies the amount of white space around the object as measured in pixels.
- **Quality**   Specifies the appearance quality of the Flash file. A higher setting looks better but requires a faster computer processor to render. There are four possible settings: Low sacrifices appearance to accommodate slower computers, whereas High favors appearance at a penalty for slower computers. Auto Low accommodates slower computers but will improve appearance when possible. Auto High accommodates any computer, if possible, but sacrifices appearance when necessary (when running on a slower computer).
- **Scale**   Defines how the movie displays within the parameters set for width and height.
- **Align**   Specifies the alignment of the movie within the page.
- **Bg**   Specifies the background color of the Flash movie.
- **Play/Stop**   Allows you to preview the Flash animation.
- **Parameters**   Opens a dialog box for entering additional custom parameters.

5. Press F12 or choose File | Preview in Browser | *browsername* to view the Flash movie in action.

This example shows how to insert a Flash animation into your document, but you can easily adapt the instructions to any media type by simply substituting the appropriate Insert bar button or Insert menu command in place of Flash. After you insert a media object into your document, Dreamweaver displays the object's properties in the Property Inspector panel. The properties for each media type vary, but those shown here for Flash animations are fairly typical.

## Play with Sounds

Adding sounds to a web page isn't a whole lot different from adding images. The main difference is that there are a lot more sound-file formats to deal with and several different methods for incorporating them into a page. Which format you decide to use and how you go about adding the sound depends on how you want the sound to be presented, who your audience is, the size and quality of the sound file, and, of course, old faithful: browser compatibility.

> **TIP** *To add a short sound bite to your page, use .wav or .aif files. They're the best-supported formats for web sounds. Most browsers can play these formats without an additional plug-in. Any good sound-editing application will allow you to save a sound file in .wav or .aif format. Just make sure you don't add any compression options when saving the files.*

Sound files tend to be large, and anything more than a few seconds of sound can take a very long time to download off the Web. To combat the long download times, longer sound samples, like whole songs, often use a technology called *streaming*, which allows them to play while they download. Streaming formats also incorporate very heavy compression in order to decrease file size. Streaming sounds usually requires special encoding software running on dedicated servers to deliver the sound files, as well as player plug-ins such as Real Player to play the sound in a browser. Shorter sound files, delivered as .wav or .midi files, can play natively within a browser, without extra plug-ins or dedicated servers.

## Link to an Audio File

The easiest way to add a sound to a web page is to simply create a hyperlink to the audio file. It's also the least obtrusive method because it allows your viewers to decide whether or not they want to listen to the file, rather than the sound playing automatically. (A site that plays a sound over and over when you visit the page, without providing the option to turn it off, can be downright annoying.) You can link to any of the sound formats listed in Table 10-1 by linking directly to the source file.

The process for creating the link is just like creating a link to an image or another web page. The result is a hyperlink between the linked text or image on the web page and the sound file. When the visitor clicks the link, the browser downloads and plays the sound file.

## Embed an Audio File

Embedding an audio file is useful when you want a sound to play automatically as background music or if you want to include a sound player (with play, stop, pause, and volume controls) directly on the page. To embed an audio file, you start by inserting a plug-in media object into your page. And when Dreamweaver gives you the opportunity to select a file, specify the sound file you want to insert. Dreamweaver (and the visitor's browser) will automatically use the appropriate plug-in for the sound file format, provided the plug-in is installed (see Figure 10-2).

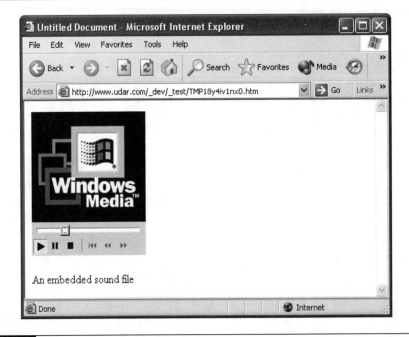

FIGURE 10-2    Sound file embedded in a web page

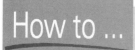 ... **Embed a Sound Without Displaying the Player Controls**

You can also embed a sound file into your web page without including visible player controls. Here's how:

1. Insert a sound file into your Dreamweaver document using the Plug-in media type.

2. In the Property Inspector, set the height and width of the plug-in object at 2 pixels. (Even though you want the controller to be invisible, some browsers require you to still set a visible height and width.)

3. Click the Parameters button to open the Parameters dialog box.

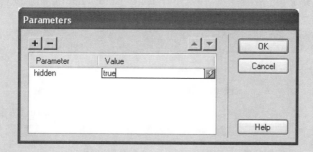

4. Click the Add (+) button to add a custom parameter.

5. Enter **hidden** in the Parameter column. Press TAB to go to the Value column, and enter **true.** The Hidden=True parameter means the player will remain hidden.

6. Click OK to close the Parameters dialog box.

When the page is viewed in a browser, the sound will now play without a visible audio controller—a perfect situation for including automatic background sound on your web page.

 *Use this technique with discretion! If you embed a sound in your page without any visible controls, the visitor will not have any convenient way to prevent or stop the sound playback—except by leaving your page.*

## Get Flashy Without Using Flash

Most of the Flash animations you see on the Web are created using Flash, a separate program. However, Dreamweaver has some Flash-creation capabilities too. With Dreamweaver you can create simple buttons and text objects to include in your web sites.

10

## Insert Flash Button Objects

Flash is a great application for creating animated movies, but if you don't have access to Flash, or your needs are too simple to justify the cost and steep learning curve of another program, you might get by with some of Dreamweaver's built-in Flash capabilities. Dreamweaver includes more than 40 professionally designed, customizable Flash buttons, allowing you to add Flash content to your pages without ever leaving Dreamweaver. Just like regular image buttons, a Flash button can include a link to other pages or media. Flash buttons share the advantages of other Flash objects in that the file sizes are very small, and you can resize the button without any loss of quality or increase in file size.

**1.** In Design view, place your cursor on the page at the place where you want the Flash button to appear.

**2.** Choose Insert | Interactive Images | Flash Button, or click the Flash Button icon in the Media category or the Insert bar. The Insert Flash Button dialog box appears.

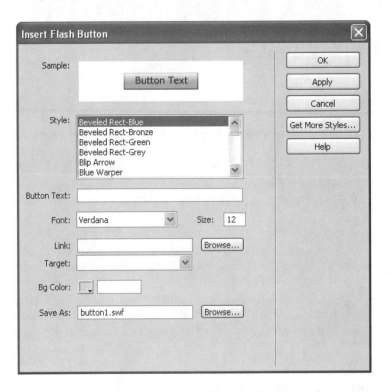

**3.** Use the up and down arrow keys to scroll through the different button styles in the Styles category; then select a style that you like. The selected style appears in the sample window, allowing you to preview it.

**TIP** *You can add more button styles by clicking the Get More Styles button in the Insert Flash Button dialog box. Clicking this button will launch your browser and take you to a section of the Macromedia site where you can download additional button styles.*

**4.** Enter the text for the button in the Button Text field. You can also customize the display font and font size in the corresponding fields.

**5.** Enter the path and filename for the file you want the button to link to. You can type it into the Link field or click the Browse button to open a dialog box, in which you can locate and select the file. Optionally, you can specify a target frame in the Target pull-down menu.

**6.** Apply a background color using the pop-up color picker in the Bg Color field. Usually you select the same background color as your web page so that the button blends in correctly.

**7.** Type a filename in the Save As box, or click the Browse button to open a dialog box where you can select a folder location and enter a filename for the file. Remember to save it in the same site folder as your current site.

**TIP** *If you use a consistent naming scheme for all your Flash buttons, they'll be easier to find and work with in your site. I like to preface all button filenames with btn_ as in btn_buttonname.swf.*

**8.** Click OK to close the Insert Flash Button dialog box. The button appears on the page in Design view (see Figure 10-3).

**FIGURE 10-3** Flash buttons can be scaled up or down without affecting image quality.

After you create a Flash button, you can resize it by simply selecting the button and dragging the sizing handle. Unlike GIF and JPEG images, the image quality of the Flash button doesn't suffer by being resized, so there's no need to reoptimize the button after changing its size. If you need to make other changes to the button, just double-click it to reopen the Insert Flash Button dialog box and edit any of the settings there.

## Insert Flash Text Objects

Dreamweaver's Flash text objects allow you to create simple text-only Flash objects using any font available on your system (not just standard web fonts). A Flash text object looks pretty much like a text graphic. Flash text can include a hyperlink to another file, and you can easily incorporate rollover effects so that the text changes color when the pointer passes over the text. Again, the benefits of Flash vector graphics also apply to text: you get smaller file sizes than with bitmapped images, and you have the ability to scale up or down without loss of image quality.

1. In Design view, place your cursor on the page in the place where you want the Flash text object to appear.

2. Choose Insert | Interactive Images | Flash Text, or click the Flash Text icon in the Media category of the Insert bar. The Insert Flash Text dialog box appears.

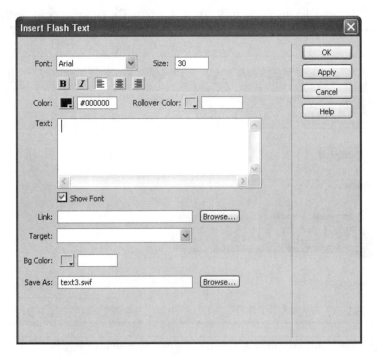

3. Select the font, type size, and other attributes in the appropriate fields. If you want the text to change color when a user rolls their mouse over it, select a different color in the Rollover Color field.

4. Enter the text in the large Text box. Check the Show Font option box to preview the text in the selected font and color.

5. Enter the path and filename for the file you want the button to link to. You can type it into the Link field or click the Browse button to open a dialog box in which you can locate and select the file. Optionally, you can specify a target frame in the Target pull-down menu.

6. Apply a background color using the pop-up color picker in the Bg Color field. Select the same color as your web page background if you want the text to blend in. If you select another color, it creates a rectangular box big enough to enclose the text.

7. Type a filename in the Save As box, or click the Browse button to open a dialog box where you can select a folder location, and enter a filename for the file. Once again, remember to save it in the same site folder as your current site. The Flash text object appears on the page in Design view.

# Work with External Editors

Designing and developing a web site is a multifaceted project that typically requires the web author to work with a variety of different programs. Even a program as powerful and versatile as Dreamweaver can't create and edit all the different image and media file formats that you deal with. However, switching from program to program can be a time-consuming drag.

Suppose you need to modify an image after placing it in your Dreamweaver document. If you haven't defined an external editor in Dreamweaver, you would need to note the filename of the image and then get out of Dreamweaver (either minimize or exit the program), open your image editing program, locate and open the file you want to modify, make the changes and resave the image, quit the image-editing program, reopen Dreamweaver, and reopen or refresh the document to view the updated image. That's a lot of steps to go through.

But suppose Dreamweaver knows what program you want to use to edit a given file type, such as the image we just mentioned. In that case, the workflow goes like this: You double-click the image in the Dreamweaver document. Dreamweaver automatically sends the necessary commands to launch the external editor and load the image file. You use the external editor to make the necessary changes and then resave the file. When you switch back to Dreamweaver, the updated image appears in the Document window.

Launching the external editor from within Dreamweaver doesn't enable you to do anything you couldn't do manually before. What it does do is automate some of the steps, thus making this oft-repeated process go faster and smoother, and that saves you time and hassle.

10

## Configure an External Editor for Media Objects

Most computer users are accustomed to being able to double-click a file icon on the desktop or in a file manager window (Windows Explorer or Mac Finder) and have the operating system launch the associated program and load the file for editing. Dreamweaver supports the same feature in the Site window file lists.

In addition, Dreamweaver maintains its own list of file types and the external programs you like to use to edit them. Dreamweaver's external editor list offers some advantages over your operating system's file type associations:

- Dreamweaver's external editors work when you double-click an object in Design view as well as in the Site window.

- You can associate multiple editors with a given file type and select the one you want to use from a Dreamweaver menu.

- Dreamweaver automatically updates the Design view display when you return to it after editing a file with an external editor launched from within Dreamweaver.

To associate a given file type with an external editor in Dreamweaver, you edit the File Types/Editors category in the Preferences dialog box. Here's how:

**1.** Choose Edit | Preferences to open the Preferences dialog box and select File Types/ Editors from the Category list.

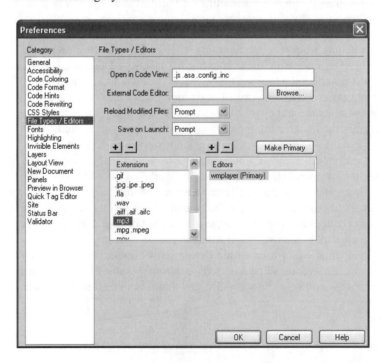

2. Select a file extension in the Extensions list box. If the file extension you want isn't in the list, click the + button above the Extensions list to add a blank line to the list and then type in the new file extension. The default editor for the selected file type appears in the Editors list. In some cases, more than one program may be listed.

3. Select the program you want to use as the main editor, and click the Make Primary button to make it the primary editor for the file type. If the desired editor doesn't appear in the Editors list, click the plus sign (+) above that list to open the Select External Editor dialog box. Use this dialog box to locate and select the application to associate with the file extension; then click the Open button to close the dialog box and add the program to the Editors list.

4. Repeat steps 2 and 3 as necessary to define your preferred editors for other file types.

## Launch an External Editor

After you define an external editor, using it to edit files from within Dreamweaver is a simple process. Here are the basic steps, as they apply to most external editors:

1. In the Dreamweaver Document window, select the image or other element that you want to edit with an external editor.

2. Use any of the following techniques to launch the external editor and instruct it to open the image or media file associated with the selected page element:

   ■ Click the Edit button in the Property Inspector panel. (If the Edit button isn't visible in the Property Inspector panel, click the arrow button in the lower-right corner to show the expanded options.)

   ■ Right-click the image and choose Edit With *Editorname* to use the primary editor.

   ■ Right-click the image and choose Edit With | *Editorname* to launch one of the secondary external editors instead of the designated primary editor.

3. Edit the file in the external editor and save the changes.

4. Switch back to Dreamweaver. The revised image appears in Design view.

# Use Fireworks from Within Dreamweaver

You can assign any program you might have in your graphic design arsenal as an external editor for a given file type. However, setting Macromedia Fireworks as the external editor for images is an obvious choice because of the strong symbiotic relationship between Dreamweaver and Fireworks.

NOTE    *If you install Fireworks MX along with Dreamweaver MX as part of the Macromedia Studio MX package, Fireworks is automatically configured as the primary external editor for images in Dreamweaver.*

## Launch Fireworks from Within Dreamweaver

When you use Fireworks as your external editor for image files, the process is basically the same as using any external editor. But Fireworks introduces a couple of wrinkles. Because you normally save a Fireworks document in one file and export to another file format to create a web graphic, Fireworks prompts you to identify the original Fireworks document for editing and re-export instead of simply opening the image file from the web document. Also, the Document window in Fireworks shows evidence of the tight integration with Dreamweaver with a prominent reminder that you are editing an image from Dreamweaver. Here's how it works when you use Fireworks as your external image editor:

1. In the Dreamweaver Document window, select the image you want to edit with Fireworks.

2. Click the Edit button in the Property Inspector panel, or use any of the other techniques described earlier for launching an external editor. As Fireworks opens, the Find Source dialog box appears (see Figure 10-4).

3. Click the Yes button if you want to open the existing Fireworks document (PNG file) that is the basis for the image you want to edit. Fireworks displays the Open dialog box. If there is no existing Fireworks document associated with the image, click the No button and skip the next step.

TIP        *If you don't want to see the Find Source dialog box each time you launch Fireworks, you can change the setting in the Fireworks Source Files list box at the bottom of the dialog box. Select Always Use Source PNG to go straight to the Open dialog box. Select Never Use Source PNG to skip both dialog boxes and open the web image in Fireworks.*

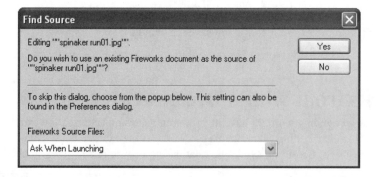

FIGURE 10-4    Find Source dialog box

**4.** Locate and select the Fireworks PNG file in the Open dialog box; then click the Open button to close the dialog box and open the document. The document to be edited appears in a Fireworks Document window.

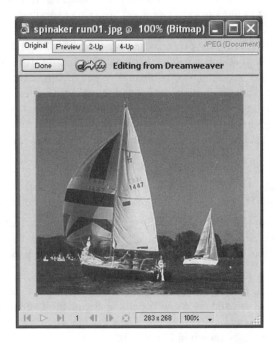

Note that the Fireworks Document window looks a little different. There is a Done button and a reminder immediately above the image that says Editing from Dreamweaver.

**5.** Edit the image in Fireworks.

**6.** After you complete your edits, click the Done button. Dreamweaver reappears immediately with the edited image updated in the Dreamweaver Document window.

## Optimize and Edit Images Within Dreamweaver

Nowhere is the symbiotic relationship between Dreamweaver and Fireworks more apparent than in the ability to access Fireworks' image-optimizing features from within Dreamweaver. With a single command, you can go directly to the Fireworks Optimize/Export Preview dialog box without even opening the full Fireworks program. There, you can optimize, crop, and resize the image quickly and efficiently and then get right back to Dreamweaver. It's almost as though the Optimize dialog box from Fireworks has been grafted onto the Dreamweaver program.

## Optimize Your Image

Web surfers are an impatient lot. They seem to enjoy the visual richness of sites with a lot of graphics, but they're not willing to wait very long for those images to load in a browser window. So, if you want the visitors to your site to have a good browsing experience, every image on your page must load as quickly as possible and deliver maximum impact.

Toward that end, it's essential that you *optimize* your image files. Optimizing an image means to create an image file that is as small as it can possibly be and still display the image with adequate quality. Smaller files require less download time and therefore reduce the time visitors have to wait for your page to appear in their browser. You optimize a file by experimenting with different file formats and settings in order to find a combination that produces the best compromise between file size and image quality.

To optimize an image that you have placed on a web page in Dreamweaver, follow these steps:

**1.** Select the image in the Dreamweaver Design view window.

**2.** Choose Commands | Optimize Image In Fireworks, or right-click the image and choose Optimize in Fireworks. The Find Source dialog box appears (see Figure 10-4).

**3.** Click the Yes button if you want to open the existing Fireworks document (PNG file) that is the basis for the image you want to edit. The Open dialog box appears. If there is no existing Fireworks document associated with the image, click the No button and skip the next step.

**4.** Locate and select the Fireworks PNG file in the Open dialog box, and then click the Open button to close the dialog box and open the document. Dreamweaver opens the Optimize dialog box (the same dialog box you see when you choose File | Export Preview in Fireworks), as shown in Figure 10-5.

**5.** Select a preset combination of file format and settings in the Saved Settings box located above the preview image. Here's a list of the default settings and what they mean:

- **GIF Web 216**   GIF format that forces all the colors in the image to change to the 216 web-safe colors.

- **GIF WebSnap 256**   GIF format that uses a 256-color palette and automatically converts all non-web-safe colors to the closest web-safe color.

- **GIF WebSnap 128**   Same as WebSnap 256, only this selection uses a palette of 128 colors.

- **GIF Adaptive 256**   GIF format that uses the actual colors present in the image for the color palette—up to 256 colors.

- **JPEG—Better Quality**   JPEG format with a quality setting of 80 and no smoothing. Produces a high-quality image with only minor file compression. The result is usually a larger file size than other JPEG settings.

- **JPEG—Smaller File**   JPEG format with a quality setting of 60 and smoothing of 2. Creates a significantly smaller file than the JPEG Better Quality setting. The image quality is impaired, however.

**FIGURE 10-5**   The Optimize dialog box

Note the status display above the preview image and to the left of the Saved Settings box. This area shows the key settings, the resulting file size, and an estimate of the download time for the image. Also note the visual effect of your settings on the preview image.

6. Further adjust the Format and other settings near the top of the Options tab. (When you select a file format in the Format box, the options below that box change to show the appropriate settings for the selected format.)

7. Repeat steps 5 and 6 as needed to produce the best-looking preview image with the smallest file size.

8. Click the Update button to close the Optimize dialog box. Dreamweaver/Fireworks automatically saves the file with your selected settings. The updated image appears in the Dreamweaver Design view window.

## Crop an Image

When you crop an image you remove superfluous material by trimming unwanted image area from the outer edges. The idea is to get rid of portions of an image that detract from the main subject matter by drawing attention away from the subject—for example, too much open space above a person's head.

The same dialog box you use to optimize images with Fireworks includes a Cropping tool (called Export Area) that you can use to crop an image from within Dreamweaver. Here's how:

1.  Follow steps 1–4 in the preceding instructions for optimizing an image. (Right-click the image and choose Optimize With Fireworks. Locate and select the Fireworks PNG file if appropriate.) The Optimize dialog box (see Figure 10-5) appears with the selected image displayed in the preview pane.

2.  Click the Export Area button below the preview image. A dashed rectangle with cropping handles (small boxes) at the corners and in the middle of each side appears surrounding the preview image.

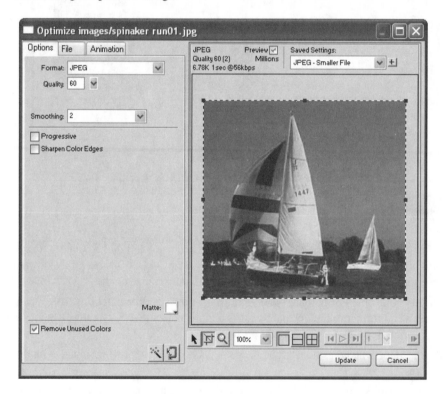

3. Drag the cropping handles toward the center of the image to reduce the image area. Adjust the various cropping handles to achieve the desired effect.

4. Click the Update button to close the Optimize dialog box. Dreamweaver/Fireworks automatically saves the file, without the superfluous area you cropped out. The updated image appears in the Dreamweaver Design view window.

**CAUTION**    *As you edit and optimize an image for the Web, make sure that you create a copy of the image and record all edits in the copy, not in the original image file. Cropping, resizing, and optimizing the image all discard image data that you may need if you ever reuse the image at a different size.*

## Resize an Image

Very often an image that you have scanned, shot with a digital camera, or acquired from another source is too large to fit into the designated space on your web page. Then you need to resize the image so that it fits on your page and doesn't take an inordinate amount of time to download to a browser.

**CAUTION**    *Resizing an image means that you change the dimensions of the picture—and you can use the resize tools to make an image larger as well as smaller. However, for bitmap images, you can only reduce the dimensions safely. You can't make a bitmap image larger without adversely affecting the quality.*

As with cropping an image, you can resize an image using the Optimize dialog box. Here's how you do it:

1. Select the image on your page in Dreamweaver's Design view window.

2. Resize the image to fit your layout using the sizing handles on the bottom and right edges of the selection box around the image (or type dimensions into the H and W boxes in the Property Inspector panel). (See Chapter 4 for more information on sizing an image.) This instructs the browser to enlarge or reduce the image display to fit certain dimensions; it doesn't affect the actual size of the image recorded in the image file. Note the height and width measurements shown in the Property Inspector panel.

3. Follow steps 2–4 in the preceding instructions for optimizing an image. (Right-click the image and choose Optimize With Fireworks. Locate and select the Fireworks PNG file if appropriate.) The Optimize dialog box (see Figure 10-5) appears with the selected image displayed in the preview pane.

10

**4.** Click the File tab and check the image dimensions shown in the Scale area. Confirm that they match the desired image dimensions you noted in step 2. If the dimensions don't match, enter the desired dimensions in the W and H boxes.

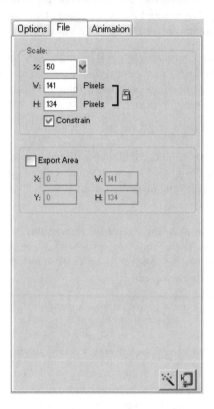

**5.** Click the Update button to close the Optimize dialog box. Dreamweaver/Fireworks automatically saves the file, reduced to the new dimensions. The updated image appears in the Dreamweaver Design view window.

*For best results when performing multiple operations on an image, first crop, then resize, and finally optimize. Working in this sequence ensures the best quality by maintaining maximum image information in preliminary steps.*

## Create Graphic Effects with Fireworks

In addition to the tight integration with Dreamweaver for optimizing images, Fireworks offers some special features and tools designed specifically for creating web graphics. In contrast to the image-optimization process, in which you start with an image in Dreamweaver and turn to Fireworks to alter that image, you create these web graphics in Fireworks, save them, and then place the resulting graphics onto your web page in Dreamweaver.

One of the cool features of Fireworks is its ability to produce the multiple image files and the HTML code required to implement effects such as buttons with rollover effects. You design the base button graphic and the variations for the different button states in a single Fireworks document, and then export a collection of separate image files plus the (automatically generated) HTML code needed to implement the effect. Fireworks can create both images and HTML code for effects such as rollover buttons, navigation bars, sliced images, image maps, and pop-up menus. The HTML code contains references to all the image files related to the effect, tables to assemble multipart images, JavaScript script code for rollover effects, and so on.

## Work with Fireworks HTML in Dreamweaver

The tight integration between Dreamweaver and Fireworks shows in Dreamweaver's ability to import the images and HTML code generated by Fireworks and incorporate everything into your web page in one operation. Without the Fireworks HTML code, you would have to recreate the effect by writing the code or rebuild the effect using Dreamweaver Behaviors. Since the code usually contains scripts, integrating it into your Dreamweaver documents isn't as simple as cutting and pasting a few HTML tags into Code view. The code for the tables containing sliced images can be quite complex, and blocks of JavaScript code often need to be inserted into the document header.

Fortunately, Dreamweaver includes an intelligent import feature for Fireworks HTML code that takes care of all the details for you. Here's how it works:

**10**

1. Open your Dreamweaver document and position the insertion point at the location where you want to insert the Fireworks button, pop-up menu, sliced image, or whatever.

2. Choose Insert | Interactive Images | Fireworks HTML. The Insert Fireworks HTML dialog box appears.

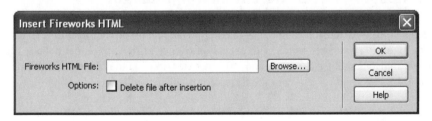

3. Enter the path and filename of the Fireworks HTML file, or click the Browse button to open the Select Fireworks HTML File dialog box (a standard File Open dialog box), where you can locate and select the file.

**NOTE**   *Check the Delete File After Insertion option to have Dreamweaver automatically delete the Fireworks HTML file after inserting its contents into your document's source code.*

**4.** Click the OK button to close the dialog box. Dreamweaver reads the Fireworks HTML file and automatically inserts the code into the appropriate locations in your document's source code. The Fireworks-created button (or other graphic) appears in the Design view window.

# Add Features to Dreamweaver with Extensions

Extensions are objects, commands, Behaviors, and so on that have been created by Macromedia and by other Dreamweaver users to automate certain tasks. There is a lively exchange of these extensions on the Macromedia web site and elsewhere.

## Where to Find Extensions

Macromedia set aside a special section of its web site, called Macromedia Exchange, as a clearinghouse where Dreamweaver users can go to find and download extensions. At Macromedia Exchange, you can view lists of extensions for Dreamweaver and other Macromedia programs, check out descriptions of the extensions, and download extensions that you want to try.

The Dreamweaver section of Macromedia Exchange is located at http://www.macromedia.com/exchange/dreamweaver/. You can also go to Macromedia Exchange from within Dreamweaver by choosing Commands | Get More Commands or Help | Dreamweaver Exchange. If you're working in the Behaviors panel, clicking the + button and choosing Get More Behaviors from the menu that appears has the same effect.

At the Macromedia Exchange web site, you can browse through the ever-expanding list of available extensions for Dreamweaver, sorted into various categories. Click an extension name to drill down to the detail page with a description of the extension and its function. Then, with a click of your mouse, you can download the extension file and save it in a convenient location on your system. (If you haven't already registered at the Macromedia web site, you'll need to do so before downloading extensions.)

## Install Extensions with the Extension Manager

Installing extensions in previous versions of Dreamweaver could be a chore, but Dreamweaver MX includes a utility—Extension Manager—that automates the process of installing extensions. Macromedia Extension Manager works with extension package files (.mxp) that contain all the files you need to install and use the extension. All the extensions on the Macromedia Exchange web site are in MXP format for use with the Extension Manager utility.

NOTE
*Depending on your browser, you may have the option of opening the extension package file from its web location without downloading it first. If you choose to go this route, the Extension Manager application opens automatically to install the extension. Although this direct-install method works, I can't recommend it unless you enjoy an exceptionally fast and reliable Internet connection. Even then, you sacrifice the convenience of having the .mxp file available to reinstall.*

After you download an extension, follow these steps to install it with Extension Manager:

**1.** Launch the Extension Manager utility: choose Start | Programs | Macromedia | Macromedia Extension Manager. The Macromedia Extension Manager window opens.

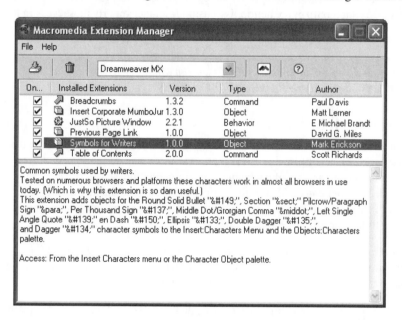

**2.** Select Dreamweaver MX from the list box in the Extension Manager toolbar.

**3.** Choose File | Install Extension, or click the Install New Extension button in the toolbar. The Select Extension to Install dialog box appears ( a standard File Open dialog box).

**4.** Locate and select the MXP extension file you want to install.

**5.** Click Install to close the Select Extension to Install dialog box and start the installation process. The Extension Manager may display one or more message boxes asking you to accept license terms and/or confirm file replacements. Macromedia Extension Manager displays a message after it successfully installs the extension and adds the extension to the list in the Extension Manager window.

> **NOTE** *Depending on the extension, you may need to shut down and then restart Dreamweaver to make the extension functional.*

When you select an extension in the Installed Extensions list in the Extension Manager window, a description of the extension appears in the bottom half of the window. The description text for some extensions is pretty skimpy, but you will almost always see a short description of the extension and information on where to find it in Dreamweaver (on the Command menu, in a certain category of the Insert bar, or whatever). Some extension authors display helpful instructions on how to use the extension in this space.

If you decide that you want to remove an extension from Dreamweaver, simply select the extension name in the Extension Manager window and click the Remove Extension button in the toolbar. Click Yes to confirm the action. Extension Manager reports its success in another message box.

 *You can disable an extension without removing it by simply clearing the check box beside the extension name in the Extension Manager window. Click the check box again to reenable the extension.*

## List of Popular Extensions

There are a lot of extensions available on the Macromedia Exchange web site (more than 500 at the time of this writing). The following list is a rather capricious and random sampling of what's available. It's not intended as an endorsement or recommendation of specific extensions. Instead, this list is intended to give you an idea of the variety of extensions that are available and to encourage you to check Macromedia Exchange for extensions that might make your work with Dreamweaver a little faster and/or easier.

 *Not all the extensions available on Macromedia Exchange are compatible with Dreamweaver MX. Some extensions only work with previous versions of the program. As time goes by, more and more extensions will be updated to support Dreamweaver MX.*

- **Add to Favorites Extension**    A Behavior that enables visitors to automatically add your page to their Internet Explorer Favorites list.

- **Alternate Table Rows Extension**    Formats a table with rows of alternating colors.

- **Button Rollover Extension**    Creates and applies CSS styles to convert normal text links into buttons, complete with rollover effects.

- **Calculate Form Extension**    A Behavior that enables you to perform calculations using the contents of form fields and display the results.

- **Check Spelling on Save Extension**    Automatically runs the spell checker before saving your document.

- **Form Builder Extension**    An assortment of prebuilt pop-up menus for use in forms. Menus include marital status, age group, date of birth, education, occupation, and so on.

- **Insert Corporate MumboJumbo Extension**    Inserts dummy text into your document for use on mock-up pages. The text reads like notes from a corporate board meeting full of the latest buzzwords. Very funny!

- **JustSo Picture Window Extension**    Creates a pop-up image window for displaying a higher resolution version of an image. The pop-up browser window is automatically sized to the image.

- **Layer Transitions Extension**   A collection of preconstructed transition effects for moving layers on or off the page.

- **News Ticker Extension**   Creates a news ticker or marquee to display scrolling text from an external text file.

- **Super Countries Extension**   Inserts pop-up menus into forms preloaded with values such as a list of countries or U.S. states.

- **Symbols for Writers Extension**   Adds buttons for a bunch of extra symbols (such as the en dash (–), ellipsis (…), and (¶) to the Characters pane of the Objects panel.

- **Table of Contents Extension**   Automatically creates a table of contents linked to either anchors or heading paragraphs in the page.

- **Word Count Extension**   Finds out how many words are on the current web page, excluding the HTML code.

# Part IV

# Expanding Your Horizons

# Chapter 11

## Create and Use Style Sheets

## How to...

- Create Cascading Style Sheets
- Link to an external style sheet
- Reformat an entire site using Cascading Style Sheets
- Convert Cascading Style Sheets to HTML tags
- Set CSS Style Preferences

If you've spent any time trying to control the look and layout of text in a web document, you've no doubt been frustrated by the lack of precision layout capabilities provided by HTML tags. *Cascading Style Sheets* (CSS) address the shortcomings of HTML design by giving web designers much greater control over the look of their pages.

With standard HTML, the only way to control the font and formatting characteristics of text is through limited `<font>` tag attributes or equally limited formatting tag elements such as bold (`<b>` or `<strong>`) and italic (`<i>` or `<em>`). These attributes and elements provide some means of control over font faces and font style, but they have little ability to control size and positioning. Similarly, table formatting is limited to `<table>` or row/cell tag attributes. Changing the appearance of a site becomes a time-consuming, cumbersome project, as each tag attribute and element must be modified individually.

Cascading Style Sheets are a kind of "extended HTML" that provide a way to control the appearance of a site much more precisely. They enable you to apply formatting changes to an individual page, multiple pages, or even to an entire site simply by changing the definitions in a single *style sheet*—which is just a set of CSS styles. Besides providing text formatting and layout control, CSS provides a way to specify and control such features as layer positioning, special effects, and mouse rollovers. However, this chapter concentrates on using CSS to provide advanced text formatting.

Despite the obvious advantages of CSS, web designers have been slow to embrace style sheets. That's undoubtedly because, until recently, browsers offered incomplete and inconsistent support for CSS. Now that the current versions of the major browsers have greatly improved CSS support, many developers are finally starting to enjoy the benefits of style sheets.

Although CSS is fairly simple to learn, the syntax and rules involved in coding CSS differ from those of HTML coding. Fortunately, Dreamweaver provides a simple and intuitive interface for accessing and implementing virtually all the powerful text-formatting features of CSS without having to master this syntax.

# What Are Cascading Style Sheets?

CSS allows you to define new rules that affect how a browser renders HTML tags. These rules define how the browser displays text or how it interprets HTML tags, even to the point of overriding the normal rules of HTML. Each time you create a style sheet using CSS, you can define a new set of rules, and the document that uses the style sheet knows which rules to follow because you've instructed it to do so. You can embed these instructions within individual HTML tags, add them to the page as part of the `<header>` tag, or save the style sheet instructions in an external file (called an *external style sheet*) that can be linked to one or more web documents. Using CSS, you can specify font sizes based on absolute measurements such as pixels, points, picas, inches, millimeters, and more. You can also set line heights, font weights, and upper- or lowercase letters, to name a few customizable options.

## The CSS Styles Panel

The CSS Styles panel (see Figure 11-1) is your main access point for creating and editing style sheets in Dreamweaver. To open the CSS Styles panel, choose Window I CSS Styles or press SHIFT-F11.

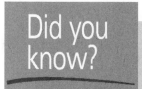

## The Difference Between HTML Styles and CSS Styles

Dreamweaver includes another kind of style—HTML styles, which are covered in Chapter 3. Like CSS styles, HTML styles provide a way to control text attributes in Dreamweaver. However, HTML styles are very different from CSS styles.

- HTML styles are a shortcut for applying a group of normal HTML text attributes all at once. They are limited to the standard HTML text attributes, such as `fontface`, `color`, `bold`, `italic`, and so on. CSS styles give you far greater control over the formatting and layout of type, plus control over layers and other new web document features.

- HTML styles work only in Dreamweaver. The effects of applying an HTML style are viewable in any web browser, but the styles themselves are available only when you are working on a site in Dreamweaver. CSS styles, in contrast, are an industrywide standard that is independent of Dreamweaver. CSS style sheets that you create in Dreamweaver can be used and edited by other applications or HTML editors.

- Modifying an HTML style affects only subsequent applications of that style. Modifying a CSS style affects all instances where that style is used throughout the document or site. When you change CSS attributes, the change is automatically reflected in all text or pages that utilize the CSS rules.

- HTML styles are compatible with all commonly used browser versions. The use of CSS styles requires newer browser versions.

11

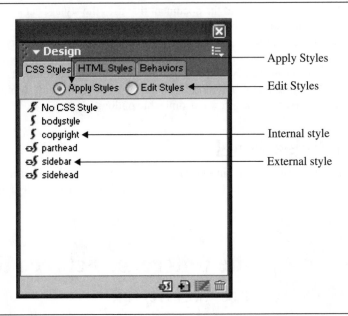

**FIGURE 11-1**    The CSS styles panel

The CSS Styles panel lists any styles currently associated with the document. There are also four commands that enable you to create new style sheets, attach external style sheets, and edit and delete existing style sheets. These commands are displayed as buttons in the lower-right corner of the panel and are also accessible in the pop-up menu that appears when you click the menu button in the upper-right corner of the panel or right-click within the panel.

The Edit Styles button at the top of the panel changes the CSS Styles panel to list every style accessible from the current page, including both internal and external styles, as shown in Figure 11-2. (Internal and external styles are covered later in this chapter.) This view shows which style sheets are associated with each style and also shows the style's attributes.

# Using the Property Inspector with CSS Styles

Dreamweaver MX not only allows you to create and set styles using the CSS Styles panel, it also enables CSS Styles in the Property Inspector. Accessing these features requires changing the Property

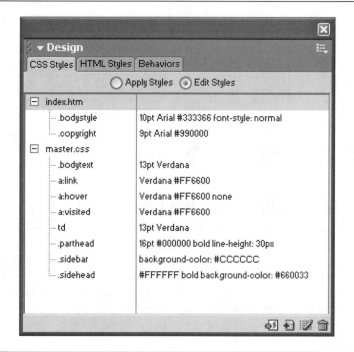

**Design**

CSS Styles | HTML Styles | Behaviors

○ Apply Styles  ● Edit Styles

| ⊟ index.htm | |
| --- | --- |
| .bodystyle | 10pt Arial #333366 font-style: normal |
| .copyright | 9pt Arial #990000 |
| ⊟ master.css | |
| .bodytext | 13pt Verdana |
| a:link | Verdana #FF6600 |
| a:hover | Verdana #FF6600 none |
| a:visited | Verdana #FF6600 |
| td | 13pt Verdana |
| .parthead | 16pt #000000 bold line-height: 30px |
| .sidebar | background-color: #CCCCCC |
| .sidehead | #FFFFFF bold background-color: #660033 |

**FIGURE 11-2**     The Edit Styles view of the CSS Styles panel

11

Inspector to CSS Mode using the Toggle CSS/HTML Mode button, as shown in Figure 11-3. (In the default HTML formatting mode, the button appears as the letter A.)

The Property Inspector's CSS mode operates in much the same way as the CSS Styles panel, and you can use the two interchangeably to apply styles. You can also create and edit styles from the Property Inspector. You'll notice that most of the HTML-based formatting options are removed from the Property Inspector in CSS mode, since the use of CSS implies you'll be using style sheets more or less exclusively for formatting. If you need these formatting options, click the Toggle CSS/HTML Mode button.

NOTE

*In most cases, you'll probably find yourself using the CSS Styles panel to create and maintain style sheets, leaving the Property Inspector for quickly applying styles to selected text.*

Toggle CSS/HTML Mode

FIGURE 11-3    The Property Inspector in CSS mode

# Create a CSS Style Sheet in Dreamweaver

You can create two different kinds of CSS style sheets: internal style sheets and external style sheets. An *internal style sheet* is a collection of styles embedded in the code of the existing web document. *External style sheets* reside in an external file that can be referenced much as you reference another HTML page using a hypertext link. If your site is small and there are style differences between pages, you'll probably want to use internal style sheets for each page. If, however, you're trying to create a consistent appearance for your entire site, you can create an external style sheet and apply it to multiple pages (or even multiple sites), thus simplifying the formatting of those pages considerably.

In each type of style sheet you can also create three different and distinct kinds of styles:

- Custom styles
- Redefined HTML tag styles
- CSS Selector styles

To work with CSS styles, you first need to open the CSS Styles panel (see Figure 11-1) or the CSS Mode of the Property Inspector (see Figure 11-3). You can define styles for your document or site in either place.

## Create a Custom Style

Custom CSS styles are what people usually think of when they imagine a style sheet. If you've worked with Dreamweaver's HTML styles, the concept is similar, but the capabilities of Custom CSS styles are far greater than those of HTML styles. With a custom style, you can create and modify a diverse set of attributes and apply them to any text selection on your page.

For example, you might create a custom style to use for the top-level headings in a document that makes them 14-point Verdana, bold, and blue. Then, whenever you want to apply that style, you just highlight some text and apply that heading style. If later you decide to change the color to red, just change the custom style, and all the top-level headings in your document automatically change to reflect the updated style specification.

In CSS parlance a custom style is referred to as a *class*. This term refers to a collection of CSS *rule declarations* (a list of formatting specifications) that you create and save—either in your existing document or in an external file. When you name a custom style, you can use pretty much any name you want, as long as it begins with a period. To create a custom style, follow these steps:

1. Open the New CSS Style dialog box, shown in Figure 11-4:
   - ■ Click the New CSS Style button in the CSS Styles panel.
   - ■ In the CSS mode of the Property Inspector, select New CSS Style from the CSS Style drop-down menu.
   - ■ From the menu, select Text | CSS Styles | New CSS Style.

2. Select the Make Custom Style (Class) radio button.

3. Enter a name for your style in the Name box. All class styles begin with a period, such as .bodytext or .copyright. If you forget to type the period yourself, Dreamweaver will add it for you.

*When naming custom style classes, avoid using names that are used by HTML tags, such as "head," "body," "title," and so forth. If you want to use those names to jog your memory as to the purpose of a custom style, use it combined with another term, such as ".mytitle."*

4. Select the This Document Only radio button. This saves your style information in an internal style sheet in the current web document. (For information on saving external styles, see "Create an External Style Sheet," later in this chapter.)

5. Click the OK button to open the CSS Style Definition dialog box, shown in Figure 11-5. This is where you define the actual attributes for your new style.

11

**FIGURE 11-4**   New CSS Style dialog box

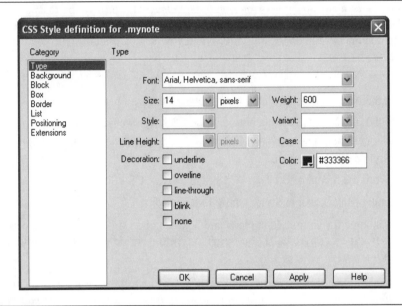

FIGURE 11-5 CSS Style Definition dialog box

6. Click Type in the Category list. Adjust the Type settings in the CSS Style Definition dialog box to define the text formatting attributes for your style:

■ Enter the name of the font you want to use for your style, or select one from the Font pop-up menu.

■ Enter a font size in the Size box, and select a measurement in the pop-up menu to the right of the Size box.

*Many designers like to use points to specify text size with CSS because points provide the most consistent size appearance across computer platforms. This is one of the more compelling reasons to use CSS.*

■ Select other options and attributes using the fields in the CSS Style Definition dialog box. Click Help for descriptions of each field and the available attributes.

7. Click OK to close the CSS Style Definition dialog box and finish creating your style. Dreamweaver adds the style definition to the internal style sheet for your document and also adds the style name to the list of styles shown in the CSS Styles panel and the drop-down list of CSS styles in the Property Inspector panel.

*Support for Cascading Style Sheets varies from browser to browser, particularly with older versions. Some of the attributes in the Style Definitions dialog box are not supported by all browsers. Always preview your styles in different browsers to assure the attributes you specify will display properly.*

The preceding steps describe how to create a style that controls text attributes. However, you can also create custom styles for any other category listed in the Style Definition dialog box; see Table 11-1.

## Apply Your Style

After you create a style, applying it to text in your document is easy. Here's how:

1. Make sure the CSS Styles panel is visible by choosing Window | CSS Styles. If you're using the Property Inspector, toggle the CSS/HTML Mode button to display CSS mode.

2. Select the text to which you want to apply the style. You can highlight a block of text in the Document window, or you can simply click anywhere within a paragraph or table cell to apply the style to the whole paragraph or cell.

3. Click the style you want to apply in the CSS Styles panel. Dreamweaver applies the new style to the current selection or, if no text is selected, to the entire paragraph.

**TIP**   *To remove CSS formatting from a text selection, choose the No CSS Style option from the CSS Styles list in either the panel or the Property Inspector.*

**11**

| Category | Description |
|---|---|
| Type | Allows you to specify text formatting attributes such as font, size, and weight. |
| Background | Allows you to specify background images or colors within a style. |
| Block | Allows you to alter options such as word or letter spacing, and alignment and justification of paragraphs. |
| Box | Allows you to use CSS to alter spacing around elements (such as images) in much the same way that tables do. |
| Border | Allows you to control the characteristics of border elements around objects, including text, images, and other media objects. |
| List | Gives you control over bullet points for lists, allowing you to customize the bullet or even substitute your own graphic in place of a standard bullet. |
| Positioning | Gives you exact control over positioning of elements on the page using a variety of measurement systems. |
| Extensions | Includes advanced-level CSS options such as defining page breaks, specifying a custom cursor, and enabling special effects with filters. |

**TABLE 11-1**   Style Categories Available with CSS

## Redefine HTML Tags

In addition to defining custom styles from scratch, CSS enables you to redefine the attributes of the standard HTML tags. Redefined HTML tag styles allow you to change the way existing HTML tags are rendered by the viewer's browser. This feature can be very useful for making quick, global changes to a page or a web site. For example, when you apply the bold attribute to text by clicking the Bold button in the Property Inspector, Dreamweaver marks the text with the `<strong>` tag, which instructs the browser to render text in boldface. However, by using redefined HTML tag styles, you could specify additional attributes for the `<strong>` tag, and all text marked with the `<strong>` tag would take on the new attributes. For example, you could redefine the `<strong>` tag such that any text marked with that tag displays in red as well as boldface.

To create a Redefined HTML tag style, follow these steps:

1.  Open the New CSS Style dialog box, shown in Figure 11-4:
    - Click the New Style button in the CSS Styles panel.
    - In the CSS mode of the Property Inspector, select New CSS Style from the CSS Style drop-down menu.
    - From the menu, select Text | CSS Styles | New CSS Style.

2.  Select the Redefine HTML Tag radio button.

3.  Select an HTML tag to redefine from the Tag list box. The list shows all the available HTML tags without the angle brackets that normally surround them.

4.  Select the This Document Only radio button. This saves your style information in the internal style sheet for the current HTML document.

5.  Click the OK button to open the CSS Style Definition dialog box, shown in Figure 11-5, where you define the attributes for your new style.

6.  Click Type in the Category list. Then adjust the Type settings in the Style Definition dialog box to define the text formatting attributes for your style:
    - Enter the name of the font you want to use for your style, or select one from the Font pop-up menu.
    - Enter a font size in the Size box, and select a measurement in the pop-up menu to the right of the Size box.
    - Select other options and attributes using the fields in the Style Definition dialog box. Click Help for descriptions of each field and the available attributes.

7.  Click OK to close the Style Definition dialog box and finish creating your style. Dreamweaver adds the style definition to the internal style sheet for your document.

No further steps are necessary to apply the style; it will automatically apply to any text currently surrounded by the HTML tag you have redefined.

## Modify a CSS Selector

In a way, CSS Selector styles combine both custom styles and redefined HTML tag styles. With CSS Selector styles (also called *pseudoclasses*) you can change the attributes of the <a>, or anchor tag, used to create a hypertext link. This feature allows you to change how links appear in a browser and how they react when the mouse hovers over them or when the user has already visited the link.

To create CSS Selector styles to control link colors and rollover colors follow these steps:

1. Open the New CSS Styles dialog box, shown in Figure 11-4.

2. Select the Use CSS Selector radio button.

3. Select a click state from the Selector list box. For example, select "a:active" to set the appearance attributes for active links. These are the available states:

   - **a:active**   The way the link appears when the user clicks it
   - **a:hover**   The way the link appears when the pointer is hovering over it
   - **a:link**   The way the link appears normally
   - **a:visited**   The way the link appears after the user has visited it

4. Select the This Document Only radio button to save the style in the document's internal style sheet.

5. Click the OK button to open the CSS Style Definition dialog box, shown in Figure 11-5, where you define the formatting attributes for your link.

6. Click the Type category and enter the text attributes for the link text. Remember that you're setting the way a link should appear in a particular state—active, hover, normal, or visited. Usually you'll want to select different colors for each state.

7. Click OK to close the New Style dialog box and apply the style.

This procedure defines the attributes for one state of the <a> tag. Repeat the steps to create style definitions for the remaining link states, to complete the effect.

## Selector Styles Are the Most Common CSS Styles

CSS Selector styles for the <a> tag are one of the most commonly used CSS implementations on the Web, since they allow you to create text rollover effects without using JavaScript or creating extra images. Large web sites such as Microsoft's and others make common use of this CSS feature.

 *The CSS Selector styles applied to the <a> tag do not display in older browsers. Internet Explorer 4 and later or Netscape Navigator 6 and later are required to view them properly.*

# Create an External Style Sheet

The CSS style definition procedures covered earlier in this chapter describe how to create an internal style sheet that is saved within the current web document. But you can also save styles in an external style sheet. An external style sheet differs from an internal one only in that the code used to define the styles is saved as a separate text file instead of within the current document.

Saving style information this way provides one of the most powerful and compelling reasons to use Cascading Style Sheets: you can link to the external file from multiple pages, rather than having to include the style information on each page. This feature allows you to apply consistent styles to an entire site and update the entire site simply by making a few changes to the external style sheet. Many large web sites—such as Yahoo!, CNN, and Microsoft—use external style sheets to achieve consistent styling and formatting throughout their sites.

One of the easiest ways to create an external style sheet is to simply select the external style sheet option when you create a new style. Here's how:

1.  Open the New CSS Style dialog box, shown in Figure 11-4.

2.  Select the appropriate type of style: Custom Style, Redefine HTML Tag, or CSS Selector.

3.  Instead of selecting the This Document Only radio button, click the radio button next to Define In, and then choose New Style Sheet File in the list box. Then click OK to open the Save Style Sheet File As dialog box.

4. Locate the folder where your want to save your new style sheet file, and enter a name for the file. Dreamweaver automatically adds the extension .css to the end of the name when you enter it. Click Save to close that dialog box and open the CSS Style Definition dialog box, shown in Figure 11-5.

*A .css file is a text file containing all the style sheet information.*

5. Set the attributes for your new style in the CSS Style Definition dialog box. Then click OK to close the dialog box and create the style. Dreamweaver saves the style definition in the external style sheet file instead of embedding it in the header of the current document.

This procedure creates an external style sheet consisting of a single style and automatically links that style sheet to the current document. You can also use the same basic technique to add a style to the collection in an external style sheet. First make sure the external style sheet is linked to the current document (see the next section) and then follow steps 1 and 2 above. In step 3, select the linked style sheet name in the Define In list. Skip step 4 and then complete the style definition as instructed in step 5.

*You must save the external CSS style sheet in a location that is accessible via the Web if you expect visitor's web browsers to use it to display pages.*

## Link to an External Style Sheet

Since an external style sheet is a separate file, you need to create a link between your web document and the external style sheet to apply the formatting specified in the external .css file to the current document. When a browser accesses a web document that references an external style sheet, the browser retrieves the information from that style sheet to correctly render the page. The style sheet information can reside on the same server as the web document or anywhere else on the Web.

To link the current web document to an external style sheet, follow these steps:

 1. In the CSS Styles panel, click the Attach Style Sheet button in the lower-right corner of the panel. This opens the Link External Style Sheet dialog box.

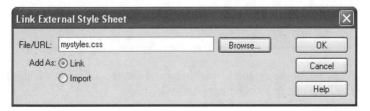

2. Locate an existing style sheet (.css), or enter an external URL if the style sheet resides somewhere on the Internet.

3. Choose Link to establish a link between the current document and the external style sheet.

4. Click OK to close the dialog box and finish attaching the style sheet.

11

*You can also use this option to import the styles from the external style sheet into the current document. This is commonly used to copy styles from an external style sheet you created for one site into a particular document on a different site. To import the styles rather than link to the external style sheet, choose Import in the Add As area of the Link External Style Sheet dialog box.*

## Export an External Style Sheet from Existing Internal Styles

If you've created CSS styles in an internal style sheet in the current document, you can easily export those styles to an external style sheet. Here's how:

1. Choose File | Export | Export CSS styles (this option is grayed out if the current document does not contain any style sheet information). The Export Styles As CSS File dialog box appears.

2. Enter a filename for the external style sheet, and locate a folder in which to save it. Click Save to close the dialog box and save the style sheet.

3. Follow the instructions in the previous section for linking the current document to the external style sheet.

NOTE

*Filenames for CSS style sheets must be lowercase and cannot contain spaces.*

## Edit a Style Sheet

One of the greatest advantages of style sheets is the ability they give you to quickly change the appearance of your pages by simply editing the styles. To edit a style in an internal style sheet, follow these steps:

**1.** In the CSS Styles panel (Figure 11-1), click the Edit Styles button at the top of the panel.

**2.** Select the style you want to edit.

**3.** Click the Edit Style Sheet button in the lower-right corner of the panel. This brings up the CSS Style Definition dialog box, shown in Figure 11-5.

**4.** Change the style attributes in the CSS Style Definition dialog box as needed.

**5.** Click OK to close the CSS Style Definition dialog box and update the style sheet.

Editing an external style sheet is similar to editing an internal style sheet; the only difference is that you need to have access to the external style sheet in order to make the edits. You can edit only those style sheets that reside locally on your computer. To edit a style sheet on a remote site, you must first copy the style sheet file to your computer, where you can make the edits. Then you upload the revised style sheet to the remote server. Once you edit an external style sheet, any changes you make will automatically be reflected in all pages that are linked to it. This is a great way to update an entire site—simply edit a single style sheet that it is linked to. Here's the procedure for editing an external style sheet.

**1.** In the CSS Styles panel, click the Edit Styles button at the top of the panel.

**2.** Select the style sheet you want to edit.

**3.** Click the Edit Style Sheet button in the lower-right corner of the panel. This brings up the Edit Style Sheet dialog box, which lists the available styles in the external style sheet.

**11**

**Edit Style Sheet**

mystyles.css (link)
.bodystyle
.copyright
.mynote
.galleryhead
h1
a:active
blockquote blockquote
blockquote

Link...
New...
Edit...
Duplicate...
Remove

File contents

.copyright, .gallerytext, a:active, a:hover, a:link, a:visited, h1

Done        Help

4. Select the individual style to edit, and click the Edit button to open the CSS Style Definition dialog box, shown in Figure 11-5.

5. Edit the style definition as needed, and then click OK to exit the dialog box. Dreamweaver returns you to the Edit Style Sheet dialog box.

6. Repeat steps 4 and 5 to edit another style, or click Done to close the Edit Style Sheet dialog box.

# Convert CSS Styles to HTML Tags

CSS styles are powerful formatting tools, but your site visitors must use an up-to-date browser to properly view web pages that include CSS styles. Dreamweaver gives you the option of creating a copy of your web page that has the same formatting but doesn't rely on CSS. This option converts your CSS styles to HTML tags that are compatible with a wider range of browsers.

Of course, while this process attempts to convert all the CSS style attributes into standard HTML tags, it isn't 100 percent successful. Not all CSS style attributes will convert because HTML has much more limited type-display capabilities. Still, if you need to make a 3.0-browser-compatible version of your page, the Convert command streamlines the process.

 *Any CSS styles that do not have HTML equivalents are ignored when you use this command.*

To convert CSS styles to HTML, follow these steps:

1. Open an existing web document that contains CSS style sheet specifications. The document can contain styles from internal or external style sheets or both.

2. Choose File | Convert | 3.0 Browser Compatible to open the Convert to 3.0 Browser Compatible dialog box.

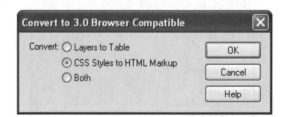

3. Select CSS Styles to HTML Markup, and click OK. Dreamweaver closes the dialog box and creates a copy of the current page with CSS styles converted to HTML tags. The converted document appears in a new Untitled Document window.

To avoid having to repeat this process numerous times, do not convert CSS styles to HTML tags until the CSS-formatted page is complete. Any changes you make to the CSS-formatted page after the conversion will not be reflected in the HTML-formatted page.

# Setting CSS Style Preferences

Certain CSS styles can be coded in a form of shorthand. These shorthand CSS definitions cannot always be correctly interpreted by older browsers, but most of the current browsers can correctly render styles coded in shorthand. The CSS Styles category of the Dreamweaver Preferences dialog box (choose Edit | Preferences) allows you to set which styles should be coded in shorthand. If you're not familiar with CSS shorthand, you should probably stick with the default settings.

**Preferences**

| Category | CSS Styles |

General
Accessibility
Code Coloring
Code Format
Code Hints
Code Rewriting
CSS Styles
File Types / Editors
Fonts
Highlighting
Invisible Elements
Layers
Layout View
New Document
Panels
Preview in Browser
Quick Tag Editor
Site
Status Bar
Validator

When Creating CSS Styles:

Use Shorthand For: ☐ Font

☐ Background

☐ Margin and Padding

☐ Border and Border Width

☐ List-Style

When Editing CSS Styles:

Use Shorthand: ◉ If Original Used Shorthand

○ According to Settings Above

[ OK ]   [ Cancel ]   [ Help ]

11

# Chapter 12 Work with Layers

## How to...

- Create layers
- Use layers for precise page layout
- Manage multiple layers
- Convert layers to tables
- Use the timeline to create animated layers

Chapter 11 covers using Cascading Style Sheets (CSS) to control text formatting on a web page. But CSS can do more than format text. An extension of the original CSS specification offers the same level of control for additional page elements, including images, tables, forms, media objects, and almost anything else you can include on a web page. This specification is called CSS-P, or Cascading Style Sheets-Positioning. CSS-P is the foundation of a web design feature more commonly known as *layers*, which allows pixel-level control of almost any element on a page.

Like CSS, CSS-P has had some difficulty gaining wide usage (at least among nongeek web design folks). Programming layers takes a pretty high degree of coding skill. Nonetheless, thanks to Dreamweaver's easy and intuitive layers implementation, all the benefits of layers are readily accessible to Dreamweaver MX users. Layers offer a level of design and interactive capability that is just not possible with plain HTML.

# What Are Layers?

Although the raw code needed to create and manipulate layers is quite complicated, the basic concept behind layers is simple. Think of a layer as a kind of container within a web page. This container can be sized and positioned independently from the web page and can contain pretty much anything a web page can contain—images, text, tables, media files, etc. The layer itself is invisible when viewed in a web browser—only the contents of the layer are visible. You can move the layer around wherever you want on the page using precise, pixel-accurate measurements. For example, you could create a layer, insert an image, and then position the layer exactly 100 pixels from the top of the page and 100 pixels from the left of the page. Layers provide the exact kind of page layout control that web designers have been clamoring for.

In addition to providing exact positioning capabilities, layers also enable you to overlap items, animate them, and control their appearance and behavior using Dynamic HTML (DHTML) and scripting languages such as JavaScript. You can use layers together with Dreamweaver Behaviors to add many advanced special effects and interactive capabilities to your web pages, without the need for external plug-ins or media applications.

# Manage Layers with the Layers Panel

The Layers panel, shown in Figure 12-1, is the main access point for creating, editing, and managing layers in Dreamweaver. To bring the Layers panel into view, simply choose Window | Others | Layers, or press F2.

# Compatibility Problems with Layers

Many of the great advanced tools available to web designers have at least one drawback, and layers is no exception. The biggest problem with layers is that they don't work with browsers earlier than version 4.0. Pre-4.0 browsers simply don't understand layers, so they ignore them. Anything in a layer just disappears on a 3.0 version browser.

Another compatibility problem with layers involves a different layer specification introduced by Netscape when it first released version 4 of its browser. Most layer examples you see on the Web today use the original layer specification proposed by the W3C, which is based on the `<div>` and `<span>` tags. Early on, Netscape introduced a system of creating layers that relied on different tags: `<layer>` and `<ilayer>`.

When layers first appeared, nobody knew which standard would gain the widest acceptance. Over time, the original W3C spec has gained wide usage, while the Netscape spec has slipped into oblivion. While Dreamweaver still recognizes layers created using the Netscape tags, it will only allow you to create layers using `<div>` and `<span>` tags. Netscape itself has even abandoned the old tags in the latest version of their browser, Netscape 6.

12

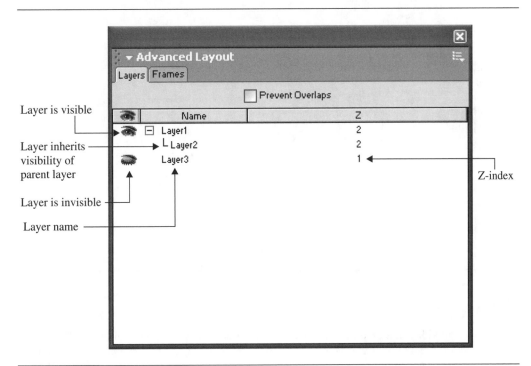

Layer is visible

Layer inherits visibility of parent layer

Layer is invisible

Layer name

Z-index

FIGURE 12-1    The Layers panel

## The Layers Panel

The Layers panel lists all the existing layers in the document and enables you to control their appearance and behavior. You can include as many layers as you want in your document; the Layers panel provides the interface for managing them. You can easily control layer visibility, Z-index, and overlap in the Layers panel. You can also use the Layers panel to select a layer to edit further in the Property Inspector panel.

## Set Layer Preferences

Layer preferences define the default characteristics of any layers you create in Dreamweaver. You can set your own default layer settings using the Layers category in the Preferences dialog box (choose Edit | Preferences). The defaults establish the properties of a newly created layer, but you can still change all those properties after you create a layer.

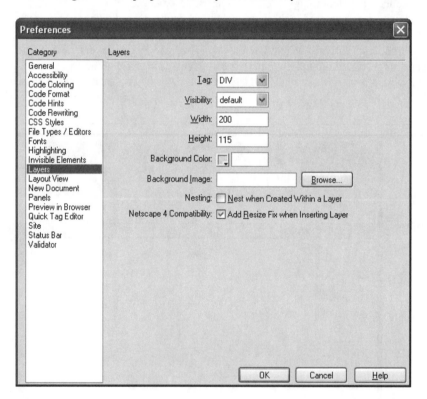

# Create Layers

Dreamweaver provides an incredibly simple interface for accessing the power of layers. It may be difficult to appreciate this if you've never coded layers by hand, but you can take a look at the HTML source code for some layers to see what I mean.

Using Dreamweaver's visual tools, you can create and position layers precisely by simply dragging them around on the page or by entering exact measurements into the Property Inspector panel. Dreamweaver even includes rulers and a grid to further facilitate layout (see Chapter 1 for information on the rulers and grid).

## Insert a Layer

There are two ways to insert a layer into a page in Dreamweaver. You can draw a layer using the Draw Layer tool, or you can use the Insert Layer command. If you've ever worked with page design programs such as QuarkXPress, PageMaker, or Microsoft Publisher, you're probably familiar with the concept of creating a text box on a page and later filling it with content. Drawing a layer is a similar process:

1. Click the Draw Layer button in the Common category of the Insert bar. Your pointer becomes a crosshair cursor.

2. Click anywhere in the document and drag the cursor diagonally to create a rectangular shape approximating the size and positioning of your desired layer. When you release the mouse button, Dreamweaver creates the layer.

Use these steps to insert a layer into your web document using the Insert Layer command:

1. Choose Insert | Layer. Dreamweaver automatically places a new empty layer in the upper-left corner of the document. The layer's default size is 200 pixels wide by 115 pixels high, unless you change the setting in the preferences.

2. Move or resize the newly created layer as needed.

*After you insert a layer, a blinking cursor appears inside the new layer to indicate that you can insert content. If you immediately insert another layer using the Insert | Layer command, the second layer will become nested within the first. To create a non-nested layer, click outside the first layer before inserting a new one. (See "Create Nested Layers," later in this chapter for more information.)*

When you insert a new layer with Dreamweaver, two new objects appear on the screen. In the upper-left corner of the page you'll notice the layer icon, a small yellow square with the letter C inside. This is an invisible element that anchors the layer onto the page. Like other invisible elements, you can cut, copy, paste, and reposition the element anywhere else on the page, but the layer itself does not move when the icon moves. Moving the icon simply moves the source code for the layer to another location in the HTML without affecting the functionality of the layer (though generally it's a good idea to keep layer icons together in one location on the page). Deleting the icon deletes the layer and all its associated code from the page.

The second object that appears when you insert a layer is the *layer bounding box*. This box indicates the size and the position of the layer, and you can use it to move and resize the layer.

12

## Move and Resize Layers

After you create a layer, you can move it by clicking and dragging the selection handle, which appears anytime you click inside the layer. To select the layer for resizing and other manipulations, click the selection handle or the layer border to make the sizing handles appear. You can resize the layer by clicking and dragging any of the resizing handles.

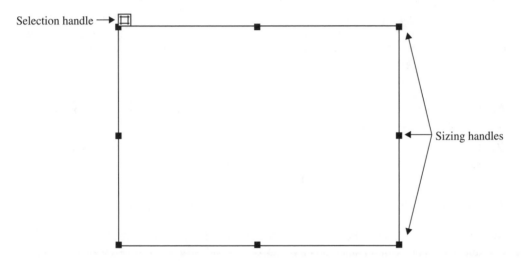

You can also move or resize layers by selecting the layer and typing new coordinates into the Property Inspector panel. When you select a layer on the page, the Property Inspector panel displays its size and location on the page in the corresponding Property Inspector fields. (See "Set Layer Properties" for an illustration of the panel and descriptions of the layer properties.)

## Insert Content into Layers

Layers are basically containers—containers that can hold almost any kind of content, including text, images, tables, forms, media objects, and even other layers. By placing your content into a layer, you can control its exact placement on the page when you reposition the layer. Another great advantage to working with layers is that you can overlap them on a page. Thus, even though you can't place an image on top of another image using ordinary HTML, you can place images into separate layers and position one layer on top of the other to achieve the desired effect.

Inserting content into a layer is exactly like inserting content into a regular web document. You can drag and drop, use the Insert command, type text from the keyboard, or click buttons in the Insert bar to insert objects into a layer. However, before you insert anything into a layer, make sure the layer is selected and that the cursor is blinking inside it.

To insert items into a layer you can:

■ Insert text by simply typing or by copying and pasting

■ Insert images and other media by dragging and dropping them into the layer, or by clicking any of the insert object buttons in the Insert bar

# Set Layer Properties

Layers have many different customizable properties that you can access through the Property Inspector panel.

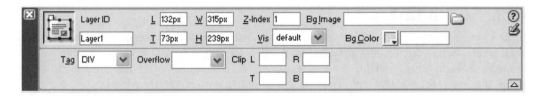

The following are the layer property options available in the Property Inspector panel:

- **Layer ID**    The ID uniquely identifies each layer as a document object and for use with scripting. Dreamweaver supplies default names for each layer, but you can replace the name with your own.

- **L (Left)**    Specifies the distance of the layer as measured from the left edge of the page.

- **T (Top)**    Specifies the distance of the layer as measured from the top edge of the page.

- **W**    Specifies the layer's width.

- **H**    Specifies the layer's height.

- **Z-Index**    Specifies the stacking order of the layer in relation to other layers. Layers with higher numbers will appear in front of layers with lower numbers.

- **Vis** (visibility)    Specifies whether the layer is visible or not. The inherit option takes on the visibility of the parent layer when a layer is nested.

- **BgImage**    Specifies the background image for the layer.

- **BgColor**    Specifies the background color for the layer.

- **Tag**    Specifies the HTML tag used to define the layer. (Unless you have a reasons not to, use the default `<div>` tag.)

- **Overflow**    Specifies how the contents of a layer should be displayed when they are larger than the dimensions of the layer. The Scroll option adds horizontal and vertical scroll bars, enabling the user to scroll the hidden content. The Auto option adds scroll bars only if needed. Selecting Hidden will cause any overflow to be clipped by the layer boundaries.

- **Clip**    Specify the region of a layer (left, top, right, bottom) that you want cropped from view by entering numerical values as measured from each edge of the layer. If no values are specified, the layer displays in its entirety. Clipping is a useful feature for creating interactive and animated effects that change over time.

12

*Enter negative values into the L and T fields in the Property Inspector panel to position the layer off the page. Use this technique combined with animation effects to create a layer that moves into view from somewhere off screen after the page has loaded. See "Animate Layers," later in this chapter, to learn how to achieve this effect.*

## Create Nested Layers

*Nesting layers* is a technique in which you insert new layers inside of existing layers, sometimes several levels deep. Nested layers are often described as having a parent-child relationship: the outer layer is the parent and the inner layer is the child (see Figure 12-2). One of the main benefits of nesting layers is that child layers usually move in unison with the parent as you move the parent layer around the page. Using nested layers, you can move complicated multilayer structures around as a unit, just by moving the parent layer.

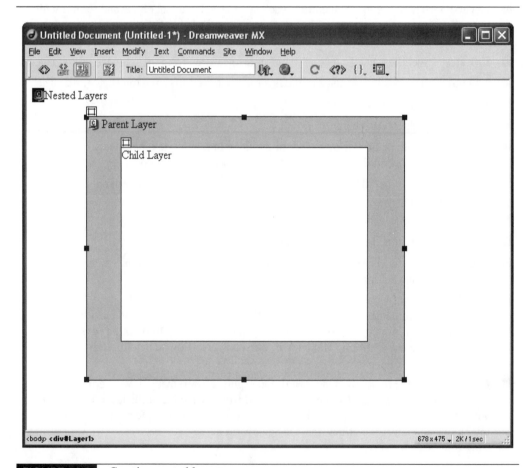

FIGURE 12-2    Creating nested layers

**CAUTION** *Nested layers use the upper-left corner of the parent layer as their origin point for ruler measurements, instead of the upper-left corner of the document.*

To nest a new layer into an existing layer:

1. Place the cursor inside the existing layer so that you see a blinking cursor in the upper-left corner of the layer.

2. Choose Insert | Layer to create a new child layer inside the parent layer. After creating the child layer, you can reposition it by clicking and dragging the selection handle to move it anywhere else on the page.

To nest an existing layer inside another existing layer:

1. Make the Layers panel visible by choosing Window | Layers or pressing F2.

2. Press and hold the CTRL key as you click and drag the name of the layer in the Layers panel that you want to make the child and drop it onto the parent layer. Note that the Layers panel now shows the name of the child layer indented beneath the parent layer.

**NOTE** *Child layers don't have to be located inside their parent layer. They can be located anywhere on the page but will still always use the upper-left corner of their parent layer as their origin point instead of the upper-left corner of the document.*

# Work with Layers

In order to work with layers you need to be able to modify and manipulate them in a variety of ways. Many of the layer features and functionality are accessed through various interface tools unique to Dreamweaver, such as the Layers panel and the Timelines panel.

12

## Select Layers

To manipulate and modify layers you need to be able to select them. You can tell when a layer is selected because the selection and sizing handles appear around it, and the Property Inspector panel displays the layer properties for the selected layer. Basically, there are two ways to select layers in Dreamweaver:

- Click anywhere on the layer in the document window and then click the selection handle or layer border so that the sizing handles are displayed. To select multiple layers, hold down the SHIFT key as you click other layers.

- Click the layer name in the Layers panel to highlight it. To select multiple layers, SHIFT-CLICK on other layer names.

**TIP** *Using the Layers panel to select layers is usually easier and more efficient when several layers are stacked on top of one another in the document. Otherwise, it can be difficult to click on the correct layer in the Document window.*

 *When you are selecting layers containing images or other content, it's easy to accidentally select the content inside the layer instead of the layer around it. If the layer-selection handle and resizing handles are visible after you click the layer, the layer itself is selected. If they are not visible, you may have selected only the layer's contents.*

## Change Layer Visibility

Layers include a visibility attribute that enables you to make them either visible or invisible on the page. The main reason to make a layer invisible is to allow special interactive effects, such as turning a layer on or off when the user clicks a button or interacts with the page in some other way. You can also use this feature to facilitate design and layout by temporarily hiding a layer to make it easier to work with other layers on the page.

You control layer visibility through the Layers panel (see Figure 12-1). The first column in the layers panel shows an eye icon. To change a layer's visibility, click the eye next to a layer. An open eye indicates that the layer is visible. When the eye is closed, the associated layer is invisible. When no eye icon is visible, it means that the layer inherits the visibility status of its parent layer. In the event that the layer is not a child layer, no eye icon means that the layer is visible, since the parent is the document itself, which is always visible. By clicking the eye icon at the top of the column, you can control the visibility for all the layers in the document.

## Change Layer Stacking Order

One benefit of using layers is the ability to overlap content on a page. Dreamweaver uses a stacking order to determine whether a given layer is in front of or behind other layers. This stacking order is also referred to as the *Z-index* (shown in Figure 12-1). The Z-index simply uses a numerical value to determine the position of a layer along the Z-axis, which runs from the front of the page to the back. Layers with a lower Z-index number are stacked closer to the back, while layers with a higher Z-index are stacked closer to the front. For example, a layer with a Z-index of 2 obscures a layer with a Z-index of 1 where the two overlap (assuming the top layer's contents are not transparent). If you assign two layers the same Z-index, they stack in the order in which they were created. As you begin working with layers you will find that controlling their stacking order is an important function.

The Z-index is displayed for each layer in two different locations: the Z-index field in the Property Inspector panel and the Z-index column in the Layers panel. You can change the Z-index value in one of three ways:

- Enter a new value in the Z-index field in the Property Inspector panel.

- Enter a new value in the Z-index column in the Layers panel.

- Click and drag a layer's name in the Layers panel up or down the list of layers. Layers listed at the top of the panel have the highest index, and layers at the bottom of the panel have the lowest. When you move a layer into a new position in the Layers panel, Dreamweaver automatically adjusts its Z-index accordingly.

# Use Layers for Page Layout

Layers are a powerful tool in the web designer's toolkit. Using layers, designers can mimic most any design created in traditional design. Unfortunately, a significant drawback to using layers is that some older browsers can't view layer content. The number of people still surfing with pre-4.0 browsers is steadily diminishing, but they still exist in significant numbers. Fortunately, there's a way to design pages using layers and then convert the layers to tables for compatibility with pre-4.0 browsers.

## Convert Layers to Tables

Dreamweaver includes a handy Convert Layers to Tables feature that enables you to take a layout created with layers and automatically convert all the layers in the document to tables. A page created with this feature will look similar to the layers version but will still be viewable in pre-4.0 browsers.

To convert a page that has been designed using layers to a page that uses tables instead, choose Modify | Convert | Layers to Tables. This opens the Convert Layers to Table dialog box, which presents you with several options for outputting your tables.

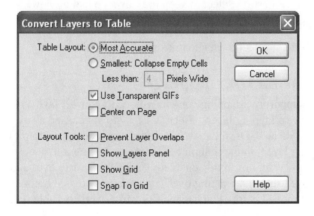

*Since the Convert Layers to Tables command modifies and replaces the existing document, apply the command to a copy of your layers page if you want to preserve a version of the page that uses layers as well.*

The following options are available when converting tables to layers:

- **Table Layout** These options affect the construction of the new table:
  - **Most Accurate** Most closely mimics the layout of the layers-based page. Use this option when you want to match the layers-based layout as closely as possible, regardless of the complexity of the resulting table.

12

- **Smallest**   Simplifies the table structure by joining adjacent empty cells into single cells. You can set a number to specify the size of the cells that get joined. The higher the number you enter, the simpler the table structure (fewer cells) but the less accurate the layout compared to the layers version. Use this option when you want to avoid creating an overly complex table and you're willing to sacrifice a degree of accuracy in matching the layers-based layout.

- **Use Transparent GIFs**   Uses transparent GIF images to fill the empty cells in the layout as spacer cells. This guarantees a greater degree of uniformity across browsers. The default setting is to use transparent GIFs.

- **Center on Page**   Centers the table in the browser window instead of the usual position at the upper-left corner.

- **Layout Tools**   These options affect the attributes of the document after the conversion to tables takes place. Any of these options can still be turned on or off after the layers have been converted.

  - **Prevent Layer Overlaps**   Select to enable this option for the document (refer to next section for more information about overlapping layers).

  - **Show Layer Palette**   Select to keep the Layers panel in view.

  - **Show Grid**   Select to turn the grid on.

  - **Snap to Grid**   Select to enable this option for the document.

## Prevent Layers from Overlapping

Because tables do not support overlapping content, you can't convert layers to tables if the document contains any overlapping layers. Since it's easy to get carried away with layers and overlook the effects of overlaps, Dreamweaver includes a special option to prevent you from creating any overlapping layers in the first place. To enable this option, choose Modify | Arrange | Prevent Layer Overlaps. With this option enabled, you cannot create overlapping layers in your document. Note, however, that any existing overlapping layers created before this option was enabled still need to be moved before you use the Convert Layers to Tables command.

# Animate Layers

Using layers to achieve accurate page design is a compelling enough reason to use layers. But there's another great reason to use layers: the ability to animate layers.

Layers are actually page objects that can be manipulated and moved around the page interactively, even after the page has already been loaded into the browser. This is made possible via an extension to HTML called *Dynamic HTML* (DHTML). Like layers, DHTML displays only in 4.0 and later browsers. DHTML works in conjunction with JavaScript—a scripting language—to enable designers and programmers to create dynamic, interactive content on web pages. Normally programming in DHTML and JavaScript requires a high degree of scripting knowledge and experience. However, once again, Dreamweaver enables mortal web designers to access much of the power of DHTML and layers using easy-to-understand visual tools.

## Use the Timelines Panel

Dreamweaver's layer animation capabilities are based on a timeline metaphor. If you've ever used a program like Flash or Director, you may be familiar with how a timeline works. It's basically a way to control animation frame by frame over time. Traditional cartoon animators use a similar process to create frame-by-frame animations with drawings. New frames appear several times per second, each with a slightly different drawing. Over time, the illusion of motion is created. The Dreamweaver timeline allows you to move layers, frame by frame over time, to create the same illusion.

To access the timeline, open the Timelines panel: choose Window | Others | Timelines (see Figure 12-3).

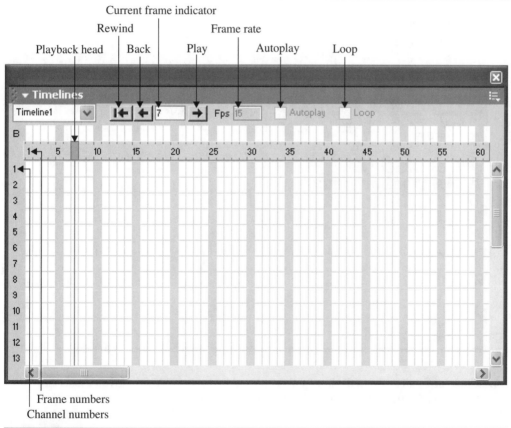

**FIGURE 12-3**    The Timelines panel

## Create a Timeline Animation

Timeline animations allow you to change the size, position, visibility, and stacking order of layers over a specified period of time. You can also change the source file of images in a layer or add Behaviors to create rollovers and other interactive effects.

1. Choose Window | Others | Timelines to make the Timelines panel visible.

2. Select a layer on the page to animate. You may want to insert text, images, or other content into the layer first.

3. Choose Modify | Timeline | Add Object to Timeline, or simply click and drag the layer from the page onto the first cell of the Timelines panel. Dreamweaver adds a bar to the first channel of the timeline, labeled with the name of the layer you just added.

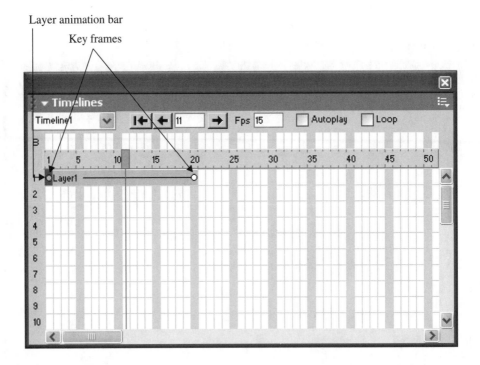

4. Click the small circle in the last frame occupied by the bar. This circle represents a keyframe. *Keyframes* are starting, ending, or intermediary points in an animation.

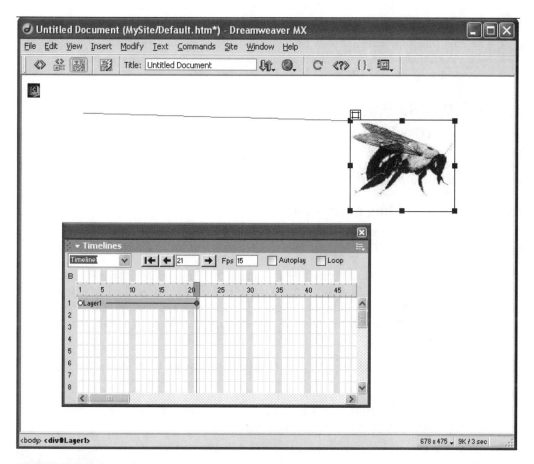

**FIGURE 12-4**   Moving the layer at the last keyframe in the animation to create a motion path

12

5. In Dreamweaver's document window, drag the layer somewhere else on the page. After you move the layer, a line appears representing the motion path of the layer between frame 1 and the ending keyframe of the animation (see Figure 12-4).

6. Click and hold the Play button to see the layer move across the page.

7. Repeat steps 1–6 if you want to add additional layers to the timeline. When you add additional layers, each new layer occupies a different channel in the timeline, identified by its layer name. Channels are displayed as the horizontal numbered rows across the Timelines panel.

 *You can also add images to a timeline by dragging them from the Document window into the Timelines panel. Though you can't animate images on a page unless they are placed in a layer first, you can add Behaviors to them to create rollovers and other interactive effects (see Chapter 13).*

## Modify a Motion Path

You're not limited to just straight motion paths between animation keyframes. To create more interesting animated movements, you can customize the motion path of your layer either by adding new keyframes or by having Dreamweaver automatically record the onscreen path of the layer as you move it around the page.

### Define a Path by Adding a Keyframe

The previous example shows how to create a timeline animation with two keyframes and a straight path. This example shows how to modify such a path by adding additional keyframes.

1. Click anywhere near the middle of the layer bar in the Timeline panel to select a frame somewhere between the first and the last frames. When you select the frame, the playback head moves to that frame, indicating that it is the current selected frame. The layer also changes its position in the document window to reflect where it is at that point in the timeline.

 *You can also CTRL-click the layer bar where you want to add a key frame.*

2. Choose Modify | Timeline | Add Keyframe, or press the F6 key. This places a new keyframe into the timeline at the current frame.

3. Reposition the layer to alter its motion path (see Figure 12-5).

4. Repeat steps 1–3 as needed to further modify the path. You can continue to add keyframes and alter the motion path until the desired path is achieved.

### Define a Path by Recording Mouse Movement

When you need to create a complicated motion path, it's sometimes easier to draw the path with your mouse pointer and let Dreamweaver record the motion automatically. This works really well when it's too difficult or involved to create the path by inserting new keyframes and moving layers around. An example might be an animated image of an insect circling the page a few times before landing.

1. In the document window, select the layer whose path you want to record and drag it to its starting position on the page.

2. Choose Modify | Record Path of Layer. This opens up the Timelines panel if it is not already visible.

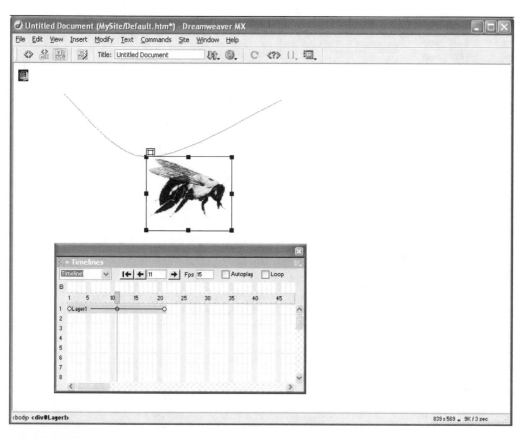

**FIGURE 12-5**   Modify the animation page by creating a new keyframe and repositioning the layer.

**3.** Click the layer again, and drag it around on the page to define the movement path (see Figure 12-6). As you draw, Dreamweaver creates keyframes to capture the movement. The more slowly you move the mouse, the closer the keyframes are spaced together. The faster you move the mouse, the farther apart they are spaced.

**4.** Release the mouse button to stop the recording and complete the motion path.

**5.** Press and hold the Play button in the Timeline panel to preview the animation effect.

## Refine the Timeline

The timeline uses total number of frames, total number of keyframes, and the positioning of the layer in each keyframe to define the way the animation appears over time. You can make further refinements to the animation by modifying any of these components.

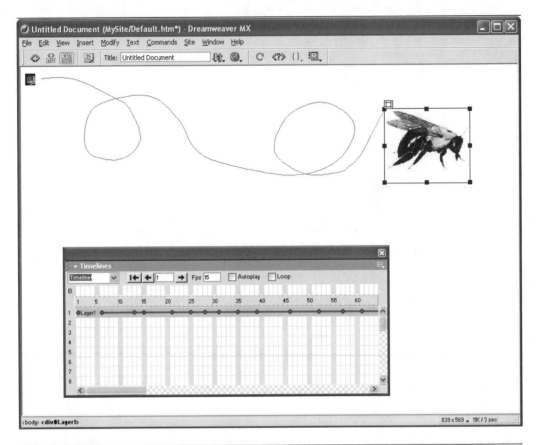

FIGURE 12-6    Use the Record Path of Layer command to manually create a motion path
using your mouse.

## Change the Animation Speed

Frame-based animation works by tricking the eye with a rapid succession of changing images.
To achieve a smooth animation, a certain number or frames per second must be displayed; this
is the *frame rate*. To modify the frame rate, enter a value in the timeline's Fps (frames per
second) field, found just to the right of the Play button in the Timelines panel. Motion picture
animation usually runs at 24 to 30 frames per second. Web-based layer-animation frame rates
depend on the speed of the computer running the browser, and while fast computers may be able to
display 30 frames in a second, slower computers just can't keep up. As a result, it's better not to
go too much higher than the default frame rate of 15 frames per second, which is usually fast
enough to produce smooth animation without degrading too significantly on slower computers.
In fact, you might get by with 8 to 12 frames per second, which approximates the speed of
animated cartoons.

Another factor that affects the speed of an animation is the number of frames used. By clicking the last keyframe in an animation and dragging the bar out to the right on the timeline, you can increase the number of frames used. The number of frames displayed each second remains constant, so the more frames there are in the animation, the longer it lasts. Moving the last keyframe to the left has the opposite effect: it shortens the animation by reducing the number of frames.

### Modify the Position of Layers in the Time Sequence

Keyframes define the position of a layer at a given point in the timeline sequence. To change the position of a layer, simply select a keyframe and reposition the layer in the document window. Whenever you reposition a layer in a keyframe, Dreamweaver looks at the position of the layer in that keyframe and the one preceding it to automatically calculate the layer positions for intermediate frames. For example, to move the beginning position of the layer in an animation, change its position in the first keyframe. To move to the ending position, change the position in the last keyframe. Move the position in any middle keyframes to change the middle positions.

## Use Multiple Timelines

For creating more complicated layer animations, you can use additional timelines. However, only one timeline can be displayed in the Timelines panel at any given time. To add a new timeline, choose Modify | Timeline | Add Timeline. A new blank timeline appears, which Dreamweaver automatically names Timeline2. You can continue to add timelines in this manner and modify each one to create multiple timeline animations. Use the pop-up window to select which timeline to view in the Timelines panel. To delete a timeline, select it using the pop-up window, and choose Modify | Timeline | Remove Timeline. You can rename timelines by either typing in a new name in the Name field or by choosing Modify | Timeline | Rename Timeline.

## Apply a Timeline

When you view a timeline in a browser, nothing happens unless you instruct the timeline to begin playing after the page loads—it won't play on its own. The normal way to tell a timeline to begin playing is to select the Autoplay field in the Timelines panel. Autoplay instructs the browser to begin playing the animation as soon as the page has loaded. Normally, the animation plays once and stops at the last frame in the animation. If you want the animation to continue playing over and over, select the Loop option.

Another way to control when a timeline begins playing is to *call* (start playback of) the timeline using a Behavior. When you use a Behavior to control when a timeline plays, do not check the Autoplay option. Using Behaviors is covered in Chapter 13.

12

# Chapter 13

## Work with Rollovers and Other Interactive Elements

## How to...

- Understand the technology and process behind Behaviors
- Add interactive elements to your page
- Plan for browser compatibility
- Create interactive buttons, navigational elements, and menus

Dreamweaver helps implement real interactivity in your web sites in many ways—one of which is *Behaviors*. Behaviors enable you to take your site from the realm of "digital magazine" to full-blown multimedia showcase. Behaviors unlock the power of JavaScript and add visual effects, navigational tools, and rich media control to your web site.

# Understand and Work with Behaviors

For many people, JavaScript crosses a line between the relative ease of HTML coding and hard-core script programming. Scripting can be like playing chess—you need to think several moves ahead in order to construct code in the proper order and obtain the desired result. This is more than some web developers want to take on. Even if they are willing to deal with the structured nature of scripting, the script language itself is intimidating for many web authors. The good news is that Dreamweaver makes it relatively easy for designers, writers, and editors (read: nonprogrammers) to make a transition to the technical side of web development in a user-friendly, visual environment.

You're probably aware that Dreamweaver automates the process of creating web documents; you don't have to spend hours hand coding the HTML tags that tell a browser how to interpret your design. What you may not know is that Dreamweaver can also produce scripts that respond to the way users interact with your web site. These scripts are called Behaviors, and you access them through the Behaviors panel.

## What Are Behaviors?

The term *Behaviors* is self-explanatory: in the most basic sense, Behaviors tell elements of a web page how to act or behave. Think of Behaviors as a set of instructions that you can apply to text, graphics, buttons, links, timelines, and other web page elements. After you select an object on your page (let's say a button graphic), you use menus in the Behaviors panel to define the way this button acts when someone points to it or clicks it. Meanwhile, Dreamweaver automatically inserts these instructions into your web document.

Behavior "instructions" are added to your document as lines of JavaScript code. Like HTML, JavaScript tells the web browser how to display a web page. The difference is that JavaScript can convey more complicated instructions than plain HTML. As you probably guessed, Dreamweaver handles all the scripting automatically. So if you are daunted by hand coding but impressed by the functionality JavaScript can provide, Behaviors are definitely for you.

If you are new to web development, you may not be aware of the flexibility and sophistication that JavaScript can add to your site. This powerful language has an enormous variety of applications, many of which go beyond the scope of this book. However, Dreamweaver Behaviors serve as an excellent introduction to JavaScript; they enable you to expand the interactivity and user friendliness of a web site. You can use Behaviors to do the following:

- Create rollover button effects
- Create navigational elements and pop-up menus
- Open a new browser window
- Toggle images on and off
- Play a sound
- Control animations
- Manage frames and hyperlinks

This list is not exhaustive by any means. Dreamweaver ships with a large assortment of Behaviors, and you can add more. A good source for Behaviors is the Macromedia web site, http://www.macromedia.com.

As an example, consider the use of Behaviors with buttons. From a design standpoint, buttons on a web page can be visually appealing, and they offer a clear means of accessing information. Buttons are a metaphor from our physical world; we use buttons every day to summon an elevator or make a telephone call. Buttons are interactive. We push them and something happens. This concept translates well into the realm of digital media. What does not translate, however, is the sensory experience of pressing the button. In the real world, a combination of sound, light, or resistance offers feedback and tells you that the button has performed its duty. You can use Behaviors to provide this feedback from a digital button. Behaviors allow buttons to

- Change appearance when the mouse is positioned over the button
- Change appearance when it is being "pressed"
- Play a sound to acknowledge the mouse click

## Understanding Events and Actions

As stated, a Behavior is nothing more than a set of instructions that causes an element of your web site to change in response to the requests of a user. Each behavior has two major components: an *event* and an *action*. The event is the catalyst, the trigger that sets a sequence of instructions in motion. Clicking or pointing the mouse, pressing a key, and loading an HTML document into memory are events. An action is a programmed response to the event, and it is handled by JavaScript.

## Did you know?

### Fancy Effects Aren't Always Good

Behaviors, and the effects they offer, are some of the "bells and whistles" of web development. While they can add a level of sophistication and "wow" to your site, they do not ensure that your message will get through to your audience. As the web designer you have a responsibility to communicate the message and information offered by your site as clearly as possible. Just because you *can* add fancy effects with Behaviors doesn't mean you *should* add them. Before using a Behavior, ask yourself if the Behavior reinforces your message or distracts from it.

Behaviors monitor events and provide appropriate responses. For example, a behavior can change a graphic when triggered by a *mouseover* (the mouse passing over an object in the browser window). The behavior is attached to a graphic to create the illusion that the button changes appearance when the mouse rolls over it. In reality, the original button graphic is switched and replaced with a slightly different image. It works like this: When the user's mouse passes over the button with the behavior attached, the browser sends a message: "The mouse has just pointed to an element of this web page; is there anything that is supposed to happen?" The Behavior responds: "Yes, according to the JavaScript instructions, you need to replace the graphic file the mouse crossed over with a new one named buttonOver.gif." Obviously, no such chat actually takes place within your computer, but in a basic sense, a Behavior manages this communication.

**TIP**    *It is common practice for designers to use multiple images for a single button—one for each state or condition of the button. For example, a button could have three states: normal (up), over (standby), and down (active).*

Another Behavior could be attached to the button image to control what happens when the button is clicked. When the Behavior receives that message from the browser, it swaps in the image that represents the button in its down state.

The sequence described here provides a good example of the conceptual framework on which all Behaviors are based. After you grasp this idea you can create and apply a variety of other Behaviors on your own.

### Use the Behaviors Panel

The Behaviors panel (Figure 13-1) enables you to apply and work with Behaviors. It normally appears as a tab in the Design panel group. If the Behaviors panel is not already open, choose Window | Behaviors or press SHIFT-F3. The Behaviors panel allows you to attach Behaviors to elements of your web page. After you attach a Behavior to an element, Dreamweaver displays the element's HTML tag near the top of the Behaviors panel.

Actions button

Delete Actions button

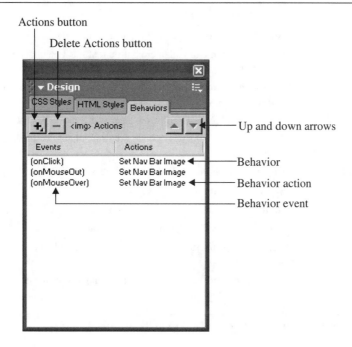

Up and down arrows

Behavior

Behavior action

Behavior event

**FIGURE 13-1**   The Behaviors panel showing three behaviors attached to an object.

**NOTE**   *Behaviors are not separate tags that you insert into your document like a graphic or a link. Rather, they are placed within the tag for the element, similar to an attribute.*

In addition, the Behaviors panel displays the event and action that make up the Behavior. If there is more than one set of events and actions, the Behaviors panel lists them from top to bottom either alphabetically or in the order in which they occur. If a tag has no Behavior attached to it, then the Behaviors panel is empty.

The Behaviors panel contains several buttons that allow you to edit the Behavior parameters. Most predominant is the Actions button, represented by a large plus (+) sign. This button opens a menu of JavaScript actions that are available to you in Dreamweaver. (See Table 13-1 for a partial list of available actions.) Although actions are the second component in a Behavior sequence, you attach Behaviors by first defining the action. Next to the Actions button is the Delete Actions button, represented by a minus (–) sign. Clicking this button removes any selected (highlighted) Behaviors in the panel.

13

| Action | Description |
|---|---|
| Jump Menu | Allows a menu object to perform as a jump menu |
| Jump Menu Go | Inserts a jump menu with a Go button that must be clicked before jumping to the selected entry from the menu |
| Open Browser Window | Opens a new browser window with the properties (size, menu bar, and so on) that you specify |
| Play Sound | Action that plays a sound when cued by a Behavior event |
| Preload Images | Action that loads images that are not immediately displayed on a web page |
| Show Pop-Up Menu | Displays images and text you specify as a pop-up menu |
| Show-Hide Layers | Sets the visibility property of a layer |
| Swap Image | Action that switches one graphic with another |
| Swap Image Restore | Resets a swapped image to its original source |
| Timeline | Actions that start, stop, and move the Timeline playback head to a specific frame |
| Validate Form | Action that confirms that all text field data has been entered correctly and is in the right format |

**TABLE 13-1**     Some of the JavaScript Actions Available in Dreamweaver

If a Behavior is selected in the panel, a small button appears beside it. This is the Events menu. Click it to display a list of events that will set the action in motion. Table 13-2 lists the more commonly used event triggers Dreamweaver recognizes.

**TIP**     *The Events menu displays some events in parentheses, such as onClick. These events are to be used for links only. For more details, see "Use Behaviors with Text and Links," later in this chapter.*

| Event | Description |
|---|---|
| onBlur | Initiated when the element is no longer the main object of user interaction—the opposite of onFocus |
| onClick | Initiated when the user clicks an element such as a button or a link |
| onDblClick | Initiated when the user quickly clicks the mouse twice on an element |

**TABLE 13-2**     Some Event Triggers Available in Dreamweaver

| Event | Description |
|---|---|
| onFocus | Initiated when an element becomes the main object of user interaction—the opposite of onBlur |
| onHelp | Initiated when the user selects the Help option from a browser button or a menu |
| onLoad | Initiated when an image or HTML document finishes loading |
| onMouseDown | Initiated when a user presses the mouse button |
| onMouseOut | Initiated when the user moves the mouse away from (off of) the specified element |
| onMouseOver | Initiated when the user moves the mouse over (onto) the specified element |
| onMouseUp | Initiated when a pressed mouse button is released |
| onSubmit | Initiated when a user submits a form |
| onUnload | Initiated when a user exits a page |

**TABLE 13-2**    Some Event Triggers Available in Dreamweaver *(continued)*

The final two components of the Behaviors panel are the up and down arrows. These do not apply to all Behaviors, but they are extremely useful for reordering the actions that make up some multi-Behavior sequences. To reorder a Behavior, simply select it from the list and use the up or down arrows to change its position in the list. For Behaviors where order is not relevant, the up and down arrows are disabled.

## Attach a Behavior

Using the Behavior panel to attach Behaviors to objects on your web page is a simple process involving a few quick clicks of the mouse. Before you begin, be sure that both the item that requires a Behavior and the Behavior panel are visible. Then follow these steps:

13

1. Select the element of your web page where you wish to attach the Behavior. Both the Tag Inspector and the Behaviors panel (Figure 13-1) indicate the element's HTML tag.

NOTE    *If you want to attach a Behavior to a link, you can either select the entire link or just click anywhere within the link text.*

2. Click the Actions button in the Behavior panel and select the desired action from the menu of possible actions that appears. A dialog box appears, in which you can select the various options for the specified action. The options in the dialog box vary depending on the action you select.

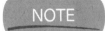 *Some actions in the menu will be dimmed. This simply means that they do not apply to the document you are currently editing. For example, the Drag Layer action will be unavailable if your document does not contain layers.*

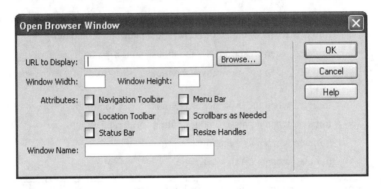

3. Define the action by entering and selecting options in the dialog box. Click OK to close the dialog box and return to the Behaviors panel. The Behaviors panel displays the action alongside the default event that triggers it.

4. Choose the event that sets the Behavior into motion. To do this, simply click the arrow for the Events menu in the Behaviors panel and select the desired event. Again, some of the options may be dimmed either because the events are not applicable to the object to which you are attaching the Behavior or because the events are not recognized by some browsers. (See "Behaviors and Browser Compatibility," later in this chapter.)

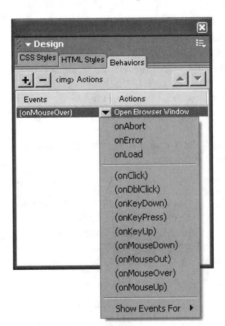

You can't preview Behaviors in Dreamweaver. To test your new Behavior you must preview the document in a web browser. Choose File | Preview In Browser | *browsername*. (For additional information on previewing Dreamweaver documents, see Chapter 1.) When the document appears in the browser window, you can test your Behavior and see that it performs properly.

## Modify a Behavior

After you attach a Behavior, you may wish to edit its attributes. Within the Behavior panel you can make changes to actions and the events that trigger them. To do so, make sure the Behavior panel is open, select the object that has an attached Behavior you would like to modify, and then do any of the following:

- To edit action parameters, double-click on the action to display its dialog box. Make any necessary changes and click OK.
- To change an event, select the event in the Behaviors panel. Click the arrow for the events menu and choose a new event from the list.
- To remove a Behavior, select it and press the minus (–) button or press the DELETE key.
- To add to a Behavior, select a new action, assign its parameters, and choose an event to serve as the trigger. Behaviors appear on the list in alphabetical order by event name. When a single event has two or more actions associated with it, use the up and down arrows to sort the list from top to bottom in the order you want the actions to occur.

## Use Behaviors with Text and Links

Not all portions of a web page can pass event messages to the web browser. Text is one such element. Within an HTML document, text is usually surrounded by a tags such as `<p> </p>` or `<blockquote> </blockquote>`. These tags are for display and formatting purposes only and don't provide a feedback channel to detect user actions. As a result, you can't attach a behavior to the tags or to the text itself. To apply a Behavior to text, you must first insert a tag that enables the text to communicate with the browser and access the JavaScript necessary to perform a Behavior. You normally do this with a link tag—the same tag you use to create a hyperlink to another web page.

To attach a Behavior to a word or section of text, follow these steps:

**1.** Select the text. The Property Inspector panel changes to reflect any formatting that may be applied to the text already.

**2.** In the Link field of the Property Inspector panel type **javascript:;**. This creates a *null link*—a link that goes nowhere. The purpose of a null link is to tell the browser that the link will be handled by the JavaScript of the attached Behavior.

13

*Notice the colon ( : ) and semicolon ( ; ) following* `javascript` *in the null link. You must type the link exactly as shown.*

**3.** In the Behaviors panel, choose the action you wish the Behavior to perform and select an event to trigger it. For more details, see "Attach a Behavior," earlier in the chapter.

*Because the selected text is now tagged as a link, the text will look like other linked text in the document. To change the appearance of the text—either to match surrounding text or to stand out differently from other links—you can create a CSS style and apply it to the text. See Chapter 11 for more about CSS.*

## Use Behaviors with Images

Dreamweaver Behaviors include several JavaScript actions that you can use to manage images and the graphic interactivity on your web site. You can use image-related Behaviors to create interactive diagrams, navigational menus, and buttons.

The most common use of JavaScript in relation to images is the rollover button. In its most basic form, a rollover button changes appearance when a user moves the mouse pointer over the button, and it reverts to its original appearance when the pointer moves away. To complete this effect a button must have two different Behaviors attached to it: Swap Image and Swap Image Restore.

- **Swap Image** Changes the `src=` portion of the `<img>` tag to display a new graphic file within the same tag.
- **Swap Image Restore** Resets images to their original state.

*For detailed instructions for creating rollovers, refer to "Create Rollover Effects," later in this chapter.*

A rollover button is only one use for these Behaviors. The Swap Image action can be applied to any image on the web page to create most any effect you imagine. For example, you can use a Swap Image action to switch between before and after views of an architectural project. The action also allows you to switch multiple images, meaning that one button can alter several graphics on the basis of a single trigger event. For example, on a shopping site, you might attach a set of behaviors to a button to select an item and configure those behaviors to change the images for multiple views of the selected item.

*Preload Images, which loads images into a browser's cache, is also a key component of the Swap Image action because it facilitates an instantaneous swap of images in response to the triggering event instead of a delay as the new image loads. Because this behavior is so often used in conjunction with the Swap Image behavior, the Swap Image dialog box includes a check box that allows you to automatically attach a Preload Images behavior at the same time you add the Swap Image Behavior.*

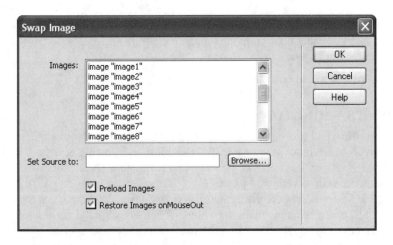

## Use Behaviors with Frames

As discussed in Chapter 7, frames provide a useful means of dividing a web page into sections that can be controlled independently. Frames allow web designers to load new information into one area of the browser window while leaving other areas (such as navigation menus or site maps) untouched. However, it is possible that your design scheme demands that multiple frames change simultaneously. To do this, you must use a Behavior.

The Go to URL action is most helpful when it comes to managing frames. Since Behaviors allow you to trigger multiple actions from a single event, you can create a Behavior that, when triggered by the correct event, loads new content into multiple frames. Use these steps to create and attach the Behavior:

1. Select the link or button you wish to use to target several frames. For more details, see "Attach a Behavior," earlier in the chapter.

2. From the Actions menu, select the Go to URL action. The Go To URL dialog box appears, showing where the link can be opened. You can choose the main window or any frame on the page.

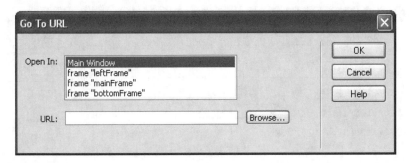

3. Select the frame you want to target, and then either type the URL for the linked document or click the Browse button to locate the file you want.

13

4. Click OK, and the Go to URL action appears in the Behavior panel beside an event. Since you will be using this action in conjunction with a link or a button, the default event is either onClick or onMouseDown.

5. Repeat steps 1–4 to add other target frames to the link.

## Use Behaviors with Layers

Like frames, layers are a tool that can help with the layout and design of your page. (See Chapter 12 for more on layers.) Layers offer a great deal of flexibility by allowing designers to position layers, and thus their contents, at exact pixel coordinates. Combining Behaviors with layers can add exciting interactive flair to your web page.

The Show-Hide Layers action controls the visibility of a layer. You can use it to create complex rollover responses, dynamic maps with hidden overlays, digital dress-up dolls, and so on. Once you attach this kind of Behavior to an element of your page, that element becomes a kind of switch that turns a layer on or off. The kind of switch depends on the event you assign to the Behavior.

Another interactive JavaScript command that you can use in Dreamweaver Behaviors is the Drag-Layer action. The Drag-Layer action allows users to physically move the graphic and text elements that reside in the layers of an HTML document. This makes the action ideal for creating digital jigsaw puzzles and board games, moveable interface controls, and so on. In addition to the interactivity afforded by moveable graphics, the Drag-Layer action allows you to define parameters such as the following:

- **Movement**   Unconstrained or bounded by pixel coordinates.
- **Drop Target**   Defined by pixel coordinates; sets layers to "snap" to coordinates when they are within a particular range.
- **Drag Handle**   Defines the area where the viewer can click and drag to move the layer.
- **Stacking**   A layer can change stacking order when it is dragged.
- **JavaScript**   Calls additional JavaScript code while the drag is in progress or when a layer is dropped.

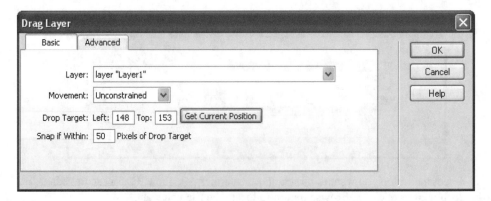

## Use Behaviors with Timelines

In Dreamweaver, Timelines allow you to animate the contents of a layer. You can use layers to create quick intro animations, "slide show" picture sequences, and other kinds of visual changes over time. (For more on Timelines, see Chapter 12.) By incorporating Behaviors into a Timeline you can control the animation or use animation sequences as events that trigger other Behaviors.

Use the Play and Stop Timeline actions for Behaviors that control Timeline animations. These Behaviors are often attached to a link, a button, or the <body> tag of the web page. When the element receives an event message, such as a mouse click, the event triggers the Timeline animation to either begin or stop playing.

You can also create Behaviors that allow you to jump to any point in an animation. To do this, use the Go to Timeline Frame action. When cued by an event, this action causes the Timeline to automatically advance to the frame number specified in the Behavior. Think of this as a means of creating fast-forward and rewind buttons for your animation.

Many times, these Behaviors are attached to elements outside the Timeline, such as buttons and links. However, it is also possible to attach Behaviors to frames of the Timeline itself (Figure 13-2), using the Behavior Channel in the Timeline panel. Events are defined by frame numbers. When

Timeline panel

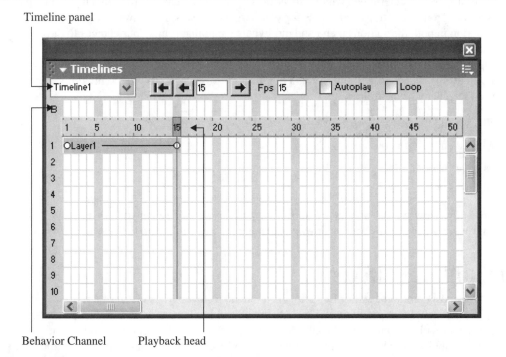

Behavior Channel        Playback head

**FIGURE 13-2**    Attach Behaviors to a Timeline using the Behavior Channel in the Timeline panel.

13

the playback head reaches the event frame, the action is executed. In this case, the event is onFrame15.

Placing a Behavior (or more accurately, an action) in the Timeline creates a timed event. When the playback head arrives at the designated frame, the JavaScript action executes. In Figure 13-2 there is an animation on Layer 1 that lasts 15 frames and a Go to URL action in frame 15 of the Behavior Channel. When frame 15 is played, the action executes, and a new URL is launched. This technique is useful for causing an introductory animation to immediately open a home page when the animation is complete.

# Behaviors and Browser Compatibility

Dreamweaver Behaviors provide a wide range of effects, but unfortunately they have limitations. Not all web browsers are able to interpret the events and actions associated with Behaviors. Some browsers do not support JavaScript at all, and even among those that do, there are differences in the way various browsers interpret it. Macromedia has taken steps to ensure that the JavaScript generated by Dreamweaver Behaviors functions on as many platforms and browsers as possible, but it's still best to test your site on a variety of machines and browsers to ensure both design and functional consistency.

Macromedia has determined which browsers support what Behavior functionality. To help you select appropriate actions and events for your target browsers, Dreamweaver provides a menu option in both the Actions menu and the Events menu that limits your choices to the browser(s) you select.

Open either the Actions (click the + button) or the Events menu (click the arrow button beside an event), and choose Show Events For | *browser* to select a browser compatibility level. You can select any of the following:

- 3.0 and Later Browsers
- 4.0 and Later Browsers
- Internet Explorer 3, 4, 5, or 6
- Netscape 3, 4, or 6

Select the browser your audience is most likely to use when viewing your web site. Dreamweaver grays out any actions or events that are incompatible with the selected browser.

# Create Rollover Effects

One of the most common uses for Behaviors is to create rollovers. The effect of a rollover can be impressive, although it is really quite simple to create and implement in your web page design. Dreamweaver will, of course, handle all the JavaScript. But what it can't do is produce the necessary graphics. At a bare minimum, you need two: one for the idle state and one for the rollover state. To create these you must use a separate graphics program such as Macromedia Fireworks or Adobe Photoshop.

Once your graphics have been created, you should be ready to add them to your web page and create the rollover. This is how you do it:

*Before bringing rollover graphics into the Dreamweaver environment, place them in your local site folder or one of its subfolders.*

**1.** Position the insertion point in your document at the location where you want to insert the rollover button.

**2.** To insert the rollover image, do any of the following:

■ Click the Rollover Images icon on the Insert panel (in the Common section).

■ Drag the Rollover Images icon from the Insert panel onto your document.

■ Choose Insert | Interactive Images | Rollover Image.

The Insert Rollover Image dialog box appears.

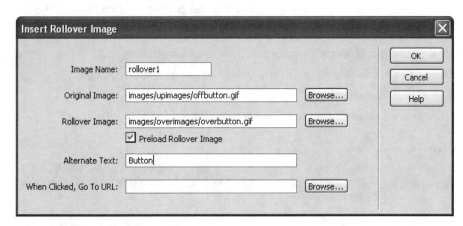

**3.** Select the options for your rollover image:

■ **Image Name**  Type a name for the rollover here. (This is not mandatory, but it can be helpful if you plan to use several rollovers in a single document.)

■ **Original Image**  Type a path or click Browse to select the "idle state" image.

■ **Rollover Image**  Type a path or click Browse to select the "active state" image.

■ **Preload Rollover Image**  Check this option to preload your rollover image (recommended).

■ **Alternate Text**  Type a description of the image to make your site accessible to those with visual impairments.

■ **When Clicked, Go to URL**  If your rollover is a hyperlink button you can enter the link's URL in this field.

13

4. Click OK to close the Insert Rollover Image dialog box. The rollover image you defined appears in the Document window. To test the rollover, preview your page in a browser.

This procedure streamlines the process of attaching Behaviors for a rollover effect. Dreamweaver automatically inserts the image and attaches the necessary Behaviors to create a rollover image with the link you specify. You can also insert the image into your page manually and attach three or four separate Behaviors, but this procedure requires more work.

## Create a Navigation Bar

Navigation bars offer an immediately recognizable, clear means of exploring a web site. Navigation bars (or nav bars) serve as both a bookmark and a table of contents (Figure 13-3). The navigation options are listed horizontally or vertically on the web page and offer two kinds of information: the visitor's current location and other primary locations that can be visited within the site.

As with rollover images, you must create nav bar graphics in an external imaging program. Nav bar components can have up to four states:

- **Up**   Idle or inactive state
- **Over**   Ready state when the cursor is pointing to the nav bar selection
- **Down**   Active state that marks a selection
- **Over While Down**   Ready state for a selection in the down position

---

**FIGURE 13-3**   This navigation bar sits horizontally across the top of the page. Visitors click the different selections to navigate the site.

Basically, a nav bar is a set of rollover buttons. As you can with single rollovers, you could manually insert the base images for each button and then attach behaviors to each one, but it's a lot easier to use Dreamweaver's Insert Navigation Bar feature to automate much of the process. Here is how to create a navigation bar:

1. Position the insertion point cursor in your document at the location where you want to insert the navigation bar.

2. To insert the navigation bar you can either:

   ■ Click the Navigation Bar button in the Common category of the Insert bar panel.

   ■ Choose Insert | Interactive Images | Navigation Bar.

   The Insert Navigation Bar dialog box appears.

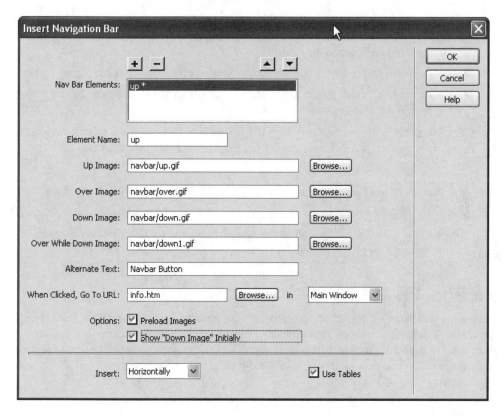

3. Dreamweaver lists the first Nav Bar Element as "unnamed1." Click the Browse button for the Up Image field, and select the graphic you wish to use for the idle state of the first nav bar element.

4. Click the other Browse buttons to select graphics for the remaining states (as desired): Over Image, Down Image, and Over While Down Image.

5. Click the Browse button for When Clicked, Go To URL to select the linked document and choose a location for the new link from the "in" pop-up menu.

6. If you want an element to be in the active (down) state when the nav bar is first loaded, check the box next to Show "Down Image" Initially. Dreamweaver tracks this by inserting an asterisk next to the element.

7. To add more elements to the nav bar, click the plus (+) button and repeat steps 4–7. Click the minus (–) button to remove elements, and use the up and down arrows to reorder them.

   Other options in this dialog box do the following:

   ■ Preload Images attaches the necessary Behaviors to load nav bar graphics into the browser's cache before they are used. This option prevents lag when the graphics change from one state to the next.

   ■ Choose horizontal or vertical orientation for your nav bar from the Insert pop-up menu.

   ■ Check the Use Tables option to instruct Dreamweaver to create a table to control the position of the various nav bar buttons.

8. Click OK to close the Insert Navigation Bar dialog box. Dreamweaver inserts the images into your page, attaches Behaviors to the images, and adds the necessary code to your web document.

To make changes to an existing navigation bar choose Modify | Navigation Bar and edit as needed.

**NOTE** *You can only have one navigation bar per page. If you are working with a frameset, be sure to select the correct frame before inserting or editing a nav bar.*

# Create a Pop-Up Menu

Pop-up menus are one of the hottest features on the web, and they're also the newest feature in Dreamweaver's Behaviors arsenal. These dynamic menus can be linked to text or images, and are often used as submenus for nav bars (see Figure 13-4). This enables visitors to link to a particular page of interest without having to wade through intermediate pages.

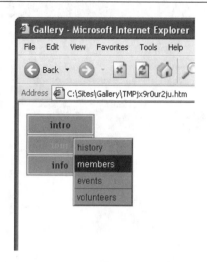

**FIGURE 13-4**   This pop-up menu is triggered by the mouse moving over the main navigational menu. The pop-up menu is hidden when the mouse moves away from the menu.

To add a pop-up menu to a page:

**1.**  Position the insertion point cursor in your document at the location where you want to insert the pop-up menu. If you're attaching the menu to a text element, you first need to establish a null link, as described in the Use Behaviors with Text and Links section earlier in this chapter.

**2.**  Choose Show Pop-Up Menu from the Actions list in the Behaviors panel. The Show Pop-Up Menu dialog box appears.

**3.**  Use the following options to complete your menu:

■   The Contents tab establishes the menu items. Click the plus (+) sign to add a menu item and link. Click the Indent button to add a submenu to your pop-up menu.

**13**

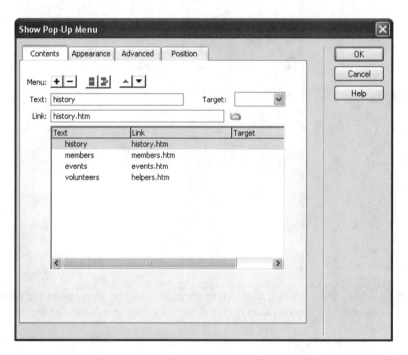

■ The Appearance tab determines the font, color, and up and over states for the menu items.

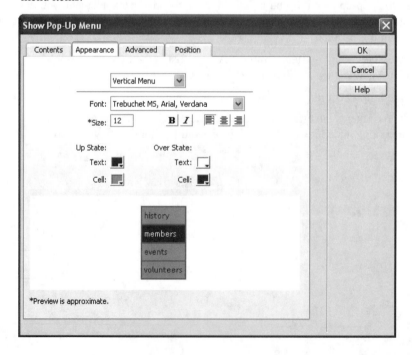

■   The Advanced tab controls the menu table, including the cell dimensions, border width and color, and the position of the text within the cells. This tab also enables you to set the delay between the mouseover and when the menu appears.

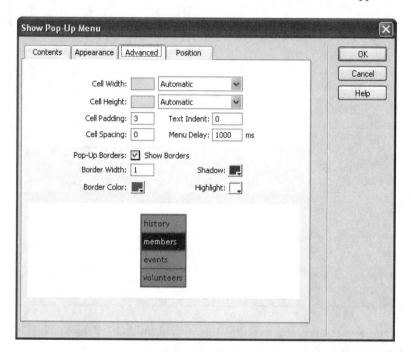

■   The Position tab controls the positioning of the pop-up menu in relation to the image or text that triggers it. The positioning can be set using one of four preset options, or by manually typing coordinates that represent the distance in pixels from the top-left corner of the menu.

**13**

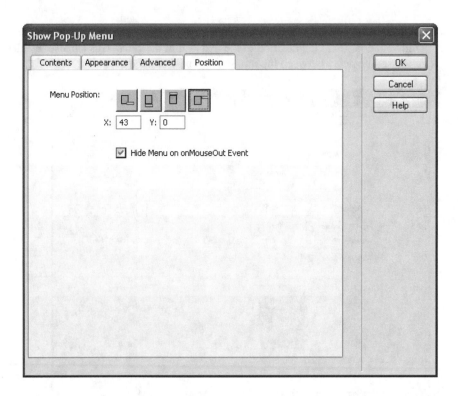

The trigger image or text becomes a link to the pop-up menu, so it will take on the formatting of other links in your document. If you wish to change this appearance, you can create a CSS class (see Chapter 11) and apply it to the trigger text.

NOTE *Pop-up menus will not appear over forms or other active content that solicit user interaction. If you want to use a pop-up menu on a page with active content, position the menu carefully to avoid overlap, or you risk the menu not being functional.*

# Chapter 14

## Program Dynamic Web Pages

## How to...

- ■ Create pages using server-side scripting technologies
- ■ Connect to databases
- ■ Add server Behaviors to your pages

As web technologies mature, web surfers expect more from the web experience. Just about every major site these days has one thing in common—they don't rely on plain web pages or even client-side scripting to provide content. Today, database-driven web applications are the rule rather than the exception on big web sites, and the technology is spreading fast among many smaller sites as well. Macromedia recognized this trend and made its own move in this direction by merging what were previously two separate products, Dreamweaver and Dreamweaver UltraDev, into Dreamweaver MX. Now all Dreamweaver MX users have access to the same tools for tapping into the power of dynamic database-driven web programming.

Creating database-driven web pages and developing web applications are advanced topics that are well beyond most beginning-to-intermediate Dreamweaver users. However, since Dreamweaver MX includes such a large set of features devoted to supporting server-side programming, this book would be incomplete without at least acknowledging the existence of these features. If you plan to use Dreamweaver only to produce basic HTML web pages, you can skip this chapter. However, for those readers who have the background to understand the underlying technologies and may have the need to use them, this chapter can give you a glimpse at the tools Dreamweaver MX puts at your disposal when you're ready to take your web development to the next level.

# Understand Web Application Technologies

There was a time when designing for the web was pretty straightforward—you used a design tool or even just a text editor to place the HTML tags on each page, and published them on a web server. If you wanted to get fancy you could add some JavaScript code to your page and maybe a Java applet or two. Server-side processing was strictly limited to CGI programs handling form data.

These days, however, some of the focus for web development has shifted from creating sites consisting of individual static pages to building sites full of dynamically generated pages that combine to perform some useful function, such as an online store. This collection of pages has come to be known as a *web application,* so named because of the similarity to traditional desktop applications. The main difference between a desktop application and a web application is that the web application is distributed. The majority of the application logic, as well as the data storage and retrieval, occurs on web servers accessible over the Internet, while the user interface is presented as an HTML document in a browser window on the client.

NOTE    *A detailed explanation of SQL (Structured Query Language) databases is outside the scope of this book. The Using Dreamweaver MX help file provides a basic overview of how databases are organized and how to make SQL calls to access a database.*

## Did you know?

# A Word About Databases

While it is possible to develop powerful dynamic web applications using just the server-side code and maybe a data file or two, you won't be tapping into the full power of server-side scripting until you add a database. Most of the objects and behaviors that Dreamweaver provides for server-side use are designed to work with database connections and recordsets.

As with most things pertaining to web site development, there is no one way to develop web applications. There are a lot of choices for server-side development environments available now, and more are coming all the time. Dreamweaver MX's strength is that it can work with several of the most popular server-side technologies, including Active Server Pages (ASP), JavaServer Pages (JSP), PHP, ColdFusion, and ASP.NET. This support allows you to design and develop web applications no matter what server technology you may choose.

The web application technology you choose to use may depend on several factors, including the type of server you are running your site on and your comfort level with various scripting languages. For instance, if your company uses Windows 2000 servers and you are familiar with the Visual Basic language, you may decide to use ASP or ASP.NET, since they are integrated well with Microsoft's web server, IIS, and can be programmed using VBScript or VB.NET respectively. On the other hand, if you are developing applications that you want to distribute to others to run on their sites, you might choose PHP due to its widespread availability on several server platforms. The following table shows the web application technologies supported by Dreamweaver MX and the server platforms required to run them.

| Server Technology | Supported Languages/Application Servers |
| --- | --- |
| ASP | Microsoft's original server-side technology. Server-side code can be written in either the VBScript or JScript scripting language. It is supported on Microsoft's IIS and PWS web servers. |
| | Sun's Chili!Soft ASP brings ASP to other platforms and web servers as well, including those running Apache, iPlanet, and Zeus. Chili!Soft can be found at www.chilisoft.com. |
| ASP.NET | The next generation of server technologies from Microsoft. Currently the only server supporting it is IIS 5.0 running on Windows 2000 or XP, or .NET Server. Applications can be written in a variety of languages, including Visual Basic.NET, C# (C Sharp), C++, and JScript.NET. |
| | To install ASP.NET, you must download the .NET Framework from Microsoft at asp.net/download.aspx . |

14

| Server Technology | Supported Languages/Application Servers |
| --- | --- |
| ColdFusion | Requires Macromedia ColdFusion 5 or ColdFusion MX Server. While ColdFusion is an extra-cost option compared to the other technologies listed here, ColdFusion is well integrated with Dreamweaver MX and merits consideration. More information about ColdFusion, as well as a fully functional developer edition, can be found at Macromedia's ColdFusion site: www.macromedia.com/software/coldfusion. |
| JSP | JavaServer Pages requires a JSP application server to be installed. Popular ones include:<br>• Macromedia JRun: www.macromedia.com/software/jrun/<br>• IBM WebSphere: www-3.ibm.com/software/webservers/appserv/<br>• Jakarta Tomcat : jakarta.apache.org/tomcat/ |
| PHP | Both a language and a server technology, PHP is available for many popular web servers, including Apache, IIS, and Netscape servers. More information about PHP can be found at www.php.net/. |

# Define an Application Server

Once you've decided on a server technology, you must tell Dreamweaver which technology you are using for testing purposes. The Site Definition wizard provides a page that lets you do just that. You can specify the server technology when you first create your site or go back later and choose a different one.

To modify your server settings or set some of the advanced details for the server environment, you use the Advanced tab of the Site Definition dialog box. To set up a testing server using the Advanced tab, follow these steps:

NOTE    *These steps assume you have already set up the local and remote information for your site. If you haven't, do so before proceeding. See Chapter 2 for more information about configuring a site.*

1. Choose Site | Edit Sites. Select the site you want to edit, and click the Edit button. You can also create a new site from this dialog box. Dreamweaver displays the Site Definition dialog box.

2. Click the Advanced tab at the top of the Site Definition dialog box, and select Testing Server in the category list to display the options shown in Figure 14-1.

3. Choose a server-side scripting model in the Server Model drop-down list.

4. If your site has legacy ColdFusion 4 pages generated by a previous version of Dreamweaver, choose one of the following options in the This Site Contains box:

   ■ **Dreamweaver MX Pages Only**    Dreamweaver MX will modify existing ColdFusion pages to generate Dreamweaver MX's improved ColdFusion code.

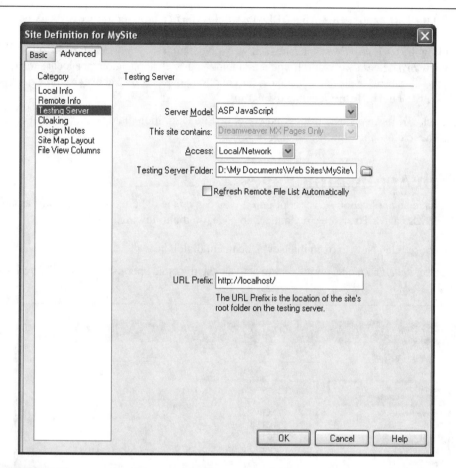

**FIGURE 14-1**    Setting testing server options using the Site Definition dialog box's
Advanced tab

- **Ultradev 4 Pages Only**    Existing and new ColdFusion pages will continue to generate the same code as Ultradev 4.

- **Both Versions**    Existing ColdFusion pages will be generated with Ultradev 4 ColdFusion code. New pages will use improved ColdFusion code.

**5.**    Edit the server settings as needed. Dreamweaver automatically duplicates the server settings from the Remote Info category. If those settings are correct for your development environment as well, you can leave them alone. If your application server is separate from your web server, you can specify the appropriate settings here.

6. Set the URL prefix. This is the URL you would type in a browser to access your web application, without the filename. For instance, if your web application is accessed using the URL http://www.mysite.com/webapp/default.asp, you would type **http://www.mysite.com/webapp/**. If you are running your web application on a local server, you can substitute the name localhost for your domain name. The above example run locally would be **http://localhost/webapp/**.

7. Click OK to save your settings and close the Site Definition dialog box, and then click Done to close the Edit Sites dialog box.

# Create Web Application Pages

Once you have an application server configured, you can create dynamic web pages just as easily as static HTML pages. To create a dynamic web page, do the following.

1. Choose File | New to open the New Document dialog box.

2. Select the Dynamic Page category to activate the dynamic options, as shown Figure 14-2.

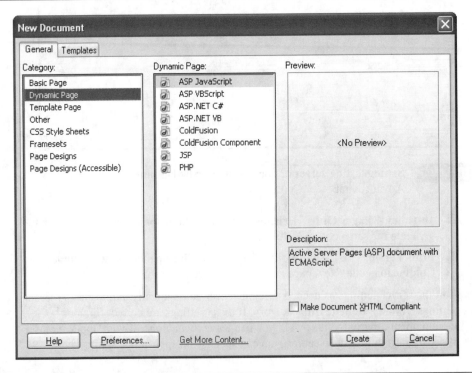

**FIGURE 14-2** Create server-side pages just as easily as static HTML pages.

**3.** Choose the server-side scripting technology you want to use from Dynamic Page list.

**4.** Click Create to open the new page in the Design view.

That's it! You've just created a server-side dynamic page. Now comes the hard part, writing the code. Dreamweaver MX helps with that by providing special objects for each supported server-side technology.

# Use Active Server Pages (ASP)

Microsoft's Active Server Pages (ASP) is a well-established technology on Windows NT and 2000 web servers, if for no other reason than that it's built in. ASP works by embedding server-side script (written in VBScript or JavaScript) into a web page with special tags that mark it as server code. The web server executes the script and then sends the combination of the script output and the page's HTML code to the browser. This is a straightforward approach that is easily understood by people already familiar with client-side scripting.

There are some disadvantages to ASP as well. Since script code is interpreted at run time, performance isn't as high as it would be using one of the compiled application technologies such as ASP.NET, PHP, or JSP. However, ASP's ubiquitous distribution and ease of programming make it a compelling choice, especially for people new to server-side programming. Besides, performance can be improved by writing some computationally intensive portions of an ASP web application in Visual Basic or C++.

When you edit an ASP page in Dreamweaver, the Insert bar shows a new category populated with special objects just for ASP pages. (You can also access the same objects choosing Insert | ASP Objects | *object*.) The objects are the same whether you are editing a VBScript ASP page or a JavaScript ASP page. Dreamweaver knows which code to generate based on the default language chosen for the page. Here's a brief description of the ASP objects:

■ **Server Variable** ASP provides many different built-in variables that provide information about the server environment. This object inserts a reference to one of these variables into the code, either as a script reference or as an output block that will display the value of the variable.

■ **Include** Inserts a server-side include in the head of the document. You must type in the file name path yourself in Code view. Server-side includes allow you to put common code that you want to access from many different pages in a separate file and just reference that file instead of copying the code into each page.

■ **Code Block** Inserts a code block at the current cursor position. Code blocks are special tags that tell the server that the enclosed code is server-side script. The tags are formatted with special tags (`<% %>`) and are a shorthand way of using a server-side `<script></script>` tag.

■ **Output** This is similar to a code block, but an equal sign at the start of the tag shows that ASP should evaluate the expression contained in the block and output the result to the document. For instance, `<%= Date %>` in VBScript will call the Date function and output the result, the current date, to the document. Any expression will work here, from function calls to variable names.

14

- **If, Else, Elsif, End** These buttons insert control-execution blocks into the code. These let you display different items depending on the result of an expression. For example, you could use an if-then block to completely customize a page depending on values inserted in a query string or depending on values obtained from the query string appended to the URL, or you could display a message instead of a table if a retrieved database recordset is empty.

- **Response.Write** Inserts a Response.Write() call into a script block (you must make sure that the cursor is inside a script block in Code view). Response.Write() is the method that ASP uses to write information to the document. The string data inside the Response.Write() call can be text, HTML tags, or whatever you wish to output to the document as is.

- **Trimmed Form Element** If the ASP page is processing a form submission, this button provides a way to automatically add the code needed to retrieve a form value by name. The value is also trimmed to remove any white space from the beginning and end.

- **Trimmed Querystring Element** This is similar to Trimmed Form Element; however, it provides access to a value passed in on a querystring variable appended to the URL in the form `http://www.mysite.com/mydoc.asp?var1=val1&var2=val2`.

- **Server.CreateObject** This is an advanced ASP feature used to create external objects. It's commonly used to create objects needed for database connectivity such as connections or recordsets.

- **More Tags** This button is common to all of the Insert bar categories for server-side technologies. It opens the Tag Chooser dialog box, where you can select any of the many less common tags for insertion into your document. (To open the dialog box from the menus, choose Insert | Tag.)

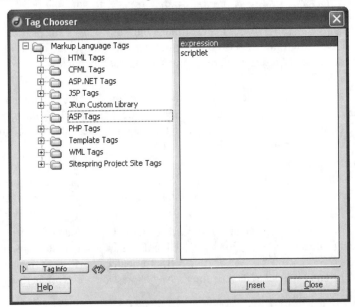

## Define ASP Database Connections

While ASP is good at generating dynamic content all by itself, it really begins to shine when you add a database to the mix. ASP database connections typically are made through an Open Database Connectivity (ODBC) driver or an Object Linking and Embedding database (OLE DB) provider. In most cases, you will use a Data Source Name (DSN) to connect to the database. You (or the system administrator) will need to create the DSN on the server where your web application is running. The database can be any that you have a driver installed for, from Access to SQL Server to Oracle.

Once you have a DSN created for your database, you can create a database connection in Dreamweaver to use that DSN to access the database. To create a database connection using a locally created DSN, follow these steps:

**1.** Open an ASP page (either JavaScript or VBScript), or create a new one in Dreamweaver.

**2.** Open the Databases panel (Window | Databases). All of the connections created for the site are displayed.

**3.** Click the plus (+) button and choose Data Source Name to open the Data Source Name dialog box.

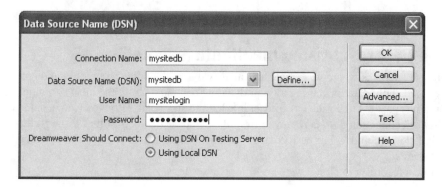

**4.** Enter a name for the connection.

**5.** Select the Using Local DSN option at the bottom of the panel to use a DSN on your local machine, or select Using DSN on Testing Server to create a connection to a database on a remote server.

**6.** Enter the DSN name and the user name and password (if required) in the appropriate boxes.

14

**7.** Click Test to validate the connection. If the connection works, click OK. Dreamweaver adds the new connection to the Databases panel.

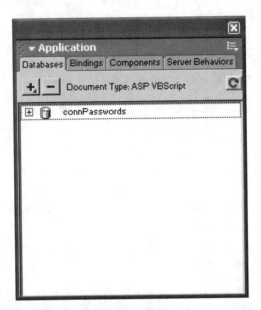

# Define a Recordset Using the Bindings Panel

The Bindings panel is is where you create and modify dynamic content sources, add them to your pages, and apply data formatting to your dynamic content. One of the most common uses for the Bindings panel is to define a recordset in which to store data retrieved from a database. A *recordset* is a collection of data retrieved from the database (as the result of a query) that is temporarily held in memory. For performance reasons, it is only held as long as it is needed, and then it is discarded.

To define a recordset in Dreamweaver, follow these steps:

**1.** Open the Bindings panel (Window | Bindings).

**2.** Click the plus (+) button and choose Recordset (Query) to open the Recordset dialog box.

**3.** Enter a name for the recordset in the Name box.

**4.** Choose a connection from the Connection drop-down list. (Click Define if you haven't created the connection yet.)

**5.** Choose the table from which you want to retrieve the data.

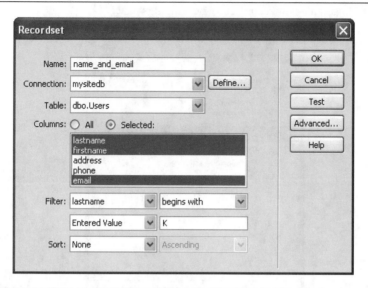

**FIGURE 14-3**   The Recordset dialog box is an easy way to query a single database table without having to write any SQL queries.

**6.** Select the column(s) you want retrieved as part of your query. CTRL-click to select multiple columns.

**7.** Fill in the Filter section if you want to limit the number of records retrieved, say by searching for a name that starts with a particular letter, as shown in Figure 14-3.

- In the first drop-down box, choose a column to filter by.

- In the second drop-down box (to the right), choose an expression to compare against the values in the first column.

- In the third box, select Entered Value.

- Enter the value to test against in the fourth box.

**8.** In the Sort box, select the column you want to sort the data by, and then choose Ascending or Descending. Select None if you don't want the data sorted.

**9.** Click Test to see if the query is successful (and returns the results that you thought it would).

**10.** Click OK to add the new recordset to the Bindings panel.

> TIP
>
> *While it's tempting to always have a query return all columns in a recordset, you can achieve better performance by narrowing the query to those columns you really need. You can always create multiple recordsets that access the same table for different needs.*

## Add Server Behaviors

Server behaviors are the quick and easy way to add dynamic data-driven content to your pages. You can use server behaviors to display data retrieved from a database, add or edit data in a database, authenticate users, and more. You can add server behaviors to your page from the Server Behaviors panel (choose Window | Server Behaviors to open the panel) or from the Applications category of the Insert bar.

The following server behaviors are available:

- **Recordset** Another way of defining a recordset from an existing database. This has the same effect as adding a recordset through the Bindings panel.

- **Repeated Region** This lets you display multiple records on a page. If you have individual dynamic text items on a page, you can apply this behavior to make it repeat a specific number of times. Once a repeated region has been added, you can select it in the editor and use the Repeat Region Property Inspector panel to modify the settings.

- **Dynamic Table** Creates a table associated with a recordset. You can choose to display all rows in the recordset or a limited number. All columns selected for the recordset are displayed in the table. Figure 14-4 shows the Design view display of a dynamic table.

  - **Dynamic Text** Inserts a dynamic text object. This text object is associated with an item from an existing recordset.

  - **Recordset Navigation Bar** Adds a set of controls that the viewer can use to move through a recordset collection.

  - **Recordset Navigation Status** Inserts a line of information about the current row in the recordset. Figure 14-5 shows this object, along with a recordset navigation bar and a dynamic table in a Design View window and in a browser window.

  - **Master/Detail Page Set** Inserts a table showing selected columns from a recordset. This server behavior also adds a second page with more columns displayed, which the viewer can see by clicking on one of the items displayed in the master page table.

  - **Record Insertion Form** Creates a form that allows the browser to insert new records into a table.

  - **Record Update Form** Creates a form that allows the browser to update existing table records, as shown in Figure 14-6.

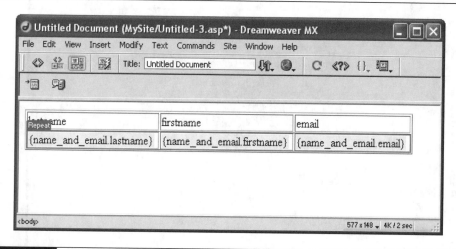

**FIGURE 14-4** A dynamic table makes it easy to display data from a recordset.

14

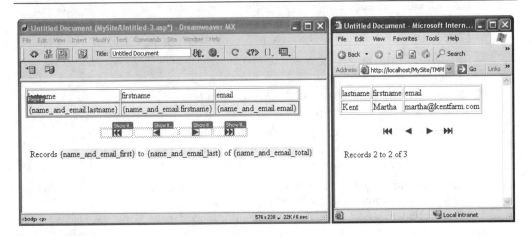

**FIGURE 14-5** A dynamic table, recordset navigation bar, and recordset navigation status control in both Design and Preview views.

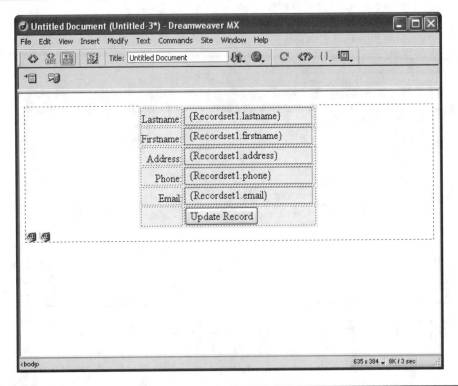

**FIGURE 14-6** A Record Update form will automatically update a table record with new information.

In addition to the server behaviors available on the Insert bar, the Server Behaviors panel adds a few more options.

- **Dynamic Form Elements** Creates form elements that automatically set their values to data from a recordset.

- **User Authentication** Lets you restrict access to certain areas of your web site. You define a table where valid user authentication values are stored.

- **Edit/New Server Behaviors** Allows you to edit existing server Behaviors or create new ones.

- **Get More Server Behaviors** Links to the Macromedia Exchange site, where server Behaviors created by others can be downloaded.

# Use ASP.NET

The .NET framework is Microsoft's next-generation platform for creating all types of applications, from desktop apps to full-blown data-driven web applications using ASP.NET. ASP.NET goes way beyond ASP in features and functionality. Instead of being limited to essentially two scripting languages, ASP.NET allows you to write server-side code in modern object-oriented .NET languages such as VB.NET, C#, and JScript.NET. This code is automatically compiled into native code by the server the first time the page is accessed. No manual compilation step is required.

Although the script code is compiled, writing ASP.NET applications is in fact very similar to writing ASP applications. You can still embed your server-side scripts directly into your web page. (Actually, ASP.NET gives you the option to separate your server code and HTML into separate files, but this approach isn't supported by Dreamweaver MX.)

Another huge advantage to using ASP.NET instead of classic ASP is the .NET Framework classes. While ASP provides a smattering of objects such as Response and Request for use in your scripts, ASP.NET has a full-blown object framework consisting of thousands of classes, which provide such functionality as XML, encryption, communications protocols like TCP/IP and SMTP, and much more. Best of all, you can use this framework with any .NET language you like, because .NET languages share a common run-time element that makes them compatible at the object level.

The ASP.NET category of the Insert bar provides the following objects useful to web application developers:

- **Register Custom Tag** An advanced feature of ASP.NET is the ability to define custom tags, complete with attributes, that are bound to a server-side class file that generates content to replace the tag in the document. The Register Custom Tag button inserts the Register directive into your page, which allows you to specify the information for any custom controls.

14

- **Import Namespace**　You can group .NET classes into collections of related objects, and give each a unique *namespace*. This button inserts an Import directive, which explicitly imports the namespace into the page. This makes all classes in the namespace available to the page.

- **Trimmed Form Element**　This is similar to the ASP item of the same name—it provides the code necessary to access a form item value in a form-processing page. The difference is that the language generated here is either VB.NET or C#, depending on what you chose to use for this page.

- **Trimmed QueryString Element**　Provides a way to access a query string variable and trim white space from the start and end, in either VB.NET or C#.

- **Runat Server**　This inserts an attribute that specifies that an object will run on the server before the page is sent to the browser.

- **Bound Data**　Inserts a tag that can display a data value obtained from a data source such as a database.

- **Page_Load**　Inserts a server-side script block with a Page_Load function defined. This function is called on the server before the page is sent to the browser.

- **asp:button, asp:checkbox, asp:checkboxlist, asp:dropdownlist, asp:imagebutton, asp:label, asp:listbox, asp:radiobutton, asp:radiobuttongroup, asp:textbox**　These objects insert special versions of common form tags that have server-side components. These objects allow you to generate forms with existing data filled in, among other features.

When you add an ASP.NET form object to your page, the Tag Editor dialog box appears, as shown in Figure 14-7. This dialog box lets you set just about every possible attribute, style, event, and data-binding option for a tag.

# Use ColdFusion

ColdFusion is a web application technology that has been around for a number of years now, the latest incarnation of which is ColdFusion MX. Because ColdFusion and Dreamweaver MX are both Macromedia products, it's not surprising that Dreamweaver MX supports ColdFusion more thoroughly than most other server-side technologies.

One difference between ColdFusion and most other server-side technologies is that it doesn't require that you use a traditional programming language for the dynamic portions of a page. Instead, you use a set of custom tags, functions, and variables known as ColdFusion Markup Language (CFML).

ColdFusion Markup Language looks similar to HTML—The tags are surrounded by angle brackets, and they have start and end tags with a forward slash preceding the name of the end tag. All CFML tags start with "cf" for ease of identification.

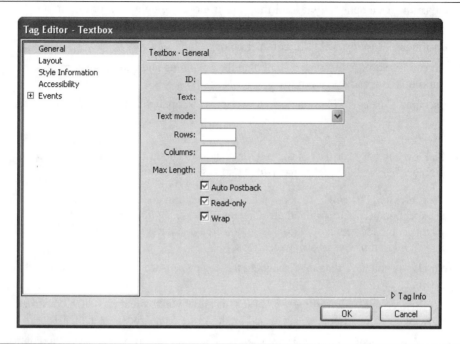

**FIGURE 14-7** The Tag Editor lets you set ASP.NET tag properties.

## CFML Basic

ColdFusion is so well supported in Dreamweaver MX that the Insert bar has to have three separate categories to display all of the provided tags. The first one is the CFML Basic category, which contains some of the most useful data and script operations.

- **Server Variable** This is much like the ASP equivalent: it provides access to server variables showing many server configuration values. The server variable you choose is wrapped in a ColdFusion variable so that it is accessible to CFML.

- **cfquery** Defines a general database query. Specify the data source connection information as well as the SQL commands to execute as the query.

- **cfoutput** Used to display the results of a database query or some other operation such as a cfdirectory (see "CFML Advanced").

- **cfinsert** Used to insert new records in a data source based on form results.

- **cfupdate** Similar to cfinsert, except that it's used for updating existing records.

- **cfinclude** Embeds a reference to an external ColdFusion file.

- **cflocation** Stops the current page execution and loads a new page.

- **cfset** Used to define a ColdFusion variable and set a value.

14

- **cfparam**   Can optionally test for the existence of a variable, test for the variable's being of the proper type, and specify a default value to set the variable to if it does exist.
- **Comment**   Inserts an HTML comment block.
- **Surround with #**   Inserts a # symbol at the beginning and end of the current selection, marking it as a variable reference.
- **cfscript**   Creates a CFScript block. CFScript is a scripting language similar to JavaScript.

## CFML Flow

The CFML Flow category consists of those items that have conditional execution. These include if-then-else blocks, try-catch blocks, and switch and case statements.

- **cftry, cfcatch, cfthrow**   Exception handling tags. Put code that might potentially throw an exception between cftry and cfcatch tags. If the exception occurs, execution will resume at the cfcatch, assuming it is set to catch that particular exception. The cfthrow tag is used to throw your own exceptions.
- **cflock**   If you have data that is shared, this tag can ensure that only one access occurs at a time.
- **cfswitch, cfcase, cfdefaultcase**   These tags allow you to create a switch construct, allowing execution to take place based on the value compared at each cfcase.
- **cfif, cfelse, cfelsif**   These tags are used to create an if-elseif-else construct to control execution flow based on the result of the expression being compared in the cfif.
- **cfloop**   Used to execute a loop, such as over the rows of a recordset.
- **cfbreak**   Used to break out of a cfloop.

## CFML Advanced

The CFML Advanced category consists of more complex CFML tags:

- **cfcookie**   Defines a web browser cookie, including the expiration options, security, and domain information.
- **cfcontent**   Lets you specify a MIME type for the content of the current page. Optionally, allows you to specify a file for download with the page.
- **cfheader**   Allows you to create custom HTTP response headers for the page. The tag editor allows you to enter the name and value for the custom header.
- **cfapplication**   Allows you to set ColdFusion application settings, including whether to use client or domain cookies, session management, and application and session time-out values.
- **cferror**   Displays a custom HTML page when an error occurs.
- **cfdirectory**   Allows you to manage directories from ColdFusion. Options include List, Create, Delete, and Rename actions and the directory to perform the action on. This tag must be enabled in ColdFusion Administrator.

- ■ **cffile**    Manages file interactions. Allows common file operations such as read, write, create, delete, and upload files. This tag must be enabled in ColdFusion Administrator.

- ■ **cfmail**    Sends mail containing the results of a query to a specified address.

- ■ **cfhttp**    Executes standard HTTP POST or GET operations to retrieve files.

- ■ **cfhttpparam**    Specifies a parameter for an HTTP POST operation created by a cfhttp tag.

- ■ **cfldap**    Provides access to an LDAP (Lightweight Data Access Protocol) server.

- ■ **cfftp**    Performs FTP operations, such as listing the directory, getting and putting files, and more.

- ■ **cfsearch**    Performs a search against data indexed in a collection. The collection is typically created with the cfcollection tag.

- ■ **cfindex**    Indexes data in a cfcollection.

- ■ **cfmodule**    Invokes a custom tag. It references a file containing a custom tag definition.

- ■ **cfobject**    Instantiates ColdFusion components, or calls methods in COM, CORBA, or Java objects.

- ■ **cfgraph**    Displays a graph based on a database query. This tag is deprecated in ColdFusion MX. Use cfchart, cfchartdata, or cfchartseries instead.

## Define ColdFusion Database Connections

Unlike other server-side technologies that can connect directly to a database using a System DSN, ColdFusion databases must be defined in the ColdFusion management console, ColdFusion Administrator.

While you can't add database connections directly in the Database panel, you can access the ColdFusion Administrator by right-clicking on a data source listed in that panel (in Windows) and choosing Modify Data Sources.

# Use JavaServer Pages (JSP)

14

JavaServer Pages (JSP) is a server-side technology that uses the power of the Java programming language, allowing web developers to create impressive web applications. JSP uses XML-like tags and scriptlets written in Java to provide the logic that generates dynamic page content. Application logic can also reside outside of the page in other server-side resources, such as JavaBeans objects.

JSP pages are an extension of Java Servlets technology. JSP pages are compiled into Java Servlet modules, which are in essence Java classes. This gives JSP pages the advantages of Java—platform independence, reusability, and access to the wide range of Java APIs out there. Being Java classes, JSP pages are compiled into Java bytecode. Although Java bytecode is typically not as fast as native compiled code, it will still blow the doors off interpreted script code like ASP.

The JSP category of the Insert bar provides several common objects useful to JSP developers:

- **Page Directive**   Inserts a page directive, which specifies the page content type, language, and other settings.
- **Include Directive**   Inserts an include directive, which specifies an external JSP file.
- **Taglib Directive**   Specifies a tag library file.
- **JSP Declaration**   Inserts a code block that can be used to declare new methods.
- **JSP Scriptlet**   Inserts a code block that is placed within a base method in the generated servlet.
- **JSP Expression**   Places code within the base method that is appended to the output stream of the generated page.
- **JSP Use Bean**   Used to instantiate a JavaBean component.
- **JSP Set/Get Property**   Used to set or get properties in a Bean.
- **JSP Include**   Includes a static file or the result from another web component.
- **JSP Forward**   Forwards a request to a web service.
- **JSP Plugin**   Downloads a plug-in to the client browser to execute an applet or Bean.
- **JSP Params/JSP Param**   Specifies parameters for a JSP plug-in.
- **JSP Comment**   Inserts a comment. Comments are ignored by JSP and not rendered in the final document.

## Define JSP Database Connections

JavaServer Pages communicates with databases using a JDBC driver. While some databases have native JDBC drivers available for them, you can also use an ODBC-JDBC bridge driver to connect to any ODBC-capable database, such as Microsoft Access. Here's how:

1. Define a Data Source Name (DSN) on your Windows server.
2. Open or create a JSP page in Dreamweaver.
3. Open the Databases panel by choosing Window | Databases.
4. Click the plus (+) button, and choose Sun JDBC-ODBC Driver (ODBC Database) from the menu. The Sun JDBC-ODBC Driver (ODBC Database) dialog box appears.

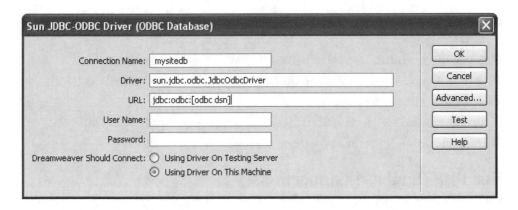

5. Enter a name for the connection.

6. In the URL box, replace the portion of the URL in square brackets with the name of your DSN, for example, jdbc:odbc:*mysitedsn*.

7. Enter your user name and password, if required.

8. Specify the location of the JDBC-ODBC Bridge driver, either your local machine or a testing server.

9. Click OK to close the dialog box.

# Use PHP

One of the more popular server-side technologies—especially in the non-Windows world—is PHP. PHP started out as a modification to the Perl language that let it be embedded in HTML documents. It has evolved on its own since then, and now it is its own language that borrows syntax ideas from C, Perl, and others.

The PHP category of the Insert bar provides the following common objects useful to PHP developer:

- **Form Variables**   Gives access to a global associative array containing HTTP POST data, HTTP_POST_VARS.

- **URL Variables**   Gives access to a global associative array containing HTTP GET data, HTTP_GET_VARS.

- **Session Variables**   Gives access to a global associative array containing session variables, HTTP_SESSION_VARS.

- **Cookie Variables**   Gives access to a global associative array containing cookie variables, HTTP_COOKIE_VARS.

- **Include**   Includes PHP code from an external file. Fails with a warning if the file isn't there.

14

- **Require** Also includes PHP code from an external file, but fails with a fatal error if the file isn't there.
- **Code Block** Inserts an empty PHP code block.
- **Echo** Outputs one or more strings to the client browser.
- **Comment** Inserts a comment.
- **If** Inserts the PHP conditional statement if.
- **Else** Inserts the PHP conditional statement else.

## Define PHP Database Connections

Dreamweaver's database support for PHP is limited to the MySQL database system. This is not entirely a bad thing, as PHP and MySQL make a great combination. They are both free and available on the widest array of platforms of any server-side technology.

To create a database connection to a MySQL database, do the following:

1. Open or create a new PHP page.

2. Open the Databases panel by choosing Window | Databases.

3. Click the plus (+) button, and choose MySQL Connection from the pop-up menu.

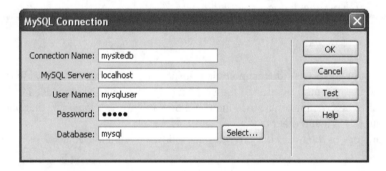

4. In the MySQL Connection dialog box, enter a name for the connection. Make sure there are no spaces or special characters.

5. In the MySQL Server box, enter the name of the computer hosting MySQL. This can either be a host name or an IP address. If it's the same as the current computer, enter **localhost**.

6. Enter your MySQL user name and password.

7. Click Select, and choose your database from the list.

8. Click Test to test your connection. If the test fails, check all of your settings and try again.

9. Click OK to close the dialog box. Your MySQL connection appears in the Databases panel.

# Part V

# Managing Your Site with Dreamweaver

# Chapter 15 Publish Your Site

## How to…

- Prepare your site for publication
- Publish your site to a web server
- Keep your site up-to-date

You have your site built. All the pages are done, and the links are in place. You're ready to show your creation to the world—or are you?

First, you need to examine your site and all its pages to check for browser compatibility issues and common code errors so that you can detect and correct those problems before you publish the site for all to see. Second, you need to get all the files that make up your web site transferred to a web server where they will be available to the Internet population (or to a server on your corporate intranet). Then you need to keep the site content fresh by updating it on a fairly regular basis. This chapter describes how to do all that—make the final preparations before uploading, upload the site, and perform incremental updates after the site is online.

# Prepare Your Site for Publication

Before transferring your site to your web server, you need to make sure that everything is working correctly. It is one thing to create pages in Dreamweaver, but to see the site as your visitor will see it, you need to check the pages for browser compatibility. You need to look at how various browsers render the HTML codes and the scripts in your pages and confirm that all the links work as expected.

 *The techniques described in this section all identify and report potential problems with your web pages, but they don't automatically make any changes in the HTML source code. It's up to you to decide what, if any, action to take to correct the reported problems.*

## Check Pages for Browser Compatibility

Each browser, be it Internet Explorer, Netscape, Opera, AOL, or any of several other, less well-known browsers, has its own way of displaying content. Default font sizes might be different. Certain HTML tags and attributes might be rendered differently. Certain scripts might or might not be recognized. Browsers vary from brand to brand and from version to version. So you need to test your site carefully before posting it in order to find and eliminate the many small—and not so small—glitches that invariably turn up and cause your pages to display improperly.

### Set Browser Preview Options

Dreamweaver's Preview in Browser feature is your first line of defense in your effort to ensure that your pages appear as intended. The browser preview enables you to quickly preview your page in a browser window as you work. When you install Dreamweaver, it automatically configures itself to use your default browser for previews. However, if you're going to produce web pages for others to view, you need to check those pages in other browsers in addition to your own favorite. Naturally, you'll need to have those other browsers installed on your system. You also need to tell Dreamweaver how to find those other browsers so you can use them to preview pages as you work. Here's how to add browsers to Dreamweaver's preview list:

1.  Choose Edit | Preferences to open the Preferences dialog box, then click Preview in Browser in the Category list. Dreamweaver displays the following options.

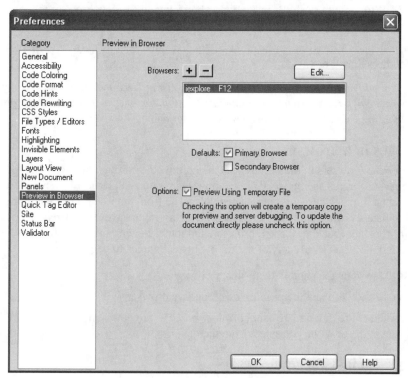

2.  Click the + button above the Browsers list to open the Add Browser dialog box.

15

3.  Click the Browse button to open a file open dialog box where you can locate and select the executable file for the web browser you want to add. When you select the file and

close the dialog box, Dreamweaver adds the path and filename to the Application box in the Add Browser dialog box and copies the filename to the Name box as well.

4. Edit the Name setting to make it more descriptive. (This is the name that appears on the Dreamweaver menu.) Optionally, check Primary Browser or Secondary Browser if you want to use a shortcut key (F12 for primary or CTRL-F12 for secondary) to preview pages in this browser.

5. Click OK to close the Add Browser dialog box and add the new browser to the Browsers list.

6. Repeat steps 2–5 to add other browsers to the list, and then click OK to close the Preferences dialog box.

*You can add multiple browsers to the Browsers list in Dreamweaver. Only two of the browsers can have shortcut keys associated with them, but you can access the others by choosing File | Preview in Browser | browser name.*

## Preview Pages in a Browser

Once you set up the browsers in the Preferences dialog box, they are readily available for previewing your web pages as you work in Dreamweaver. You can preview a web page as you're working on it in a document window or select a file from the Local Files list in the Site window and initiate a browser preview from there. Dreamweaver saves the current document to a temporary file, launches the selected browser, and loads the temporary file for viewing in the browser window. You can use any of the following techniques to begin the preview:

- Press F12 to view the page in the primary browser
- Press CTRL-F12 to view the page in the secondary browser
- Choose File | Preview in Browser | *browser name* to preview the page in the browser you select from the menu.

## Check Pages Against Target Browsers

As useful (and essential) as the Preview in Browser feature is, it can't test a page for all the various browsers and versions of browsers that site visitors might use. You can't keep that many browsers installed on your system; even if you did, it wouldn't be practical to preview every page in every version of each browser.

Dreamweaver's Check Target Browsers feature addresses this problem by providing a way to check your pages against a series of *browser profiles*. A browser profile lists browser characteristics for a specific browser, such as what HTML tags and attributes the browser supports. Dreamweaver can scan the source code for your pages, compare it to the browser profile for a given browser, and generate a report listing any known problems such as unsupported HTML tags.

The Check Target Browsers feature is quite versatile. Dreamweaver has browser profiles for several versions of the major browsers, and other profiles are available as extensions that you can download and install. You can use Check Target Browsers to check a single document, selected files, all the files in a selected folder, or all the files in an entire site.

Here's how to run a target browser report:

1. Select the file or files that you want to check against one or more browser profiles. You can use any of the following techniques to select the web documents to check:

   ■ Open the document you want to check in the Dreamweaver Document window.

   ■ Select one or more files in the Local Files list in the Site window.

   ■ Select a folder in the Local Files list in the Site window to check all the files in the folder.

   ■ Select the root folder of the Local Files list in the Site window to check the entire site.

2. Choose File | Check Target Browsers. Dreamweaver opens the Check Target Browsers dialog box.

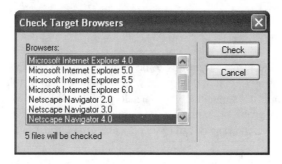

3. Select one or more browsers in the Browsers list. (CTRL-click to select additional browsers.) You can select from the following choices plus any additional browser profiles you've installed:

   ■ Microsoft Internet Explorer 2.0, 3.0, 4.0, 5.0, 5.5, 6.0

   ■ Netscape 2.0, 3.0, 4.0, 6.0

   ■ Opera 2.1, 3.0, 3.5, 4.0, 5.0, 6.0

4. Click the Check button to close the Check Target Browsers dialog box and begin the check. Dreamweaver displays a message box showing the status of the process. When the checking process is complete, Dreamweaver opens the Results panel and displays its findings on the Target Browser Check tab (see Figure 15-1).

 *Checking a single file against one browser profile takes only a few seconds, but checking multiple files against multiple browser profiles can take several minutes. The progress bars showing the status of the browser check aren't very informative. Be patient. Give Dreamweaver time to do its thing.*

The Target Browser Check report lists the filenames of files with potential problems and displays the line numbers where you can find the offending tags and/or attributes in the source code. There's also a short description of each problem and an icon to indicate its severity.

**15**

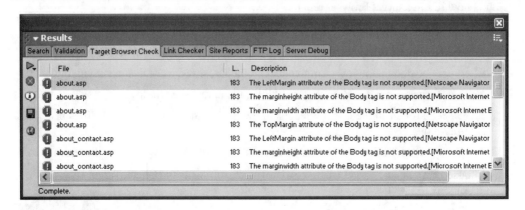

**FIGURE 15-1**    The results of a Check Target Browser scan

The Target Browser Check report requires some interpretation. The report points out potential problems, but it's up to you to determine whether a particular problem is serious enough to require action or if it's something you can safely ignore. In other words, just because the report lists a potential problem, such as an unsupported tag or attribute, that doesn't necessarily mean your page will crash or fail to display correctly. It just indicates something you need to check on.

For example, Internet Explorer and Netscape support different attribute names for page margins. It's common practice to insert duplicate margin settings into the <body> tag, one set for IE and one for Netscape. Each browser sets its margins according to the attribute it recognizes and ignores the unsupported attributes. The Target Browser Check correctly points out the unsupported attributes, even though they are intentional.

    *Double-click an item in the Target Browser Check (or any of the tabs in the Results panel) to open the related file in a document window and automatically highlight the problem area of the code.*

## Validate Your Code

NEW IN MX    In addition to the ability to check your web documents against target browsers, Dreamweaver MX adds a new feature that allows you to check your documents for compliance with the published standards for the various markup languages Dreamweaver supports. So, for example, you can run a check on your document's source code to make sure all the tags are valid according to the HTML 4.0 specification from the W3C (World Wide Web Consortium). You can also run a separate check on a Dreamweaver document to validate it as XML code.

## Set Validation Preferences

Dreamweaver can validate your document code against a long list of standards specifications.
It's impractical to check your pages against all of them, so you'll want to select which ones
Dreamweaver uses when validating a page. You make that selection in the Validator category of
the Preferences dialog box. (Choose Edit | Preferences to open the dialog box, and then select
Validator in the Category list.) Check items in the Validate Against list box to select one or more
specifications to be included in the page validations. (You can select more than one specification,
such as HTML and ColdFusion, but you can select only one version of each.) Click OK to close
the dialog box and record your validation settings.

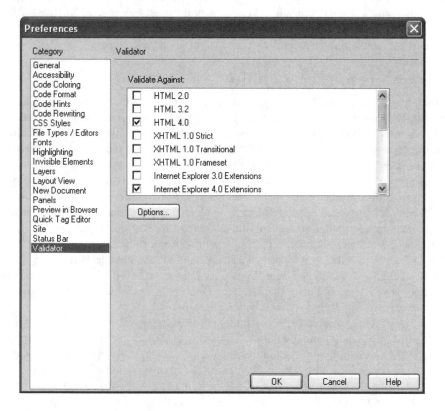

## Check Your Document Code

After you select what standards you want to use to validate your code, you're ready to check
pages against those specifications. The process is similar to checking pages against a target
browser. You select the page or pages you want to check, issue the command to start the
validation scan, and then view the results in the Validation tab of the Results panel.

15

- ■ To validate the document in the current Document window, choose File | Check Page | Validate Markup or press SHIFT-F6.
- ■ To validate documents from the Site window, select one or more files in the Local Files list and choose File | Validate or press SHIFT-F6.

### XML Validation

Dreamweaver includes XHTML among the options for the standard validation check. But you can also run a more generic XML validation on your documents. Oddly, XML validation is only available from the menus in the Document window, which means that you can only perform an XML validation on the current document. To check your document for invalid XML tags, choose File | Check Page | Validate as XML. As with the regular validation check, Dreamweaver displays a list of invalid tags and attributes in the Validation tab of the Results panel.

## Check Your Site for Accessibility

Making your web site accessible to the largest possible audience involves more than making sure your pages display correctly in the major web browsers. That's a start, but many people access the web with assistive technologies, such as the screen readers used by the visually impaired. You'll want to make your web site accessible to them as well. In fact, you may be required to do so if you work on a web site for a government agency or a large corporation.

Just as Dreamweaver can check your web documents for browser compatibility, the program can also check your documents for compliance with accessibility guidelines such as the W3C Web Accessibility Initiative and Section 508 of the Federal Rehabilitation Act. The accessibility check scans your pages for things such as missing alt text attributes for images.

To run an accessibility check on the current document in a document window, choose File | Check Page | Check Accessibility. You can also check one or more documents from the Site window by selecting files in the Local Files list and running a site report with the Accessibility option checked (see the next section of this chapter). Dreamweaver displays the results of the accessibility scan in the Site Reports tab of the Results panel.

One of the helpful things about the accessibility report is the way it is linked to both the source code of the document(s) and to related information in the Reference panel. You can select any reported accessibility problem in the Site Reports tab and click the More Info button. Dreamweaver pops open the Reference panel and displays an explanation of the related accessibility guideline. Then you can double-click the item in the Site Reports tab to open the document with the problem section of the source code highlighted and ready for editing.

## Run a Site Report

In addition to the browser checks and code validations, Dreamweaver includes a report you can run to check your web documents for several other potential problems before publication. The Site Report feature includes eight different reports that cover everything from the Design Notes attached to web documents to a number of common HTML code errors and omissions. You can select which reports to run, and you can elect to run the reports on the current document, selected files, all the files in a selected folder, or your entire site. Here's how to do it:

1.  Select the file or files on which you want to run site reports. You can use any of the following techniques to select the web documents for checking:

    ■ Open a document in the Dreamweaver Document window.

    ■ Select one or more files in the Local Files list in the Site window.

    ■ If you want to run reports on the contents of a folder or the entire site, you don't need to preselect the folder—you can do that in the Reports dialog box.

2.  Choose Site I Reports to open the Reports dialog box.

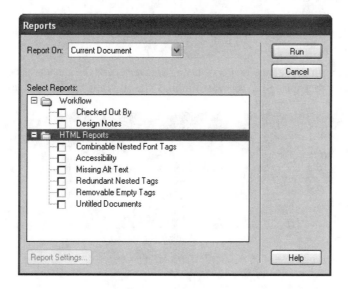

3.  Select the subject of the report from the Report On list box. You can select Current Document, Entire Current Local Site, Selected Files in Site, or Folder. If you select Folder, another text box appears below the Report On list box. where you can type in the folder name. Or you can click the folder icon beside the text box to open the Choose Local Folder dialog box, where you can locate and select the folder.

4.  Select one or more reports in the Select Reports box by clicking the check box beside the report name. You can select any of the following reports:

    ■ **Checked Out By**   Lists files that are locked by Dreamweaver's Check Out feature and shows who checked out the file

15

- **Design Notes**　Lists the files that have Design Notes attached and shows the contents of those notes
- **Combinable Nested Font Tags**　Lists nested font tags that could be combined to clean up the source code
- **Accessibility**　Lists errors and omissions in your source code that don't comply with accepted accessibility guidelines
- **Missing Alt Text**　Lists images that lack alt text attributes
- **Redundant Nested Tags**　Lists instances of a tag nested within another tag of the same kind, to no effect
- **Removable Empty Tags**　Lists empty tags that could be removed to clean up the source code
- **Untitled Documents**　Lists documents that still have the default "Untitled Document" title

**5.** Click Run to run the selected reports. Dreamweaver opens the Results panel with the Site Reports tab displayed to show its findings after it scans the selected documents.

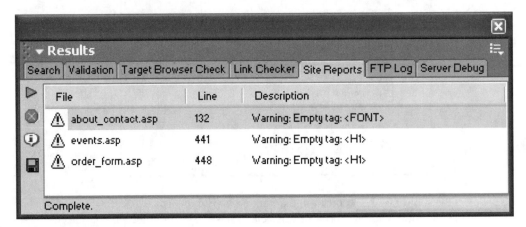

# Publish Your Dreamweaver Site to a Web Server

After you have made sure all the elements of your site are working correctly, it's time to publish your site by placing it on a web server. To publish your site, you need to duplicate the local site that you worked so hard to develop on the remote site. The remote site is usually a directory on a web server at your Internet service provider (ISP) or a web hosting service, although it can also be a web server on your local area network. Typically, you access the web server via the Internet using FTP (file transfer protocol). Dreamweaver includes built-in FTP capabilities that handle all file transfer duties necessary to publish and maintain most web sites, so there's no need to use an external FTP utility program.

## Define the Remote Site

To publish your site to the remote server with Dreamweaver, you must supply Dreamweaver with some information about the server location and the settings you use to access it. This is all part of the Dreamweaver site definition; you may have completed it when you originally defined your site in Dreamweaver using the wizardlike Basic tab of the Site Definition dialog box (see Chapter 2). However, if you didn't define the remote site earlier, you must do so now. Here's how to enter the remote site settings directly into the Advanced tab of the Site Definition dialog box:

**1.** Choose Site | Edit Sites, or select Edit Sites from the Site list box in the Sites window toolbar. Dreamweaver opens the Edit Sites dialog box.

**2.** Select the site you want to publish from the list box in the Edit Sites dialog box and click Edit. Dreamweaver displays the Site Definition for *sitename* dialog box.

**3.** Click the Advanced tab; then select Remote Info in the Category list to display the settings for the remote site.

**4.** Select the appropriate access mode in the Access box. Normally, that's FTP, but you can also select Local/Network, RDS, SourceSafe Database, or WebDAV. Dreamweaver

15

displays options for the selected access mode in the dialog box. The FTP options are shown here.

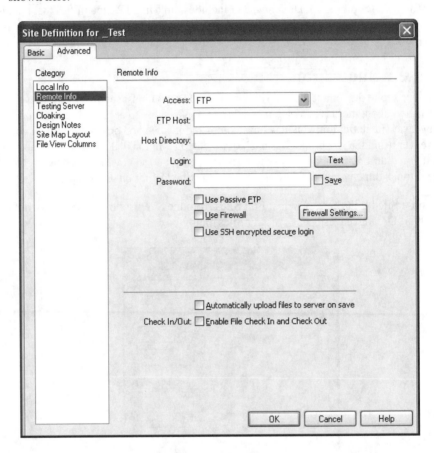

5. Enter or select the information as needed. Here is what you will need to supply for an FTP connection:

   ■ **FTP Host**    The address for the host FTP site. This address is usually in the form of ftp.*hostname*.com.

   ■ **Host Directory**    The directory on the host system where web documents are stored—the root directory of the web site. You may not need to enter anything here if the FTP host address points directly to the web root directory. Otherwise, you need to enter a directory path from the FTP host root to the web root—for example, *~username/webroot/*.

   ■ **Login**    This is your user name for access to the FTP/web server. It's usually the same as your account user ID for this service provider.

- ■ **Password**   Input the password for FTP access—usually the same as your master account password for this service provider.

- ■ **Save**   Check this option to have Dreamweaver remember the password so you don't have to enter it manually each time you connect.

- ■ **Use Passive FTP and Use Firewall**   If your Internet access goes through a firewall that requires special passive-mode FTP operation, check one or both options. If you're not sure, leave these options unchecked for the time being. If you later have a problem establishing an FTP connection, consult with your network system administrator for the proper settings.

- ■ **Use SSH Encrypted Secure Login**   Check this option if the FTP server requires an encrypted login.

- ■ **Automatically upload files to server on save**   Check this option to have Dreamweaver automatically copy your file to the FTP server when you save your document.

- ■ **Check In/Check Out**   Check this option to enable the file checkout feature (see Chapter 16). This feature is for workgroups collaborating on web site development. If you work alone, ignore it.

6.  Click the OK button to close the Site Definition dialog box and record the remote site access settings.

## Transfer Site Files to the Remote Site

Once you have the access information for the remote site configured, you're ready to transfer your files to the host server. Dreamweaver uses the remote site definition to take care of all the mechanics of establishing a connection to the remote site and transferring files. All you need to do is tell Dreamweaver what files to transfer. Here's how to do that:

1.  If the Site window isn't already displaying the site you want to publish, choose Site | Open Site | *sitename,* or select the site from the Site menu in the Site window toolbar.

2.  Choose Site | Site Files, or click the Site Files toolbar button to display the lists of remote and local site files (instead of the site map) in the Site window.

15

 3.  Choose Site | Connect or click the Connect button in the toolbar. Dreamweaver establishes a connection to the remote site (usually via an FTP connection over the Internet) and updates the Remote Site files list. The Connect button changes to show the two plugs connected. (This step is unnecessary if the remote site is located on your local area network.)

NOTE   *You must have an established connection to the Internet in order to connect and transfer files to the remote site. Depending on your system configuration, you may need to initiate a dial-up connection outside Dreamweaver.*

4. Select the files in the Local Folder file list that you want to transfer to the server. To upload the entire site, select the root folder of the local site.

*Make sure all your files are saved before you transfer them. Dreamweaver prompts you to save any unsaved files before the transfer begins.*

5. Choose Site | Put or click the Put button in the toolbar to begin the transfer. If you selected the entire site for upload, Dreamweaver prompts you for confirmation before proceeding. Dreamweaver begins copying files and folders from your local site to the remote server. Dreamweaver automatically creates folders on the remote site as needed to duplicate the folder structure of your local site and copies files into the correct folders. The Site window status bar shows the filename of each file as it is transferred to the remote site.

*If you select individual folders or files for upload instead of the entire site, Dreamweaver displays a message box asking whether to include dependent files. Click Yes to have Dreamweaver automatically transfer those files along with your web pages.*

6. When the transfer is complete, click the Connect button again, or choose Site | Disconnect to break the connection to the remote site. (If you accessed the Internet via a dial-up connection, you may also want to end the modem connection outside Dreamweaver.)

*Check with the system administrator or webmaster for your web host to find out if it's necessary to change or set file-access permissions for the files you upload to your remote site in order to make them available to anonymous web surfers. If you do need to adjust permission settings, you'll need to get instructions on how to do so.*

## Did you know?

# Dependent Files

In Dreamweaver parlance, *dependent files* are the images, buttons, media objects, and other page elements that are stored in separate files and referenced by your web documents. Dependent files are often stored in folders on your web site separately from the main web documents. Dreamweaver automatically scans your web pages before uploading or downloading them and offers to copy dependent files along with the web pages.

# Keep Your Site Up-to-Date

After you initially publish your site by copying all the files and folders from the local site folder to the remote server, you'll rarely need to go through a full-site transfer again. But that doesn't mean you just load your site onto a web server and forget it. Web sites, like pets, need constant care and feeding in the form of frequent updates to freshen content, repair broken links, and add new pages and features.

## Upload and Download Files

The same Dreamweaver tools you use to publish your site in the first place also help you maintain it. You can establish a connection and transfer files back and forth between the local and remote sites at any time. The procedure is essentially the same as outlined previously for publishing the site. The only differences are in the files you select to transfer and the choice of the Put or Get command.

■ To transfer (upload) selected files from the local site to the remote site, select the files you want to transfer in the Local Files list and choose Site | Put, or click the Put button on the toolbar.

■ To transfer (download) selected files from the remote site to the local site, select the files you want to transfer in the Remote Site list and choose Site | Get, or click the Get button on the toolbar.

■ To delete files or folders from the remote site, select the files or folders you want to delete in the Remote Site list; then right-click one of the selected files and choose Delete from the context menu that appears. (You can do the same in the Local Files list to delete files from the local site.)

TIP    *When you transfer files to or from a remote site, Dreamweaver creates a transfer log that you can refer to if a problem occurs. You can even show your client this record after you have uploaded or changed files on the site. To view the log, choose Window | Site FTP Log from the Site window or click the FTP Log button on the Site window toolbar. Dreamweaver displays the FTP Log tab in the Results panel, as shown in Figure 15-2.*

15

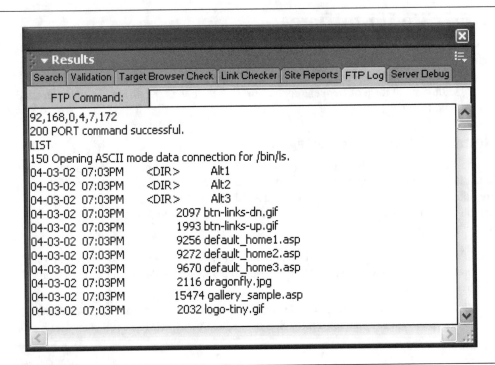

**FIGURE 15-2**    The FTP Log tab shows a record of Dreamweaver file transfers.

## Synchronize Files

Web sites can quickly become quite large. It is not uncommon to have hundreds of files to keep track of. In addition to the web pages themselves, you have all the image files, slices of image files, buttons, animations, and other dependent files to worry about. Identifying which files have been changed and need to be updated can make the process of maintaining a site rather tedious.

Dreamweaver includes a special feature to automate the process of synchronizing the files in your local and remote sites. When you use the Synchronize command, Dreamweaver compares the file dates for the selected files in the Local Files list and the Remote Site and transfers only the files that have changed, not files with the same modification date. The Synchronize command works for transferring files in either direction between the local and remote sites. You can synchronize an entire site or only selected files.

Here's how to synchronize your files:

**1.** Choose Site | Connect, or click the Connect button in the toolbar to establish a connection to the remote server. (This step isn't necessary if the remote site is located on your local area network.)

**2.** Select the files you want to synchronize in the Dreamweaver Site window. (If you want to synchronize the entire site, you can skip this step.)

**3.** Choose Site | Synchronize. Dreamweaver opens the Synchronize Files dialog box.

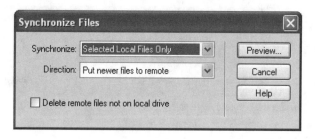

**4.** In the Synchronize box, select either Entire *sitename* Site to synchronize the entire site or Selected Local Files Only to synchronize only the files you selected in step 2. (If you selected files in the Remote Site file list, the option reads "Selected Remote Files Only.")

**5.** Select the appropriate option in the Direction box. Your choices are as follows:

- ■ **Put newer files to remote**   Replaces outdated files on the remote site by uploading newer versions from the local site but ignores any newer files that may be located on the remote site

- ■ **Get newer files from remote**   Replaces outdated files on the local site by downloading newer versions from the remote site but ignores any newer files that may be located on the local site

- ■ **Get and Put newer files**   Uploads and downloads as necessary to replace all outdated files with newer versions

**6.** Check Delete Remote Files Not on Local Drive if you want Dreamweaver to automatically delete files from the remote site if there isn't a matching file on the local site. This option is useful if you've deleted some old files from the local site and need to make corresponding deletions on the remote site. (This option changes depending on the selection in the Direction box. If you choose Get Newer Files from Remote, the option is Delete Local Files Not on Remote Server. If you select Get and Put Newer Files, this option is unavailable.)

**15**

7. Click the Preview button. Dreamweaver closes the Synchronize Files dialog box, scans and compares the files in the local and remote sites, and then displays a dialog box listing the files it will synchronize.

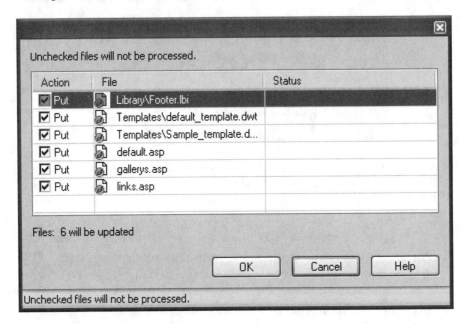

8. Review the proposed synchronization actions in the dialog box. The dialog box lists each file transfer and/or deletion Dreamweaver deems necessary to implement your instructions. You can cancel an individual action by clearing the check box in the first column.

9. Click OK to start processing the files. Dreamweaver updates the list to show the status of each file as it is transferred or deleted.

10. When synchronization is complete, click the Close button to close the dialog box.

## Cloak Files You Don't Want to Synchronize

Cloaking is a new feature of Dreamweaver MX that instructs the program to ignore certain files and folders when it performs operations in the Site window, such as transferring files to the remote site. This enables you to store original images, text documents, and other source files in folders within the local site and yet automatically exclude them from uploads to the remote site, and vice versa.

To cloak a file or folder, select the file in the Local Files list and choose Site | Cloaking | Cloak or just right-click it and choose Cloaking | Cloak from the context menu. Cloaked files and folders display a red slash through their icons in the file list. Later, you can remove the cloaking by selecting the file and choosing Site | Cloaking | Uncloak.

You can also specify that files with certain extensions (such as the .png extension used by Fireworks) be cloaked automatically. The sitewide cloaking settings are in the site definition. The quick way to access those settings is to choose Site | Cloaking | Settings to open the Site Definition dialog box with the Cloaking category of the Advanced tab already selected. To cloak certain file extensions, check the Cloak Files Ending With check box and enter the file extensions you want to cloak in the adjacent text box. Click OK to close the Site Definition dialog box. Dreamweaver marks all the files with the specified extension as cloaked.

# Chapter 16

# Maintain Web Sites and Collaborate with Others

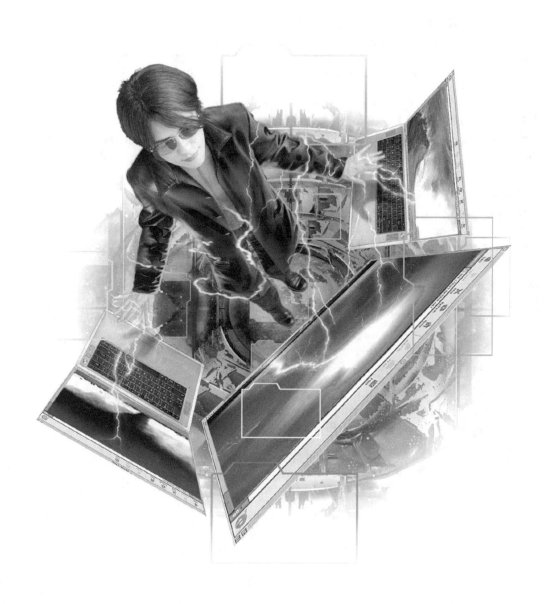

## How to...

- Manage links in your site
- Back up and share your site definitions
- Use file check out and check in
- Use Design Notes

Dreamweaver excels in link maintenance and workgroup collaboration. Dreamweaver automatically assists you in updating changed links and makes it easy to alter links in the Site window. When it comes to collaboration, Dreamweaver's Design Notes remind you of a task's status and keep other members of your workgroup informed.

# Manage Links in Your Site

Chapter 4 described how to create links in your site. But links often don't remain static; they need to be updated and changed periodically. Fortunately, Dreamweaver makes it easy to do just that.

## Change Links in the Site Map

One of the fastest and simplest ways to change links in your site is to make your changes in Site Map view. The site map, shown in Figure 16-1, is a graphical representation of the links between pages in your site, so it's a logical place to go when you need to update those links. To change an existing link in the site map, follow these steps:

TIP    *Remember that the site map shows links between pages as lines connecting page icons. The page containing links is at the top of the map, and the linked pages are in the next row below. You can click the + beside a page icon in the row to show the links in that page as a column of smaller icons beneath the page icon. However, it's usually easier to right-click a page icon and choose View As Root to elevate that page to the top position and work with the linked pages in the wide row beneath it.*

1. Navigate through the site map so that the page containing the links you want to change is displayed in the root position, at the top of the map. (Right-click a page icon in the site map and choose View As Root.)

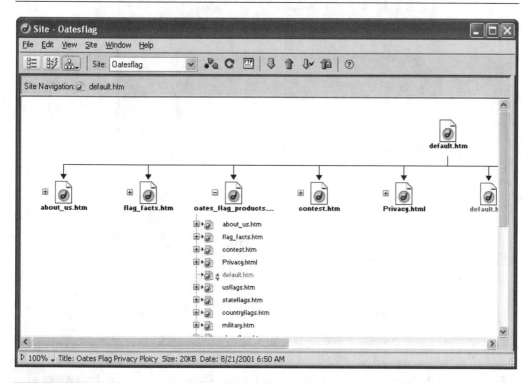

**FIGURE 16-1** The site map is a natural place to update links.

**2.** Locate the icon for the link you want to change in the wide row beneath the root. Right-click the page icon and choose Change Link from the context pop-up menu that appears. Dreamweaver displays the Select HTML File dialog box.

16

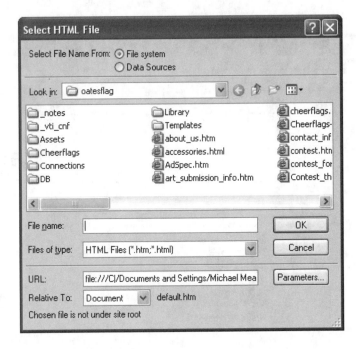

3. Locate and select the new file you want the link to point to. Select the appropriate option in the Relative To box to finish defining the link.

4. Click OK to close the Select HTML File dialog box. Dreamweaver opens the Update Files dialog box, shown in Figure 16-2.

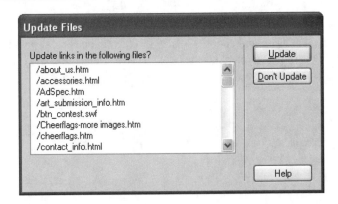

FIGURE 16-2    The Update Files dialog box

5. Click the Update button. Dreamweaver changes the link in the page that appears in the root position in the site map and also in all other pages listed in the Update Files dialog box. (Depending on your preference settings, Dreamweaver may skip this confirmation step and update all the links automatically.)

## Change Links Sitewide

Another way to change a link throughout your site is to use the Site | Change Link Sitewide menu command in the Site window. When you use this command, Dreamweaver performs a search-and-replace operation on all the HTML files in your site. The program searches for any link to a given filename and changes it to another filename. Here's how it works:

1. Choose Site | Change Link Sitewide from the menu in the Site window. Dreamweaver opens the Change Link Sitewide dialog box.

2. Enter the URL of the link you want to change in the Change All Links To box. You can type the URL or click the small folder icon to open a dialog box where you can select the linked file. (If you selected the old linked file before opening the Change Link Sitewide dialog box, Dreamweaver enters its URL in the Change All Links To box automatically.)

3. Enter the path and the filename for the replacement linked file in the Into Links To box. You can either type the path and the filename or click the folder icon to the right of the text box to open a dialog box where you can locate and select the file.

4. Click OK to close the Change Link Sitewide dialog box. Again, Dreamweaver displays the Update Files dialog box shown in Figure 16-2.

5. Click the Update button. Dreamweaver changes the link in all the other pages listed in the Update Files dialog box. (Depending on your preference settings, Dreamweaver may skip this confirmation step and update all the links automatically.)

## Test Your Pages for Broken Links

Broken links—links that point to invalid URLs—are an ongoing challenge for webmasters. Links can be broken in any number of ways. The most common cause is files that are moved or renamed.

16

Dreamweaver tries to prevent broken links from happening in the first place. If you move or rename a file within Dreamweaver's Site window, the program tracks the effect the change will have on links to and from that file and offers to update those links automatically. However, if you or someone else moves, deletes, or renames a site file outside Dreamweaver, the links to that file are broken. Likewise, Dreamweaver can't automatically update your site files to reflect changes to links to files outside the local site.

Obviously, you will need to test your site for broken links from time to time. Dreamweaver provides a link checker for this task. Here's how to check the entire site for broken links:

1.   Choose Site | Check Links Sitewide from the menu in the Site window. Dreamweaver scans the source code for all the pages in the site, checking all the links in each page. When it is done, Dreamweaver displays the results on the Link Checker tab of the Results panel.

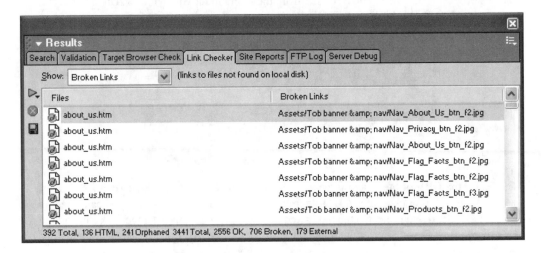

2.   To fix a broken link, click on the filename in the Broken Links column, type in the correct URL, and press the ENTER key to make the correction. (You can also click the folder icon that appears when you click the filename in the Broken Links column to open a dialog box where you can locate and select the file.) If the URL is referenced from more than one file, Dreamweaver displays the Update Files dialog box, shown in Figure 16-2.

*You can double-click a file name in the Files list to open that document for editing. Dreamweaver automatically selects the problem object in the document window so you can edit the link in the Property Inspector panel.*

3.   If the Update Files dialog box appears, click the Update button. Dreamweaver changes the link in all the other pages listed in the dialog box.

# Back Up or Share Your Site Definition

Your Dreamweaver site definition contains a lot of important detailed information about your web site. The site definition includes not only the site's URL and the exact location of the site files on both the local and remote systems but also all the settings needed to access the remote site for maintenance and testing, plus various preference settings and the like.

Having all this information stored in the site definition is a great convenience, but entering that information is a tedious task. That's why the ability to import and export site definitions is a welcome addition to Dreamweaver MX. Now you can export your site definition data and save it as a file that you can keep for backup purposes or share with coworkers. And you can import a site definition to restore settings that were lost or damaged or to set up a site definition on a different computer without reentering all the settings.

To export a site definition, open the site in the Site window and follow these steps:

1.  Choose Site | Export from the menu in the Site window. Dreamweaver opens the Export Site dialog box.

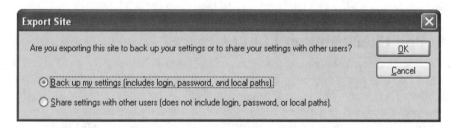

2.  Select one of the two options in the Export Site dialog box and click OK. The "Back up my settings" option saves all the site settings while the "Share settings with other users" option omits logon IDs, passwords, and local folder settings that you may not want or need to share with a coworker. Dreamweaver opens another dialog box (also titled Export Site) that's similar to a standard Save As dialog box.

3.  Select the location and filename for the site definition file, and click Save. Dreamweaver saves the file with the extension .ste.

If you need to recreate a site definition on another computer or restore a site definition from a backup, you can import the data from a site definition file by following these steps:

1.  Choose Site | Import from the menu in the Site window. Dreamweaver opens the Import Site dialog box, which is really a standard File Open dialog box.

2.  Locate and select the site definition file you want to load, and click Open. Dreamweaver creates a new site definition using the data from the file. If the site definition file was created using the sharing option, Dreamweaver prompts you to select a local folder for the site.

16

The result of importing a saved site definition file is essentially the same as creating a new site with the site definition wizard, except that Dreamweaver gets all the settings from the file instead of from your input into the wizard. The site definition includes the information about file locations and the settings required to access the remote site. However, importing a site definition does *not* copy site files into the site's local folder. You'll need to do that in a separate step. You can copy the files into the local folder from your LAN, from a CD or other media, or download (Get) them from the remote site.

# Use the Collaboration Features

Dreamweaver is versatile enough to be used by an individual or by a megacorporation's web design team. After all, the basic web page design process is the same whether you're working solo or as part of a team. The difference between the two work environments is that a solo web author does everything alone, whereas the design team typically assigns different tasks to different team members. The collaborative nature of a team environment requires communication to keep everyone informed of the project's status. To facilitate communication Dreamweaver includes two key features—Check Out/Check In and Design Notes.

## Manage File Check Out and Check In

One of the problems that a development team runs into when collaborating on a web site is the possibility that two (or more) team members might be editing the same file on their local systems at the same time. Then, when they upload the edited files to the common remote site, the changes made by one team member overwrite the changes made by another team member.

The accepted solution to this problem is to institute a *checkout* system on the remote site. That's what Dreamweaver does with its Check Out/Check In feature. When the feature is enabled, you check out a file from the remote site before editing it. Dreamweaver locks the file on the remote site so no one else can change it and marks the file so that other team members know who has the file checked out. While the file is checked out, other team members can view the file, but they can't make changes. When you complete your edits, you check the file back in, which uploads the changed file to the remote site and releases the lock so that the file becomes available for edits by other team members. This system effectively eliminates the problem of conflicting updates being posted by different team members.

## Check Out Files for Editing

Although file checkout sounds like it could be complicated, the process is actually quite simple. When file Check Out/Check In is enabled, Dreamweaver activates two buttons—Check Out and Check In—on the Site window toolbar. To use the file checkout feature, use those buttons instead of the Get and Put buttons. Dreamweaver takes care of the rest.

To check out a file for editing, select the file in the Site Files list and click the Check Out button. Dreamweaver downloads the latest version of the file from the remote site (like a Get operation) and marks it as checked out to you. A green check mark appears next to the filename on your screen, and a red one appears on your partners' screens (see Figure 16-3).

*If you activate the Check Out Files When Opening option (see the following section, "Set Up Check Out and Check In"), Dreamweaver automatically checks out the file from the remote site when you open it for editing. You can skip the manual checkout step and simply open the file.*

To check in a file after editing it, select the file in the Site Files list and click the Check In button. Dreamweaver uploads the file to the remote site (like a Put operation) and clears the lock created by the checkout status. The check mark beside the filename in the Local Folder file list changes to a padlock to indicate that you can't edit the file unless you check it out again.

*Don't forget to check in each file when you finish working with it. Remember that other team members can't update the file if you've got it checked out.*

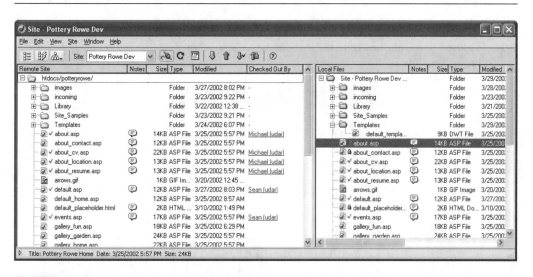

**FIGURE 16-3**    A Site window showing checked out files

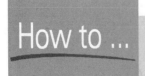

## How to ... Inquire About a Checked-Out File

Sooner or later, you'll need to edit a file only to find it locked because someone else has it checked out. You need to contact that person to find out when the file will be available for editing. Dreamweaver can help. The program not only marks checked-out files in the file lists in the Site window, it also lists who has the file checked out in the Checked Out By column. (You may need to scroll the file list horizontally to see the Checked Out By column.) The name in the Checked Out By column works like a mailto link; click the name to open a preaddressed e-mail message. Type your message, and click Send to send the message to the person who checked out the file.

### Set Up Check Out and Check In

The file Check Out/Check In feature is usually enabled at the time the site is first created. However, if you have a site that you want to change from a solo project to a group project, you can follow these steps:

1. Choose Site | Edit Sites from the menu in the Site window. Dreamweaver opens the Edit Sites dialog box.

2. Select the site you want to alter from the list; then click the Edit button. Dreamweaver opens the Site Definition dialog box.

3. Select Remote Info in the Category list to display the options shown in Figure 16-4.

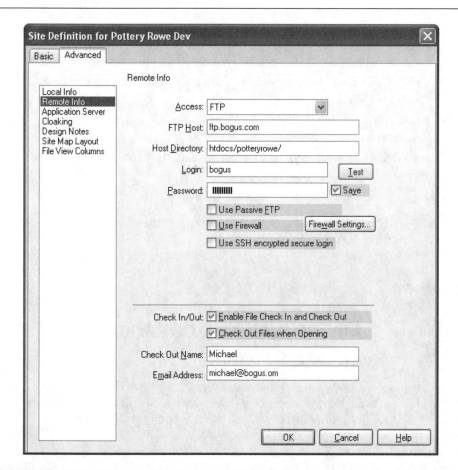

**FIGURE 16-4**    Remote Info options for an FTP connection in the Site Definition dialog box

NOTE    *The Remote Info options vary depending on what type of remote connection you are using. Figure 16-4 shows the commonly used FTP connection version. All the Check In/Out options don't appear until you enable that option.*

16

**4.** Click the Enable File Check In and Check Out option and select or fill in the other Check In/Out options:

- **Check Out Files When Opening**   Enable this option to have Dreamweaver automatically perform a file checkout when you open a file for editing. This eliminates the need to manually check out a file before you edit it. The drawback is that Dreamweaver doesn't know whether you are opening a file to make significant editing changes or just opening the file to view its contents. It checks out the file in either case, thus making it unavailable to other team members.

- ■ **Check Out Name** Enter the name you want to appear on the remote site identifying the files you check out.
- ■ **Email Address** Enter your e-mail address, so team members can contact you to inquire about a checked-out file.

5. Click the OK button to close the Site Definition dialog box and return to the Edit Sites dialog box.

6. In the Edit Sites dialog box, click the Done button.

From here on in, all you have to do to check a file out or in is click on the Check Out or Check In button in the Site window.

# Manage Web Site Collaboration with SiteSpring

While features such as Check In/Check Out and Design Notes provide many Dreamweaver users with all the workgroup collaboration capabilities they're likely to need, you might want more robust collaboration tools, especially if you need to coordinate the efforts of a geographically diverse team working on large projects.

Macromedia SiteSpring is a workgroup collaboration product designed specifically for web-development teams. It includes features for project management, team communications, file versioning, client communications, and tracking approvals and changes—all accessible through a web interface. SiteSpring is a powerful tool that Macromedia touts as being appropriate for web-development projects large and small, but it really comes into its own when managing larger teams and projects. Dreamweaver MX integrates into the SiteSpring development environment by allowing you to see and work with your SiteSpring tasks and associated files in Dreamweaver. For more information about SiteSpring, see the Macromedia web site at www.macromedia.com.

# Use Design Notes

Design Notes are Dreamweaver's equivalent of stick-on notes. They allow you to attach notes
to various files so that you and others can know about any special requirements relating to those
files. You can use Design Notes as a reminder of what needs to be done next on a given file, as
a place to store information on the location of source files, or as a way to track approvals and
changes to a web page. To add a Design Note to a file, follow these steps:

1.  Right click on the file in the Site window file list; then choose Design Notes from the
    pop-up menu that appears, or select a file and choose File I Design Notes. Dreamweaver
    opens the Design Notes dialog box, shown in Figure 16-5.

2.  Select an entry from the Status drop-down list.

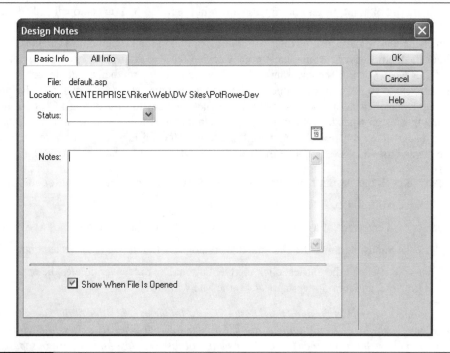

**FIGURE 16-5**    The Design Notes dialog box

16

3. Expand the note with comments, a date, or detailed information:

   ■ Type comments in the Notes text area.

   ■ Click the calendar icon to enter the current date (Windows only).

   ■ Check the Show When File Is Opened option to have Dreamweaver automatically display the Design Note when the file to which it is attached is opened.

   ■ To enter more detailed customized information, click on the All Info tab. You can add a new field by clicking on the plus button and then entering the field's name in the Name text box. Finish by entering the corresponding value in the Value text area and then pressing the TAB key. You can add any number of new name/value pairs to your Design Note using this approach.

4. Click the OK button to close the Design Notes dialog box.

After you add a Design Note to a file, the Local Files list in the Site window indicates its presence with a balloon symbol in the Notes column, as shown in Figure 16-3. You can open and edit the Design Note by simply double-clicking that symbol in the Site window.

If you check the Upload Design Notes for Sharing option in the Design Notes category of the site definition, Dreamweaver automatically copies design notes to the remote site along with the associated files when you Put or Synchronize files. The design notes are then available for viewing by other members of your workgroup either by double-clicking the design note icon in the Remote Site file list or by automatically downloading the design note along with a file during a Get operation and viewing the design notes from their local folder. On the other hand, if you don't check that option, the design notes you create remain confined to your local folder for your reference only.

To delete an individual Design Note in Dreamweaver, follow these steps:

1. Double-click the Design Note symbol in the Site window to open the note for editing.

2. Click the All Info tab.

3. Select each entry one at a time (unfortunately, you can't select all the entries as a group).

4. Click the minus button in the Design Notes dialog box to remove the selected entry.

5. After you delete all the entries, click the OK button. Dreamweaver deletes the entire Design Note, and it no longer appears in the Site window.

NOTE *Dreamweaver stores Design Notes in the _notes/ folder, a subfolder of the site's local folder. The folder doesn't appear in the Site window but is easily accessible with Windows Explorer or other file-management utilities. The design notes are in separate files with filenames corresponding to the file to which they belong and identified with the added .mno extension. You can delete the design notes for a given file by deleting the corresponding .mno file from the _notes folder.*

# Index

## G

General category (Preferences dialog box), 40
Get button, 391
Get File button, 61
Getting (downloading) files, 60-61, 391
GIF files, 280
Go to URL dialog box, 341
Graphical submit button, creating, 232-233
Graphics. *See* Images (image objects)
Grid Settings dialog box, 18
Grids, 17-18

## H

Head Content pane, 150
Heading styles, 95
Heading tags, 94-96, 149
Helvetica font, 90
Hidden Field button, 233
Hidden field markers on a form, 234
Hidden fields, adding to a form, 233-234
Highlighting category (Preferences dialog box), 41
Hints (code), 146
History panel, 36-38
History panel group, 34
Home page, 48, 63
HomeSite+, 162
Horizontal rules, inserting in a document, 86-87
Hotspot Property Inspector panel, 133
Hotspots (image)
    in Design view, 133-134
    explained, 131
HTML code. *See* Code (HTML code)
HTML documents, opening and editing, 83-84
HTML editors, using external, 162
HTML forms. *See* Forms
HTML 4.0 specification, 382
HTML head content in Design view, 149
HTML (Hypertext Markup Language), 68
HTML style formatting, clearing, 106
HTML styles, 100-106
    applying to text, 105-106

based on existing text, 102
based on HTML styles, 103
creating, 102-104
creating from scratch, 104
vs. CSS styles, 101, 295
editing and deleting, 104-105
HTML Styles panel, 100-101
HTML tables. *See* Tables
HTML tag list, 148
HTML tag style, CSS Redefined, 302
HTML tags, 22, 308.
    *See also* Code (HTML code)
HTML text, importing from Microsoft Word, 84-85
Hyperlinks. *See* Links (hyperlinks)
Hypertext links. *See* Links (hyperlinks)

## I

I-beam pointer, 79
Image borders, 128
Image bounding box, 124
Image files, optimizing, 128, 280
Image hotspots, 131
Image links, buttons as, 130-131
Image map, creating, 131-134
Image placeholder, creating, 125
Image Placeholder dialog box, 125
Image properties, setting, 128-129
Image Property Inspector panel, 126
Image sizing handles, 124
Images (Fireworks), optimizing within Dreamweaver, 279-284
Images (image objects), 121-137
    adding alt text for, 129-130
    adding to a page, 122-124
    as links, 130-134
    background images, 134-135
    cropping, 281-282
    dragging and dropping, 124
    Fireworks graphic effects, 284-286
    inserting in a document, 122-124
    positioning, 126-127
    resizing, 127, 283-284

# INTERNATIONAL CONTACT INFORMATION

**AUSTRALIA**
McGraw-Hill Book Company Australia Pty. Ltd.
TEL +61-2-9417-9899
FAX +61-2-9417-5687
http://www.mcgraw-hill.com.au
books-it_sydney@mcgraw-hill.com

**CANADA**
McGraw-Hill Ryerson Ltd.
TEL +905-430-5000
FAX +905-430-5020
http://www.mcgrawhill.ca

**GREECE, MIDDLE EAST,
NORTHERN AFRICA**
McGraw-Hill Hellas
TEL +30-1-656-0990-3-4
FAX +30-1-654-5525

**MEXICO (Also serving Latin America)**
McGraw-Hill Interamericana Editores S.A. de C.V.
TEL +525-117-1583
FAX +525-117-1589
http://www.mcgraw-hill.com.mx
fernando_castellanos@mcgraw-hill.com

**SINGAPORE (Serving Asia)**
McGraw-Hill Book Company
TEL +65-863-1580
FAX +65-862-3354
http://www.mcgraw-hill.com.sg
mghasia@mcgraw-hill.com

**SOUTH AFRICA**
McGraw-Hill South Africa
TEL +27-11-622-7512
FAX +27-11-622-9045
robyn_swanepoel@mcgraw-hill.com

**UNITED KINGDOM & EUROPE
(Excluding Southern Europe)**
McGraw-Hill Education Europe
TEL +44-1-628-502500
FAX +44-1-628-770224
http://www.mcgraw-hill.co.uk
computing_neurope@mcgraw-hill.com

**ALL OTHER INQUIRIES Contact:**
Osborne/McGraw-Hill
TEL +1-510-549-6600
FAX +1-510-883-7600
http://www.osborne.com
omg_international@mcgraw-hill.com

# New Offerings from Osborne's
# How to Do Everything Series

**How to Do Everything
with Your Palm™ Handheld,
2nd Edition**
ISBN: 0-07-219100-7
Available: Now

**How to Do Everything
with Your Scanner**
ISBN: 0-07-219106-6
Available: Now

**How to Do Everything
with Your Visor,
2nd Edition**
ISBN: 0-07-219392-1
Available: October 2001

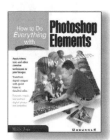

**How to Do Everything
with Photoshop Elements**
ISBN: 0-07-219184-8
Available: September 2001

**How to Do Everything
with Your Blackberry**
ISBN: 0-07-219393-X
Available: October 2001

**How to Do Everything
with Digital Video**
ISBN: 0-07-219463-4
Available: November 2001

**How to Do Everything
with MP3 and Digital Music**
ISBN: 0-07-219413-8
Available: December 2001

**How to Do Everything
with Your Web Phone**
ISBN: 0-07-219412-X
Available: January 2002

**How to Do Everything
with Your iMac,
3rd Edition**
ISBN: 0-07-213172-1
Available: October 2001

**HTDE with Your Pocket PC
& Handheld PC**
ISBN: 07-212420-2
Available: Now

 **OSBORNE**
www.osborne.com